ETHNOGRAPHIC STUDIES IN SUBJE

Tanya Luhrmann and Steven Parish, Editors

Unsettled

Kenya and its neighbors. This map shows places mentioned in the text.

Unsettled

Denial and Belonging
among White Kenyans

Janet McIntosh

UNIVERSITY OF CALIFORNIA PRESS

University of California Press, one of the most distinguished university presses in the United States, enriches
lives around the world by advancing scholarship in the
humanities, social sciences, and natural sciences. Its
activities are supported by the UC Press Foundation
and by philanthropic contributions from individuals
and institutions. For more information, visit
www.ucpress.edu.

University of California Press
Oakland, California

Library of Congress Cataloging-in-Publication Data

Names: McIntosh, Janet, 1969– author.
 Title: Unsettled : denial and belonging among white
Kenyans / Janet McIntosh.
 Other titles: Ethnographic studies in subjectivity ; 10.
 Description: Oakland, California : University of
California Press, [2016] | "2016 | Series: Ethnographic
studies in subjectivity ; 10 | Includes bibliographical
references and index.
 Identifiers: LCCN 2015043971 | ISBN 9780520290495
(cloth : alk. paper) | ISBN 9780520290518 (pbk. : alk.
paper) | ISBN 9780520964631 (ebook)
 Subjects: LCSH: Whites—Kenya—History. | Kenya—
History—1963– | Kenya—Social conditions—1963–
 Classification: LCC DT433.545.B74 M35 2016 | DDC
305.809/06762—dc23
 LC record available at http://lccn.loc.gov/2015043971

25 24 23 22 21 20 19 18 17 16
10 9 8 7 6 5 4 3 2 1

For Tobias and Theo, with love beyond words

Contents

Acknowledgments

I am indebted to many people for their support during the research and writing of this book. For their contributions to and comments on material related to the book, I give heartfelt thanks to Mark Auslander, Misty Bastian, Ann Biersteker, Jacob Boersema, Rob Blunt, Manduhai Buyandelger, Neil Carrier, Jennifer Cole, Jean Comaroff, Joanna Davidson, Peter Dreyer, Paulla Ebron, Caroline Elkins, Elizabeth Ferry, Jim Ferguson, Susan Gal, Perry Gilmore, Angelique Haugerud, Anita Hannig, Nick Harkness, Simon Hawkins, Rachel Heiman, Jane Hill, Dorothy Hodgson, David McDermott Hughes, Lotte Hughes, Nancy Rose Hunt, Jennifer Jackson, Alexandra Jaffe, S. Lochlann Jain, Karega-Munene, Anderson Kasiwah, Stanslous Kiraga, Maxwell Kombe, Smita Lahiri, Sarah Lamb, Ann Marie Leshkowich, Katherine Luongo, Dillon Mahoney, Lisa Malkki, Adeline Masquelier, George Paul Meiu, Norma Mendoza-Denton, John Mugane, Joseph Mwarandu, Elinor Ochs, Kwame Onoma, Heather Paxson, Rory Pilossof, Jennifer Roth-Gordon, Danilyn Rutherford, Rick Schroeder, Becky Schulthies, Brett Shadle, Parker Shipton, Jim Smith, Ann Stoler, Megan Styles, Ajantha Subramanian, Noah Tamarkin, Katja Uusihakala, Danelle van Zyl-Hermann, Deanne van Tol, Chris Walley, Margaret Weiner, and Brad Weiss. Several of those mentioned are members of the Cambridge Writer's Circle, a group that has furnished me with so many years of great company and astoundingly good feedback. I am positive I have forgotten some who should be on this list; no doubt after this book goes to press I will remember my gratitude to you again.

Based on a fragment of the material that is now in this volume, Tanya Luhrmann put her faith in my project. I am grateful for the chance to work with an estimable anthropologist so fascinated by what unfamiliar experience might feel like, and one dedicated to expressing ideas in such fine prose. Tanya, thank you so much for your discerning eye, your insistence on clarity, and your perfectly timed, fortifying words. And to Reed Malcolm at University of California Press: thank you for trusting in this project.

I would like to make special mention of the members of the Anthropology Department at Brandeis. It was my great good luck to begin my career at Brandeis while writing my dissertation fourteen years ago. Since then I have been reminded almost daily how fortunate I am to work in a department busy with over a hundred enthusiastic majors and dozens of wonderful graduate students, anchored by a superb administrator, Laurel Carpenter, and populated by faculty who are exceptional scholars and profoundly decent people with senses of humor. I recognize that our departmental dynamic is a luxury in academia, and I thank my colleagues for making it possible.

Writing about a cultural milieu as diverse and subtle as Kenya has been challenging, and I assume I have gotten some things wrong—at the very least, anyway, wrong from some vantage points. In speaking to me, most settler descendants knew that I was unlikely to see things the way they do, or to represent them in a way they find flattering, yet they nevertheless engaged with me and assisted me, often repeatedly. Doing so required politeness, generosity, and bravery. I am grateful, but I cannot thank them by name because I have promised to keep their identities confidential. Those respondents who can be named are Tom Cholmondeley, Richard Leakey, and the exceptional artist Sam Hopkins, whose work and words I discuss briefly in the Conclusion. For special acts of generosity (and with no assumption that they agree with the contents this book), I thank Doreen Hartley, David Obura, Ann and Ian Robertson, and Hilda Tucker. For their kindness and friendship over many years, I thank Lorna Depew and Ian Gordon. My gratitude goes to Olivia Spalletta and Rachana Agarwal for their help with literature reviews on South Africa and on the ethnography of elites. Particular thanks again to Anderson Kasiwah and Maxwell Kombe for their research assistance, and to other friends in Kenya who were instrumental in supporting my early research efforts, including Abdallah A.M. Alaussy, Emmanuel Safari Chai, and Kaingu Kalume Tinga.

I am grateful for the solidarity of several others not yet mentioned, some of whom have had utmost meaning in my life since long before this book was conceived: Rosa Brooks, Chris Demars, Jim Dawes, Barbara Ehrenreich, Kelly Flynn, Rachel Meyer and Jim Herron, Laura Nooney, Nira Pollock, Christine Rayner, Antony Seely and Carla Power, Diana Bermudez and Merrick Hoben, Laura Kunreuther, and Karen Strassler. I must single out Elizabeth Ferry, Rachel Heiman, and Smita Lahiri as especially generous friends and colleagues over many years. I would like as well to acknowledge Jennifer Jackson, my beloved friend. She exemplified a full heart and vibrant, indelible life in the face of unthinkable challenges, and she was a brilliant inspiration.

These thanks can't be complete unless I mention the dozens of fellow parents and children in Brookline and Cambridge who have given my family a community of warmth, good humor, and playdates. And to Kate and Sanden Averett, Renee and Mark Gruen, and the care-givers and teachers at Peabody Terrace Children's Center and the Devotion School: thank you for taking great care of our children while we work.

My parents-in-law Aniko and Bob, my sister Kate, my niece Janet, and my nephew Kenneth have been lovely and unwavering sources of good cheer and support. My parents have been wonderful in many ways, including, sometimes, diverting the children while I have tapped away at my computer on their sofa. Dad, for all the music, for your humor and integrity, for the sourdough pancakes and that bacon, I am forever grateful.

And I must give special acknowledgement to my mother, Peggy McIntosh, who in the late 1980s wrote a now well-known paper about white privilege before that became a household phrase. I worked my way around to this project accidentally, after happenstance conversations with white Kenyans while conducting research on my first project on ethnicity and religion on Kenya's coast. As I got more interested in settler descendants, I focused initially on their awkward relationship to the African occult, and subsequently on their tenuous task of finding their place in Kenya when the structure that their ancestors supported has been exposed—and widely re-presented—as deplorable. Perhaps in the way of children who imagine themselves as to be wholly original, it took me a long time to admit that my project was (at least partly) about whiteness. I am sure my mother saw it before I did. While I have been grateful to her and my father for all these years of support of every kind, now I am particularly grateful for her intellectual influence.

Finally, at the very heart of things are my husband Tom and our sons Tobias and Theo. Tom, thank you for unwavering support of this project; you are one of the most talented people I know, a tremendous editor, and the ally everyone would love to have—plus, you just keep making me laugh; what gives? And Tobias and Theo, this book is dedicated to you both. Each of you is so distinct, yet you are both so ebullient, funny, thoughtful, sensitive, clever, and big-hearted. Also loud (take it outside, please). Your radiant smiles and laughter are the very greatest joy there is.

The research and writing for this project were made possible with the help of the National Endowment for Humanities; first, from a Summer Stipend (2004), and subsequently a year-long Faculty Research Award (2008–9) that gave me the chance to conduct longer term fieldwork. Other fieldwork and writing time were supported by several Norman Awards from Brandeis University, and by a Faculty Research Leave at Brandeis University.

Some of the material in chapter 5 appeared previously in "Linguistic Atonement: Penitence and Privilege in White Kenyan Language Ideologies," *Anthropological Quarterly* 87, no. 4 (2014): 1159–93. Portions of the material in chapter 4 appeared in "Autochthony and 'Family': The Politics of Kinship in White Kenyan Bids to Belong," *Anthropological Quarterly* 88, no. 2 (2015): 251–80. And portions of chapter 6 appeared in "'Going Bush': Black Magic, White Ambivalence, and Boundaries of Belief in Post-Colonial Kenya," *Journal of Religion in Africa* 36, nos. 3–4 (2006): 254–95, as well as in "Stance and Distance: Ontological Doubt and Social Boundaries in White Kenyan Narratives about the African Occult," in *Stance: Sociolinguistic Perspectives,* ed. Alexandra Jaffe, 72–91 (New York: Oxford University Press, 2009).

1

Unsettled

In late September 2006 prison warders escorted Thomas Cholmondeley (pronounced "CHUM-lee") into a wood-paneled courtroom in Nairobi, where he pled "not guilty" to a charge of murder. He wore a cream-colored linen suit, blue paisley tie, and handcuffs, and his 6-foot-6-inch frame and pale complexion cut quite a figure in this courtroom largely packed with black barristers, spectators, and journalists. Cholmondeley, heir to the colonial-era Delamere family fortune and a vast swathe of coveted land in Kenya's Rift Valley, had been charged for the second time in about a year with shooting an indigent Kenyan dead on his own ranch.

In the first case, in April 2005, Cholmondeley had reportedly believed that he was being robbed, and prosecutors had dropped the charges, accepting his claim of self-defense. But the deceased, a Maasai man, had been an undercover ranger with the Kenya Wildlife Service who was investigating illegal game cropping on Cholmondeley's property. The Kenyan public was appalled at the idea of an Eton-educated scion of a wealthy colonial family killing a Maasai father of eight. When Cholmondeley was released, flashing a double thumbs-up to cameras, the outcry was so intense that the then president of Kenya, Mwai Kibaki, reportedly ordered the chief prosecutor sacked.

In 2006, after Cholmondeley pulled the trigger again and was charged with murdering a man poaching wildlife on the Delamere family ranch, the Kenyan media went into overdrive. He insisted upon his innocence, but a headline of Kenya's *Daily Nation* deplored, "Oh No,

1

Not Again!" and editorials approvingly invoked Zimbabwe's violent campaign of redistributing white-owned farms. Kenyan bloggers suggested that Cholmondeley killed indigent blacks for sport, and Kenyans and British journalists alike reminded readers of the early twentieth-century "Happy Valley" era of Cholmondeley's great-grandfather, the third Baron Delamere, when prominent colonials in Kenya notoriously indulged in epic gin-soaked parties, wife-swapping, and lavish lifestyles.[1] As Cholmondeley's trial dragged on for nearly four years, public reactions sounded a wake-up call for some whites with family roots in Kenya. They realized that he was not only a symbol of a bygone era but also, fairly or not, a stand-in for the rest of them. And they could not help but detect the subtext to the media outcry: colonials, go home.

But for many aging former settlers and their descendants, Kenya *is* home. True, the Europeans who came to East Africa a century ago didn't always imagine it that way. However enticing they found the golden savannah and teeming wildlife, however embroiled they were in carving a life out of the bush, Kenya, or as it was pronounced in those days, "Keenya," was a site where Britain would inscribe and magnify itself as an emissary of civilization and enforcer of empire. The microcosmic aspects of European life replicated there—country clubs, polo matches, tea parties, churches, medical clinics, and schools—remind us that Britain, for most, was the touchstone of their identity. Though some settlers had other European roots, English culture suffused their institutions, as did racial exclusion. Settler children sometimes had African playmates when they were little, but they were eventually segregated with other Europeans in elite schools, or sent abroad to boarding school where they could learn to enact the "prestige" that would uphold whites' civilized image.[2] Although here and there one could find a settler with an unusual affinity for "the natives," most considered Africans to be intellectually inferior, vaguely polluting, and potentially dangerous. No wonder that even those settlers who would leave their bones in Kenya still called England "home," many referring to themselves as "British Kenyans" or simply "British."

Many of today's settler descendants have, however, adopted a Kenyan nationalist discourse of shared future aspirations. After political power shifted into African hands in 1963, settler families went from brazen race-based entitlements to sharing power and resources with a growing elite and middle class of African and Asian descent. The transition was so destabilizing that tens of thousands of whites emigrated for fear that their fortunes would fall. Of whites who are citizens of Kenya today, those with family roots in the colonial era number only between about three and five thousand.[3] Eager to differentiate themselves from the image of the vilified colonialist, many I spoke to insist that their families had remained in Kenya because of the emotional impossibility of leaving it. Their very being, they say, is connected to the landscape and people of Kenya, and they consider themselves dedicated to the nation's future. They wish that ethnic divisions and ethnoterritorialism—called "tribalism," in Kenya—would give way fully to liberal nationalism; if that happened, the nation would be at peace, they feel, and perhaps they would stop being reminded that, in the eyes of some, they are always interlopers.

Broadcasting their sincerity, energetic young and middle-aged settler descendants tell me they are devoted to helping "develop" Kenya, working with Kenyans of all backgrounds to move its economy forward. They have valuable know-how, they say, because they understand the place and its people and bring modern managerial expertise to bear on their projects, whether fund-raising, conserving wildlife, managing a hotel, or running a library well. They passionately describe their families' charitable efforts, conservation forums, and businesses, which (sometimes) conspicuously offer employment to some of Kenya's neediest groups—beadwork for single Maasai mothers, for instance, or training for indigent youth in the basics of restaurant service. They call their domestic staff "part of the family," and consider these relationships evidence that their lives are braided together with those of black Kenyans. (I use the phrase "black Kenyans" with hesitation, realizing it may rub some Kenyans the wrong way, since they are accustomed to being called simply "Kenyan"; however, racial categories and perceptions are important to my analysis and I often need to clarify which group I am discussing.)[4] And many younger whites insist that, unlike many of their settler forebears, they speak Kiswahili, Kenya's national lingua franca, with pride and affection, using it as their "language of connection" with their fellow citizens. In light of all this, when the incumbent president Mwai Kibaki rigged the December 2007 elections in his favor and the country exploded into violence, white Kenyans wrung their hands. Their promising nation seemed on the brink of disaster, and their lives had been destabilized, they told me. Most of them felt "Kenyan, through and through."[5]

The public stance of many white Kenyans has shifted from identification with Europe to proud Kenyan nationality. But beneath the surface, this change has been fraught with ambiguity. For one thing, history has left most of them with trappings of privilege, and for all of their efforts to support those in poorer communities, they prize their lifestyle of manicured gardens and cheap domestic help. "I could never live this way in Europe," says a middle-aged Nairobi businessman I call Simon, with a hint of sheepishness in his glance. Like many whites in the Nairobi suburbs, Simon lives in a beautifully kept, airy home behind concrete fences, with Maasai or Samburu security guards at the gates. Some settler descendants in the Rift Valley occupy sweeping ranches replete with zebra, elephants, and wealthy Western tourists; meanwhile, retirees on the coast swim and fish in turquoise, palm-fringed waters. Those with the energy and means enjoy rally driving, polo, and windsurfing. One young man said he adored "driving like a maniac across the country" and the feeling of commanding wide open spaces. "You couldn't get away with that anywhere else," he told me. "It's exhilarating." Although there is some wealth disparity among settler descendants, their vision of an acceptable standard of living still far outstrips the possibilities for millions of black Kenyans. All of those I met, for instance, have at least the means to employ domestic staff to clean their homes, launder their clothes, or prepare their food. Some may say they love Kenya selflessly, but they also know it is possible for them to live "like kings" there, as one put it.

And they realize their privilege has not gone unnoticed. History has marked them for reminders that their claims to belong are tenuous, and they could lose much should grievances be aimed in their direction. To be sure, they haven't seen the nadir of loss faced by white Zimbabweans forcibly removed from their farms over the past decade and a half in Robert Mugabe's violent campaign of land reform. Nor have they faced an economic restructuring like that in South Africa, where racist apartheid-era protections for white employment were replaced by an affirmative action program to empower blacks. Still, the Cholmondeley trial and other recent events have been powerful reminders that, in the eyes of some, white Kenyans risk looking like the archaic residue of a dead world order. They are legal citizens, in other words, but without the more elusive imprimatur of full cultural citizenship.[6]

And so, for instance, when Jason Dunford, great-grandson of the renowned Lithuanian Jewish settler and hotelier Abraham Block, proudly carried Kenya's flag into the Olympic Stadium in 2012 as a member of Kenya's swim team, social media lit up as some Kenyans watching the ceremonies on television expressed shock and dismay. "WTF??" one participant in an on-line sports forum typed. "The Kenyan flag was just carried in by a white swimmer?!" An onlooker interviewed in Nairobi, Sebastian Murunga, summed up a common objection: "He does not really represent Kenyans. Kenyans are black while he is white." While other black Kenyans defended Dunford, deeming him a worthy choice as a committed athlete and a Kenyan citizen, it was clear that for some, his race made him unsuitable as a representative of the nation.[7]

Such issues of belonging have arisen again and again for settler descendants in recent years.[8] Mary, whose British family were influential coffee farmers before they sold their land at Independence, told me of the bad feeling in the air when the Cholmondeley scandal was at its height. A week or so after the second shooting, Mary was shopping in Nairobi when she passed a young man hawking magazines on the street. She called him out, she says, for selling back issues of *National Geographic*. "That's supposed to be subscription only," she said indignantly. (Like many settler descendants, Mary sees the rule of law as an important contribution from the colonial era, and takes offense at both political corruption and rule-breakers.) As she recalls it, the young man retorted, "You keep your nose out of this. You know, it's like Zimbabwe; you're just a visitor here. We can get rid of you." Her lined face looked exasperated as she remembered her reaction. In her own mind, her life trajectory gave her just as much belonging as his lineage. She had been born in Kenya, and was clearly his generational senior. "I thought to myself, Oooohhh! Well, *I've* lived here *longer* than *you!*"

Nationalist gestures, resented privileges, and acute defensiveness—all are components of what it can mean to be a white Kenyan today. In this ethnography, I explore the subjective lives and stances of white Kenyans descended from colonial families as they navigate their unsettled sense of identity in the nation today. I don't aspire to offer a comprehensive account of this diverse group; rather, my material emerges from participant observation among roughly 150–200 individuals of middle- to upper-class status, about fifty of whom I interviewed. Seeing themselves as seen by their critics has been unsettling for them, and some of my respondents seem to ricochet between an embryonic sense of embarrassment and a frustrated, defensive reaction. They continue to enjoy enormous privileges, but their self-consciousness and uncertainties suggest that in some respects, they are of two minds about their entitlement to belong.

A phrase that captures the unease of some white Kenyans is "moral double consciousness."[9] When W. E. B. Du Bois first defined double consciousness to characterize African American subjectivity in the early twentieth century, he described it as "this sense of always looking at one's self through the eyes of others, of measuring one's soul by the tape of a world that looks on in amused contempt and pity."[10] It would be absurd, of course, to draw a direct comparison between Du Bois's subjects and my own; double consciousness among African Americans emerged from their legal, economic, and cultural immiseration, whereas settler descendants in Kenya are still reaping the benefits of white privilege. But scholars such as Linda Martín Alcoff (1998, 2015) in her discussion of white American crises of identity have extended the concept to encompass situations where a privileged social group reckons internally with the judgments of its critics, destabilizing it, even if not critically injuring its members. As Marc Black (2007) notes, white double consciousness may have promise, for unlike the often degrading double consciousness of people of color and colonized populations, it can open the possibility of much-needed self-critique as whites encounter epistemic friction.[11] That said, the first glimmers of double consciousness in elites seem just as likely to result in a defensive reaction that attempts to shut down its associated discomforts and revert to an emotionally safer pole of consciousness—namely, the evaluative stance they started with. (Du Bois describes a similarly protective maneuver of denial and repression in his characterization of the fragile white American ego when challenged by even the slightest recognition of black humanity; see Watson 2013: 31–35.) Among former settlers and their descendants, their nascent double consciousness stems from an unsettling of the colonialist notion that whites are paragons of humanity, and a realization that to some, they and their history represent injustice. True, unlike any subaltern group, most white Kenyans have the luxury of moving toward or away from this discomfiting awareness of their critics. But when they experience the shock of seeing their community being seen, they see themselves "othered," that is, refracted through essentialist stereotypes that portray them as part of an undesirable, alien social mass. This, indeed, speaks to another prong of the "two-ness" Du Bois described, in which African Americans struggled to reconcile "two warring ideals," namely, their identity as American and their identity as "Negros."[12] Though white Kenyans are hardly disenfranchised, they do face an awkward tension between their ethnoracial and national identities in a nation where, in public discourse, entitlement to belong and to own land increasingly hinges on having deep ancestral roots in local soil.

For many of my white Kenyan respondents, then, this embryonic double consciousness is a morally confusing experience. Most of them had been raised to think that their settler family members were good,

giving people who lived bravely and sacrificed much, and that the colonial endeavor had been engineered to uplift Africa. Now they are
informed that their forebears were oppressors, and that perhaps in some
fashion they are too—and while they don't have to internalize this view
of themselves, it has made inroads on their awareness. The resultant
embarrassment, frustration, and (sometimes) anger have meant they
have sometimes had to struggle to compose themselves.[13] Some have
had enough close brushes with critics to taste the edges of humiliation
about the settler past and their privileges in the present. But shame is
not a comfortable dwelling place, and many settle into a defensive
stance, reclaiming their comfort zone and mystifying their structural
advantages. Some dance around the tension by focusing on their felt
bonds to Kenya and black Kenyans and insisting that their personal
intentions and feelings take priority over history and structural inequalities. A few, though, a small minority, have come to soul-search, questioning their received truths and seeking new, more empathic ways of
understanding the perceptions of their black fellow citizens.

Seeing inner conflict and self-doubt in colonial whites is not an altogether new project. We find inklings of the same idea, for instance, in
the work of Albert Memmi, an Algerian Jew who famously excoriated
colonial psychology in the mid 1950s. To Memmi, colonialists knew
"deep down" that they were "usurpers," but strenuously defended their
own legitimacy. The racist devaluation of the colonized was crucial to
this dynamic, including an angry hostility toward Africans, whose
oppression "made [of the colonialist] a tyrant."[14] In this model of white
supremacy, colonials made draconian claims about racial superiority,
not so much out of conviction as to defend against the lurking suspicion
that they were unfit to rule. Other scholars, too, such as John Lonsdale,
Bruce Berman, Frederick Cooper, and Ann Stoler have plumbed uncertainties among the agents of empire, arguing that although colonial
states posed as reasoned and rational, administrators wrestled with
their own confusions and with the unruly behavior and feelings of the
very settlers who were expected to represent European superiority.[15]
Self-deception, mixed feelings, and contradictory practices all led to the
nagging suggestion that European "common sense" was based on fragile conceits.[16] The historian Brett Shadle pinpoints a kind of double
consciousness among settlers in Kenya in the early twentieth century.
In his keen depictions of their anxieties and sometimes vicious racism,
we see, not only fear of black contamination and insubordination, but
also a fear of being found out. White settlers in Kenya, he argues,

"constantly observed themselves through . . . the eyes of the dominated. Their fear was that Africans would measure the white soul with the tape—a tape the settlers had made—and find that soul lacking."[17]

If white anxiety in the colonies is an old story, what has changed? One striking shift is that today, instead of asserting white supremacy, many settler descendants I spoke to are striving to fit into a liberated Kenya as morally accepted nationals. This isn't to say that chauvinism among them is dead, but when it's alive, it must lead a more clandestine existence.[18] One could argue, in fact, that there has been a related sea-change for whites globally, who continue to enjoy untold advantages, but some of whom find that the confidence of white supremacy has been punctured by global liberation and civil-rights movements. And so Alcoff insists on the importance of exploring the "ongoing but rarely named struggle" of anxious double consciousness among some American whites who wish to move beyond the notion of a white master race but find themselves grasping for self-esteem.[19] Former settlers and their descendants in Kenya, while distinctive to their history and place, are part of this broader historical fabric.

That said, in Kenya, white vulnerabilities are perhaps more keen. Though white Kenyans enjoy friendly relationships with plenty of black Kenyans, whites have lost political sovereignty, epistemological credibility, and control over the plotline of Kenya and the narration of its colonial past. And while most whites in the West enjoy the luxury of racial invisibility as part of their "whiteness," Kenyan whites are conspicuously marked as an ethnoracial minority and, depending on the context and the historical moment, as outsiders. Although Kenya entered Independence with a public ideology of civic nationalism, in which citizenship and rights would be conferred across racial and ethnic groups in egalitarian fashion, the stark truth is that the idea of (essentialized) ethnic differences has stalked the political landscape. The colonial administration scored sharp, institutionalized lines between "tribes," despite histories of intermarriage and (often) different ways of dividing the social pie (subsistence, lineage, clan, or trading partnerships, for instance), and used tribal designators to determine different potentials for social mobility. Today Kenya has as many as seventy or more ethnotribal[20] groups, depending on how they are counted; the largest of these are Kikuyu, Luo, Luhya, Kamba, and Kalenjin—but there are subgroups of each, with their own internal divisions.[21] With the chronic inequality and land hunger of the post-Independence era, politicians often frame conflicts over resources in ethnic and ethnonationalist terms.[22] In 2008, for instance, with encouragement from political players, Kikuyu and Kalenjin clashed over which group had deeper roots in and hence more entitlement to Rift Valley lands;[23] meanwhile, thousands of South Asians fled Kisumu to escape violent attacks on their places of business, and some coastal Mijikenda floated the idea of chasing Kikuyu and Luo out of Coast Province in a reprisal of earlier clashes in 1997.[24] Whites intersect in a strange way with these national subdivisions; typically, they aren't rhetorically discussed as a local "tribe" (though, as I discuss later, occasionally they wish they could claim a tribal identity so as to better fit in); rather, they are treated alternately as emissaries of Westernization or as interlopers—in either case, representing the West rather than another local group. Unfortunately for them, as in many sub-Saharan African nations, Kenyan ethnonationalism turns again and again to autochthony as grounds for belonging and landownership—and here is a criterion whites just cannot meet.[25] Although the Kenyan state hasn't endorsed the forcible removal of white landowners, stakeholders such as Maasai in Laikipia have publicly challenged whites' rights to hold land, while the Cholmondeley scandals that began in 2005 prompted a national discourse that sometimes asserted that settler descendants should go back to Europe. Whites can sputter, then, about civic nationalism and wanting to be part of a "multicultural Kenya," but they also know that some black Kenyans reject them as cultural citizens, on mingled grounds of race, class, and history. If, in the colonial era, beleaguered colonized subjects struggled for credibility among white elites, perpetually seen, in Homi Bhabha's famed phrase, as "not quite/not white,"[26] now settler descendants are the ones who risk disdain. Their imperative is no longer to rule, but to belong.

Evidently, my respondents live in complex conditions of ethnic nationalism and amidst national memories that threaten to condemn them. And their moral double consciousness, when they experience it, leaves them with a jumble of questions. How should they now understand the colonial past, and the beloved friends and family members implicated in it? How should they relate to black Kenyans in the present? Can they fit into Kenya as accepted cultural citizens? How "African" are they—and how African do they want to be? How can the love they say they feel for Kenya—its landscapes, its people, its languages—be so discounted? Is it possible that, as one put it to me, they're "not right the way they are"?

STRUCTURAL OBLIVION AND ETHNOGRAPHY OF ELITES

If colonial racism was, as Memmi argues, a response to colonials' anxieties that they were not fit to rule, settler descendants' moral nationalism emerges from a somewhat different insecurity, one concerned about holding onto their residue of privilege while currying a modicum of public acceptance. In some of these chapters, then, I describe settler descendants' anxious responses to their critics, and their protestations that they are in fact good nationals who belong in Kenya. They talk of their stewardship of land and wildlife, which they feel displays responsible regard for Kenya's resources; their charitable care for needy Kenyans; the kin-like affection they have for domestic servants, which they hope will be irreproachable; and the connection they say they feel to other Kenyans through effortful cultivation of Kiswahili, the national language. The worst of the colonial past is sometimes renounced, sometimes held at arms' length as a product of another time and another attitude, or sometimes denied altogether. These announcements of loyalty and protestations often seem heartfelt, but they are also adaptive efforts to belong in the face of having the wrong sort of history and the wrong lines of descent.

Locating their comfort zone—that mode of moral consciousness in which white Kenyans use their *own* yardstick—requires particular dismissals and blind spots, and particular ideas of the good. To capture these, I have coined the phrase "structural oblivion." Structural oblivion is a state—a subject position—of ignorance, denial, and ideology that emerges from an elite social structural position, and it is constituted by the refusal of certain implications of social structure. In particular, structural oblivion includes refusing the experience of and/or reasons for the resentment of less privileged groups, and overlooking the ways in which one's ideologies, practices and very habits of mind continue to uphold one's privilege. Structural oblivion is constructed at a variety of scales, ranging from the institutional structuring of information flow (as in, for example, a colonial administration's whitewashing of its own human rights violations); to collective myths, ideologies, and discourses that skew interpretations of the social world; to psychological mechanisms that surely sometimes include denial and the repression of unpleasantries. Structural oblivion thus may require certain kinds of "work," but this does not mean any given individual's condition of oblivion can readily be called "deliberate." Through structural oblivion, the line between deliberate and unwitting oppression blurs, as elite actors can channel a colonial residue without being fully aware of how it is problematic. If double consciousness has precipitated a minor crisis of identity for some settler descendants, structural oblivion is what allows them to shake it off.

The concept of structural oblivion articulates with certain recurrent themes in whiteness studies—including Peggy McIntosh's (1988) and Shannon Sullivan's (2006) work on white privilege as habitual and unconscious, and Charles Mill's (1997: 18) suggestion that a tacit "racial contract" produces for whites an "epistemology of ignorance . . . producing the ironic outcome that whites will in general be unable to understand the world they themselves have made." Melissa Steyn dubs this dynamic "The Ignorance Contract," and contends that white South African ignorance of the depredations of apartheid "must be studied as a social accomplishment, not just as a failure of individual knowledge acquisition."[27] I locate systematic ignorance as well among some of my respondents, but with the phrase "structural oblivion" I highlight the architecture of elite ignorance, self-deception, *and* ideology, a crucial component. Most people of European descent take for granted a very particular, hegemonic model of the way the world is or should be, a model so all-permeating that it includes the economy, the political and material world, and the person. For instance, like most people of European descent, my white Kenyan respondents presume a liberal, individualistic model of personhood in which persons are (ideally) self-determined and rational; a largely capitalist model of economy in which private property structures access to resources and land should be made "productive"; and a model of civic nationhood, in which ethnicity and descent should be irrelevant to rights. In the moral domain, they presume that a person's intentions are or should be crucial to the adjudication of their morality, while individual deeds should be central to one's entitlements. Such assumptions cluster together again and again, and their logic privileges European expertise by envisioning an ideal, "developed" Kenya that looks more like the West, eschewing customary African modes of organization and power (collective land rights, expansive kinship structures and attendant structures of reciprocity and obligation, ritual healing, or respect for occult agency, to name but a few) and actively marginalizing the colonial past, deeming it irrelevant; after all, if the individual is sovereign, the son does not inherit the sins of the father, and belonging is (or should be) established at the individual level rather than by descent. To be sure, it is possible that some of these liberal individualistic ideologies—held by some black Kenyans as well as whites—might hold the seeds of a less ethnically turbulent Kenya. But white Kenyans are not in an especially good position to proselytize, and they also have difficulty seeing the world through alternative lenses to grasp why (for instance) many Kenyans' feelings about collective redress are so acute. Theirs is a model of a good nation, then, in which colonialism would be neatly forgotten—yet they live in a moment when popular discourse and politics in Kenya are suffused by invocations of grievances past.

Structural oblivion, of course, is hardly exclusive to white Kenyans; many of us live in contexts of profound inequality in which elites have limited understanding of the sources and human implications of their own privilege. If "hegemony" is a system in which all social strata are implicated in the process of oppression,[28] then not only do the subaltern sometimes unwittingly collude in their own oppression, but, too, the powerful oppress not only deliberately but sometimes unwittingly— even if their conscious, explicit ideologies (e.g., of multicultural enthusiasm, or love for Kenya) might suggest otherwise. This is not to suggest that oppression is never witting, or that elites should be let off the hook, or that elite ignorance and denial are completely innocent. Being "out of it" requires a certain self-interested kind of work—refusals and erasures at many levels, including, no doubt, at the level of the psyche, where denial can sweep undesired fears and discomforts out of sight. But the engines of elites' self-deception are also bigger than they are; they have often been supported by state institutions, widespread social narratives, and collective amnesia. (To offer but one example: when one elderly former settler living on the coast griped about coastal Mijikenda threatening violence against elite landowners in 2008, I tried to contextualize events by reminding her that for several decades Mijikenda, like so many other "natives," had been excluded from landownership by the colonial government.[29] It turned out not to be a reminder after all. "Really?" she replied incredulously. "I find that very hard to believe.") The phrase structural oblivion clarifies that elites don't always grasp what they have brushed aside or the depth of what they don't know, and they tend not to recognize the machinery of power that has structured their selective lens on the world. It clarifies one way in which elites can be implicated in hegemony.

Structural oblivion runs deep through the material that follows. Many white Kenyans I spoke to about Laikipia landholdings, for instance, know little about precolonial modes of land tenure, the ecological facts of precolonial pastoralism, or the details of colonial-era land appropriation, blind spots that help them feel comfortable with whites' landownership (chapter 2). In their relationships with domestic staff, which they describe as kin-like and affectionate, they maintain a structure of paternalism with colonial echoes (chapter 4). Even in young white Kenyans' embrace of Kiswahili as a "beautiful" language, they sustain an unconscious linguistic hierarchy that marks English as more prestigious (chapter 5). And at the same time younger settler descendants frame themselves as culturally tolerant and cosmopolitan, their enduring resistance to other modes of personhood—acceptance of the occult, for instance (chapter 6), or the mingling of marriage with economic need (chapter 4)—places limits on how much they are willing to take on cultural traits that colonials marked as "African." While there are exceptions—a young activist who strives to preserve indigenous ethnobotanical medicine, for example, or another who undertakes anthropological studies at university—many former settlers and their descendants share a developmentalist mentality founded on a culturally bounded vision of what constitutes a good society with many Westerners, while largely unaware of the merits of other possible social worlds that by now have been marginalized by colonialism, neoliberalism, and global capitalism. Among many I spoke to, then, their self-presentation broadcasts their nationalism and care for their fellow citizens, yet a residue of colonial hegemony and a dose of ethnocentrism still shape their opinions. Structural oblivion helps to explain why these elites are in disfavor to begin with, and also explains why it's so hard for them to see their way out.

And yet structural oblivion on its own does not account for all the aspects of white Kenyan subjectivity I explore. The less reassuring pole of their double consciousness is home to that critical voice that prods them, reminding them of the pain and depredations imposed by the colonial order, and suggesting that they need to reckon with various African vantage points in new ways. While some settlers and settler descendants have heard this critical voice intermittently over the years, it was especially loud at the historical moment in which I conducted my work. I began to focus on white Kenyans around the time of the publication of two widely publicized volumes criticizing the British administration's moral conduct during the 1950s anti-colonial "Mau Mau" revolt, a moment that put white Kenyans in an uncomfortable spotlight. I was there during the incarceration and trial of Tom Cholmondeley, during which some whites felt conspicuously re-racialized. Many of my interviews were conducted just after the post-election violence of 2007–8, when Kenya exploded into politically sponsored ethnoterritorial

conflict, and whites wondered if they might be targeted next as alloch-
thons, or interlopers. The ethnic violence of 2008 sharpened whites'
alarm at the prospect of being treated as outsiders, and (ironically)
highlighted the fact that precisely because they disapprove of Kenyan
tribalism, they are misaligned with the many Kenyan citizens who
believe in collective historical redress. A decade or two before, then,
whites arguably had felt more comfortably situated in the country. But
the events of the 2000s shook the structural oblivion of some, and I was
able to capture some of their ambivalence and confusion. Although
almost none of my respondents were able to see past hegemonic Western ideas of progress and development, and very few put their noses
deep into history books about colonial oppression, some had expanded
their sense of possible moral truths compared to those of earlier generations. While there may have been a strategic element to these preliminary concessions to African points of view, the struggle to reconcile the
idea of themselves (and their colonialist forebears) as good people with
black Kenyan grievances marks a new and sometimes uncomfortable
way of being white in Africa today. That struggle is central to this book.

Ethnographies of elite groups are somewhat unusual; most cultural
anthropologists prefer to explore the experiences of people who don't
have much of a voice (as I did in my first book, about coastal Giriama
people). As Joel Robbins (2013) has noted, recent decades have seen the
anthropological lens zero in on those he calls "suffering subjects"; groups
subject to oppression, exploitation, and discrimination. What then justifies putting ethnographic energy toward studying a privileged group?
One reply can be found by harkening back to the anthropologist Laura
Nader's 1972 essay "Up the Anthropologist," in which she challenged
anthropologists to swivel their lens and "study up."[30] Nader argues that
although power is lodged in the political and economic realm, we can't
fully understand it unless we understand how the elite make their privilege feel credible to themselves. She also urged anthropologists to complement these efforts by "studying down" in order to understand all the
strata in the social field. There I have failed her—and indeed I have failed
laterally as well, since Kenya's elite stratum now includes wealthy African and Asian Kenyans. While I include a limited number of African
Kenyan voices in these chapters, furnishing a richly class-conscious
understanding of diverse black Kenyans' interactions with and opinions
of whites would have meant writing another book altogether. But
though my focus may be limited, I take up part of Nader's challenge, and

question the presupposition that my respondents are easy to understand from afar, or simply abhorrent and thus not worth studying. Such characterizations flatten them out, and fail to understand that they act and justify their position in the world through complex, internally fraught frameworks of meaning, rather than, say, sheer malevolence or simple greed. Other ethnographers have come to similar realizations in communities that outsiders are tempted to pigeonhole as "the repugnant other," to invoke Susan Harding's phrase in her exploration of American Christian fundamentalists.[31] Even Kathleen Blee, in her study of women in the Ku Klux Klan, ultimately concluded that understanding them meant realizing that their pathological racism started at the community level rather than in the psychology of already-twisted individuals.[32] Such work reminds us again and again that tidy villains make for good stories but inadequate scholarship. Perhaps some simplified portrayals of elites stem from anxiety; if one concedes the moral complexity of the persons involved, including ways in which they may believe themselves to be doing the right thing, one risks being misunderstood as endorsing the system they subscribed to. But as the anthropologist Renato Rosaldo reminds us about the ethical limits of cultural relativism, "To understand is not to forgive. Just because you come to terms with how something works in another culture doesn't mean you have to agree with it; it means you have to engage it."[33]

Some scholars of colonialism, too, have argued that we must not succumb to a version of critical history in which agents of empire are reduced to mere caricatures.[34] Vincent Crapanzano, in his discussion of white South Africans anxiously awaiting the end of apartheid in the early 1980s, contends that to understand white domination, one must come to grips with the complexity of whites' attitudes.[35] Others, such as Terence Ranger and Alasdair Pennycook, have eschewed limited stereotypes of European colonials, seeing them instead as both human and complicated—and thus immediately relevant to elites currently living in, and rationalizing, social hierarchies.[36] Such works have helped set the stage for a recent flowering of scholarly interest in whites in South Africa and Zimbabwe, where whites have had reason to feel more destabilized, more unsettled, than perhaps ever before.[37] I allude to some of this work as I go, and much later, in the conclusion, I discuss the rather airy concept of "whiteness," after I have covered enough ground to make whiteness seem both more concrete and less homogeneous among whites in Africa.

NOTES ON METHODS

I began to think about settler descendants in earnest during my dissertation fieldwork over the course of several years in the late 1990s, while I was studying the interactions between Swahili and Giriama groups on the Kenya coast.[38] By day I was conducting ethnographic research among Giriama living in mud-and-wattle dwellings on the fringes of coastal towns, or with Muslim Swahili in the dense town centers. But sometimes I would unwind at a coastal resort where settler descendants would turn up for a swim, a drink, or a buffet lunch under the red blossoms of the flame trees. I was a conspicuous presence, a solitary American amidst the clusters of local whites, and some of them took an interest. Several had decided, perhaps based on my modest graduate student attire, that I needed their intervention: they invited me to parties and dinners, lent me novels, and even, at one point, sat me firmly down to trim my split ends. Some were curious about my fieldwork, plying me with gin and tonics to ask what I was finding out about the ways of life that played out just a few hundred yards from their own gated residences. A few seemed to bristle, such as the elderly woman who shook a cane at me as she said: "I don't know how you do it, grubbing about with those people." But what struck me the most, at first, anyway, was that when we got onto the topic of the many spirit mediums, healers, and accusations of witchcraft that swirled around the coast, some white Kenyans would lean in to tell me, sotto voce, about an encounter they had had with these occult forces themselves.

Now I had glimpsed not merely whites' relative wealth, but also a strange, push-pull force field in the ways settler descendants interacted with African Kenyan lifeways. I began to wonder how things had changed for their community since Kenya's independence, and how they interacted with other Kenyans in a place where they stood out so conspicuously. In 2004 and 2008, then, I returned to Kenya to learn more, expanding my questions to examine their felt relationships to the colonial past and to black Kenyans, as well as their responses to bad publicity, which mounted over the course of the decade. I included settler descendants living in the Nairobi, Naivasha, and Laikipia areas in central and northern Kenya, as well as my contacts on the coast. The people I spoke to can't be treated as a "representative sample," for I came to them through a method best visualized as a tree growth. As one person referred me to another, my contacts radiated like branches, to the point that I came to know not only clusters of friends and family, but also some groups of white Kenyans who did not know one another. Ultimately, I was a guest in at least thirty white Kenyan homes, sometimes for dinner parties or other gatherings, and I accompanied white Kenyan contacts to workplaces, restaurants, clubs, shopping centers, yoga classes, polo matches, horticultural events, and elsewhere. The quoted material within these pages comes from both offhand remarks during ordinary interactions and, when lengthy or detailed, from interviews with approximately fifty individuals, recorded with permission and in the location of my respondents' choice (including their homes, their offices, and cafés and restaurants). These interviews were semistructured and open-ended, revolving initially around certain key topics I wished to discuss, but usually digressing as respondents guided the conversation to matters that were on their mind. Some of these encounters were with people I didn't know well, but plenty were conducted with individuals I had socialized with, and some took place over several sessions. Everyone knew I was an anthropologist conducting research and rightly divined that my academic (and American) background gave me progressive leanings and an inclination to be critical of colonial projects, but as I discuss later, I also sensed that my respondents presumed we shared a commitment to Western ideals of rationality, pragmatism, and the liberal individual. This presumption may have made them feel free to expand on their vision of what was right for Kenya, and what was going wrong as well.

I complemented my research in Kenya with work in the United Kingdom in 2007, when I interviewed former settlers and administrators who had left Kenya at some point after Independence, and I also followed up remotely with some of my respondents and interviewed some settler descendants while they were visiting the United States (2009, 2010, 2014). I further augmented my material with interviews—some conducted by research assistants, some by myself—with Kenyans who had experience working as domestic staff or occult practitioners for settler descendants. Along the way, I followed the requirements of my discipline by promising my respondents that I would conceal their identities with special care. In this small, tight-knit population, and in a book that will be discomfiting to some of them, it was vital that nobody be able to detect those they knew. As ethnographers generally do in these situations, I have rejiggered not only names, but also sometimes, when it does not obviously affect the analysis, identifying details such as locations, vocations, and very occasionally the genders of my informants.[39] In several instances, like other ethnographers, I created composites out of more than one respondent to further protect their identities.[40] The individuals I identify are those on public record (as in journalists' accounts) and some of those already in the public eye, including Tom Cholmondeley and Richard Leakey, whose identities are crucial to situating their words, and who consented to my quoting them by name.

I encountered a breadth of ages among my respondents, who ranged from their twenties to their eighties, which became important as I realized the importance of generational differences in how much my respondents cared about matters such as racial integration. However, most white Kenyans I met were comfortably well-off and some were downright wealthy, which means my sample doesn't include Kenya's poor whites, though there are not many of those nowadays. There is some diversity in ethnonational descent among my respondents; most had at least some family background in the United Kingdom, but some have strands of other influence as well—a Greek, Scandinavian, or Italian parent, for instance, and Jewish (usually Eastern European) heritage in a handful of cases. But British culture has been influential on all of my respondents, all of whom speak English with a British-sounding accent. (I did not, incidentally, include in my studies the population of whites of Italian descent who socialize primarily with Italian expatriates, since they emerge from a different historical and cultural crucible.) I didn't have enough respondents to make meaningful comparisons between certain groups, such as those of purely Anglo descent versus those with continental European influence; fifth-generation versus second-generation Kenyans; or the descendants of farmers versus those of administrators or missionaries. Nevertheless, settler descendants have a loose cultural coherence; many of their extended families are braided together, many have heard of one another through their social networks, and many move between home bases in different white communities (in rural Laikipia, urban Nairobi, and the coast, for instance), so they aren't geographically isolated from one another. Perhaps most important, all of them—unlike more recent arrivals—feel personally connected to, and sometimes implicated in, Kenya's colonial era. This group has enough common background that, while I found diversity in their perspectives, I also found narrative strands that circulate widely through their community—what anthropologists would call shared discourse, or common ideology.[41] Still, I am mindful that I have interpreted only some voices from a much larger and more multivocal story; there are white Kenyans who defy the patterns I describe in these chapters. I can only describe the part of the story that I grasped and focused on, and reiterate that it was not the whole.

IN THE FIELD OF PRIVILEGE: THE ETHNOGRAPHER AND
STRUCTURAL OBLIVION

My comfort level shifted over time as I did this work. In fact, my encounters went to the heart of a dynamic ethnographers often experience: what the anthropologist Antonis Robben calls "ethnographic seduction," in which ethnographers develop a certain sympathy as a result of being embedded in the world of their respondents.[42] Ethnographic seduction can make it harder—especially while in the field—for ethnographers to situate their respondents in the structural context of society, history, and power dynamics. At the same time, however, it can be a tool; humanizing those with privilege can help the ethnographer better understand the inner lives of their subjects, including where their blind spots are, and how they find their own worldview credible. In some ways, in fact, my own experience mirrored the structural oblivion of some of my white Kenyan respondents, perhaps making it a little easier for me to grasp why they aren't always mindful of the structures that buoy them and elicit resentment from others.

When I began this work, I had been taken aback by white Kenyans' lavish lifestyles, since I had spent many months working among Giriama, one of the most indigent groups in Kenya. My understanding of settlers and their descendants had also been shaped by the latter-day scholarly literature that catalogues the paternalism, cruelty, and disenfranchisement perpetrated by colonial administrations and settler culture. I had a hard time wrapping my mind around the privileges elderly former settlers and their descendants enjoyed, for they seemed to live in a cabinet of luxuries. I was struck by the contrast between their gated residences and the tremendous poverty just a short stroll away—dilapidated mud-and-wattle huts, children wearing scraps of clothing, youth dying of preventable illnesses—and dismayed by the low wages so many pay their domestic servants. At first, too, I could hardly believe that some whites could drive around Kenya's towns and countryside for years and not know certain elementary things about life outside of the isolation bubble of their Land Rovers, such as the greeting rituals in the Giriama language, or what Swahili eat for dinner. Undeniably, there were parallels to my existence in the United States, where I live a comfortable life that benefits from (indeed, continues to be built on) the labor of underserved, undercompensated people whose lives I know relatively little about. In Kenya, though, I was intimately familiar with those lives. It felt untenable, even physically unsettling, to move between socioeconomic scales so sharply distantiated but so available to my imagination.

But when I began fieldwork in earnest among white Kenyans, the indignation that had made me so queasy seemed to shift. Our shared white privilege, my relative youth, and my background—Anglo-American, middle-class, familiar with the country—made it fairly easy to be pulled into their orbit. As I socialized more with whites and saw less of those who are marginalized, my discomfort with being among the elite began to ebb, even though my principles remained in the abstract. The elderly former settlers and younger settler descendants who at first had seemed like museum pieces became real, human, and, in some cases, likeable. No doubt their self-presentation to me made this easier. Though there were exceptions, most of those I encountered hadn't directly participated in the atrocities of (say) the crackdown against Mau Mau in the 1950s (most were too young, and most of my elderly respondents were female); most did not wish to be perceived as bigoted by others or indeed by themselves; and most did not enact the boorish persona of the hard-line white supremacist.[43] In fact, there *was* cultural racism (sometimes crashing, sometimes subtle) underpinning some of their views, and I analyze it extensively in these pages—but most of what they presented to me did not appall at the time. And as I shared their meals, rode their horses, and had affable conversations with many of them, I understood by the end of it how some of them could enjoy life so much. It's not that I didn't know about the brutality of the colonial regime that got their families there; it's that it was harder to keep it in my field of vision. I was reminded all too keenly why it is unusual for people to step out of their social bubbles to engage in critique of their structural advantages, to understand how others see them, or to live in a chronic state of aching compassion for others who still suffer because of the deeds of their forebears. The path of least resistance for most people living in comfort is simply to enjoy one's privilege—a luxury I both respond to, and feel uncomfortable with.

All of this meant that, as an ethnographer in their midst, I had to work harder to reestablish my critical distance—something that was easier once I returned from the field. Although this work was discomfiting, it was instructive. My hope is that the concept of structural oblivion will be understood to apply not simply to my white Kenyan respondents, but also, potentially, to anyone in a position of privilege, including myself and many others in the global North and beyond. And my experiences in the field furnished a reminder that ultimately, our task as ethnographers is to move back and forth between subjective worlds and broader political contexts, proceeding with sympathetic skepticism and skeptical sympathy.[44] We must try, in the inevitably partial way of an outsider, to approximate what it might be like from the insider's point of view (often called the "emic" perspective), and at the same time reserve the right to be critical of what is treated as "common sense" among our informants. The chapters that follow, then, tack between the words and feelings of individual white Kenyans, and the broader historical, social, and (multi)cultural contexts that help us analyze their words and stances.

THE UNFORGETTABLE PAST

Remembrance of the past is central to Kenyan life, particularly in contemporary talk about ethnic entitlements and redress. Such collective memories are contested and shifting—after all, as Ernest Renan (1882) first noted, a core aspect of nationalism is the selective retelling of history, and the same can be said for ethnic identity formation. As in many parts of sub-Saharan Africa, memories of past conflicts and seizures of land rise to the surface or recede, depending on the historical moment.[45] In recent decades, the project of memorializing the nation's past has been increasingly fragmented along regional and ethnic lines. Local heritage sites in Kenya, for instance, have been held up as not only symbolic capital, but also possible avenues to group autonomy, while museums commemorating the anti-colonial Mau Mau rebellion sometimes privilege the sacrifices of certain group over others, typically in the interest of Kikuyu nationalism.[46] To be sure, there is also a rising appetite for pan-ethnic Kenyan-hood, which white Kenyans fervently would like to be part of, but time and again pigment politics or ethnic divisiveness flare up, and in service of such grievances, the past is invoked with special force. This is perhaps especially true when it comes to matters of land, as will be seen in chapters 2 and 3.

Some of the whites I spoke to struggle with how to represent their own past. Certainly they would prefer to encourage civic nationalism and a peaceable country, and most of them resist narratives of their ancestors as land-grabbers. Should they therefore ignore the history of white settlement in Kenya, by way of encouraging Kenyans to drop old grievances and move into a more tolerant future? (The issues resonate with race relations in the United States, where some whites have argued that between the end of slavery, the Civil Rights Movement, and the election of Barack Obama, the nation should "move on" from racial grievances, particularly since sons proverbially shouldn't be held responsible for the sins of their fathers.) Or should they partake, however feebly, in the popular discourse of autochthony and entitlement by touting their family's lineage in Kenya, but then risk being conflated with settler history? Should they admit that racial politics continue to shape Kenya, but condemn colonial offenses, to signify their distance from settler values? Or should they celebrate the initiative and grit of early settlers, as still reflected in their own deeds and their strenuous efforts to help Kenya "develop"? My respondents moved variously between these strategies, nervously wondering when they would next be aligned with the colonial era (and thus, they worried, be unfairly maligned as brutal, racist settlers).

When former settlers and their descendants broadcast that they are "proudly Kenyan," they are implicitly distancing themselves from the era when settler colonialism was justified by a backdrop of Social Darwinism and "scientific racism," in which supposedly scientific theories supported the domination of the white race. In the late nineteenth century, as economic recessions and imperial hubris in Europe motivated the "scramble for Africa," Europeans widely presumed that intrinsic white superiority entitled them to commandeer land and people alike. In 1895 Britain formally acknowledged its commercial interests in the area with the establishment of the East Africa Protectorate. The next year, the British government began work on a sweeping railway that would ultimately link Mombasa on the coast to Lake Victoria in the interior, cutting through Maasailand on the way. Known as "the Lunatic Line" by colonial tabloids and "the Iron Snake" by some Africans, the project barreled across uneven terrain at a terrible human cost. Many hundreds of indentured laborers from India (called "coolies"), as well as African workers, expired of disease and injury. At least one hundred others died in the jaws of an infamous pair of lions that cultivated an unusual taste for human flesh.[47] Imperialists, however, looked past the human sacrifice to the economic hope of bringing raw goods out of the interior and British commodities to an East African market.

To fund the project's exorbitant expense, the Crown encouraged white settlers to claim farms in the highlands, producing tea, coffee, and other commodities for export. The region had an appealing climate and what seemed like limitless game and agricultural land—particularly if one disregarded those living on it. The British embarked on a period of bloody "submission by bullets," as the East Africa Protectorate's first commissioner, Sir Arthur Hardinge, wryly called it, massacring those who put up a fight, and sometimes even those who didn't.[48] The Crown seized enormous tracts of land from African pastoralists and herders—singling out the cool, green highlands in particular as "white man's country"—with near-total disregard for both the communal land arrangements already in place and the spiritual significance, for many Africans, of their ancestral lands.[49] Another former commissioner of the East Africa Protectorate, Sir Charles Eliot, remarked in 1918 that he had a "clear conscience," since his administration paved the way for settlers. It was the inevitable fate of "Maasai and many other tribes," he said, to "go under" as Europeans had their way.[50]

By 1914 there were more than 5,000 whites in the region, and the numbers grew quickly after the colony of Kenya was officially founded in 1920.[51] By the mid-1920s, 50,000 square miles or marginal land had been gazetted as "reserves" for Africans.[52] Administrators found it convenient to parse the more than three million Africans into rigidly defined "tribal" groups, in spite of their history of porous group boundaries.[53] Settlers and officials then spent decades honing stereotypes of each tribe and the labor and rights they felt each was best suited for—thus setting the stage for ethnic inequalities and divisiveness that still trouble the nation today.[54] Africans were denied landownership and taxed by the household (or "hut"), squeezing many into migrant labor roles. Large populations, especially Kikuyu in Central Province, found themselves squatting on settler land and required to labor for white owners as compensation for tilling their own small plots.[55]

So who were the white newcomers benefiting from this semi-feudal arrangement?[56] Kenya appealed to the British aristocracy, including second and third sons who wouldn't inherit their family estates in England and wished to prove their mettle shooting elephants and lions in an exotic land. Many of these were educated at elite public schools such as Eton. Oxford and Cambridge trained colonial officials in the arts of administrating people they did not much understand. Some aristocrats, such as Lord Delamere and the brothers Berkeley and Galbraith Cole, would leave an indelible stamp on the colony through their farming experiments and pungent opinions. Other British were attracted by the "soldier settlement schemes" in the wake of the two world wars, which offered the promise of a new life to hundreds of demobilized military men from Britain and its colonies.[57] An eclectic mixture of newcomers hailed from the lower and middle classes fleeing British inflation in favor of free land.[58] Afrikaners arrived from the south before World

War I and during the campaign against Deutsch-Ostafrika (German East Africa), and stayed to work in Kenya's service industry.[59] And there were migrants from elsewhere—Irish, continental Europeans; Anglos from North America, Australia, and India; and a small but socially significant European Jewish contingent.

Within their diversity, settlers found meaning in performing their prestige—a concept that presumed white superiority, but also made fine-grained distinctions among types of whites. Envy and social climbing could be found among all classes, and working farmers and tradesmen resented Kenya's dominant aristocrats (Shadle 2015). The hubris was parodied by one cynical editor who, in his 1922 report on Kenyan social events, teased plantation owners for their overdrafts, joshed about the "Engagement of Mr Highup-In-The-Air," and offered congratulations to the new parents "Mr and Mrs Title-Angler."[60] In their status-conscious crucible, Anglos tolerated western Europeans, but aimed their distaste at southern and eastern Europeans and indigent Afrikaner migrants ("Boers"), who were not the right kind of white.[61] Meanwhile, many whites looked down too on the thousands of Asians who stayed on after their Lunatic Line days and made lives as merchants and entrepreneurs. This group would find tremendous commercial success, but only marginal representation in the colonial administration. Most Europeans regarded Asians with suspicion, treating them as impediments to African progress.[62]

But the most vituperative prejudice was reserved for Africans themselves. Particularly in the early decades, most settlers and administrators were "supremely confident," as Shadle puts it, "that civilization, race, and fitness to rule could not be pulled apart."[63] Whatever their intentions, whatever personal gestures of goodwill individual settlers made, they lived in a structure that encouraged racism. The law gave European employers draconian control over employees, and some workers were subject to physical and psychological abuse.[64] Settlers cultivated anxiety about "alien infiltration" from the black populace, resulting in a system of identity cards, ordinances, passes, and segregation that looked like a prototype for apartheid.[65] Meanwhile, with white purity at stake, settlers beat back the feared (if largely mythical) "black peril" of African men who would rape white women.[66] Whites topped this off with an elitist club culture, and the infantilization of domestic servants.[67] The Kikuyu writer Ngugi wa Thiong'o would later lacerate the settler community as a "Draculan idle class" with "a culture of legalized brutality" that treated Africans as "instinctless, unlovable, unredeemable, sub-animals merely useful for brute labor."[68] Despite their advantages, settlers sometimes framed themselves as victims of the colonial administration, regarding it as overly concerned with African welfare and unsympathetic to their wishes.[69]

If the official colonial agenda was concerned with building a solid British settler community while bringing civilization to the poor African, what that could mean was a source of some contention. Eugenicist ideas of white biological superiority were in the air, but could the natives be improved if they were intrinsically inferior?[70] Shadle argues that in the early twentieth century, some settlers entertained an ideology of Lamarckian evolutionism—the inheritance of acquired characteristics, one African generation after another, on a march forward from their infantile state.[71] As administrators put resources into uplifting initiatives, the word "civilize" fell out of favor, supplanted by the still-current term "development," which sounded less like imperial triumphalism and more like a means of enhancing African quality of life.[72]

By the 1950s a few formally educated Africans were rising in the ranks, and a sense of global change was in the air. Although most settlers held fast to the system that had benefitted them, some more liberal settlers had come to question the racism behind Kenya's land policies, segregation in hotels and restaurants, and the total exclusion of Africans from politics.[73] For decades, too, and in growing numbers, Africans had been politically organizing for rights, dignity, and independence. Anti-colonial discontent—especially among the many thousands of Rift Valley denizens who had lost much of their prized land—finally caught fire with the Mau Mau revolt in Central Province in the 1950s. The administration cracked down on what it saw as an insolent, half-deranged, and deeply threatening resistance movement. Many thousands of Kikuyu, Meru, and others were killed or incarcerated, and the details of their treatment are horrifying; castration, mutilation, sexual humiliation, and beyond.[74] The suppression of the Mau Mau, however, did not save the colony. Nationalist movements were striding across Africa, and critics in Britain were clamoring for change. "By the 1960s," the historian Fred Cooper observes, "a normative transformation had taken place on a worldwide level; the colonial empire was no longer a legitimate or viable form of political organization. This transformative process took in not only political structures but the very way in which people and roles could be talked about and understood."[75]

Whites in Kenya were nervous about what might happen when black Kenyans took power, but some took heart in 1963 when the new premier, Jomo Kenyatta, resolved to effect a peaceful transition. An elderly Kikuyu, Kenyatta had been a political prisoner for seven years, indicted by the colonial courts for "managing" the Mau Mau in spite of the fact that he had not endorsed the movement's violence.[76] But now, wearing a grizzled grey beard, a three-piece suit, and a decorative states-man's cap, he delivered an oration that would be remembered as his "Forgive and Forget" speech. He encouraged Kenyans to bury their dif-ferences and focus on the future, welcoming white settlers to stay on and work for an independent Kenya. "We are not to look to the past—racial bitterness, the denial of fundamental rights, the suppression of our culture," he famously urged. "Let there be forgiveness." In the same tone of conciliation, Kenyatta declined to forcibly seize white farms, preferring instead the "willing buyer, willing seller" arrangement subsi-dized by the World Bank and the British government. Though the dynamics of land transfer would come to disproportionately favor Kikuyu and therefore wrack Kenya in the coming decades, whites were mostly able to slip under the radar as Kenya built itself under a new administration.

One elderly former settler, Lucy, looked at the sea from her beach-front porch as we discussed the era when the British flag came down and the Kenyan flag was raised in its stead. She told me what a relief Kenyatta's words had been for the settlers considering staying on. "We took hope, in that moment, that the past would not be dredged up," she said wistfully. "And I will admit," she went on, "that we'd hoped bygones would be bygones." She sounded almost betrayed that resent-ment against colonialism was still relevant, still raising its head, more than forty years later.

VULNERABLE PRIVILEGES: WHITE KENYANS IN THE POST-INDEPENDENCE ERA

If some white Kenyans bristle when the colonial past is invoked, they also know that in some respects, they haven't lost much. Political power is in African Kenyan hands, and whites are sometimes criticized, but nevertheless, they still enjoy astonishing social status. Some details of their socioeconomic privilege, along with some vivid accounts of their sometimes perilous sense of belonging, will help set the stage for the rest of this book.

As I spent time among settler descendants, I saw again and again how they were treated in public—and I recognized it well since, as an

Anglo-American, I had often been treated in a similar way. Most whites have ready access to the private clubs that require social connections for membership—and even if they don't, it won't usually be hard for them to breeze into the common area for a drink. Doors open, literally and figuratively, as they approach; taxi drivers and helpful employees pick up their bags as they set them down; clerks and domestic workers are almost unfailingly polite and friendly; police wave away minor infractions such as speeding. In the post office in a coastal town, I once watched a young white Kenyan man hold up a long line as he complained about the slow pace of his mail deliveries; the clerk responded with respectful haste, but dressed down the next (black Kenyan) customer for failing to bring enough money to post his package.

In spite of nationalist critiques of white dominance, these habits of white social hegemony are tenacious. Eleanor, a sixty-something woman from an old family of settler agriculturalists, looks unassuming enough with her pilling brown cardigan and unkempt hair, but finds herself treated regally when she goes to her local Barclay's Bank in Nairobi:

> Quite often it's embarrassing that you, you get shown to the front of the queue because maybe they feel you're busier or you care more about getting somewhere. Quite often people will *expect* you even to move to the front of a queue. You have to reflect: is it us? That we've projected onto them that our time is worth more than their time? Or is it that they're just *such* polite people and there is a colonial hangover still? It's difficult to know where it comes from.

Malcolm, a middle-aged manager at a dairy products company, agrees that whites often get the benefit of the doubt, particularly in situations where red tape threatens. Gesturing out the window of his office at the busy Nairobi street, he tells me: "I think we get treated with amazing respect in many situations where indigenous Kenyans wouldn't, be it a roadblock, or a government office. Even if you get pulled over you say, 'I'm really sorry, I'll be a good boy next time,' and they smile and let you go. That is *not* what happens to indigenous Kenyans and Asian Kenyans."

Clearly, too, white Kenyans continue to enjoy elite economic status in the post-Independence era. They work side by side with well-to-do African and Asian Kenyans, but whites are disproportionately advantaged, and can count on their cultural style conjugating with status. They do very well in the private sector, enjoying prominence in the luxury tourism industry, for instance, and having privileged access to trade permits in floriculture (there is a small cottage-industry of white flower farmers in the Naivasha region).[77] Some flourish in arenas such as business, import/export, and air transport; others work the land as farmer managers, horticulturalists, and ranchers. Those who devote themselves to conservation attest to deep emotional ties to Kenya's wildlife and open spaces, but they can conserve and protest poaching precisely because they own so much land, unlike their neighbors who sometimes rely on bush meat to feed their children. The younger generation also includes a contingent to whom some of my informants refer derisively as "trust fund kids," who don't have to think much about employment and can indulge to excess in parties, deep-sea fishing, and jet-setting. Still, some white Kenyans live at a more ordinary middle-class standard, troubleshooting the same rickety Land Rover for many years on end. A few of my respondents have so little cushion—little, anyway, by the standards of middle-class Westerners—that they fret aloud about which possessions they will sell to make ends meet in the event of an economic dip. Nevertheless, Kenya does not have a white underclass like the many thousands of Afrikaners who—in spite of enduring prosperity for most South African whites—now live in shacks and squatter camps.[78] While there are surely some indigent settler descendants tucked away from ordinary social circles, not many Kenyan whites inherited poverty from their parents or grandparents, in part because colonial officials long preferred to repatriate the impoverished whites who had embarrassed the race's prestige and the civilizing mission.[79]

Settler descendants' relative wealth sometimes detracts from their being accepted as legitimate participants in the nation. In a discussion of Kenyan whites on the UKENTV web site in March 2012, one commentator berated them for their failure to integrate with workaday Kenyans and participate in civic life, while attributing their wealth to colonial exploitation:

> If they are Kenyans, then why don't we see them in the streets when we are complaining that *unga* [maize meal] prices have gone up? Do we see them board a *matatu* [mini-van; a kind of public transportation] to go town to look for work? Why didn't we go to the same schools with their kids? Because we don't belong together. I am Kenyan; that is why I participate in Kenyan issues . . . they have unfairly acquired wealth on Kenyan soil; that is why they don't feel the pinch.

The next commentator responded that the same could be said of wealthy Kenyans in general, including the Kenyattas and "anybody related to MPs," saying: "You are describing a divide created by wealth, not race."[80] Indeed, moneyed black Kenyans and Asian Kenyans also travel in rarified circles, attend elite schools and clubs, and so forth. But just as Asian Kenyans are sometimes singled out as economic exploiters and outsiders, white Kenyans' colonial history marks them as easy targets for grievances—"out group" members who weren't born from the soil, but instead, stole it (their ancestors did, anyway). Even if land-grabbing has been perpetrated by members of several ethnic groups, all black Kenyans can point to the small white minority without jeopardizing the felt coherence of a nation wracked by ethnoterritorial conflicts.

My respondents bristle at suggestions they might not belong on grounds of racial appearance. One middle-aged woman of English descent, Nicola, tells me she "definitely definitely" considers herself Kenyan, but she recognizes not everyone perceives her that way. She finds it maddening that her belonging could be judged on the basis of her lineage rather than her felt affinity for the country of her birth:

> The one thing that really irritates me is you're driving along and you've got someone shouting out "*Mzungu, mzungu, mzungu* [white person, white person]"![81] And [sometimes] you get somebody nasty saying: "Go back to your country." And it *really* gets on my nerves; it's just—This *is* my country! So I do *definitely* feel very Kenyan.

Yet in spite of their affinity for Kenya, their uneasiness has meant that many settler descendants have kept an exit option open. In her sprawling garden on the fringes of Nairobi, Lorrie sits back in a chair and scratches the scruff of her dog's neck while a Kikuyu housekeeper pours two glasses of lemonade. Speaking on behalf of the wider community of white Kenyans, she says: "Our country, in a way, it was taken away from us, at a certain cutoff point in history—but that doesn't make us *feel* any less for that country. You know, although we—I sort of regard us as guests in the country and I've always got one eye out, just in case."

Like quite a few white Kenyans I know, Lorrie hedges her bets. She holds both a Kenyan passport and a British one to cover any contingencies: in case Kenyan politics head into another vortex; in case the economy irretrievably breaks down; in case sentiment turns violently against those perceived as elite interlopers. Malcolm, from his Nairobi office, explains this freedom with mingled candor and embarrassment: "We have an exit strategy in our wallet, though it sounds awful to say it." This exit strategy was not legal, for most, until 2010. At Independence, Europeans, Asians, and other immigrant groups were allowed to apply for Kenyan citizenship provided they renounced other citizenships. Some whites opted not to apply for Kenyan passports at all (though this filled their work lives with extra red tape, it felt like a safer option), while others obtained Kenyan passports and found ways to hold European ones too (through *jus sanguinis,* or "rights of blood," laws) under the table. But Kenya's new 2010 constitution formalized the right to dual citizenship, so settler descendants can now be legally Kenyan *and* European. Socially, many were both already. Their kin ties and friendships outside of the country, cultivated through schooling, travel, and Facebook pages, had given them the luxury of cosmopolitans who, in principle, anyway, have somewhere else to land. In truth, some say, the peculiar feeling of being both nationalist and supranational inspires a trace of guilt, for unlike most other Kenyan citizens, they would not be forced to stick it out in place if political chaos broke out.

Even with their Kenyan passports, settler descendants know that concepts of indigeneity loom large in conflicts over who belongs, all over sub-Saharan Africa.[82] In Zimbabwe, for instance, white commercial farmers heard President Mugabe deem them "true Zimbabweans" in 1980, but by the 1990s political elites were pronouncing Zimbabwe a "black nation," and new discourses of indigenization, along with Mugabe's apparent need to shore up his political support, legitimated the violent seizure of many white-owned farms.[83] A similar specter arose in the rhetoric surrounding a Nakuru-based white farmer in his sixties, Malcolm Bell, who was engaged in a protracted lawsuit against the former Kenyan President Daniel Arap Moi over the past decade. Moi owns a large plot of neighboring land, and in the 1980s agreed that if Bell's father gave Moi one hundred acres, Moi's staff would connect electricity, drill a borehole, and construct a cattle dip. When Moi's camp failed to live up to his end of the bargain and threatened to strip Bell of all his land if he complained, Bell sued for trespass, winning the case in 2012. The verdict was vexing to the Kenyan public, many already cynical about the wealth of the former president, but still more dismayed at the prospect of a white Kenyan winning back land from the courts. On postings responding to an NTV report on the case, dozens weighed in against Bell: "I thought white settlers were long gone. So we still have 100+acres of land for them?" Others wrote, "Why take land from a Kenyan to a white settler?" and "How can a settler claim the land? We should get advice from Mugabe [in Zimbabwe]." Another poster invoked the Mau Mau revolt as an historical moment that ought to have culminated in the total expulsion of colonials and their descendants:

"MAU MAU means *mzungu aende ulaya mwafrika apate uhuru* [the white people should return to Europe and the African should get freedom]."[84]

Such responses were not lost on Bell, who, as the journalist Wanjiru Macharia notes, "gets upset at being referred to as a white settler." As if to counteract the stigma of this term, Bell repeatedly recites his life history, "reiterat[ing] that he is a Kenyan, born in Mombasa and brought up in Nakuru." In his emphatic claims to belong, Bell adduces not only *jus soli*, the rights of someone born on particular soil, but also his cultural credentials in having attended local schools for many years; he "only" went to Europe, he says, to study agricultural engineering at university. He reaches back into his line of descent, explaining that his mother was born and brought up in Rongai, and that his mother and grandfather are buried at the Nakuru North Cemetery, while his father is buried "on this farm." These words indirectly evoke widespread African ways of thinking about land entitlement, in which one hopes to be buried in one's ancestral homeland, to dwell alongside the spirits of one's forebears. If the term "settler" implies an outsider, Bell underscores that his entitlement began before his birth through ancestral ties. But many onlookers felt he still counted as a colonial interloper.[85]

Perhaps some intermingling of pride and anxiety about belonging prompted so many white Kenyans, in conversation with me, to tout the fact that they are "third-," "fourth-," or even "fifth-generation Kenyan"—though as often as not, the description only works for one branch of their ancestry. It is a very tenuous autochthony, measured in countable generations, compared to that of black Kenyans who date their ethnic group's roots in a given province (justly or not) "since time immemorial." In light of whites' limited time-depth in the country, they sometimes draw on a foil, a contrast group, among those they call "two-year wonders"; expatriate Europeans and Americans who come to Kenya for just a few years, and, say my respondents, fail to understand the place and its people. "Two-year wonders" may try to put their oar in, but their superficial grasp of things inevitably reveals itself. Hence, for instance, when settler descendants in the Naivasha floriculture industry also find themselves in competition with European (e.g., Dutch) flower-farmers, they frame themselves as the *real* stewards of the lake, by virtue of their long-standing history in Kenya and deeper understanding of its dynamics.[86]

But no matter the depth of their involvement in Kenyan farming, conservation, or the wider economy, workaday Kenyans can see how removed most white Kenyans are from Kenya's political process. "We keep our heads behind the parapet" of Kenya's political life, as one middle-aged white farmer puts it to me. This distance is thrown into relief by the exception to the rule: Richard Leakey, the grandson of Christian missionaries and son of the famous founders of paleoanthropology, Louis and Mary Leakey. Louis had famously claimed he identified more with Kikuyu than with settlers, and Richard, whom I interviewed in 2014, considers himself an outlier in his own way. His skin at sixty-nine is mottled from years of equatorial sun, no doubt intensified by the early years he spent in his parents' footsteps scouring the dry areas of northern Kenya for hominid fossils. Leakey moved on to other wide-open spaces, serving for several electrifying years as the director of Kenya Wildlife Service, where he curtailed the ivory trade by arming his wardens with automatic weapons and authorizing them to shoot poachers on sight. Detractors accused him of caring more about wildlife than people (a common charge, it should be said, against white conservationists in Kenya), and he had enough enemies that in 1993, when his single-engine Cessna crashed mysteriously, many suspected an assassination attempt. Leakey lost both legs in the disaster, but soon learned to walk on prosthetics, and forged undeterred into politics. In 1995, fed up with Kenya's crumbling infrastructure and the corruption of Moi's regime, he co-founded a new opposition party called Safina. His political enemies branded him racist and colonialist, and at one point he was attacked and whipped severely on the campaign trail, reportedly by thugs hired by Moi.[87] He displayed long red welts across his back to press cameras.

Rather than throwing support behind Leakey, other white Kenyans feared he would attract political retribution to their entire community. Leakey's brother Philip (himself a member of Parliament) led a contingent of eighty-eight white businessmen, agriculturalists, and ranchers to the lawn of the State House in Nairobi, where they pledged allegiance to Moi's administration. But Moi reassured them that his only target was Richard Leakey.[88] The latter won enough votes to be elected MP, and, in a political turnaround, Moi later appointed him head of the civil service.

All in all, Leakey's political career exposes the political invisibility of other settler descendants. Today, most lie low; they are loathe to discuss which candidates they voted for, and some don't even bother to vote. Leakey himself is grumpy about the white Kenyan community, telling a journalist, "These people bore me stiff and I'm not part of that set at all. . . . Some of them are pretty racist people deep down. They don't mix and have very negative attitudes to their fellow Kenyans. I keep them at arm's length and I find them offensive." In conversation with me, he describes himself as having put his body on the line for Kenya, unlike settler descendants who've sought out security and comfort. In fact, he doesn't think of himself as particularly white. "Everything that anyone can do, I've done" he says cheerfully. "From activism and politics, to burning police cars, to starting riots, to being locked up—and I've never been singled out as a white guy. I've been singled out as a troublemaker." This is a simplification—Leakey's political enemies have been delighted to highlight his race—but he's also right that he stands apart from most settler descendants. He tells me he was asked, recently, if he'd like to be put up for membership at the Muthaiga Club—a gorgeously manicured colonial remnant that, though now multiracial in membership, remains heavily influenced by white socialites from old Kenya families. A white club secretary urged him not to apply, saying that it wouldn't end well; the members wouldn't admit him, and the club would be embarrassed by the drama. But I had the sense that to Leakey, this pre-emptive rejection was a badge of pride. The Muthaiga whites may belong to the club, but Leakey belongs to Kenya.

Leakey feels satisfied with himself morally, having plunged headfirst into the fray of black Kenyan movers and shakers. He also takes pride in his father's gadfly role among settlers; although Louis publicly denounced the Mau Mau rebellion, he was also a sometime advocate for African rights. But unlike the Leakeys, many settler descendants find it a struggle to cope with the loss of the moral standing their forebears assumed they had. As Social Darwinism and scientific racism gave way to liberal notions of equal rights, elderly Kenyans who had been instrumental to empire felt the sting of judgment against them. Some younger whites felt the confusion of questioning their families' old assumptions about the social universe. Today, many of the former settlers and settler descendants I spoke to found it upsetting to hear the colonial past invoked, or to see themselves through the eyes of critics.[89]

As a leftist American academic, my very presence put some of them defensive. The Nairobi-based businesswoman Nicola, for instance, hosted me for coffee in her living room one day, and when I remarked on a beautiful arrangement of roses on her coffee table, muttered, "Well, I hope you won't take this as a sign that we're exploiters." I must have looked surprised, so Nicola went on to describe the shock of a friend who had hosted an English house guest and later discovered the guest had written up her impressions on-line:

The blog was slagging the family off, saying they were colonial and they all live like aristocrats and they all drink red wine. And just like that, I got a lot of grief in England; people said "You have slaves in your house! And I'd say, "You mean our staff? How are they slaves? [They get a] monthly salary and they're lining up for this job!" . . . And it also gets simplified here because when you sort of chat to locals about it, they haven't been told any of the good side. [I'll] get a debate going and they'll be like "You guys have done this, took our land and exploited." And I'll be like: "[It] wasn't actually your land and they did bring all these crops." My uncle started the probation service, taking naughty youths and giving them education!

Like Nicola, other white Kenyans would play down critiques of the colonial system by playing up the infrastructure it brought—roads, schools, clinics, large-scale agriculture, rule of law, and state bureaucracy. Similarly, some white Zimbabweans on the defensive protest that, far from coming to "Rhodesia" to exploit it, they came to teach and bring the benefits of civilization.[90] Settler descendants also argue repeatedly that their forebears should be exonerated because they *thought* they were doing the right thing. Mary, who had the prickly confrontation with the magazine seller, reflected on her great uncle, who was instrumental in establishing the coffee industry in Kenya:

I've always been very proud of what he did. And then when I hear people say [she adopts a low, muttering voice] "Oh those dreadful old colonials," I must say it does, it hurts! I think: "*Oh!* Don't don't talk about him like that! He's a *wonderful* man! Who took Kenya a step up!" You know, in agriculture and this sort of thing. So I think that's been quite hard. . . . I believe he came with good intentions. . . . I believe a *lot* of them came with good intentions.

Mary laughed weakly and added a concession: "Whether, whether it was all carried out right, I mean, that's beyond me." But, she says, "I hate hearing that people came to exploit the Kenyan people or the country. Because I really believe that the majority did not. That they came with the right intentions."

Yet occasionally, I met a settler descendant who expressed discomfort or even a degree of chagrin at the colonial history that benefited them so. Jos, for instance, is the middle-aged descendant of a well-to-do colonial family that sold their farmland at Independence and bought estates in the Nairobi area. As we sat at a café on the outskirts of Nairobi, Jos ran his hand through a thick shock of light brown hair and peered around to be sure that none of his acquaintances were in earshot. "I'm unusual," he said, "because I think this country's still in a caste system from the way it got set up." He leans in, lowering his voice as he alludes to his parents' and grandparents' generations: "I think they all kind of built a country, somehow, built a country for white people on the backs of black people, let's not forget that . . . I think they didn't even humanize them, you know, they were just an inconvenience. . . . That was the way people thought. That was the way people thought."

Jos repeatedly implored me to conceal his identity, since his opinions would be so unpopular with even his close friends. The more people I spoke to, the more I could see why. For most of them, confessionals about colonial ills had to be quickly followed by protestations that their family was now giving back to Kenya, or denials that the colonial past should even matter.

As my conversations with white Kenyans unfolded, I grew to anticipate the muddle of moral double consciousness I encountered again and again. My respondents were clearly aware that as an American academic, I would be steeped in critiques of colonialism, and they sometimes framed their responses accordingly. The environmental anthropologist Megan Styles had a similar experience in her study of flower farmers around Lake Naivasha. She found that white Kenyan farmers would routinely, preemptively deliver what Styles called "the speech," a defense of their community, framed with the assumption that Styles's vantage point would be both liberal and critical of them, stoked and (mis)informed by Western news outlets such as the BBC.[91] I noted too some of the smaller verbal gestures that suggested my respondents were grappling with others' judgments. Several self-consciously put scare quotes around controversial phrases from the colonial era, such as "the white highlands" (prime land the British expropriated from Africans), or "half-caste" ("a horrible phrase. . . . Today we would say "mixed-race").[92] Elderly interlocutors threw a glance in my direction while sheepishly framing their actions of half a century ago: "I suppose it all looks so awful in the light of today." Others, with rueful humor, dubbed themselves "just dreadful old colonials," evidently unreconstructed, yet perhaps—if they could make such a quip—not as bad as all that. Even younger white Kenyans, more influenced from a young age by liberal attitudes, sometimes expressed a degree of chagrin about their own habits. In the words of a thirty-something informant describing their relationships with their domestic servants: "I guess probably we're, um, probably not right in the way that we are." And Tom Cholmondeley himself, who spoke with me in Kamiti Prison in July 2008, occupied a tactfully ambiguous stance between condemnation and defense of colonialism. "I'm not an apologist," he said, half-amused, half-indignant, "but it seems a little odd to use modern standards to judge what happened forty-five years ago."

This shadow on the conscience, a sense of being judged or haunted by forces external and, sometimes, internal, is common among the white Kenyans I spoke to. Even the act of framing one's self in virtual scare quotes as an "old colonial" is no minor matter; it suggests that the weight of historical change has inflected white Kenyans' subjectivity, in spite of the privileges they retain. They feel themselves straddling two historical eras that have been pitted against each other. And unlike South Africa, Kenya has had no official forum—no Truth and Reconciliation Commission, for instance—through which to confront and contend with the colonial past, or to define a national vocabulary for talking about race and redemption. In spite of Kenyatta's speech, settler descendants have found that not all has been forgotten or forgiven after all, and that history and enduring racial inequalities sometimes surge into popular discourse to work against their full belonging. Some are in search of a sense of legitimacy, wishing they could be embraced more fully as part of the nation. They cast furtive glances backward at the uglier aspects of the colonial past, and frame themselves as key to Kenya's economic and environmental future. And through all of it, the question of how they are represented and how to represent themselves arises again and again.

SELECTIVE REPRESENTATIONS: STRUGGLING WITH HISTORIES

Kenya's settler past has been a source of fascination to many. In this section I discuss some of these outsiders' portrayals, as well as my respondents' rejoinders to them. Ultimately, I find that recent histories of the Mau Mau rebellion evoked some of the most anguished but mostly defensive responses among those I spoke to, pulling to the surface acute white Kenyan anxieties about their families' histories and their own entitlement to belong. The haunting of white Kenyans by Mau Mau encapsulates many of the dynamics that return in chapters to come: unpalatable and controversial colonial deeds, their second life in twenty-first century Kenya, and white Kenyans' complex responses to them, involving a blend of moral double consciousness and structural oblivion.

White Kenyans have long struggled with popular images of them, which have been profuse and unflattering. For decades, Western audiences have been riveted by media portrayals of early twentieth-century European aristocrats shooting lions on the savannah and conducting extramarital affairs on zebra-hide rugs. The so-called Happy Valley set, immortalized in a 1987 BBC television drama of the same name, were rendered as a lotus-eating group caught up in a miasma of drink, drugs, and scandal. The figures included settler pioneers such as Hugh Chol-mondeley, the third Baron Delamere, and his son and heir, the fourth Baron Delamere; extraordinary women such as Karen Blixen, whose Danish accent and independent spirit were later captured on film (*Out of Africa*) by Meryl Streep in 1987; wanton and adventuresome heir-esses such as Lady Idina Sackville; and the philandering Lord Erroll, whose 1941 murder, probably the outcome of a love triangle, has been the subject of ongoing speculation in print and in the 1987 film *White Mischief.*

The contemporary cousin of the Happy Valley hedonist is the pro-verbial "Kenya cowboy" (or KC). The KC prototype is an anti-intellec-tual white male who works in the safari industry, has a proclivity for fast cars and women, and brags about the generational depth of his family's history in Kenya. David Bennun's memoir of growing up in an expatriate family in 1970s Kenya satirizes the KC figure as "part squire, part redneck, and all around party animal." The American journalist Michael Hiltzik characterizes him as "the type of young white native who still [strides] firmly around Nairobi and upcountry as if he were still divine heir to this land of lush potential." And the British writer Ian Williams implies that the only energy to be found in the Muthaiga Club comes from the KC types who wrestle on the barroom floor.[93]

The Happy Valley and KC images trouble settler descendants, but they've also been handy to those of them in the tourism industry. In a bar one day, one of my contacts was ribbed by an Asian Kenyan col-league about the "nostalgic safaris" he offers his American and Euro-pean clientele, and he is far from alone. Finch Hatton's Safari Camp in Tsavo West National Park, for instance, bills itself as "reminiscent of an era that epitomized style and good taste"; its print ads feature an image of European china on display in a wall cabinet and a close-up of a paint-ing of a colonial-era "houseboy," in a stiff-collared, buttoned-up smock.[94] Bill Winter Safaris International, run by a settler descendant, promises style from "the days of old, when 'going on safari' meant packing up the family silver and dinnerware, the rifles and the ammo, and trekking off into the wild unknown."[95] Other guides, too, cultivate this gritty yet glamorous image; they can locate a pride of lions in the morning, josh with their Maasai guides while repairing a Land Rover engine in the afternoon, then enjoy a sundowner—a whisky or gin and tonic—outdoors with their international clients. Airbrushed evocations of the good old days appeal to tourists and make settler descendants look at home in Kenya. But they do less than nothing for their reputation among most Kenyan citizens.

Many elderly former settlers and settler descendants bristle at the caricatures of Happy Valley recidivists and spoiled brat KCs, preferring to portray their family members (and themselves, by extension) as hard-working pioneers. Their anxiety betrays a telling reversal. In the colonial era, it was poor whites who embarrassed the white majority, invested in their collective prestige, but today many white Kenyans I spoke to objected to being "tarred by the same brush" (in their words) as the most elite and hedonistic of their forebears. One after another, they insisted that the image of dissolute wealth among them—past and present—is unrepresentative of the majority.[96] "Our grandparents suffered drought, locusts, disease, and terrible personal losses," Nicola said, staring me fixedly in the eye. She reminded me that the Great Depression and currency problems made their economic situation precarious, and that the early years of farming in Kenya involved much trial and error. "Some families lost everything, again and again, and had to keep rebuilding their lives from the dust, up." Several elderly informants described their parents' living conditions as "gritty" or "hardscrabble," saying that their very survival, let alone their pleasures, required great tenacity and imagination.[97] As for "Kenya Cowboys," everyone recognized the stereotype, but nobody I spoke to would admit to fitting it themselves.

Still, the narratives most grating to my respondents were the scholarly ones that focus on colonial whites' exploitation, racism, cruelty, and violence. Though most settler descendants don't read academic texts, critical messages from the academy sometimes reach them from the Kenyan press or even their own youth, who occasionally come back from their schooling in the United Kingdom to shock their elders with their progressive views. In turn, some older settler descendants circulate self-justifying print material as a kind of antidote. More than one octogenarian, for instance, pressed on me a yellowed copy of the late administrator Christopher Wilson's 1952 volume *Before the Dawn in Kenya*. "This will explain to you," said one, "why it has not been all roses since Independence." Wilson's volume draws on clichés of the barbaric "lazy native" who is more animal than human, and argues that on their own Africans had starkly "fail[ed] . . . to advance," being mired in a "long

African night" of famine, illness, superstition, drunkenness, and tribal warfare. The voices calling for African self-governance, he argues, are merely sentimental, in denial of the lawlessness, cruelty, and slavery that prevailed before whites arrived.[98]

More recently, a few settler descendants have put together histories of settler lives that also circulated among some of my respondents. While these volumes leave behind Wilson's heavy-handed Social Darwinism, they tend to move from one (often affectionate) biography or anecdote to another. Erroll Trzebinski's *The Kenya Pioneers* and Christine Nicholls's *Red Strangers: The White Tribe of Kenya*, for instance, are rich with detail about colonial personalities and not uncomplicated in their rendering of colonial motives, but they give relatively little space to the displacement and disenfranchisement of Africans. Indeed, Nicholls's book opens on a defensive note: "Now it is fashionably pious to disavow the colonial years. [But] I want to evaluate their real contribution to the development of Kenya. . . . There is indeed much to condemn, but the truth remains that there was a great deal of good."[99]

Other writings—settler fiction and memoirs—have buoyed white confidence before and after Kenya's independence. The typical "Kenya novel" is a picaresque historical romance set in the White Highlands, touting the railways, roads, hospitals and schools that signified to whites the arrival of civilization on the continent that needed it the most.[100] Kenya was also was a place where remarkable women—the writers Karen Blixen (1885–1961), Beryl Markham (1902–86), and Elspeth Huxley (1907–97), for instance—enjoyed freedoms unusual for their time and documented their adventures.[101] Some of Huxley's writings celebrated the derring-do of Delamere and other settlers in the founding of Kenya Colony, though she could also be gently critical of elements of empire (indeed, she was among the few to contemplate how Kikuyu might have felt about the first settlers).[102] Perhaps the quintessential administrator's or settler's account, though, was laced with cheerfully rendered near-misses in the bush, colorful personalities, and benign negotiations with Africans.

Today, there is a small cottage industry for these reminiscences, including the nostalgic magazine *Old Africa*, published out of Kijabe.[103] Much of this material extols settler resilience—suffering through appendectomies on kitchen tables; watching homes and belongings wash away in the rainy season, losing children to snakebite, and so forth. Most remember Kenya's colonial-era landscapes, wildlife, and people through the gauzy lens of personal memory. A few describe settler terror during the Mau Mau era—mothers sitting bolt upright in their nightgowns clutching rifles, or the horror of finding a servant swinging from the neck behind the house. But it is rare for these reminiscences to step back and explore the big picture of colonial inequalities, or to imagine the vantage point of the disenfranchised. Rather, these narratives, up close and personal with European characters, foster structural oblivion.

As a result, some white Kenyans doubt the claims historians make about, for example, the disenfranchising effects of colonial policies, or the manifestations of settler racism. Some of those from former settler families seem to feel that their forebears worked so hard, risked so much, and so loved and invested in the place that surely they could not have been in the wrong. Several remarked that they know many black Kenyans who, in the words of Malcolm, "would rather be governed by the European than under the thumb of their own leaders." This claim, it should be said, isn't entirely invented; while many Kenyans hold scathing views of the colonial era, some hold it in higher regard. When the Kenyan historian Kenda Mutongi (2007) returned to her home in Western Province after years of studying colonial history abroad, for instance, she was shaken to hear elders waxing nostalgic about British governance. Mutongi concluded that their idealization of colonialism had emerged largely out of disappointment with corruption among Kenya's post-independence political leaders. Regardless, even when Kenyans merely gripe about their politicians' failures, it encourages settler descendants to feel that the British colonial authorities would have done a better job, or at the very least that Kenya should have eased more gradually into independence.

The historical event that precipitates the most anxiety among white Kenyans is the Mau Mau rebellion, which has once again become a prominent part of the national conversation over the past decade, in large part due to new scholarly accounts of the British administration's actions during the Mau Mau era. These new histories have been spun in opposite directions by my settler descendant respondents and by Kikuyu (and some other) nationalists. Many settler descendants I spoke to contend that the colonial administration has been unfairly and harshly criticized, but Kikuyu nationalists have cherry-picked the evidence in their own way for a simplified version of Mau Mau that reflects well on their community as central to the nation, while defining anyone complicit in colonial rule as an outsider.

The Mau Mau events themselves were certainly dreadful enough to stir longstanding passions. Over the course of the conflict, Mau Mau supporters killed thirty-two white settlers and, in what many historians now see as a civil war, took the lives of around two thousand Africans who were not committed to the movement.[104] Meanwhile, the colonial administration rounded up Mau Mau, suspected Mau Mau, and Kikuyu people into patrolled temporary villages and concentration camps for what they euphemistically called "rehabilitation." By the time the British declared the Emergency over seven years later, the administration had detained at least 150,000 Kikuyu, tortured or otherwise abused untold numbers of these, and, by some reckonings, killed at least 20,000 in combat.[105] Many others also died in the detention camps and the patrolled villages housing other Kikuyu.

To the newly elected Jomo Kenyatta in 1963, Mau Mau was an unwelcome, embarrassing reminder of the bloody conflicts he hoped to move past, including internecine strife between rebels and loyalists. But the suppression of its memory did not last; the Mau Mau Veterans' organization was unbanned in 2003, and its veterans began an extended bid for recognition as nationalist freedom fighters, while a subset of them filed a lawsuit against the British government for its human rights abuses during their incarceration.[106] The reframing of Mau Mau rebels as liberation heroes was facilitated by the publication, in 2005, of two histories detailing British atrocities and injustices committed during the crackdown on Mau Mau. In *Histories of the Hanged: The Dirty War in Kenya and the End of Empire*, David Anderson explains the widespread misery and underground political movements that fostered the rebellion. While he describes "atrocity and excess on both sides" of the conflict, including rebel attacks on loyalist Kikuyu, he recounts as well how the colonial court system sent over 1,000 Mau Mau suspects to the gallows, often on slim evidence. In *Imperial Reckoning: The Untold Story of Britain's Gulag in Kenya,* Caroline Elkins draws on oral histories to document extensive atrocities the colonial administration inflicted on captive rebels, which had been drastically underplayed in official accounts. She also argues that colonial authorities ultimately detained "nearly the entire Kikuyu population," and that a genocidal punishment resulted in as many as 300,000 deaths, rather than 12,000, as colonial officials claimed.[107]

Scholarly critics (British, American, and Kenyan) countered that, while the terrible abuse of captives must not be denied, Elkins misreads quantitative evidence, overestimates the number of Kikuyu casualties, ignores the loyalists and the civil war within Mau Mau, erases the participation of non-Kikuyu ethnicities in the rebellion, and pits oversimplified African heroes against cartoonish British villains.[108] But the contradictory intricacies of Mau Mau run against the grain of the triumphal nationalist narrative sought by enthusiastic portions of the Kenyan public and the administration. Elkins's book has been "used," the historian Daniel Branch argues, "as an intellectual prop" by Kenya's government in attempting to reclaim a nationalist historical narrative.[109] The popular narratives of Mau Mau now circulating give Kikuyu history primacy over the many other ethnic groups in Kenya, sidestep the complex, mixed motives of historical actors, and marginalize Kenyans who had opposed Mau Mau violence or who fear Kikuyu dominance.[110] Meanwhile, these simplified histories have neatly framed settler families as outsiders and conversely help to define what it is to be a Kenyan insider.

When I returned to Kenya in 2008, settler descendants were still feeling taken aback by the publication of these volumes, particularly Elkins's. Some selectively read the critical book reviews circulating on the Internet (particularly those by conservative British journalists) and extended them to argue, in effect, that British atrocities in the Mau Mau era had been vanishingly rare, and indeed that *most* historians' charges against the colonial regime were rubbish. They knew, after all, that their parents and grandparents were "good people." Most of those I spoke to, furthermore, relied on their community's collective amnesia about what had happened in those detention camps and patrolled villages. The administration had orchestrated an archival cover-up, and the British men involved in violent crackdowns may have downplayed them within their families. Communicating within a fairly closed circuit, settlers of that era had fixated on horror stories about those few dozen among them who had been tortured and murdered in their homes. Through governmentally sanctioned ignorance, primal fear, and the biases of settler colonialism, structural oblivion—in this case, an erasure of African experiences in the Mau Mau era—would have been sustained.[111]

It is not surprising, then, that most of my respondents had not read Elkins's book, or had rapidly put it down. Jonathan, a farm manager in Naivasha, said, "I dabbled in the book, and in fact I was going to read the whole thing, [but] I thought it was very unbalanced." Jos, the undercover critic of colonialism, summarized the apoplectic reactions of his peers. The book for them was an emotional trigger rather than a text to be read:

[T]here was *such* an objection to [Elkins's book] amongst the white community. A, a sort of gut, visceral thing—although people haven't even read it. . . . Most people won't read it. They *won't even look at it*. That's it. I haven't met *one* white Kenyan who's read it . . . 'No, no, I'm not going to read that, it's a load of crap. It's just a—She's just a rabble rouser! She's just rabble rousing! And this and that.

Jos told me he had forced himself to read both Anderson's and Elkins's books, feeling he needed to face the colonial past. He found Elkins's perilously "Kikuyu nationalist," and concluded that Anderson's was "probably fairer." Similarly, a young conservationist, Ellen, told me she had read Anderson's book and appreciated its "balanced" approach, but added that Kenya's then president Mwai Kibaki (a Kikuyu) and his fellow nationalists "must have paid [Elkins] to write that book." Fear underwrote some of these reactions, including fear that their entire community would be identified with the brutalities of the British crackdown in the 1950s. And the fear has some justification. One Kikuyu acquaintance of mine, when he heard I was conducting fieldwork among white Kenyans, informed me that his father had fought in the Mau Mau, and he was appalled that I would spend time hanging out with a community of "murderers."[112]

My respondents had many counterarguments to the new histories of the Mau Mau era. One was a defensive 2005 book, *Kenya, the Kikuyu, and Mau Mau,* by David Lovatt Smith, who arrived in Kenya in 1950 and served in the Kenya Regiment. Sybil, a former settler in her eighties now living in England, produced a signed copy. "This," she said, placing it into my hands, "provides a more objective perspective than that"—she gestured toward my copy of Elkins's book. Sybil had placed yellow post-it notes on several passages, including recapitulated arguments (popular among colonial administrators, and encouraged by figures as diverse as the psychologist John Carothers and Louis Leakey) that Mau Mau fighters were "fanatical" men, "not normal Kikuyu people."[113] Like other administrators, Smith fixates on the notoriously gory "oathing" rituals Mau Mau administered to secure allegiance to their cause. While these oaths built upon a metaphysical and ritual framework already familiar to Kikuyu in times of peace, it was easy for the British to seize upon—and, sometimes, to distort—their frightening details (sex! blood! animal entrails!) to detect an altogether other enemy. Framed in terms of bestial irrationality, Mau Mau rebels could then be portrayed as so lost, so out of control, that the only reasonable redress was containment and psychological as well as religious (putatively Christian) "rehabilitation," accompanied by sometimes violent reminders of colonial power. "Whatever the rights and wrongs of detention," writes Smith, "at the time there was no alternative."[114]

Back in Kenya, I found former settlers and their descendants similarly defensive about the British administration's actions during the Mau Mau era. "[Mau Mau] was fierce on both sides and only *one* side has been really criticized of late. I think I'm upset that the history books have been changed to some extent that shows colonialism in a bad light," the middle-aged hotelier Gordon told me. A conservationist in her late twenties told me she took an interest in learning about Kenya's past from white Kenyan friends and family members. She smoothed her blonde hair and glanced as if for approval at a friend of her father's who had stumbled into our conversation at a club and pulled up a chair. "I've talked to everyone I know who's been in Mau Mau. There was like a handful of whites who were actually killed in that and hundreds of Africans that were killed, huge. It was tribalism; Kikuyus moved into land that wasn't theirs and it was all bubbling and bubbling. They got into cults."

"My friends in Europe," she went on, "assume the Mau Mau was mainly black against white, equivalent to apartheid, when it was [in fact] mainly tribes against tribes." Jenny isn't wrong that strife between rebels and loyalists caused many casualties, but she seems to imply that Africans died only at the hands of other Africans. Mau Mau comes to look more like a movement caused by Kikuyu land grabbing, and perhaps irrational "cults," than the agonies of colonial dispossession.

Other respondents, too, seemed at pains to downplay the racial conflicts at stake. Naomi, a young businesswoman with a practical bob, implied that virtually no hard feelings about Mau Mau remain. She described an elderly friend of hers who had fought against the Mau Mau in the forests outside of Nairobi, and then several years ago was introduced to a Kikuyu Mau Mau veteran. They didn't exactly fall into each other's arms, she says, but neither did they "draw a gun," because they had "shared" something. "What one had to do tested everybody . . . the killings were pretty horrendous, yet there's a bond between you. They lived a chapter forty-five years ago that no one ever does any more. There's a huge bond of friendship." I tried to clarify: "You're talking about a bond across the lines?" "Oh yeah," Naomi continued. "Because it's *gone*. The issues are *gone*. People shared an experience and then . . . " she trailed off. Naomi would like the deeds of the past to remain in the past and antipathies to fade. But whatever such personal encounters between veterans on the two sides have been like, Mau Mau has mounted in symbolic importance and thrown whites into the spotlight.

Some older settler descendants are still apoplectic at the way the Mau Mau story has been narrated over the past decade, feeling that it negates their community's contributions. Reginald Massie-Blomfield, headmaster of a British Christian preparatory school in Nairobi has been an outspoken critic. For some years Massie-Blomfield penned near weekly letters to the editor of Kenya's *Daily Nation* in an effort to restore the reputation of colonialism in Kenya, touting, for example, the modern agricultural economy and the free press.[115] In 2013, complaining that the Mau Mau veterans suing the British government were merely out for profit, he argued that the *Daily Nation* should instead "honor the loyal Kikuyus who refused to compromise their souls by joining the Mau Mau."[116] If Kenya's schools would stop fostering "prejudices," he argued, "we would not be a tribalised society and would recognise our debt to the colonists who brought Kenya into being."[117] *Daily Nation* staff and readers thought him inflammatory, however, and one commentator referred to him as a "colonialist remnant."

Of all my white Kenyan respondents, Jos was the most inclined to step back from his community to concede that every narrative about reality emerges from a partial and political vantage point. Jos admits, too, that structural oblivion underlies the prevalent "white" understanding of colonial history:

> Whether [Elkins] inflated the figures of the people in the camps or not, I don't know. That's maybe what she did, but you know . . . *any* history is written from a perspective. So we've read the white perspective which is: [he adopts a reasonable-sounding voice] "Colonialism is great so no one suffered and blablabla." This book comes from a different perspective and now we're saying [low gravelly voice] "It's a rabble rouser; they'll hate us for it, bla blabla." [But] colonial history was blanked out in those years, [and] it was just not in the international press until all these history books were finally written *not* from the white man's perspective. 'Cause all the history books until then were, I don't know, Elspeth Huxley . . . where the whites are portrayed as the good guys. And that's what I thought when I grew up. I thought we were the good guys. Well, why wouldn't I, 'cause I wasn't told anything different? . . . [These books] really opened up my eyes on the society in which I was brought up.

While few of my informants were as wide open as Jos to other points of view, I found in other settler descendants as well—especially those in their fifties and younger—an acknowledgement that they have begun to hear multiple voices at play, even in their own minds. One narrative from Nicola, who had been so defensive about the roses on her table, sums up some of the most interesting aspects of white Kenyan subjectivity. As we chatted over lunch for perhaps the third time, I broached the subject of the Mau Mau, telling Nicola that Jos had said his white Kenyan friends wouldn't read Elkins's book. She admitted that she was among them, and mulled it over, thinking out loud:

> You know when that book came out it's kind of [she paused for a couple of seconds, then continued quietly and rapidly] yeah, all those awful things [Nicola switches back into her regular voice] but I mean, look at Germany, for Christ's sake, that's bloody awful too, yeah . . . Yeah . . . we're not that generation . . . I think our generation is, we've moved on. We're not interested. I think *that's* maybe why . . . most friends of his wouldn't bother reading the book. I think because of *that*. I think our generation's moved *on* and we're not—Yes, I do think [very quietly] we *do* in the back of our heads know these awful, awful things happened but [a little louder, but still fairly quiet, looking at the table] it's kind of like: you don't wanna know because it's not you, and it certainly wouldn't be how you would want your generation to be seen.

In this meditation, Nicola tried the suggestion that colonial ills are in the past; that her generation has "moved on" and is "not interested," seeing Mau Mau as irrelevant to their sense of self. And yet, there is another voice in her reflection, one that quietly dwells in a past that won't go away and that provokes in her the discomforts of double consciousness. Quietly, quickly, for instance, she conceded "all those awful things" before invoking the Nazi Holocaust, as if to deflect or relativize whatever transpired in Kenya. A minute later, she again adopted the quiet voice that admitted that they "*do* in the back of our heads know" about a terrible dimension of colonial history. In a moment of deeper self-scrutiny, she suggested that settler descendants may not *want* to know—because such things don't compute with their current intentions or deeds ("it's not you"), and can't easily be reconciled with their contemporary self-image.

With these subtle concessions, Nicola outlined a subjective dynamic I heard from other settler descendants as well. Their official line about who they are and even what they "know" is a profession of how they wish to be seen by themselves and others, and yet this official personage—self-determined, practical, well-meaning—is nevertheless haunted by a collectively shared ancestral past. This past is not detached from the present; rather, to manage it, settler descendants must perpetually engage in performances of detachment and shunting; mental, verbal, and social efforts that meet with varying degrees of success. Many I spoke to know this "in the back of their heads." This kind of doubleness, this affectively charged motion between structural oblivion and glimmers of greater awareness or conscience, is interwoven in my respondents' lives.

As for the British administration's own representation of the Mau Mau, it recently staged a dramatic reversal. In 2012, the British Foreign office was ordered to release its classified records from the detention camps, and archival experts uncovered a trove of many thousands of concealed documents in the Buckinghamshire countryside. The incendiary material affirmed the systematic, brutal mistreatment of Mau Mau detainees in British camps and confirmed that civil servants in London had been aware of what was going on, despite their denials. The revelation also vindicated the Mau Mau veterans who were suing the British government for reparations.

"The days of Britain having to apologize for its colonial history are over," Gordon Brown, then prime minister of the United Kingdom, announced in 2005.[118] Yet now, eight years later, the British government issued an unprecedented apology, and agreed to settle with the veterans out of court. Before a tiny live audience on their green leather seats in House of Commons in London, Foreign Secretary William Hague read aloud: "The British government recognizes that Kenyans were subject to torture and other forms of ill treatment at the hands of the colonial administration . . . [and] sincerely regrets that these abuses took place."[119] David Anderson, writing in the *New York Times,* offered a mingled appeal and prayer: "maybe we in Britain have . . . finally begun to come to terms with our imperial past."[120] How the British government's concession will reverberate among Kenyans of all backgrounds remains to be seen. For many settler descendants, it feels like yet another blow to their community's reputation. In the following chapters, I explore how the past continually rears its head in the present, defining and troubling them as they strive to belong, to defend what they have, and to puzzle through what it can mean to be a white Kenyan today.

2

Loving the Land

"Oh god, yeah, I do," says Paul. We're sitting outside a café in the town of Nanyuki, on wooden folding chairs with canvas backs. A woman walks quietly over the flagstones to set down a coffee before him, then past a tangle of magenta bougainvillea on her way back to the kitchen area. Paul's relatives own a ranch here in the Rift Valley's Laikipia County (known as Laikipia District until 2013), and run a small luxury lodge where tourists can gaze past white curtains at gazelles and cheetah on the plateau. When Paul gives guided tours, he can name every species of succulent plant, tell you about the gestation period of a wild dog, and recognize individual black rhinos by the shape of their horns. I have asked him about this land and whether he feels he "belongs in Kenya."

> It's the air I breathe, you know? I mean, since we were young . . . we would have these amazing camping safaris—we would go out for two weeks and never see another vehicle. We'd drag a carcass, like a tommy [Thomson's Gazelle] carcass near the campfire—or near the camp—so we could sit back and watch the lions eat it. I mean, you tell people this, sometimes we tell our guests [at the lodge]. They think we must have been crazy. But we did it all.

For Paul, his family's intervention in the East African circle of life sealed a kind of intimacy with the place. But his claim to entitlement is also more specific; it has to be. A few dozen former settler families own roughly 1 million acres of commercial ranchland in Laikipia—as much as half the land, though nobody seems to agree on the math—and there is a disgruntled population of several thousand Maa-speaking pastoralists, most self-identified as Maasai, in the region.[1] To be sure, thousands of settlers across Kenya gave up their lands at Independence on a "willing buyer, willing seller" basis, and the national population of those from colonial families has dwindled to less than a tenth of what it was. Many large tracts of land in Laikipia are now owned by elite Africans, Asians, and expatriates from a smattering of other nations in Europe, the Americas, and the Middle East. Yet white Kenyans in the area—especially those descended from settler families—have played a disproportionate role in conservation, some fencing in their land as wildlife sanctuaries, where they host a few well-to-do tourists at a time and protect endangered species.

They are also disproportionally symbolic. In August of 2004, Maasai activists in Laikipia drove large herds of cattle onto about a dozen of the ranches owned by whites from old Kenya families, demanding the return of ancestral grazing lands that had been taken by the British colonial government a century earlier. This striking gesture was part of a major bid for damages from the British and Kenyan governments to compensate for injuries and loss of lives, livestock, and land. Up on the ranches, Paul tells me, some of his friends were alarmed and indignant to see Maasai decked out for war, herding livestock onto their property. The situation did not last long, though. Anxious to preserve the tourism-based economy and Western aid, the Kenyan government sent in the paramilitary unit of the Kenyan Police Force to evict the Maasai. A Maasai elder, seventy-year-old Ntinai Ole Moiyare, was shot dead, several others wounded, and 120 more arrested.

These events emerged from a major and painful theme across Kenya today: conflicts over land, which are so often played out in terms of "which ethnic group was here first." Ethno-territorialism was terribly exacerbated by colonial policies and their aftermath; the British administration encouraged the idea that ethnic identities are essential divisions and fostered conflict and competition between these newly reified groups. Both Maasai and Kalenjin, for instance, were displaced from areas of the Rift Valley, and in the colonial era came to regard both whites and other ethnic groups in these regions—including many Kikuyu squatters—as foreign occupiers. Making things worse, when the Crown Lands were turned over to Kenya's first President Jomo Kenyatta in 1963, political patronage meant that Kikuyu were disproportionately favored, and pastoralist grievances went largely unaddressed. In Laikipia and other areas, Kenya is now a crucible of tension over which group is entitled to which place, often on grounds of supposed autochthony.[2]

Paul knew Maasai had grievances, but he couldn't accept their claim that they deserve land reparations. "It's a romantic effort to recreate an impossible past," he said, tilting his chair back and picking with one finger at the chipped varnish on the table. "I think instead we just have to keep moving ahead, you know, formulating policies that are appropriate to the times." Squinting as though he's trying to read my thoughts, he continues: "In the mid 1950s, there were only six million people in Kenya. And now there are forty million, and to feed all of those bodies the economy *needs* to be agriculturally based. Pastoralism is just—it's unrealistic." He paused, and his voice began to take on an edge of irritation. "Listen, you can understand this. Some of the most marginalized people on earth are the poor Red Indians of North America! And, you know, you cannot redress these romanticized notions; we've got to move forward where we are today!"

Paul's childhood memories and sense of belonging are shot through with the intimate romance of place and connection to Kenya's wildlife, but when it comes to Maasai land claims in Laikipia, he is strictly antisentimental. Even before Independence, settlers in Kenya—indeed, across Eastern and Southern Africa—were on the defensive, needing to establish what anthropologist David McDermott Hughes calls "a credible sense of entitlement" to land in the face of African resistance and what were sometimes devastating failures (particularly in the early years) in their efforts to plant crops and rear animals.[3] Among many settler descendants I spoke to, this sense of entitlement comes at the expense of Maasai. At least a dozen white Kenyans told me Maasai land claims are illegitimate, capitalizing on what they termed "that feel good factor" or "that powerful story." Carey, the manager of a horticultural farm in the Rift Valley, said: "You've got all these NGOs who are in there drafting these policies [saying] you've gotta bend over backward to try to *de*-marginalize the marginalized people because of some romantic notion that they have, and it's completely inappropriate!"

Although Paul and Carey both frame their viewpoints as forward-thinking, I was struck by how profoundly settler descendants' views of Laikipia landownership had been shaped by old colonial narratives. To be sure, British settlers had romanticized Maasai aesthetics and their warrior tradition, but Paul and Carey forego that dimension of settler thinking to align themselves with another: in their folk histories, settlers framed themselves as pioneers while ignoring Maasai's sense of disenfranchisement. We can see their preferred narrative in a 1962 volume entitled *They Made It Their Home*, published by a popular settler charitable organization called the East Africa Women's League (EAWL) and dedicated, by Elspeth Huxley, to "the pioneers of Kenya."[4] As Independence rushed closer, EAWL enlisted its members to create colorful needlepoint illustrations of each of Kenya's districts, accompanied by a brief narrative about the area. The book is still sold to a predominantly white clientele of farmer (former settler) families at the EAWL's headquarters at Weal House in Nairobi, where I purchased a copy over Friday coffee and cookies. Its success in collective memory-making is secure; I have seen prints of the needlework designs hanging in the homes of former settler families in Kenya and England.

The book's account of Laikipia is narrated as if from the viewpoint of Satima, a mountain at the northern edge of the Aberdare range, which "has seen the history of the district unfold beneath it from ages past." Allowing a major landform to command this omniscient perspective helps the writers depoliticize Laikipia's painful history; unlike humans, geology bears no grudges. Furthermore, as D. M. Hughes (2010) notes, British colonials often identified more closely with African landscapes than with African people, and in this case, the mountain helpfully identifies with settlers' obliviousness of Maasai predicaments. In its placid way, Satima "has seen the movement of the Masai [sic] back to their southern territories by their thousands in 1912 and the slow influx of Europeans since then." There is no mention on these pages of forcible resettlement or dispossession. Instead, claims the text, "The one period when Satima did not seem to be brooding peacefully over the scene was during the Emergency, when it became a sinister place, in which lurked the Mau Mau who came down, destroying and maiming, taking away the peace from all who dwelt in the shadow of the mountain."[5]

They Made It Their Home, then, makes much of African atrocities during the Mau Mau era while ignoring British ones, and Maasai "movement" out of Laikipia appears to have been voluntary. Displacement generally is all but erased in the text and illustrations, and Huxley herself frames Kenya's colonization in terms of "the penetration of white families into hitherto unpopulated regions," a process that gradually "opened up" a "sleeping" country.[6] Meanwhile, says the text, Mau Mau destroyed the peace of the Laikipia settlers who had known how to steward the place once the Maasai left. Yes, the settlers "made it their home"; rhetorically, too, they made it their own.

A great deal has been written about the politics and ecology of land and wildlife in Africa. I focus here on the politics of affect and moral ideologies among some settler descendants as they struggle to respond to Maasai complaints coming out of Laikipia. As I listened to their fears and frustrations in the wake of the Laikipia incidents, I wondered: How and why do these respondents frame their own emotional connection to land and wildlife as authentic, but Maasai connections as inauthentic, deplorable, and destructive? Why is Maasai nostalgia for freedom illegitimate in so many white Kenyan eyes, even as a sense of freedom is central to whites' love of the land? And what variation do we see among settler descendants in their willingness to come to grips with alternative vantage points—with the reality, in other words, of African discontent?

Obviously, white Kenyan landowners who scorn the "romance of the Maasai" have material motives: They want to hold on to their title deeds. But even some of the businesspeople I spoke to in (for instance) Nairobi, those who aren't major landowners, displayed some of this derision for Maasai activism, and none of them see this dynamic as simple greed. Instead, they frame their perspectives on history, ecology, and land-and-wildlife stewardship as correct and morally superior. Many are profoundly detached from Maasai points of view, and their rhetoric—some of it dating to the colonial era—leaches empathy away from Maasai by deleting their historical presence or by representing their lifestyle as lacking integrity and focus. They also disdain Maasai distortions of fact when they find them (and such distortions can indeed be found), a dynamic that helps them feel that broader Maasai claims are disingenuous. It adds up to another instance of structural oblivion: the failure to grasp or appreciate the vantage point of those who feel oppressed, facilitated by a culturally particular ideological framework, and accompanied by the conceptual erasure of historical, cultural, and economic structures that have given rise to such grievances.

All of that said, as I describe below, recent pressures have prompted some settler descendants, however grudgingly, to begin to imagine how Maasai might view the moral landscape. This development is triggered by political, economic, and ecological pragmatics, including the global push for community-oriented conservation, but it translates into a new trend in consciousness. It signals whites' embryonic perspectivism: new recognition that their understanding of the world, and indeed of "truth," is limited by their vantage point, and that there are other possible vantage points. At the same time, however, community-based conservation allows whites to retain the stewardship of the land and wildlife, while feeling like benevolent patrons to the black Kenyans living nearby. In their uneasy movement from structural oblivion to the "second sight" of perspectivism and back again, we see whites' incipient moral double consciousness in action and the framework for fresh questions about how they might situate themselves in the land they love when other inhabitants do not always welcome their approach.

LAND ALIENATION, COLONIAL ERASURES, AND THE DISTRESS OF DISPOSSESSION

Every ethnic group, every subcommunity, in Kenya seems to have its own sense of history and entitlement, and each of these histories is both partial and highly charged with cultural and spiritual importance. There can be few places in the world where so many competing myths jostle about practically every square kilometer of land. Many Kenyans hope to be buried on their ancestral homesteads, to dwell alongside the spirits of their forebears. Their collective memories of place are often intimately bound up with a sense of group identity, so that places are much more than just commodities to be bought or sold. Among some Kenyan peoples, social identity and relations of trust are fashioned by the customary, often collective, transfer of land and the entrustment of land for use.[7] And control over land, of course, has tremendous value in a place where so many people compete over such limited resources. For many, land feels like life itself.

In the nineteenth century, the British colonial government started to expropriate East African land with disregard for existing community ownership arrangements. Although these had varied across East Africa, they were often highly structured, involving the careful inheritance or allocation of rights and obligations, and relying on an ethos of group sharing.[8] But in the eyes of officials and settlers, individual land rights, particularly on the part of Europeans, would encourage greater agricultural production and "proper" land use—a common European colonial theme across Africa and the New World.[9] And so, in the early twentieth century, the Crown Lands Ordinance of 1902 imposed English property law. Africans were to forfeit any land not occupied or developed—though interpretation of these criteria was so biased that Africans could easily be evicted and confined to Native Reserves. The state could then parcel out the so-called White Highlands of the Rift Valley to European and South African settlers, who ran their farms on the back of poorly paid Africans squeezed into labor by household taxes. Migrating in from the reserves, many such workers would become defined by their predicament as squatters.[10]

In European eyes, though, the land was in just the right hands. Colonial ideologies of land tenure were grounded in a Lockeian model in which land rights are established through a particular *kind* of labor that changes and "improves" the environment. "As much land as a man tills, plants, improves, cultivates, and can use the product of," writes Locke, "so much is his property."[11] Scholars in recent decades have noted that Locke had a vested interest in the European settlement of North America, and that his theories handily discredited customary land use among Amerindians.[12] Eurocentrism was still the order of the day a couple of centuries later in East Africa, where Commissioner Sir Arthur Hardinge held, Lotte Hughes says, "that Africans only owned land so long as they occupied or cultivated it. The moment they moved off the land it became 'waste.'"[13] The Lockeian model overlooks the ways in which pastoralists *did* transform the land, more subtly, as they grazed their animals, moved on, and returned to graze again.[14] But settler descendants still feel that they and their forebears worked hard to develop the land (and, indeed, other aspects of the nation's infrastructure). So, the feeling goes, it belongs to them, and they to it.[15] Working the land, it seems, establishes belonging through a kind of reverse autochthony; those of European descent may not be "born of the soil," but the soil was born of them.

And so, the "movement of the Maasai" out of Laikipia mentioned in EAWL's needlepoint volume was anything but benign. In the late nineteenth century, Maasai pastoralists had ranged from the Laikipia plateau to the north, down through what is now Tanzania, and West across much of the Rift Valley, including those cool, green highlands that would become so desirable to colonial settlers. They practiced transhumant seasonal migration, meaning they followed the rains to graze their cattle, and by shifting between lower and higher ground, allowed the vegetation to grow back. They had trade relationships and strategic intermarriages with their Bantu neighbors, including Kikuyu, Kamba, Embu, and Meru peoples, who were cultivators.[16] Within their subcultural groups (between fourteen and twenty-two of them, depending on how they are counted), Maasai had a complex system of rights to land, well water, and other resources. The Maasai notion of *e-rishata,* for example, distinguished zones in which certain families negotiated for rights to mingle together and graze their herds in certain areas. In the nineteenth century, British officials' maps loosely recognized Maasai proprietorship, labeling the East African highlands "Maasailand."[17]

Within a few decades, British colonial lore came to erase these entitle-ments. Although some prominent colonials such as Lord Delamere were entranced by Maasai "nobility" and their striking looks, this was not enough to preserve their way of life. Pastoralism itself, Bruce Berman and John Lonsdale contend, was unnerving to the European politics of con-trol and European morality, involving too little labor and too much movement.[18] From the early twentieth century, Britons all over East Africa were fixated on "developing" the land and, indeed, Maasai men themselves, with an eye to improving their animal husbandry and making them into "modern ranchers."[19] The notion that African animal hus-bandry would erode the land was widespread in the colonial administra-tion—in spite of the fact that early settler farming practices suffered from settlers' ignorance of the ecosystem and contributed to declining soil fer-tility.[20] A conservationist consortium in London pushed for wildlife parks, and while some colonial officials pushed back, fearing unrest and even injustice, the park system gained traction.[21] Meanwhile, officials in Kenya with their eyes on the rich Rift Valley land portrayed the Maasai as rem-nants doomed to extinction.

Lotte Hughes interprets her oral and archival British and Maasai sources cautiously in constructing her account of Maasai dispossession in Kenya.[22] Although she spots myth-making on all sides,[23] she con-cludes confidently that the following took place. In 1904, the British persuaded Maasai—apparently without force—to sign away their rights to land in the Naivasha and Nakuru areas of the central Rift Valley land. Over the next year, Maasai were moved into two reserves, one to the south and the other a very desirable grazing area in Laikipia to the north. Under the treaty agreement, the British promised these grazing areas "so long as the Masai as a race shall exist."

For a timeless contract, it didn't last long. In 1911 the administration wanted to make room for more white settlement in Laikipia, so coerced Maasai into signing a new agreement, this time with more pressure, even threats.[24] Maasai leaders balked at first, realizing those in the north would be shifted into poorly watered, low-quality land in an expanded southern reserve. When they capitulated, it was with dread. "We are sure our stock will die there, but we are prepared to obey the orders of the Government and go," one said.[25] Several colonial officials objected to what they saw as a "disgraceful" manipulation of the people, but other administrators subjected Maasai sympathizers to a "witch-hunt" of sorts, Hughes asserts, effectively silencing them.[26] Between 1911 and 1912 about 10,000 Maasai, 175,000 cattle, and over one million sheep

followed four prescribed routes to the south, with hired white settlers
and *askaris* (guards) from other parts of Africa herding them at gunpoint.[27] Government officials at the time described the Maasai as "well
behaved," but many wound up turning back because of cold, heavy
rain, and mud, and their move was postponed.[28] Oral testimony from
elders who were children during the moves suggests that there were at
least a few deaths from sickness, exposure, and the stress of travel. All
told, by 1913 Maasai had lost between 50–70 percent of the land of
which they had originally enjoyed the use.[29]

In the decades after World War I, some colonial officials did wonder
whether Africans generally had been so marginalized that they might
not have sufficient land. Their concern became integral to a long-standing tug-of-war between the Colonial Office and settlers, some of whom
agitated for a tighter hold on the land whenever they felt threatened. As
their export markets collapsed in the Depression of the 1930s, for
instance, settlers pressured the newly formed Kenya Land Commission
to ensure they didn't lose any of the White Highlands to expanded African reserves. A cornerstone of their argument was the widely circulated
European notion that African animal husbandry would erode the land.[30]
As the historian David Anderson points out, the cereal monoculture
settlers had established in the highlands had partially exhausted the soil,
but settlers drew on frightening "Dust Bowl" imagery from the south-
western United States (among other arguments) to mobilize sentiment
for their cause.[31] After much to-ing and fro-ing between the colony and
London, alarm about soil erosion became a major imperial priority,
ratcheting up convictions that pastoralists were unsuitable stewards of
the land.

Meanwhile, Maasai had felt their community's and cattle's health
deteriorating. Their bitterness at their loss was amplified by their
account of an early twentieth century "blood oath" between Maasai
elite and prominent white settlers, including Lord Delamere and possibly Gilbert Colville and others.[32] In the oath, Maasai and British had
agreed to let one another live in peace and cleave to agreed-upon territories. Unfortunately, Maasai had not recognized the difference between
charismatic settlers and the authority of the colonial government. When
the British violated the terms of the 1904 treaty, Maasai were devastated by the betrayal of what they thought was an intimate tie.[33] In
hindsight, many believed that the first move had been founded on
deception:

The British tricked us! After we had been weakened by civil wars and droughts, they claimed that our Great Laibon [spiritual leader], O'lonana, had signed an agreement in 1904 with His Majesty's Commission for the East African Protectorate, leasing Kenya to the British. The Maasai would never have accepted such a lease! This would have confined us to an arid, dusty land of thousands of miles where the threat of drought . . . is imminent.[34]

After the moves, Maasai were unable to move through the wide range of habitats that had sustained them, and the southern reserve exposed them to disease—human and bovine—and population pressures. Many could no longer reach dry-season grazing land, and as farmers and (increasingly) wildlife ranches put up fences, still more access was cut off. Maasai health suffered, the quality of their livestock plummeted, and the surrounding ecosystem was blighted by soil erosion and loss of vegetation.[35] Maasai mourned not only the loss of their livelihood but also the "bounty, freedom, and range" of their earlier lifestyle.[36] In a series of recent interviews conducted in English by the environmentalist Walter DePuy, male and female Maasai elders in Laikipia wax nostalgic about their forebears' way of life, especially their autonomy and mobility: "They were just free before these private ranches came up"; "nobody control[led] you"; "the life was okay and it was good. . . . They were just free and roaming everywhere, so the life was just simple and it was good"; "They were just free . . . there was nobody who was ruling them. . . . Because everywhere was just for them."[37]

Although their disenfranchisement is clearly documented, the question of how many deaths and how much suffering took place on the moves themselves has been hotly contested. It was a source of serious friction even among colonial officials at the time. Many Maasai now believe the British routed them to the south in a deliberate effort to kill them.[38] They are convinced that during the moves, "hundreds if not thousands of people died from starvation, disease, exposure, or gunshot wounds."[39] According to Lotte Hughes, these claims are founded in genuine loss, but also embellish the available facts, "suit[ing] the current mood for reparations."[40] Meanwhile, Maasai grudges against the British government have been stoked by the thousands of British troops who, for several decades, have trained in central and northern Kenya. Many pastoralists have been wounded by unexploded ordnance the troops have left behind, and in 2003 more than two thousand Maasai and Samburu women charged that they had been raped by British military personnel over the years (in 2006 a military investigation concluded there was insufficient evidence to bring the charges to court).[41]

Maasai have tried to find recourse for their losses. They appealed several times for the return of their northern lands, taking the case to the High Court of British East Africa in 1913 and the Kenya Land Commission in 1932, and raising the issue during independence negotiations in London in 1962.[42] But in 1963 Britain officially renounced all responsibility for further obligations to them, and since then the possibilities for recovering lands have become increasingly obscure.[43] Still, Lotte Hughes's 2002 doctoral dissertation was circulated by Maasai activists, providing fodder for the events of August 2004. Leaders of the protests included representatives from the Maa Civil Society Forum and an NGO called "The Human-Wildlife Conflict Network," as well as Maasai professionals and lawyers. Collectively, they argued that since 99-year leases had been obtained in the early twentieth century, the land should revert to the Maasai people on August 15, 2004. This logic, however, disregarded the fact that the Crown Lands Ordinance of 1915 had extended the leases to 999 years.[44]

Maasai leaders issued a press release making claims of torture and killings that exceed the evidence.[45] The question of which lost land was at stake remained sketchy, with some activists focusing on Laikipia and others, such as the then MP William ole Ntimama, the entire Rift Valley. In 2004, while the ranches were being stormed, other activists attempted to deliver petitions addressed to the Kenyan and British governments in Nairobi, Nanyuki, and Naivasha. The text demanded the return of Laikipia to the Maasai community, and urged the government of Kenya "not to extend any of the leases, which are at the verge of expiring." It also demanded compensation—land and money—from both governments for "all the historical and contemporary injustices" Maasai had been subjected to.[46] A group of leaders, including Maasai and Samburu ministers, convened in Nairobi in September 2004 to discuss what kind of compensation might satisfy the activists. The figure they quoted was 10 billion Kenya shillings (then ± U.S.$125 million) for the land lost in Laikipia alone.[47]

The pastoralists ultimately received nothing for their troubles. Up in Laikipia, the police guarded white-owned land, sometimes violently. Some white Kenyans from former settler families felt it wasn't enough. Jeremy Block, a descendant of a well-to-do settler family, told Reuters, "[Maasai] have invaded all the ranches around here, they have destroyed an awful lot of property and it is time for law and order to take control. . . . The police need to be harsher. . . . There need to be more arrests. We need quicker, more forceful action."[48]

But the police *were* harsh, meting out abuses to send a message to those who had rocked the boat. In late August, for instance, a group of Maasai were randomly assaulted. One said: "We were driving bridal animals to my friend's future wife's home at Ngare Ng'iro, when we met the police and they told us, 'You are the people who are giving us a headache' . . . I responded, 'How could we have done that while on our way to a wedding?' They attacked me, I ran off, and they threw stones at me hitting and injuring my hip and hand." Police told them "to go to parliament in Nairobi and lodge [their] complaints there," and they arrested the groom and confiscated goats and sheep (some permanently). "It's true that men my age are being arrested, and all I would like to say is that we do not need anything from anybody; we only want our land back," the groom's 76-year-old father told a journalist.[49]

Before Maasai were literally beaten back, the 2004 social drama repeatedly played to popular anti-colonial sentiment. At one point, for instance, a procession in Nairobi marched to the British High Commission, but it was closed for lunch and High Commissioner Edward Clay did not happen to be in. A Maasai activist said: "Clay's refusal to see us shows how much contempt he has for us. It smacks of colonialism."[50] Maasai spokesmen invoked another complaint dating to the imperial era; namely, that whites care more about African wildlife than they do about Africans. To link them more tightly to colonialism, furthermore, some referred to them using the colonial-era term "settlers," skirting the fact that many of them have been in Kenya for at least two generations, many have Kenyan citizenship, and some purchased their Laikipia ranches from previous owners rather than being given them by the Crown. Said John Letai, the President of the Organisation for Indigenous Peoples of Africa (OIPA): "We have the ravaging drought killing thousands of our animals while we are [sitting] on a gold mine. The land next to us is electrified with all the lush pasture. Elephants, zebras and all other herbivores are having a holiday in these *so called settler ranches* while the rightful owners whom history deprived of this gold mine are languishing in abject poverty [emphasis mine]."[51]

Ratik ole Kuyana, a Maasai tour guide, who narrowly escaped arrest during a protest, remarked, "We're now squatters on our own land. . . . I'd rather spend my days in prison than see settlers spend their days enjoying my motherland." He went on to invoke the seizures of white Zimbabwean farms: "I think Mugabe was right."[52] Placards held up during the demonstrations read: "We Demand our Land back from the British!" and "Sunset for the British and sunrise for the Maasai."[53]

Looking on as the events unfolded, the Kenyan investigative journalist Parselelo Kantai (of Maasai descent) noted that the rhetoric surrounding the Laikipia upheaval theatrically focused on early colonial relations as if they were "petrified" in time, and erased the multi-ethnic culprits in Kenya's post-independence land seizures.[54] Indeed, as the scathing 2004 Ndug'u Report on the "Illegal/Irregular Allocation of Land" observes, the families of former Presidents Kenyatta and Moi and their power brokers were prominent land grabbers throughout the country.[55] But Maasai may have felt it easier to attack "colonizers"—as a symbol antithetical to the nation—than Kenya's political power players. In so doing, they held white descendants accountable for the debts of their forebears. Contemporary white Kenyans were not legitimate citizens but colonial interlopers, relics of a dead era.

THE DEATH OF SENTIMENTALISM: WHITE KENYAN OBJECTIONS

Lotte Hughes argues that when Maasai distort the past, the distortion is a metaphor that highlights their actual disenfranchisement and loss. Settler descendants, hardly disenfranchised, respond in turn to the *threat* of loss—loss of land, loss of connection to the place they identify with, even loss of face, as colonialism, the structure upheld by their forebears, is further vilified. White Kenyans' narratives may rationalize social hierarchy and perpetuate colonial (now, in somewhat modified form, "modern") ideas about property ownership and land use, but they also emerge from vulnerability.

Although my respondents were not homogeneous in their thinking about Maasai land claims, few were in favor of compensating Maasai for lost lands by rescinding their own ownership. It didn't seem "right," it didn't seem "realistic," they said. Many portrayed Maasai as strategic opportunists rather than dispossessed victims. Hybrid perspectives, framing Maasai as *both/and,* were unusual. In fact, most white Kenyans I spoke to about Maasai activism were far more cynical than those of their colonial predecessors who romanticized the Maasai as noble or even kindred spirits. One Nairobi-based safari guide in his forties, Clem, has worked with Maasai guides for years. "My guys," as he calls them, help him with all kinds of safari logistics, from leading walks through the bush to taking care of his Land Rover. He's fond of them as individuals, and especially likes the company of Koinet, who sits in the passenger seat and comes up with wry nicknames for troublesome clients.

I had seen Clem interact generously with his workers; one of them, for example, had a sister hospitalized with cerebral malaria, and Clem had given him a loan for the clinic bill that we all knew would not be repaid. But Clem also observed cultural differences he still found mysterious—including differences over what kind of labor is familiar or even worthwhile. "Ask them to walk twenty kilometers to fetch something and it's no problem, but ask them to clean out a picnic basket and they will bungle it; they just don't *see* it the way we do." On the subject of Maasai activism, Clem snorted with laughter. "If they think there's any compensation that can be gained through those demands for restitution," he said, "well *sure* they're going to push that. And that's a *good* one, a *really* good one to try to exploit." How could Clem be so supportive of his employees in one regard, but reject their collective grievances how harshly? How did he fail to recognize or show sympathy for their sense of historical loss?

The structural oblivion begins, as it were, at the beginning, with the collective amnesia hinted at by the EAWL's needlepoint volume. Few settler descendants I spoke to have much knowledge about the Maasai moves of a century ago. Through a likely combination of actual ignorance, collective defensiveness, and perhaps even systematic administrative whitewashing, narratives circulating among earlier settler families mostly spun the events in a way that sidestepped the less palatable deeds of the colonial administration.[56] Inheriting this legacy of oblivion, some respondents told me that all of the Laikipia territories had been "fairly purchased" directly from Maasai, while others, in an even more drastic rationalization, portray Laikipia as a no-man's land at the time of settler arrival. This is an idea with a history; D. M. Hughes notes that the romantic image of "unblemished" land was widespread in British settler writing across Eastern and Southern Africa, "swe[eping] the clutter of Africans—actually traversing the savannah with cattle and goods— out of whites' imagination."[57] True to form, the Royal Geographical Society explorer Joseph Thomson wrote in the late nineteenth century that most of Laikipia was "quite uninhabited," while the influential administrator Charles Eliot declared: "We have in East Africa the rare experience of dealing with a tabula rasa."[58] While it's true the population in Laikipia had recently diminished because of a perfect storm of civil wars, disease, and drought, even Thomson reported substantial herds of cattle and other domestic animals at pasture in these areas, animals that must have been in the care of pastoralists.[59] But early twentieth century, colonials saw no permanent settlements in the highlands, overlooked pastoralists' seasonal migrations (as well as their regional migrations within seasons), and jumped to the conclusion that, in their words, "a considerable portion of Masai country was masterless" or "empty."[60]

The idea has been passed on through the generations. Certainly, it is widely acknowledged that Kenya's population has burgeoned, from about four million at the start of the twentieth century to about thirty million at the start of the twenty-first, and nearly forty-five million in 2014,[61] but to hear some settler descendants talk, most of those four million almost vanish into thin air. One Laikipia cattle rancher, Devon, still owns the farm his family received from the British administration at the end of World War I. As he narrates his life history to me, he describes himself as "bolshy,"[62] and the glowering grey eyebrows on his national ID card certainly belong to a man who doesn't live to please. In his youth, he says, he collaborated with a Somali lorry driver in an attempt to smuggle ivory across the country; he also got into trouble with British military authorities back in the day, but he crows about evading punishment. Today, at his ranch, he confronts cattle rustlers, burglars, threats, and politicians who, he says, order their cronies to graze livestock illegally on his land, but despite all the excitement he's proud not to have joined the "grannies who've retired to the coast and died of ennui." On the subject of Maasai demands, Devon is dismissive. The NGOs who advocate for pastoralists are "soft-headed," he says, agitating for "these *extraneous* things without understanding this situation." As for the 2004 protests, "It's all politics and talk. The Maasai are tremendous people for talking, but they don't stick to their word for 10 seconds. And they . . . don't really know what they're talking about, I'm sorry to say!"

I told Devon that historians had documented the displacement of Maasai, some of it under intense pressure. Devon had his own version of what had transpired. "I'm no great scholar—I don't read a lot of books—but I've got a very good memory, listening to my peers and elders talk when I was a kiddie. I can remember things that, things I heard when I was six or seven." Devon set his face with an amused attitude:

> One of the first jobs my great-cousin got, the one who came here in 1903, he got a job helping the government at the time: move the Maasai. That was one of his first jobs he got. And his big *moan* was, he was being paid by the families he moved or by the number of *cattle* he moved. . . . And his big moan was there was *nobody* to *move!* This was in 1904, I think. . . .

So he moaned about that and then he did it *again* in '11 or '12 or '13, whenever it happened again. Again he was involved in the move and again he moaned because [thumping the table] there weren't enough to move, so he couldn't make the money he thought he'd make. So that was his moan at the time.

Devon's phrase "nobody to move" downplays the magnitude of the Maasai moves to the point of erasing them. When I follow up with Clem, the safari guide with such a chummy attitude toward his Maasai guides, he, too, minimizes the numbers:

[Maasai] may have been there *first*, but then in those days there were not *nearly* so many! Like, there may have been one or two of them there but they were not, there wasn't nearly the population, what is there now, I mean 30 million [people in Kenya]? . . . So there's just that many more people . . . [and] those places didn't have people *living* on them. They might have been traditional grazing grounds where [pastoralists] would come and go to a little bit . . . say in Laikipia. I don't think there was ever somewhere there where there were people living. . . . It was more they used to come and go. And there were so *few* of them, it was *un*-inhabited more than inhabited. There was *no one*. [He chuckles softly] So it's a bit like South Africa. [When] they settled there, the white South Africans, there was *no one there!*

I didn't react much during this monologue; as Clem repeated his points, he almost seemed to be trying to persuade himself. In his portrayal, Maasai pastoralists (not to mention black Southern Africans) had barely existed in the precolonial era. There were "one or two," or perhaps even "no one there," and they had a tenuous purchase on their very existence; after all, the "coming and going" of pastoralism is not equivalent to "living." The moral reasoning here is clear; if there was plenty of uninhabited land, there was plenty to go around, so the appropriation of lands ought to have posed no problem. It is only with today's overpopulation crisis, says Clem, that moving the Maasai has come to seem like a problem.[63]

Clem treats Maasai mobility as a strike against their entitlement to landownership and, sometimes, the reality of their existence. Other respondents followed suit. Susan, a businesswoman in Nairobi who grew up in the Rift Valley, defends the land her parents were given by the colonial government: "A *lot* of the prime land was in areas that were not previously occupied or used, um, uh, a lot of unused territory. By *all* accounts . . . a lot of huge tracts of the country were pastoral." For Susan, too, pastoralism does not count as a way of "using" or "occupying" the land—and yet ecologically minded scholars have painstakingly demonstrated that pastoralists' customary use of semi-arid land is (or, as the case may be, was) not only suitable to the environment (more so than other types of land husbandry), but also gradually alters the flora and fauna without decimating it.[64] In the talk of settler descendants, a way of life seems to subsist on air, and a people and their influence vanish into the ether.

These descriptions of the land call to mind the realization of the American linguist Benjamin Whorf. While working as a fire inspector as a young man, Whorf observed that workers would treat gasoline drums labeled "empty" as wholly inert and harmless. Forgetting about their explosive vapors, the workers would blithely toss cigarette butts in their direction, triggering a disaster.[65] Carol Cohn would notice a related dynamic three decades later while conducting fieldwork among American nuclear defense strategists. Cohn was alarmed at first to find these men using dispassionate vocabulary to talk about casualties of a hypothetical nuclear attack, but after several months of learning and speaking in the same dry abstractions, she found herself less frightened of the prospect of such a war. Language, Cohn concludes, becomes a map of supposed reality in the world, and it is harder to see—and indeed harder to *feel*—outside of this version.[66] In the case of pastoralists in Kenya, the settler community and its descendants have used dismissive terms, referring to "uninhabited" or "empty" land, and erasing human life with a few syllables. If the land was "empty," if there was "no one to move," there was no human feeling there, and nobody to hurt or disenfranchise.

When white Kenyan discourse does acknowledge the presence of pastoralists, it sometimes leans toward derision. Maasai movement is portrayed as haphazard, unfocused, even wanton. These images were nourished by colonial officials; in 1933 Charles Eliot wrote grumpily, "I cannot admit that wandering tribes have a right to keep other and superior races out of large tracts merely because they have acquired a habit of straggling over far more land than they can utilise."[67] I heard similar imagery in 2004, from the Nairobi business owner Nicola, who followed the Laikipia debacle closely, phoning her landowner friends almost daily. She found Maasai claims to land frustrating because from her vantage point, their mobility was so aimless:

> You see the Maasai are a funny lot . . . they wander from place to place to place, in a certain area. Now they say that's our land. How did that suddenly become your land? *Why* have you got historical rights to that land? Just because you wandered round it for a couple of hundred years or whatever? . . . And they're saying that's our land because we've been there forever.

Yeah, you wandered about. You didn't stay in one place and say this is this is where we live. They didn't!

Another woman, whose grandparents had land near the Delameres' in the Rift Valley, similarly cited Maasai attempts to reclaim "any land they set foot on." James, an old Rift Valley farmer in his seventies, portrays the Maasai as greedy and their mobility as utterly spontaneous: "They reckon they own the whole of Kenya," he tells me, and begins to giggle at the image. "'The' Maasai just went wherever they felt like it 'cause they were really tough, wiry people."[68] Betsy, a young conservation biologist and a family friend of James's, jumps into the conversation: "So it wasn't necessarily their land, you know." James echoes her: "It wasn't a case of their owning the land. If they felt there was a drought and there was some nice green grass they'd take their cattle there, and anyone who tried to stop them just got speared, you know, like the lions did." He laughs cheerfully again at this portrait of a capricious people.

We see a similar rendering in the writings of Aidan Hartley, born into a colonial family and raised in Kenya and Tanzania. Hartley purchased a plot of land in Laikipia in the early 2000s, taking time out of his itinerant war reporter's life to build a home and *shamba* (farm), and publishing periodic essays about his adventures in the conservative British weekly *The Spectator*. His property was among those invaded by Maasai protestors in 2004, and he has since experienced periodic harassment by pastoralists who object to his landownership in the area. Like Kantai, Hartley points out that Maasai got leverage from imagining the Laikipia conflict in antiquated, racially charged terms; historically Maasai *were* disenfranchised by whites, of course, but to focus exclusively on these insults is to erase the recent decades of devastating black Kenyan land grabbing. He also claims that ever since the British government began to compensate pastoralists injured by the ordnance in the Laikipia bush, Maasai have (with the help of NGOs) concocted irrational charges that they hope will bring them more bounty. "Many feel bad about what happened to the Maasai, who attract plenty of sentimental admiration," Hartley writes, but Maasai "never settled, [and] they usually murdered other tribes wherever they found them on the road."[69]

In portrayal after portrayal of Maasai among white Kenyans, Maasai mobility is based on spontaneous "feeling" rather than deliberation or pattern. Maasai will murder anyone "in their way" like automatons, and they are driven by avarice. Straggling around and killing indiscriminately—there is no internal logic or system, no morality here. These are classic stereotypes promulgated by European travelers, missionaries, and colonialists,[70] but the portrayal contrasts dramatically with Maasai notions of territorial entitlement and historical accounts of their strategic exchange friendships with neighboring groups. Although Maasai sometimes used intimidation and violence to gain access to key grazing grounds, and they did sometimes raid to restock cattle lost through wars,[71] they also had a history of symbiotic trade arrangements with neighboring agriculturalists. Even early colonial writings don't portray them as a clear threat; Charles Eliot himself wrote that the Maasai would need more protection from the violence of settlers than vice versa. Portrayals of the Maasai as ruthless and uncompromising, then, are simplifications designed to counter equally simplified sentimental portraits.[72] Meanwhile, pastoralist mobility is taken, not as sensible interaction with the environment, but rather as aimlessness, shoddiness, and lack of aspiration.[73]

Careful ethnographic histories, however, unpack the ecological sense and social structure behind transhumant pastoralism, telling us that prior to state interventions, Maasai rangeland was carefully managed with customary laws and community sanctions.[74] Not only was the land not "unused," but it was used carefully. Pastoralists systematically moved cattle into lower lands during the dry season and in times of drought, patterns that not only extracted value—in the form of meat and milk—from the land, but also allowed the land to regenerate. As scholars such as Ian Scoones (1995) have demonstrated, pastoralist mobility and flexibility, when not curtailed by the state, works with the grain of the spatial heterogeneity of the savannah and the temporal variability of resources. (In contrast, commercial agriculture in formerly pastoralist areas has sometimes failed drastically, such as the notorious 1970s Basuto Wheat Scheme in Tanzania, which fell apart due to "unreliable rains and fragile soils.")[75] A parallel opinion has converged around the ecology of displaced Native Americans. The New England Puritans groused that "the Indians" moved around too much, worked too little, and failed to "use" the land properly—failing to see that Native American mobility, and their patchwork use of available species, had an internal logic that turns out to have been vital to the abundance of the environment.[76]

These renderings of the Maasai also contrast with European ideologies of responsible landownership and indeed personhood itself. We can see a Lockeian model of morality in another of Hartley's essays, describing how he established his Laikipia farm. Hartley's home seemed to crumble almost as fast as he could construct it, and in his self-mocking depiction of the debacle, the act of pioneering—what he calls "bush craft"—is crucial to his sense of legitimacy: "Had I been a Kenya cowboy [which Hartley defines as a "stereotypical upcountry Kenyan"] I would have had all the knowledge I needed to build up a farm with cars that work and generators that thrum. I would have known about bareface tenons, purlins, quoins, flanges, plumb lines, pinking engines, condensers and tappets."[77]

Over time, though, Hartley "earns his spurs" by overcoming numerous threats to hearth and home—elephants, termites, snakes, baboons, cattle rustlers, and more. Exhaustion, danger, and discouragement ultimately seem proof of his worthiness as a farm owner. The farm Hartley says began "in virgin bush" was "up and running": "Today we can chill a beer, flush a loo, switch on a light, sleep in a bed and have a swim . . . We've planted 20,000 trees, built three kilometres of dry-stone walls, pumped water a long way uphill and employed a large number of people."[78] (The metaphor of "virgin" land has been common since colonial times, again erasing the fact that pastoralists do change the terrain, even if it looks untouched to outsiders.) In Hartley's bravado, we can begin to see why, in white Kenyans' eyes, the itinerant behavior of Maasai, their failure to make something perceptibly new out of the land, and perhaps even the invisibility of their blood, sweat, and tears, disqualify them from holding it.

My settler descendant respondents also resent the images of Maasai available for popular consumption that, they say, stoke the sentimentality of those who contribute to their cause. Ironically, these images came to prominence during the colonial era as a result of colonial fascination. Though some imagery denigrated Maasai as bloodthirsty warriors, colonial explorers, officials, and settlers also generated romantic stereotypes of Maasai at once savage and noble, in harmony with nature, primitive, pure, and exotic.[79] Some Maasai have challenged these stereotypes, but others, in a bid for greater cultural, political, and economic rights, have reinvigorated their sense of ethnic identity, and in some cases played up their image of exotic lords of a former garden of Eden.[80] My white Kenyan respondents portrayed such representations of Maasai stewardship as deplorably "romantic"—particularly when they come from the NGOs and non-profits advocating for Maasai rights.

Several of my respondents singled out the Maasai Environmental Resource Coalition (MERC), an influential group of grassroots organizations in Kenya and Tanzania. A publicity-oriented section of the MERC website, entitled "Maasai: A Living Legacy," describes a timeless and idyllic way of life, binding together moral and environmental righteousness:

Maasai communities have lived in harmony within the rich ecosystems of East Africa for centuries. As Metitamei Olol Dapash says, "In the balance our ancestors found with the natural environment, people shared the land with elephants, giraffes, rhinoceros, and other majestic wildlife. We see ourselves as custodians of the land, which to us is a sacred living entity. . . . The land contains our history; it is the keeper of our memories and culture, and protector of our forefathers' bones. The Maasai believe that the land is entrusted to the living for safekeeping, to be passed on to future generations.[81]

If Maasai have "lived in harmony" and "balance" with the land for centuries, they are clearly its most appropriate stewards on both ecological and moral levels. In MERC's account, furthermore, the land itself is consubstantial with them, containing not only their memories and culture, but also the substance of their "forefathers' bones"—a somewhat surprising claim given that Maasai dead were customarily placed in the open to be eaten by wild animals. But the authors of this statement seem to be drawing on a sentimental rhetoric widespread among other communities (in Kenya and beyond) that do bury their dead, and are dismayed that the dwelling-place of their memories has been commodified by outsiders.[82] Meanwhile, in MERC's rendering, the Maasai and the land are locked into a relationship of mutual caregiving.[83]

For all the ahistorical gauziness of MERC's language, it must be said that the organization has a point. It is true that few ecologists would agree that Maasai today live in harmony with land or wildlife, given that they have been squeezed into marginal and overpopulated spaces. However, many have argued that in the precolonial era, pastoralists' systematic movements between grazing lands sustained their cattle, preserved the land from overuse, and avoided disease. Their relationship with wildlife, furthermore, was once compatible with conservation. While scholars caution against idealization (Maasai, for instance, are noted for killing lions to protect their livestock and as part of a warrior's rite of passage—practices that today run up against endangered species protections), they note that historically Maasai have been more tolerant than many neighboring groups of wildlife, seeing it as sharing god-given rights to grazing with their cattle.[84] This symbiosis largely died when their range was appropriated, converted to agricultural use, or adopted for game reserves.[85] But the habit of laying blame on Maasai is at least a century old. Elsewhere in East Africa, as early as the 1920s, the British administration restricted Maasai to marginal resources, but blamed the ensuing soil erosion and water conservation squarely upon

Maasai practices of "overstocking."[86] Meanwhile, while they accused Maasai of decimating wildlife, downplaying the latter's historical co-existence with it, they overlooked the often indiscriminate slaughter in Kenya's colonial history of sport hunting.[87] Generally speaking, colonial officials were very reluctant to admit guilt for undermining Maasai subsistence and their ecological balance.

Similarly, most settler descendants I spoke to found it very difficult to see that Maasai might once have engaged in ecologically responsible practices. Most make no distinction between pre- and postcolonial Maasai ecology, and argue that Maasai are inept stewards of the land, plain and simple. During my visit to one white-Kenyan owned tea estate in Limuru in 2004, for instance, my hosts around the lunch table discussed the latest reports coming from the north and opined that the Maasai "wouldn't know what to *do* with that land" were it returned to them, and that they would ultimately "destroy" it by using it unsustainably. A flower farmer in Naivasha told me he blamed the NGOs (such as "Action Aid") who "feel that the Maasai way of life has got to be preserved at all costs, and the Maasai can do no wrong, and yet through most of the Rift Valley the Maasai are doing *untold* damage." Pastoralism in the Rift Valley, he continued, is a "*highly* inappropriate use ecologically, so really they need to be cleared out."[88] And Hartley, writing out of Laikipia, argues that Maasai own abundant land in the south but have "irreparably devastated" it with their "overpopulated livestock numbers." Hartley urges Maasai to join the age of neoliberal economic choices: "In the age of private title it's up to them if they keep it or sell it. The parts they lost long ago are now occupied by millions of people attempting to build a modern economy."

In fact, some Maasai are very much part of the market. A few have become executives in multinational businesses, politicians, or academics. Others both practice pastoralism and hold regular jobs (e.g., as night watchmen, cashing in on their reputation for ferocity), put on "traditional" performances and sell jewelry to tourists, and, in some cases, run their own ecotourist lodges.[89] But rhetoric about the Maasai obscures the diversity of their lifeways.

THE LIFE OF SENTIMENTALISM: "FREEDOM," NOSTALGIA, AND STRUCTURAL OBLIVION

Given all the controversy over their privileges, why would settler descendants even stay in Kenya? Why do they feel so tied to the place?

Even as they dismiss romantic representations of Maasai connections to the land, their own relationship with the territory and wildlife is deeply emotional. If the MERC website suggests that the land "keeps" and "protects" Maasai's memories and their "bones," white Kenyan phrasing is not far off, though it is inflected by a more explicit focus on "landscape." Western notions of landscape are typically saturated with cultural ideas that aestheticize its perception, and among white Kenyans this perception is not just visual but also embodied.[90] Mary, a member of a coffee-farming family in the Rift Valley, says, "Kenya's landscape is absolutely a part of me; it is just *so* magnificent." A young man recently returned from university in the United Kingdom says that England never felt like home; "the smells and colors and the landscapes here are so much more vivid; it's like I feel more alive when I'm walking around." And Clem said in a heartfelt tone of voice:

> Yeah, for me I love the landscape. It's really . . . it's really . . . you know, it's *engrained* in you! You just *love it* to the *bone*. Especially if you go anywhere else in the world now and you see . . . how crowded their environment is. And then you, then you get involved in what I'm doing, in my business, so you see the other side of the coin, like the wildlife and the open space we have still here, then it really, *really* makes you appreciate it.

One woman who grew up in Kenya for the first twenty years of her life and then moved with her parents to the United Kingdom at Independence told me that she never really felt as though she had a "home" in England, because "Kenya was just in my blood." "What was it about Kenya?" I asked. She answered in a kind of reverie, her voice undulating:

> The smell and the birds and the red soil and the smell of rain on the red soil and the look of the valley spreading out. At school when I got out of my dormitory bed at six A.M., when the bell rang, you looked out the window and always at that time it was clear. On one side was Kilimanjaro, the other was Mt. Kenya, both snow-capped. Now, *what* a view. We thought it was a beautiful country. And of course the animals, being brought up amongst the animals—buck, rhino, giraffe, where we were. You just saw them the whole time. You were amongst them; it was one's childhood, you lived among them. You get to know which ones are dangerous and when you've got to be careful and when you've got to run from that giraffe and that sort of thing, and it's very much part of a child's life there.

She was "heartbroken" when she left, she said, and has felt "stateless" ever since, keening internally for her connection with Kenya's open spaces and creatures. Others who remain, such as Clem, say they feel the landscape inscribed on their very being. In nearly all of these accounts, Kenyan landscapes are romantic objects of contemplation, always at peril of being lost to overpopulation, misuse, the pressures of modernity, or exile, but much more as well, making an indelible impression on whites' bodily sense of identity. Losing the land can be more like losing a leg or an arm than losing a mere asset.[91]

White Kenyans also insist that they appreciate the land in ways Maasai don't. There is an irony to this appreciation, for even as white Kenyans treat Maasai mobility as a disqualification for landownership and seem oblivious of the Maasai's nostalgia for their bygone freedom to roam, their own proclaimed attachment to Kenya's wide-open spaces echoes that sentiment.[92] Karen Blixen adored gazing across the African plains from her private airplanes, and in her famous 1937 memoir *Out of Africa,* she extols what she calls the "nobility" of her lover Denys Finch-Hatton's expansiveness: "Everything that you saw made for greatness and freedom."[93] The landscape as sweeping and open is a recurrent theme in contemporary white Kenyan accounts as well. When I lunched with one elderly former settler in the United Kingdom, she presented me with a volume, *Childhood Memories of Colonial East Africa, 1920–1963,* saying, "I know American academics don't particularly like the settlers, but this will show you we were not all bad." In the narratives in the book, the trope of unfettered childhood rings like a recurring ostinato. "My sister and I had complete freedom to go anywhere"; "We had a peace and freedom that was virtually unique in this world"; "[One was] free to roam on one's bicycle with no worries of security"; "We were allowed to wander far and wide"; "We enjoyed so much freedom, so much space for our games and so much to learn from the natural surroundings"; "We children had a wonderful time; we had the freedom to climb trees [and] to explore . . . [an island near home] seemed to us to be our own private domain"; "[Life was] free and exciting . . . no fences seemed to mark the boundaries between bush and farm"; "We loved our horses and used to ride all over the plains with our Tommies [Thompson's Gazelles] and Ostriches."[94]

The theme of roaming across the bush without restraint ran through in the narratives I collected in person as well. Eleanor, now in her sixties, said of growing up in the Rift Valley: "It was a beautiful place to live in, total freedom to run around. I mean . . . *total* freedom; there were 45,000 acres, huge skies, horizons, wild animals, dogs, dairy cattle." Lucy enthused about taking her children on camping safaris and teaching them to drive in the game parks when they were as young as eight years old: "*Yeah,* eight-, nine-, ten-year-olds driving—*wonderful lifestyle.*" And on her web site, the white Kenyan artist Tanya Trevor Saunders describes a "charmed" childhood in which her "Kenyan/English" father's vocation as a maker of wildlife films gave her family special license to live inside Tsavo East National Park: "We had no garden and no faces, just our lovely wooden house looking out over Tsavo, which is a beautiful and rugged space the size of Wales . . . I grew up with elephants on my doorstep . . . all the animals became my 'friends' . . . we had the whole of Africa as our playground . . . I often wish that I could . . . feel again with adult emotions the freedom and peace and magic that I lived every day as a child."[95]

Although attachments to place often start in childhood, I was struck by how often white Kenyan attachments to the place invoke childhood memories more than adult sentiments, and I couldn't help wonder whether this twinning of the land and wildlife with their younger selves helped encourage a model of white belonging as innocent. Everyone seems absolved from political blame when you imagine them as a child. But below the level of awareness, such nostalgic enthusiasm for freedom and appreciation of East African vistas has a strategic element. D. M. Hughes has written that white Zimbabweans' rhapsodic relationship to land and wildlife constitutes "a special optic . . . [that throws] blacks out of focus while zooming in on landscape, plants and animals."[96] Among white Kenyans, too, there is an ideological selectivity to what they consider legitimate grounds for belonging. The exhilaration of moving across open land with their bodies, Range Rovers, horses, and even their gazes, is part of what has made European whites, past and present, feel so attached to it, even as they dismiss Maasai feelings about their former freedom of mobility. The double standard in these representations—innocent freedom vs haphazard straggling—calls to mind the political and economic contrast between "white hunters" and "black poachers" described by the historian Edward Steinhart.[97] For just as whites hunted Kenya's game (until sport hunting was banned in 1977) because they found it pleasurable whereas Africans hunted as a mode of subsistence, so too has white mobility been partly a product of leisurely exploration rather than a means of livelihood as it was for pastoralists. Whites in Africa have always had a home base, accompanied by sufficient wealth and technology to range around for pleasure. At the same time, their free ranging across aesthetically treasured landscapes has the effect of symbolically exempting them from the ethnic claims to particular regions that have blighted Kenya since Independence. The provincial scale of identification, after all, goes hand in hand with ethnic clashes over land rights. Those who are considered "local" (once "native") are defined as such precisely because so many of them are incarcerated in space by poverty and consumed by parochial, "tribalist" territorialism in a way that white Kenyans are not—not, anyway, in their narratives of themselves.

While Africans largely recede from view in many whites' nostalgic accounts, white children's attention was often focused on their intimacy with the animals they found in Kenya's open spaces. One after another, they reminisce about witnessing wild animals and taming orphaned ones—vervet monkeys, mongoose, honey badgers, hornbills, even warthogs and buffalo. We see a similar dynamic in earlier settler writings—consider, for instance, Blixen's sentiments about rescuing a "ladylike" bushbuck fawn from African children who were selling it by the side of the road; it lived in her home for a time and attracted her keen attention.[98] The domestication of these creatures (and, sometimes, their seizure from African hands) seems analogous to the domestication of Kenya's putatively "virgin" bush, giving whites a kind of Lockeian stewardship over the wildlife as well as the land—with implications, of course, for white adults' consuming involvement with conservation. For if white settlers were prolific hunters of East Africa's elephants and lions, in recent decades they have reframed themselves as their main protectors (from "poaching"), sometimes their tamers.[99] This concern is embodied (for instance) in the figure of the Kenya-born Briton Daphne Sheldrick, who was a co-warden of Tsavo National Park with her husband from 1955 to 1967 and became renowned for the rescue and rehabilitation of many orphaned animals. After her husband's death in 1977, she created the David Sheldrick Wildlife Trust in 1977, where many baby elephants now interact adorably with their keepers and international tourists before being released into the wild; her daughter Angela, married into an old white Kenyan family with conservation land in Laikipia (the Carr-Hartleys), is now at the helm of the Trust. (The glamorous public figures of George and Joy Adamson, who raised orphaned lion cubs and then reintroduced them to the wild, were part of this scene until their deaths, though both of them only settled in Kenya as adults. Nevertheless, such characters were part of the social scene for some white Kenyans particularly passionate about wildlife conservation.) Some white Kenyans managed to find intimacy even with animals they never tamed. One woman in middle age, Sarah, enthused about how wonderful her childhood was, largely because of the camping safaris her family undertook in the bush, experiences that "really connected me" to the place. Once a week, too, her family would enjoy a picnic breakfast in a game park: "[W]e knew where all the prides of lion were, we knew some of them by name—our *own* names. We were there *so often* that we just . . . all of them . . . we gave them our own names. Well, we would recognize one with the sort of squiff [crooked] ear or something so she would be known as 'Squiffear' and there would be Squiffear's babies and—we just—*yeah,* we just went there so much."

White Kenyans' sentimental attachments thus play out on two scales, both larger and smaller than the regional scale of loyalty conventionally attributed to black Kenyans. As part of the "special optic" identified by D. M. Hughes, whites soar across the land without boundaries at one level, while cultivating sentimental intimacies with fauna on the other. In reminiscences and representations, black pastoralists are largely erased, or blamed for abusing the land. Meanwhile, whites' affective relationships to the place are described as intimate, sensory, in the "bone," as it were. When attachments are so deeply felt, they seem to have an evidentiary force on their own. Minutely focused upon the smell of the soil or the fold in a lion cub's ear, they operate on a separate plane from structural awareness of the arc of history, of alternative ideologies of land use and ownership, of injustices, of human resentments clamoring just beyond the boundaries of a national park or privately owned ranch.

"BOTH SIDES OF THE FENCE": NEW PERSPECTIVISM

In our conversation in Nanyuki, Paul had tried to bend my mind to his—"you can understand this"—by reminding me that "some of the most marginalized people on earth are the poor Red Indians of North America." This invocation of Native Americans came up in other conversations, too, and Paul and others obviously hoped it would persuade me. The notion of returning the land directly to the "first peoples," what Maasai have demanded, seems absurd and prohibitively complex in a modern economy, Paul implies. Others concur—as Nicola put it, "Fine, give Nairobi back to the Maasai. Where do we stop? Take back the coast—just take it back! But you know history has gone fifty years now! So [the land's] been sold on and sold on and sold on—how do you sort that out? God knows." By reminding me of my own situation as a middle-class Anglo-American, furthermore, Paul may have been trying to explain his own subjectivity. If I didn't appear to wring my hands with guilt over the "Red Indians" my own ancestors dispossessed, why should he do the same over Maasai?

Time and again, settler descendants and other Westerners have been accused of reserving more of their empathy for Africa's wildlife than its marginalized human population. Time and again, they have been accused of sequestering or hoarding land that could be used for human sustenance.[100] Critics see their proprietary attitude toward African wildlife as selfish, and their views on "poaching" as racist and insensitive to the indigent. As the examples have accumulated historically, one could forgive Maasai in Laikipia for feeling that white Kenyans have simply erased their vantage points.

And yet, new structures of feeling may be in the making, for in spite of everything, at least some settler descendants today have begun to recognize alternative perspectives. To some degree, they have had to. One force behind the shift is the global turn toward "community-based conservation" (CBC) initiatives, which enlist local citizens as partners in conservation, for example, through income-generating activities that ideally are good for the environment and the people. Starting in the 1980s, the World Bank and the Asian Development Bank began to fund these "integrated conservation and development projects," and the international conversation underwent a paradigm shift.[101] In East Africa, promoters of CBC argued that tourist revenues should fund local development projects that would range from new farming initiatives to locally managed safari camps; as a result, the thinking went, local beneficiaries would have incentives to protect the wildlife themselves. In Kenya, Maasai themselves had pushed for community involvement in conservation as early as the late 1950s, forwarding an innovative proposal that local councils rather than the central government should manage the finances of Amboseli national park and Masai Mara national game reserve. While the management of these areas has been contentious, subject to corruption and infighting, surrounding Maasai communities have benefited from tourism through park revenues and the marketing of Maasai jewelry, song and dance, ecological knowledge, and other cultural attributes. The incidence of poaching has been low relative to other areas.[102] CBC schemes are controversial; each site has its unique issues, but critics have noted a range of recurrent problems: the "development" enabled by CBC is not universally welcome, local voices and critiques are not always heard, and revenue often feels like inadequate compensation for the loss of land and mobility.[103] Nevertheless, the international community has forcefully advocated for CBC, sometimes in conjunction with local players.

The shift over the past three decades has also been influenced by innovators such as David Western (of British descent, born in Tanzania, but later a naturalized Kenyan citizen), who became director of the parastatal Kenya Wildlife Service (KWS) in 1994. Western succeeded Richard Leakey, who, in defense of the threatened elephant and rhino populations, instigated a policy that authorized units could shoot poachers on sight. Mindful of the high tensions with surrounding communities, Leakey had promised that KWS would give 25 percent of park revenues to those who lived on the periphery, but the expectations he raised were impossible to meet, and Leakey was so cynical about corruption that he remarked a few years after his resignation, "I don't believe community-based conservation has a hope in hell."[104] But Western, curious about the Maasai, came to a richer understanding of how their grazing habits might complement the Amboseli ecosystem and championed a co-existence model of national parks and pastoralists that would benefit and involve the latter.[105]

In Laikipia, the conservancy that led the way since the early 1990s has been Lewa Downs, owned by the Craig family, who first came to Kenya in 1924 as part of the soldier-settler scheme. Lewa was originally a cattle ranch, but was losing wildlife quickly and failing to turn a sufficient profit. The managers turned to conservation, and in conversation with the international CBC community, they have ramped up local employment, training, education, health, micro-credit, water, road infrastructure, community forestry, livestock for community grazing, and other major initiatives in the surrounding communities. The Lewa web site touts the changes proudly: "With the changed perceptions of local people, the protection and conservation of wildlife is a source of desperately needed income rather than poaching for rhino horn."[106] While Lewa's account is unlikely to capture the full range of responses among community members, it nevertheless has a widespread reputation as a relative success story.

Lewa has also gained international approval, publicity that has altered the perspective of some other settler descendants. Its example has, in the words of one slightly edgy white landowner, "put a good deal of pressure on those who aren't doing the same thing." Trevor, a Lewa insider, delicately suggested that racism informs the mentality of those landowners who resist, and implied the racism would be well supplanted by nationalism:

[When The Maasai came through Laikipia in 2004,] other ranches said: "Well, look what you've done to us. You've just . . . stood up, you've done things . . . and we haven't. And you've left us high and dry." Which is a bit of a narrow minded way—it's, to be honest, it's a bit of a sort of, I hate to say it, a sort of Zimbabwe mentality if that makes sense . . . it's such a closed gate policy to anybody. [The policy at Lewa is]: We're Kenyan, we're a Kenyan company, we're owned by Kenyans. The guy next door is a Kenyan, what's the difference, there is no difference.

Worth noting in Trevor's words is a subtle plea, not only for white Kenyans to recognize their similarity to "the guy next door," but also for majority Kenyans to recognize them as equally part of the nation. "We're Kenyan," he insists—as opposed to white Zimbabweans, whose exclusionary racism, Trevor almost implies, contributed to their downfall. In other words, he frames CBC as a means, not only of incorporating African neighbors to augment conservation, but also of demonstrating to black Kenyans that privileged whites might plausibly belong in the mix.

By now, a number of white Kenyan property owners have felt the pressure Trevor describes, and incorporated CBC initiatives into their conservation practices. Some ranches use the profits from tourism to support schools and clinics for pastoralists and other neighboring groups, cultivating more positive relationships. Others have created trusts that pay out annually to pastoralist households living on the ranch, giving them an incentive to support the population of big game.[107]

CBC has been widely faulted on many lines, including that its proponents often fail to understand the worldview of local inhabitants—fail, in other words, to be as far-sighted or perspectivist as their publicity would suggest—and hence marginalize local knowledge claims.[108] Another complaint is exemplified by the words of a MERC founder, Meitamei Ole Dapash, who accuses white-owned ranches of using the "guise" of community-engaged ecotourism to hoard land and resources in the hands of a few families.[109] Trevor unwittingly gives this claim some credibility when he remarks that "the ranches shouldn't be given back, as long as they are managed in a way that's benefiting the local people." It's possible that "involving the community" and helping communities "develop" have become, for some progressive whites, a kind of cover story for holding onto their resources in the face of a public that objects to radical inequality. And in playing their CBC roles, whites reproduce the larger relationship of patrons to black Kenyans, rather than leveling the playing field. It is an ambiguous role, framing whites as saviors, and surely in some cases encouraging local communities to rely on whites' support for their survival, well-being, and sometimes prosperity, while re-inscribing whites in an elite position, as brokers who control the narrative of what constitutes "good use" of available resources (a narrative not all local participants are likely to concur with). Here, in fact, is a dynamic replicated on a smaller scale in white Kenyans' relationships with their domestic staff, as I discuss in Chapter 4.

But even if whites retain a kind of upper hand through CBC, the ground of white consciousness has undergone a shift, however partial and uneven. Maasai activism and the "new conservation" movement appear to have prodded some white Kenyans into the initial pangs of double consciousness, and into verbalizing at least partial concessions to the points of view of those who object to their privilege. So, for instance, even as his Laikipia neighbors urged police to crack down harder on Maasai demonstrators, a white Kenyan landowner named Michael Dyer told a journalist that he wanted to delve deeper into the history of how Maasai lost land to begin with: "Everyone knows there is a land issue here. It is causing quite a lot of distress now to the [Maasai] community. . . . My feeling would be let's get everyone around the table and let's get some proper interpretation of the Maasai agreements, and let's start the process of reconciliation."[110] Such talks never took place, and we cannot know how far empathy would have stretched if they had, but Dyer's comments show that some white Kenyans are willing to start to reckon with radically different points of view.

Indeed, ranch by ranch, other settler descendants, too, have witnessed the rise of CBC and felt the tension with resentful neighbors. Some have begun to realize that, in the words of one Laikipia landowner, "If people don't care about it and they're not part of it, it won't work. You can't simply say, 'You can't kill that.'" Lorrie, for instance, in her seventies, clearly subscribes to the notion of "development" as "progress," but within that scale relativizes common African ideologies sympathetically, saying: "for an African, coming from his place in in progress or development . . . how *can* he value an elephant higher than his *shamba* [from] which he's going to feed his family? I mean it doesn't, of course it doesn't, make sense. You can't expect people to stop cruelty to animals when they live such cruel lives themselves."

Lorrie indicates that she sees a difference in perspectives, though her way of putting it might be thought a bit patronizing—the phrase "such cruel lives" is reminiscent of colonial discourse about Africans living in an endless night, while her focus on cruelty to animals resonates with an old colonial narrative about African failures of empathy.[111] Mary, in her sixties, instead phrases the different perspectives in terms of different conditions of subsistence. She declares herself "proud" of what her forebears did to "develop" Kenya's land, particularly in the agricultural industries, and she believes in privately held game parks for conservation. Still, she describes a shift in her own attitudes. As a child, she says, "I grew up thinking, 'Ahh yeah, [I] *love* ellies!' Would never wear an elephant hair bracelet! Because I loved elephants! We would look at a giraffe *purely* as a *beauuutiful* animal. Isn't that amazing. Isn't it fabulous. Take our photographs." But another child growing up in a culture of subsistence agriculture, she says, wouldn't share her sentimental or aesthetic perspective.

> [They] would say: "Ohh—hope that can't step over our fence and damage our maize. Would that long neck reach over and eat our maize?" As opposed to seeing them as something purely ornamental. For them it's the threat of the damage it can do to them. Which is quite understandable! I mean I *love* animals! But I've heard about *shambas* [farms] in the Mara, um, and the elephants came and tore up the banana trees! You know, and they were fed up!

Mary recognizes the relatively narrow vantage point of her childhood—"I never *thought* of them like that, never *looked* at them like that!"—but as an adult she says she "understands" the logic behind local antipathy to wild animals. Even Clem, discussing hunting on protected lands, says, "If I had ten children at home and no job I'd do the same thing." While the degree of sympathy and understanding varies from one person to the next, we see in some of these remarks a strain of what anthropologists call cultural relativism; namely, a concession to the internal rationale for another group's behavior, and some effort, even if preliminary and flawed, to see the world from their perspective.[112]

In Laikipia, these concessions are bound up with a sea change in the way that some white landowners are considering their land use. Olivia, a young white Kenyan woman employed by a Laikipia conservancy, said: "Anybody living [in] this day and age on a piece of land this big has to justify their existence somehow . . . there's no way you can justify your existence without seeing it not only benefiting yourself but benefiting others." She goes on to imagine herself in the subject position of the less privileged: "Within a five kilometer radius of our boundary, the whole way round, there are close to 50,000 people . . . all looking over the fence and thinking: 'Well, they've got firewood, they've got wildlife. They've got everything we don't have.'" And Fiona, a young woman from a Laikipia family, works herself up gradually to a compromise stance in our conversation. At the same café where I spoke to Paul, she flicks her cigarette and says firmly, "The white people who own the farms, they bought the land legitimately." She reiterates the complaints I've heard many times about Maasai overgrazing. And yet, she says, most white Kenyan landowners in Laikipia now recognize that if they have a ranch, they should at least help Maasai by opening part of their farmland for limited grazing and water access during drought. And as Fiona continues, she abruptly breaks script to entertain what things may look like from their vantage point: "To be fair to Maasai, the ranchers *are* using a lot of their land, you know. And because as well all the ranches and farms are set up, the wildlife are in smaller areas as well, so they have problems with lions and cattle and elephants. . . . So it's very difficult to—I can see both sides of, of the fence there. I mean they're both right and they're both wrong, really at the end of the day."

Even Fiona's pronouns, here, suggest she's stepping back—white ranchers and Maasai both become "they." She shifts, then, from the conventional white subject position to a double awareness, suggesting that, in the end, neither side has a lock on the moral high ground. There's no doubt that my respondents may have been particularly self-conscious as they framed these admissions, seeing me as an embodiment of American liberalism. But this mindfulness also captures something in the white Kenyan zeitgeist; a new imperative to broaden one's perspective, to adjust to the political and economic imperatives of recent years. Bill, an honorary game warden authorized to help protect the wildlife and land from encroachment, makes a similar concession, however grudgingly: "You know, I hate to say it [but] I can understand their point in a way. When they're looking at a piece of land that's not doing anything, and they're not allowed onto it. They see no benefit in it. It was essentially theirs, uh not long ago. [Bill pauses] Yeah, you can *kind* of understand it."

Instead of repeating the old colonial saw that pastoralists don't "do" anything with the land, Bill here imagines them seeing a game reserve as "not doing anything." He goes on to describe an incident in 2008 when some European expatriates bought a large plot of land in Laikipia and "stuck up a great big fence" around it, cutting off the water source and all access to the pastoralists who had become accustomed to using it— what scholars now call "fortress conservation." "It doesn't work; you can't do that in this day and age, I don't think." Bill chalks the problem up to their "foreigner" status, a claim that suggests some settler descendants are framing their claim to belong not merely in terms of understanding Kenya's land and wildlife, but perhaps also, in some nascent fashion, accommodating their black Kenyan neighbors. If some white

Kenyans are beginning to pride themselves on that, the "day and age" is indeed evolving.

Jos, the urbanite in his fifties who is perhaps the most progressive of the white Kenyans I spoke to, actually feels duped by settlers' folk histories of the land. Jos grew up, he says, hearing that "the white farmers were much better farmers and the Africans were crap farmers," but has read otherwise since then. Whites' enthusiasm for conservation is "ironic", he remarks, given that before colonialism, "the animals were there, the people were there, and they lived. They somehow conserved." Then, he says, whites arrived "with their guns and hunting parties," decimating large populations of animals, "chucking lots of people off the land, and making their national parks." As we discuss the creation of conservation areas, he tacks between perspectives, making a dig at white hubris: "From our perspective, from the white—that was the right thing to do. But for the poor guy who lived in the park, and the poor guy who wants to poach—the motive behind poaching is probably poverty. . . . But if you've got one family on 60,000 acres, it's easy to conserve. You know. So. We do feel special."

Jos was one of the only settler descendants I spoke to who framed land redistribution as an idea that could move Kenya into the future. His family sold their land long ago, and Jos admits that his economic position inflects his emotions on the matter: "If I was a white land-owner I'd have anxiety but the fact is I'm not. If I was a landowner maybe I'd have a completely different view." He goes on, hesitantly:

> I *kind* of think that land should be redistributed. . . . I don't think you can hold on to a title deed that was got from an injustice system *[sic]* 100 years ago, in a colonial time, you see, 'cause the chiefs all signed it away. The unfortunate thing in this is the real losers were the pastoralists, the Maasai. And they're still losers. . . . it's a *very* inequitable system and it's one of the . . . one of the dynamics that create the instability in Kenya is there's a *vast* pool of landless people.

Jos breaks off, pauses, and shifts into a lower voice as he enunciates a familiar Western fret: "But actually, you give them the land and they'll all have babies and stuff and there'll be a new [lot], unless you deal with the population, which is a very emotive subject as well." But his voice rises again to its ordinary pitch: "Really in the end this is their ancestral land whether we like it or not . . . it's quite an unfair system where I as one person am sitting on 64,000 acres of land and, you know, [the area] outside of my electric fence is full of landless people." In his final thought, Jos' voice rises still higher: "I dunno whether redistribution of the land *would* help, I don't know. It's a simply, it's a bit of an idea whose time has come. I can't have a *real* concrete view of it, 'cause there are all different views on it." Though he remains equivocal, Jos's explicit double consciousness recognizes that structural positions shape vantage points, and to him, African subjectivities should be considered in moral judgments.

I don't mean to overplay this development. Ever since some colonial officials in Kenya objected to moving the Maasai in the early twentieth century, ever since other Europeans in late nineteenth-century Tanganyika foresaw that European-style conservation would marginalize pastoralists, there have been a few people in the colonial enterprise who have tried to see the pastoralist side of things. But there has also been an abundance of disregard, and many whites have staked their power and privilege on failures of empathy. Most settler descendants I spoke to rationalize white land ownership through structural oblivion. They do not know much about the history of Maasai displacement by the colonial government, they are in denial about the possibility that Maasai ever used the land sustainably, and they see themselves as the more responsible stewards. Where they diverge, however, is in how much they are willing to share the resources they have and how to entertain—or even *begin* to entertain—black Kenyan views about land rights and conservation. Those who do, and who share their resources, know that in the eyes of the nation and indeed the world, they have the moral high ground (and this, indeed, marks quite a difference from the "witch-hunting" of administrators who sympathized with the Maasai a century ago). Although the differences among them haven't caused a major cleavage in their collective sense of identity, they have created some resentments of the sort described by Trevor, in which conservative land-owners bristle at the "pressure" they feel to take the surrounding communities into account. Part of what they are feeling, of course, is the pressure to emerge from one historical era into another.

Still, it must be underscored that the awakening of whites' conscience has a tactical component, particularly among this group of whites anxious about their entitlement to belong in Kenya. If settler descendants are in peril of being dubbed colonial interlopers, some now realize that colonial-era ideologies of total entitlement will harm them. Conceding black Kenyan points of view, indeed, may be one mechanism that progressive settler descendants use to signal that they belong in Kenya as moral beings. But renouncing land altogether doesn't sit right with most of them, and CBC still lets them play a relatively paternalistic role vis-à-vis their neighbors. Meanwhile, in their enduring sentiments about how and why they love Kenya's land and wildlife, they entertain a sweeping vision of the nation's wide-open spaces, a vision that lets them feel they transcend petty regional squabbling about ethnic entitlements, while stewarding wildlife and land in a responsible fashion. Part of white privilege and indeed whiteness in Kenya, it seems, is the appearance (even if not the reality) of such transcendence.

Yet one aim of this book is to point out the instances and events that have shaken confident white stances. Settler descendants have been prodded from several directions to recognize or reckon with white privilege. As we shall see in the next chapter, the murder trial of Thomas Cholmondeley that began in 2006 shocked some settler descendants, who found themselves on the defensive against the collective charge of another level of colonialist brutality.

3

Guilt

By the time I visited Tom Cholmondeley in the Kamiti Maximum Security Prison outside Nairobi, he had been incarcerated for more than two years, still on remand as his trial dragged on. I hadn't sought him out, originally, but several of my contacts knew him and had urged me on: "Just go see him. He'll have a lot to say." I resisted, for reasons I did not fully understand. "I want to look at the way people talk *about* Cholmondeley," I rationalized to them. "I'm not trying to get to the bottom of what actually happened out there." Deep down I may have been worried it felt journalistic, even prurient, to interview the man himself. The very idea of him made me uneasy; he had been called an entitled brat, an arrogant aristocrat, and a cold-blooded killer. But one day I found myself accompanying a white Kenyan friend to a yoga class, where my friend pointed out Cholmondeley's long-term girlfriend Sally Dudmesh stretching on another mat. I had seen her described in newspapers as an "English beauty," and she was, but she also looked exhausted. I watched as friends approached her after the class to ask how she was holding up. The next day I worked up the nerve to call her.

Dudmesh was protective of Cholmondeley. She was infuriated by the bias journalists had shown when describing the case, citing, for instance, how they had represented the second dead man, Robert Njoya, as a "stone mason" when, she said emphatically, he was a "known poacher." (There is weighty political baggage associated with this term, to which I'll return.) She was disgusted with the way the public, politicians, and journalists repeatedly invoked Cholmondeley's family estate and colonial legacy, as if these somehow established his guilt. And, of course, she was terrified about the fate of the man she wanted to be with. She agreed I could contact him, but I'd need to email a provisional list of questions and promise I wouldn't publish material about him in non-academic contexts (the tabloid press, for instance). I told Dudmesh I would bring a consent form, and asked her if I could bring him anything to read.

Cholmondeley agreed to meet with me on a day in late June 2008. I wrestled with the contradictory accounts I had heard about the shootings and the man himself as I puzzled over what to take with me, settling on a thermos of coffee, a copy of *The Economist,* and a couple of novels that seemed tactfully irrelevant to his situation (A. S. Byatt's *Possession* and Arthur Golding's *Memoires of a Geisha*). While at the bookstore in Nairobi, I also ran my eye over V. S. Naipaul's 2004 novel *Half a Life,* which traces an Indian man's move to London and then, via a transnational romance, to Mozambique. The novel aches with postcolonial displacements, complexities of racial identity, and the pain of exile. I briefly considered bringing it too, but decided it might be too loaded.

Kamiti Maximum Security Prison is a large, squat, colonial-era structure located down Thika Road, about forty kilometers outside of Nairobi's city center. In a booth on a long driveway leading up to the complex, I handed my passport to a warden and explained who I had come to see. The warden broke into a grin, saying: "Oh, Tom is very nice." I must have looked surprised, because he added, emphatically, "He is *so* good." He directed me to the shade of a massive tree in front of the prison, where I stood feeling conspicuous among about twenty other visitors, most of them women. Male prisoners in black-and-white-striped jumpsuits were using pangas (machetes) to clear the grass to the right of the building, while others staggered back and forth to carry rusted tubs of detritus to a smoldering garbage heap. After nearly an hour's wait I was the last remaining person there, and the guards brought me into the gates. One of them plucked the thermos from my hands, murmuring that it might be returned *baadaye* (later).

My escorts and I passed a row of male prisoners crouching with their hands behind their heads in a central courtyard, and walked into a small office. It was sparsely furnished and the walls were lined with brass coat hooks that looked many decades old, probably the same ones installed by the colonial administration. Cholmondeley sat in a rickety wooden chair, very tall, with pale blue eyes and curled blonde hair peeking from behind a receding hairline. His patrician nose and amused mouth suggested his aristocratic roots, though as he stood to shake my hand I noticed he had given up on the suits and silk ties he wore in court in favor of shorts and flip-flops. We sat down to talk and I produced a consent form. Cholmondeley signed his copy and placed it in a thin plastic folder already stuffed with papers and a single book: Naipaul's *Half a Life*.

What justifies an interview with someone accused of silencing two voices at the end of his gun? Many in Kenya and beyond have assumed Cholmondeley to be such a callous, cut-and-dried colonialist that he would shoot Africans for amusement, as some of his more vicious colonial predecessors reportedly did. Yet already, in his popularity with the warden and his taste in literature, I was getting a sense of a person more complex than the media had depicted him. And irrespective of what crimes he might have committed, Cholmondeley's position seemed a high-stakes version of a more general white Kenyan predicament. I knew he would choose his words carefully, but even so I would have a chance to see how someone once so cossetted would make meaning out of the charge that he is terribly guilty.

"Guilt" is a multifaceted concept. The authorities adjudicate legal guilt; it holds a person responsible for a misdeed and implies a corresponding punishment. Legal guilt can hang over a person as they move through society, for usually they have been judged not just legally errant, but also morally guilty. But an individual's legal and moral guilt (or innocence) are often overshadowed by a broader assessment of collective guilt; a judgment of misdeeds or moral opprobrium attaching to a person by virtue of their membership in a social group. Some judgments of collective guilt are based on discriminatory stereotypes; in the United States, for instance, we talk wryly about being found guilty of "driving while black" (a presumption of collective guilt that sometimes translates unfairly into legal judgements of guilt). In some cases, collective guilt is projected as redress for structural inequalities; in contemporary South Africa, for instance, some Afrikaners report feeling targeted by projections of collective guilt, regardless of their family's history or personal intentions. This effacement of the individual is familiar in parts of sub-Saharan Africa (as in other areas of the world) where members of extended kinship networks may be held accountable for the deeds and debts of their relations, including their ancestors.[1] However, in Western traditions, not only do many consider it necessary to determine guilt and redress on an individual basis, but the term "guilt" also often refers to an individual, interior condition of feeling morally culpable: psychological guilt.[2] As part of this Western emphasis on the individual's inner states, those who have morally wrong intentions may sometimes be found legally guilty of them, and those found legally guilty are supposed to feel self-recrimination. But in spite of the ways we often link guilt to individuals, even privately felt guilt is reliant on sociocultural conditions to breathe life into it. Most early white settlers apparently felt little guilt about mistreating Africans because their racist, Social Darwinist ideological frameworks did not inspire much empathy for African suffering. It took exceptional circumstances, or an exceptional person, for elite conscience to be tweaked.

Today, settler descendants feel vulnerable to all these kinds of guilt: legal, moral, collective, and psychological. The Maasai attempts to reclaim white-owned land, for instance, projected collective guilt onto contemporary white Kenyans, hoping to hold them legally liable for the misdeeds of the British of a century earlier. For three and a half years, the very real possibility of legal guilt, followed by execution, pressed upon Cholmondeley, and of course he had his rejoinders to these (including, he claims, his morally innocent intentions). Meanwhile, the social drama surrounding Cholmondeley's trial made clear to settler descendants that, in the court of public opinion, collective and moral guilt has been projected onto them because of their collective association with him. Some whites I spoke to, for instance, were confronted by black Kenyan accusers about the trial, and were shocked by the extent of the emotional grudges that came to the surface. The notion that Cholmondeley and his peers "ought" to feel psychologically guilty, too, seems to haunt some settler descendants, a nagging feeling beneath the surface of some of the conversations I relate in this chapter. Most of them didn't buy in, but they did find themselves responding to the disturbance of it. And in seeing themselves being seen in light of the Cholmondeley trial, some whites were rattled out of some of their structural oblivion—out of their comfortable ignorance of the resentments some black Kenyans feel toward their community.

Such bitter challenges evoked a spectrum of responses among my interlocutors. Few people wish to live in a state of chronic guilt of any kind, let alone be exiled from the country they love, so many had ways of trying to hold psychological guilt at bay while talking back against the specter of collective guilt. Some distanced themselves from collective guilt by holding the Delamere family and the broader colonial past at arm's length. Others objected that their parents and grandparents should not be held guilty because they had an alibi: good intentions. Many insisted that irrespective of the past, and of anything Cholmondeley may have done, white Kenyans today should be accepted as a forward-looking group dedicated to bringing Kenya into a "developed" future. Ironically, although the Cholmondeley case challenged some of their blind spots, other kinds of structural oblivion became an important tool, for many of them, to help them make the case that neither they nor their predecessors should be held accountable for any particular misdeeds.

Only rarely did I find a white individual who settled into the discomforts of empathy for black Kenyan resentment, or into the weighty feeling of psychological guilt—and almost none of them spoke of changing structural inequalities through material transactions such as restitution. At the end of the chapter I return to Cholmondeley's own reactions, including the intermingled insight and defenses provoked by the anger directed at him, and his tentative efforts to be counted as a "son of Kenya" in spite of everything.

THE SHOOTINGS AND THEIR AFTERMATH

Until his incarceration, Tom Cholmondeley lived near Lake Elmenteita on his family's Soysambu estate, a now-48,000 acre tract of semi-arid land originally procured by the third Baron Delamere, who arrived in the colony in 1897. Despite, or perhaps because of, his reputation as a buccaneering eccentric, Delamere had immense influence. His ingenuity virtually established the cattle and farming industries in the new colony, while his charisma and ebullience—which extended to crossing Somaliland on camel, hunting lions, and shooting out chandeliers for kicks— made him the unofficial leader of Kenya's settlers. In recent decades the Delamere name has been linked to impossible glamour in Western cinema and in Kenya's tourism literature.

Yet many Kenyans associate the Delameres with colonial exploitation; this, indeed, is why Cholmondeley is so often referred to as "Delamere" in the Kenyan media and in public discourse. Contemporary Maasai, for instance, note that the third baron procured his land through blood brotherhood compacts with their ancestors, but later dramatically violated these agreements, being complicit in the notorious Maasai moves.[3] The fourth Baron Delamere, Tom Cholmondeley's grandfather, was a key player in the so-called Happy Valley set an elite group of pleasure-seeking, allegedly wife-swapping settlers of the 1920s–40s whose foibles have been held up as the worst kind of colonial self-indulgence.[4] A statue of the third Baron Delamere once dominated Delamere Avenue in central Nairobi, but it was removed in 1963 and the avenue was renamed after the first Kenyan president, Jomo Kenyatta. The statue now sits quietly on Soysambu, overlooking a cluster of pink bougainvillea bushes and the family estate.

Tom Cholmondeley was born in 1968, and educated at the British-style Pembroke School in GilGil, Kenya, then at Eton, Britain's most elite boarding school. After attending the Royal Agricultural College (now University) in Cirencester, England, he returned to Soysambu. At the time of the shootings he lived near his parents, taking an active role in the family's dairy and beef ranches while helping set up a wildlife sanctuary that protected various species, including giraffe, zebra, pelicans, and flamingoes. He loved the outdoor life, he loved zooming across (or above) the land on any kind of vehicle, and he loved to hunt. Cholmondeley co-organized the estate's venture into game ranching for profit, an experiment that provided jobs for those in the surrounding communities and reportedly cut down on illegal hunting, until game cropping itself was made illegal in 2003. In keeping with the growing concessions white landowners make to surrounding communities, Soysambu also sponsored several charitable ventures, building and supporting five schools and two medical clinics, for instance, and augmenting the water supply for nearby areas.

Still, even before the shootings, the Delamere family's relationship with the surrounding communities was tense. Soysambu is flanked by impoverished homesteads, including squatters' camps for low-wage temporary workers on the nearby flower farms, and their needs make a daily impact on the Delameres' land. Neighbors frequently trespass in search of firewood or meat, whether for subsistence or meager profit. The class differences that correlate with race have historically played into a stark double standard when it comes to killing animals in Africa; as Edward Steinhart documents, when whites do it, usually for sport, they term it "hunting," a gentlemanly endeavor; when blacks do it, it falls under the rubric of "poaching." In prohibiting various types of hunting, including African practices of hunting with nets and fire, the colonial administration destabilized many male initiation ceremonies and reduced African hunters to the role of guide or tracker for white employers.[5] They also restricted a major source of protein for many African families. But this history of dispossession is not typically discussed by settler descendants, who frame poaching as an unwanted, backward collision with conservation. The Delamere family, accordingly, regards

poaching and incursions onto their land as a major threat to their conservation agenda and their security. (Their neighbor, Lord Enniskillen,
agrees, having collected over 800 wire snares laid in stealth on his own
property.)[6] In the years leading up to the Cholmondeley accusations, the
family had also experienced numerous problems with robbery and violence, reporting no fewer than three incidents in which intruders shot
managers on the estate. Generally speaking, in fact, many settler descendants in Kenya have found "security" a growing point of stress and concern, some of them founding private security companies to help combat
their fears.[7] Cholmondeley's personal responses to trespassers were
reportedly aggressive and hot-headed. Mary Njeri, in her fifties, told a
New York Times journalist that when Cholmondeley caught her looking
for firewood in 2004, he "slapped her until she saw stars."[8] In the aftermath of the shooting incidents, reports like these would come back to
haunt him.

His real troubles began on April 19, 2005. Kenyan Wildlife Service
(KWS) officials had suspected workers at Soysambu of continuing to
deal in bush meat from the animals on the ranch—a charge that some
of my white Kenyan contacts intimated was probably true, though the
Delameres strictly deny it.[9] Three KWS rangers, including Samson ole
Sisina, a 44-year-old Maasai man, gained access to the ranch in a plain-
clothes guise and apprehended Soysambu ranch workers in the act of
skinning a Cape buffalo. Details are sketchy from here, but ranch workers apparently did not at first realize that the men who pulled guns on
them were from KWS, and one of them used a mobile phone to call
Tom Cholmondeley to the scene. When Cholmondeley arrived, revolver
in hand, he claims it looked as though strangers were holding his staff
at gunpoint, and he assumed they were being robbed—though at least
one KWS ranger has claimed that Cholmondeley recognized her.[10] Possibly, Sisina fired a shot in Cholmondeley's direction, possibly not.
Cholmondeley fired on Sisina, who died of a gunshot wound to the
neck. Cholmondeley was arrested and charged with murder, a crime
that technically may still incur the penalty of death by hanging. When
he learned the identity of the dead man, he reportedly told the police, "I
am most bitterly remorseful at the enormity of my mistake."[11]

Some settler descendants rallied to Cholmondeley's defense at the time,
arguing that fatal shootings during robberies are so common in Kenya
that many whites feel they live under a state of siege, and Cholmondeley
should be forgiven his confusion and error. Panic is easy, they reasoned,
when "security" is so poor that for many elites, even wrought-iron bars

on their windows and private security services manning the gates of their homes aren't enough to deter armed assaults. Rumors also circulated among some of my contacts that there had been a government plot to assassinate Cholmondeley, the sole heir to the land, so that the acreage could be reclaimed by the Kenyan government—in which case the KWS rangers could have been hired killers. Director of Public Prosecutions Philip Murgor was sympathetic to Cholmondeley as well, claiming that the murder charge ignored key evidence, and that powerful politicians were pressuring police to ensure a conviction. "This is all about land," he told a Western journalist; "The Delamere ranch is the [biggest tract of land] in the Rift Valley, and a lot of people want it."[12] After a month, Murgor ordered Cholmondeley acquitted and released, and in the furor that ensued he was swiftly removed from his own post, reportedly on the orders of President Mwai Kibaki himself.

The day after Cholmondeley was let go, the front page of Kenya's *Daily Nation* invoked his colonial family name: "OUTRAGE AS DELAMERE IS FREED OVER KILLING." A picture of Cholmondeley, elegantly dressed, smiling, and flashing a "thumbs-up" sign, also ran in the papers, to the dismay of many. Aggrieved members of Sisina's family and local politicians fumed about dehumanizing colonial abuse, claiming that Sisina's life had been treated "like that of a dog," and that "The Delameres were the ones who stole our land in the first place. . . . And now look at us. We've become part of the wildlife."[13] Maasai protested Cholmondeley's release outside the attorney general's office and demanded his re-arrest. Other protestors barricaded the highway between Naivasha and Nakuru, and one Maasai leader threatened to organize an invasion of Soysambu, reviving claims that the land had been deceitfully taken from them more than a hundred years earlier. The sense of tragedy was both political and personal; when Sisina's family were interviewed by the news media, it emerged that he had been the sole breadwinner for his widow, Seenoi (sometimes referred to as "Lucy") and eight children, who lived in a three-room bungalow, and had aspired to educate all of them, even the girls. The Delameres did not send a message of condolence in the days following the shooting, but even if they had, said Sisina's 16-year-old daughter Leah, "we don't want to hear it."[14]

Incredibly, history was to repeat itself a little more than a year later. On May 10, 2006, Cholmondeley was walking on Soysambu with a friend of Italian descent, rally car driver Carl "Flash" Tundo, to inspect a house site. Cholmondeley was armed, having brought a rifle, because the brushy area was thick with Cape buffalo, a species that had badly gored him in the leg years earlier and even killed a recent guest of the Delameres'. But instead of encountering buffalo, the two men stumbled upon three trespassers, among them the 37-year-old Kikuyu man named Robert Njoya.

Accompanied by dogs and carrying weapons such as bows and arrows and a panga (machete), Njoya and his companions were moving a dead antelope. Njoya's widow later told a Western journalist that her family had been on a starvation diet of greens in the weeks leading up to the incident.[15] But the sight of "poachers" surely angered Cholmondeley. Njoya and his companions may or may not have turned their dogs on Cholmondeley and his friend. In the growing dusk, Cholmondeley kneeled and fired his rifle into the dense bush, shooting, he says, only at the dogs. (Targeting hunting dogs is a widely acknowledged means of deterrence; apparently it takes at least eighteen months to train a new one). The bullets killed two dogs but somehow Njoya also took a bullet to the buttock. Cholmondeley used his handkerchief to make a tourniquet around Njoya's lower body, called the police, and loaded the man into his Toyota RAV4 to rush him to a private hospital. En route they encountered the farm's security chief, whereupon they transferred Njoya into his vehicle and Cholmondeley paid him to complete the journey to the emergency room. Sadly, fifteen minutes upon arrival, Njoya was declared dead of blood loss. Cholmondeley was arrested and charged, again, with murder.

The reaction to news of Njoya's death was swift and fierce. Kenyan newspaper headlines howled, while local and international newspapers reminded readers of Cholmondeley's glamorous but now maligned roots; the phrases "Happy Valley" and even "Trigger Happy Valley" became common currency in discussions of the case. The victim's widow, Sarah Waithera Njoya, was left to care for four young sons on their small plot adjoining Soysambu. She lamented to a British journalist: "Why does this man think he can do this again and again and not face any consequences?"[16] While some citizens and bloggers urged the public to let the legal system take its course, others called for Cholmondeley to be "lynched" if released, or, in the case of one blogger, tortured until he confessed. A commentator identified as "Kwale" wrote:

> Tom, sadly is a decadent of [sic] racist toff and his views on black people are still the same as his ancestors. One murder could have been pardonable, but two, is totally inexcusable. He should be banged up until he confess the murder, and if he confesses he should face gallow [sic]. But I am afraid

Kenya is a country full of Mzungu [white person] arse-lickers. Mzungu is seen as untouchable and that's why the idiot got the guts to commit double murder.[17]

Some citizens organized a boycott against the Soysambu dairy, deeming one of its popular products "blood yoghurt," and marching with signs reading: "We don't want his milk, we want justice." Cholmondeley's colonial background and his apparent inhumanity were twinned: "[A] great grandson of the delamere has decided that of late the shanty-dwelling folk make target practice good sport," a blogger wrote, and "Human Rights Activist, Mombasa," commented that through the boycott "we Kenyan of African origin do the just to our brother. . . . [Cholmondeley] has no regard for life of Africans, how long are we going to stomach such kind of uncouth behavior for such brutal colonialists in our own soil."[18]

Politicians upped the ante at Njoya's funeral. No fewer than seven MPs and five cabinet ministers sat in attendance at the ceremonies, and several of them called for Cholmondeley's summary execution. Deputy Immigration Minister Ananias Mwaboza invoked Zimbabwe's notorious land reform campaign to expel whites from their estates, saying: "We now know why Robert Mugabe acted the way he did." Assistant Information Minister Koigi wa Wamwere echoed him, referring to white landowners as "heartless people" and asking in an exaggerated flourish: "Which independence are we talking about if the settlers continue occupying more than half of our lands?"[19] Cholmondeley had become a stand-in for colonial injustice. Collectively, Cholmondeley and settler descendants had already been found guilty.

While Cholmondeley sat in Kamiti prison in the ensuing months, his defense lawyer Fred Ojiambo struggled to get a hearing in Kenya's turgid and antiquated court system. When he finally did, the defense revolved around two key contentions. First, although Cholmondeley had reportedly confessed to Senior Superintendent of Police Geoffrey Mwangi that he had shot Njoya "by mistake," his legal team tried to generate reasonable doubt by contending that his companion Flash Tundo was carrying a pistol and might have fired the fatal shot (apparently the ballistics evidence was ambiguous and incomplete). In court, Cholmondeley claimed not to have mentioned Tundo's pistol when he was first incarcerated because he was trying to protect his friend. Second, and more plausible, was the argument that his behavior on the scene—binding the wound, calling police, driving the victim toward the hospital—was not that of a man who intended to kill. But the settler descendants I spoke to in 2008 agreed that even if the evidence to convict him of outright murder was shoddy, there would be a national outcry if he were found "not guilty." Many felt he was likely to become the victim of a revenge killing. There were rumors of bounties on his head, including one being amassed by taxi drivers in Nairobi.[20]

Settler descendants had been shocked when they got wind of the second killing. As Cholmondeley's distant relative, the elderly Michael Cunningham-Reid remarked in the 2009 documentary film *Kenya Murder Mystery*: "Anywhere in the world where someone kills two people within one year [it] raises eyebrows. It just doesn't happen, does it?" Several white Kenyans told me of their uncanny sense that history, even destiny, might have caught up with Cholmondeley. It was so peculiar, so ironic, for this man who already embodied a history of colonial excess to have been caught up twice in the same scenario. And how could a man considered such a good shot, someone with such a masterful capacity for sight, have been so blind—both to the human being in his sightline and to the social implications of his actions? One of his friends expressed bafflement to me: "It's quite . . . it doesn't make sense; it's like fate has definitely done that to him. It's weird. . . . He won't, he won't have done it, it's not murder. It's bizarre. How *could* that happen. But how *silly* of him to even have had a gun the second time. But then he must be quite a good shot. You look at the situation and you go: *God*."

Almost nobody in the white Kenyan community thought Cholmondeley a cold-hearted murderer. A small handful even represented him as a hero who confessed (initially, anyway) to two shootings that he did not commit, in order to save the reputation of those who fired the fatal shots; a young farmhand in the first case, and Flash Tundo in the second. And some believed he was entirely justified in shooting at the dogs in the second incident, given that conservationists are perpetually tormented by the decimation of Kenya's wildlife.[21] But I met only one individual—the irascible elderly farmer Devon, mentioned in the preceding chapter—who reacted with unqualified approval.

> *Devon:* I think, from my personal point of view I think Cholmondeley did us all a favor. You've *never* heard that before I'll bet you! . . . After his first session [in court] I met him. I shook him warmly by the hand . . . and I congratulated him. I said I think you've done all us Europeans in this country a bloody favor.
>
> *Janet:* What did you mean by that?

Devon: I think he's done us a favor! Literally. *Don't mess with a European! . . .* That's how I read it. And I think *to this day* [he rapped the table, enunciating each word] with all this political nonsense going on at the start of this year, were Europeans hassled anywhere?

Devon is right in one sense: settler descendants were not directly targeted during Kenya's politically sponsored ethnic violence of late 2007 and early 2008. Devon chalks this up to Cholmondeley's display of swift retribution. But Devon was an outlier among the whites I spoke to. Far from clapping Cholmondeley on the back for his actions, the vast majority—even some of his friends and family members—told me they found the incidents reprehensible. In the most extreme statement I heard, one settler descendant in his twenties told me that when he heard of the second shooting, his first thought was, "Well, man, you should go to the gallows," until learning more about the case and coming to feel "some sympathy" for Cholmondeley.

But most of my respondents framed their feelings more along the lines of his elderly relative Tobina Cartwright Cole, who characterizes Cholmondeley's actions as "stupid, not evil."[22] One after another, white Kenyans told me Cholmondeley had behaved like an "idiot"; a "blithering idiot"; a "prat"; a "silly young man"; or a "fool." Many implied they themselves would know better how to behave in the same situation. In the wake of Cholmondeley's first scandal, for instance, they would never have carried a gun with people anywhere in the vicinity; that to do so was "asking for trouble." The wildlife manager Trevor told me that despite the perils of the bush, he himself never carries a gun on the job but has a gun bearer do it for him. These days, says Trevor, a "white face attached to a management position, putting the pressure on [with a gun] gives off the wrong impression." Several also remarked on how tactless Cholmondeley had been after his first release to put two thumbs up for a photographer. Much white Kenyan disapproval, in other words, centered upon Cholmondeley's own apparent (structural) obliviousness of what his actions would represent to the wider Kenyan public. He was insensitive to the times, they felt; no wonder he had evoked rage. Meanwhile, he had sullied his reputation forever, as well as potentially jeopardizing their own.

But concern about one's reputation is not the same as grasping the emotional perspective of the Kenyans who felt such keen resentment. Deep understanding of this anger was rare among my respondents, but I did find that in the wake of the Cholmondeley scandals, some settler descendants found themselves jostled farther along the continuum that stretches between structural oblivion at one end and empathy, perspectivism, and understanding of the historical political economy of structural oppression at the other. Such reactions were sometimes provoked by the micro-confrontations between black and white Kenyans that followed Cholmondeley's arrests, in which whites had to digest the fact that they can be viewed as morally culpable interlopers, latter-day colonialists collectively guilty in a land some feel does not belong to them.

MORAL DOUBLE CONSCIOUSNESS: BETWEEN EMPATHY AND DEFENSIVENESS

As noted in Chapter 1, some colonial-era whites recognized, however subliminally, the possibility of African resentment. The fact is that most whites were also able to sweep such dissension under the rug through a multi-pronged strategy that included legal disenfranchisement of Africans, social segregation, and psychological denial. Coming to grips with the sometimes critical sentiments of Africans is a relatively new project for many whites who live in Africa. Hence, for instance, in the introduction to his 1985 volume on white South Africans before the dissolution of apartheid, Vincent Crapanzano asserts that as whites waited in fear for seemingly imminent social revolution, "[They] lost what John Keats (in an obviously different context) called negative capability, the capability of so negating their identity as to be imaginatively open to the complex and never very certain reality around them. Instead, they close off; they create a kind of psychological apartheid. . . . In such circumstances there can be no real recognition of the other—no real appreciation of *his* subjectivity."[23]

David McDermott Hughes makes a related charge in his discussion of twentieth-century white African autobiography and literature, in which he argues that whites in Africa have fixated on embedding themselves in the African landscape, at the expense of understanding black grievances. The problem, he suggests, is not merely one of attenuated subjectivity but also of citizenship: "Nationalism and anti-white sentiment have repeatedly caught whites off-guard, marginalizing them further . . . by writing themselves so single-mindedly into the landscape, whites wrote themselves out of the society."[24]

But in the past two decades, whites in nations like South Africa and Zimbabwe have experienced a difficult reckoning, being confronted with a range of measures that extend from the Truth and Reconciliation hearings and black economic empowerment measures in South Africa to being violently, sometimes murderously, displaced from their farms in both countries.[25] Whites in Kenya haven't faced such systematic or drastic retribution, but as the Cholmondeley scandal unfolded, some white Kenyans told me of a subtler confrontation. For some, this meant experiencing the brunt of being "othered"; that is, of being assessed on the basis of negative stereotypes attaching to their group, rather than on grounds of their individuality. Consider the words of Jonathan, the owner of a flower farm in the Rift Valley, who found himself the target of projected collective guilt:

> *Jonathan:* . . . because your profile is that of . . . being white, you're tarred by the same brush [as Cholmondeley] . . . I'm a great chatter so I always will chat up and hear what they've got to say, and the, um, police force on the road [and people in the shops] would say: 'You're no better than Delamere!' *Kama Delamere, moja wao* [Kiswahili: "Like Delamere, one of them"]'.
>
> *Janet:* Did you say anything in response?
>
> *Jonathan:* Absolutely, I'd say—yeah! I'd probably think of some analogy and say, "You're not the same as [then prime minister] Raila Odinga" and, you know, huhuh [he laughs].

Jonathan's analogy has special rhetorical power in light of the ethnic clashes in the months after the December 2007 presidential election. The then incumbent President Kibaki (a Kikuyu) effectively stole the election from Odinga (a Luo), and the result was a violent upheaval widely known to have been sponsored by politicians on both sides. Thousands of people turned against one another, following an essentialist logic in which any Luo (or Kikuyu) was interchangeable with any other, and entitlement to landownership was parsed along ethnic lines. In drawing the comparison, Jonathan clearly resented the dehumanizing experience of being lumped together with Cholmondeley and presumed "guilty" merely as a member of a collective. The encounter also reminded him of the tension some perceive between white Kenyans' racial and national identities. White Kenyans may be legal citizens of Kenya, but they don't always feel fully embraced as cultural citizens because of the judgment of collective guilt leveled against them.

Jonathan was defensive. He still bristles, he says, about the process of applying to renew his national identity card, when he was forbidden from checking a box saying "Indigenous Kenyan" and forced instead to check "Other." "It's discriminatory," Jonathan rails. As we discussed the public reaction to the Cholmondeley case, he objected to the notion that he should be held guilty for being a landholder. His family earned their land, says Jonathan, and like good Kenyan nationals they use it to "contribute." His entitlement to land, he suggests, should be judged on the basis of his personal effort and personal impact, not his association with anyone else's historical deeds:

> Everything we do is designed to create as much employment as possible. And I feel passionate about trying to make Kenya work. . . . [I] watched the [British] flag go down and the Kenyan flag go up. . . . [they say] if you're a whitey you are [a landowner] by virtue of some historical injustice. Well, you know, we've acquired our own patch of land here *entirely* through our own endeavor, so you know it rankles a bit because of that. We own a *tiny* bit of very marginal land. Feel that we're contributing to the best of our abilities and provided for as many people as possible . . . [but the] conception is that there can be no whitey in Africa for any other reason than exploitation and for what they can get out of it.

For many settler descendants, the wake of the Cholmondeley drama provoked both insight and defenses. Several told me of encounters that gave them new understanding of black Kenyan perspectives, but also instilled fear of the accusations being directed at them. Here, for instance, is a relative of Cholmondeley's, a middle-aged woman named Clare from a well-to-do agriculturalist family, explaining her revelation after his second arrest:

> What I hadn't quite realized was that whites were regarded as people who *could* line up an African in the sights of their gun and blow him away. . . . That was a huge shock to me, I think. . . . That people thought that's who we were! That we could *do* that! . . . Because you'd have to be a *terrible* person to be like that. I mean, you know, there's a case in South Africa where a white African threw one of his employees to the . . . to the lions. Yeah, okay. And you think: *phuh!* Only in South Africa could people be *so* awful! And then you realize that actually that's how *you* are seen. Potentially.

Clare enacts a more innocent or naïve time when she could reassure herself that South Africa is where the real racists and racial tensions are. It was deeply uncomfortable for her to realize that some black Kenyans might perceive settler descendants as equally heartless. Her shock is compounded by the revelation that her view of herself as a good person means little in the face of the public perception of her elite role.

Yet like many of her peers, Clare has a defense, one focused on the motives and sacrifices of past colonials. She concedes that the British should not have imposed their infrastructure upon Africans, but argues that judgments against them as people have been unfair:

You can't *miss* it, really, that there is a lot written about the *evils* of the colonial system. . . . .But *so much* of what you pick up in the newspaper, *The Economist* or *Vanity Fair* [which published a long article about Cholmondeley and his family] or whatever, *so* much of of . . . uh . . . of the [low, ironic voice] "evil" that the colonialists perpetrated and how little they cared about the Africans . . . it seems to me that the people who worked for the government on the northern frontier probably for years at a time, they had a *true love* for the people.

The colonial officials who were "sent into the desert," she adds, weren't enjoying golf games or a cozy home with their families. Instead, they "dedicated their lives," because they "*really believed* in what they were doing." In Clare's moral philosophy, neither her relative Cholmondeley nor her colonial predecessors *meant* to do ill. Her model of "guilt," then, zeroes in, not on the effects of colonial structures, or on being collectively implicated, but rather on the hearts and minds of individuals; on their "love" for the people, their "belief" that they were doing good, or—in the case of Cholmondeley—his intention, which was not to kill, she believes.

Some of my white Kenyan respondents spoke back to their critics simply by resisting the idea they belonged to Cholmondeley's social group. Nicola, a Nairobi businesswoman whose parents had come from the United Kingdom in search of economic opportunity, vigorously drew a line between herself and the "worst colonial sort." She gave me a tour of her restaurant, chatting in Kiswahili with her employees, and exchanging animated jokes about the kitchen stove, which always seemed on the verge of collapse. We headed back to her home in Karen and sat under the purple blooms of a jacaranda tree in her garden. She pulled on a jean jacket against the breeze, politely asked her cook to bring us coffee, and told me about her efforts to educate her employees so they have a chance of upward mobility. Our conversation turned to the shootings, and she noted that she had felt public perception of white Kenyans sour during their aftermath. Drawing on a cigarette, Nicola parodied Cholmondeley and his type in a low, ironic voice (in italics below) with hyper-aristocratic and hyper-masculine diction:

> Yeah well . . . that's how everyone sees us. We're all mad, we're all barking, we just go around shooting; *"Look, that chap's on his land, shoot him!"* Actually, there really are people like that . . . genuine . . . hhuh! And Tom Cholmondeley sadly was one of my brother's best friends at school. But he's a little cuckoo. I certainly wouldn't relate to him. I wouldn't say: *"That's exactly what I'd do, good on him!"* In fact I don't know anyone who would say "Good on him." Huh huh!! Yes. I wouldn't relate to him. In fact I don't know him.

Apparently, the stereotypical colonial who casually shoots Africans is a "Hail fellow, well met" sort, and ostentatiously posh-sounding. Through her shift in voicing and her assertions that she neither knows nor relates to Cholmondeley, Nicola creates a flattened colonial archetype that she "doesn't relate to." Similarly Marcus, a manager in the coffee industry, called Cholmondeley a "fool" and described the British and settler descendant "aristocracy" as "inbred," adding "they all look a bit funny; eyes on the side of their head and such. I'm not very keen on them." (Like Nicola, however, he has family ties that might belie this aversion, telling me later in the same conversation that his nephew plays polo with Prince Harry.)

Generally speaking, many younger settler descendants seem at pains to avoid coming across as anachronistic, lest they be associated with the stigmas of colonial history. For just as twentieth-century white colonials famously tended to view Africans as atavistic, stuck in "tradition," and hence morally inferior,[26] white Kenyans have today sometimes found themselves represented as if frozen in colonial time and relegated to a past felt to be morally backward and deserving of extinction. Popular discourse links Cholmondeley and other descendants of settlers to the earlier sins of their colonial forebears, and press reports have also framed them as part of a "lost world."[27] No wonder some whites encourage the notion that only Cholmondeley and his family members are stuck in a different era, while aligning themselves against the outdated colonial attitudes the Delamere family supposedly represents.

A young white Kenyan in his twenties named Felix, for example, pokes fun at the regressive idiosyncrasies of Cholmondeley's father, who is known to have a large model train set at Soysambu. Felix's relaxed blonde curls jostle as he laughs: "He's a model train obsessive. . . . This incredibly wealthy guy like kind of maybe lost sight of his empire, you know!" One white farmer I spoke to described being at a cattle sale in the Naivasha area not long after the first shooting. He was conversing with a group of Maasai, when Cholmondeley's father came up to him and said in a joshing, plummy tone: "Hello old boy—shot any Maasai lately?" To the farmer, this appalling act of insensitivity went to show how "out of touch" Cholmondeley's family is. One of Cholmondeley's friends, Sylvie, defended Cholmondeley's love for country, but conceded that he did suffer from an "old" colonial attitude inherited from his parents: "[Tom is] someone who *loves* his country, and who *loves* his people. . . . Kenyans *matter* to him and wildlife matters. The problem was he was a bit too passionate about wildlife on his land. He was using an old way of land management [i.e., shooting at the poachers' dogs]."

Holding the "old ways" at arm's length, numerous white Kenyans articulate their resentment that colonial history has been so often brought up by Kenya's politicians and citizenry, especially since the Cholmondeley scandal. My respondents complain that the resurgence of anti-colonial rhetoric is a corrupt state's means of distracting attention from its own postcolonial failures. Says Clare, for instance: "Even to this day in *The Nation* [one of Kenya's dailies] you'll read articles saying the reason the roads are bad in the back of beyond is because the colonials didn't build them! An awful lot of blame gets laid at their door!" (Scholars might counter that in 1963 Kenya inherited a "gatekeeper state," and that certain colonial dysfunctions were thereby projected forward—on top of other global-economic, administrative, and cultural challenges.)[28] Far from being stuck in the past, say white Kenyans, they themselves are even more forward-thinking than Kenya's current politicians, nurturing a love of country and focusing on "developing" Kenya so it can move into the future.[29] Hence, Sylvie argues colonialism is "used" as an excuse for failure by puerile politicians and citizens:

> We've been independent for forty-six years! . . . I mean, let's move on! It's *ridiculous,* we've got a country to build, a nation to build, a million opportunities, stop blaming the past. You know, that's like being a grown up at seventy and blaming the fact that your parents didn't give you [an] opportunity earlier on. Well, you know, *pole sana* [Kiswahili: "I'm very sorry"]. Let's just move on . . . let's focus on the fundamentals and build a better nation. . . . Colonialism is a thing of the past, guys, *move on.* You know we're building a global nation. We're just one of those people in this part of the world that are committed to here . . . it's like come on guys, let's move *forward,* let's not move *backwards!*

As Sylvie uses the phrases "global nation" and "just one of those people in this part of the world," and invokes hip familiarity by addressing the wider Kenyan populace as "guys," she implies a multiracial context in which white Kenyans fit in rather than standing out. Such a context does not entirely exist, yet, but she fervently wishes to bring this vision into being.

As Sylvie vented her frustrations through gritted teeth, her sense of urgency was palpable. It is born not only of genuine passion for the country, but also, at some level, of fear. Settler descendants have a lot to lose should they be held collectively liable for the worst deeds credited to Cholmondeley and their colonial forebears. A related anxiety came up in my conversation with Nicola when she described a rumor that government officials might have offered Cholmondeley the option of exile in lieu of a trial. That Kenyan officials might even consider it implies they see him as a kind of expatriate, rather than a fourth-generation Kenyan. Nicola may say she doesn't "relate" to Cholmondeley, but in this regard, she does:

> Rumor was that [government officials] said to [Cholmondeley] "Get out. Just go. Get out of the country and never come back," and he refused. 'Cause you see this is his [country], you remember, he hasn't got anywhere to go, to be perfectly honest with you. It's like me, where have we got to go. We don't have . . . we're in a difficult situation because we don't totally belong. Yeah, we don't totally belong. We're white people in an African country.

Indeed, Felix told me that in the wake of the Cholmondeley scandals, his "burning question" was "How much I belong. What qualifies me to belong here."

Clearly, the Cholmondeley drama confronted many white Kenyans with fresh anxieties. They felt themselves conflated with a man who represented colonial brutality, and their very entitlement to belong in Kenya was questioned. Most of my respondents found it important to explain that they did not share a "colonial mentality," and were good Kenyan nationals. The very fact that they considered Cholmondeley to have been so insensitive suggests that most did not dwell in unmitigated structural oblivion, and their startling encounters with black Kenyans after his incarceration shocked some of them into still more awareness of the resentments that circulate. But because of their fears, they drew a line as to what it all should mean for them. Most were quite unwilling to accept collective guilt, and appeared to fend off psychological guilt with a fair amount of success. Few were willing to rethink the fundamental meanings and structures of the colonial era. And for many, their wish to "develop Kenya" seemed to furnish an alibi against charges that they were there as colonials. They failed to recognize the ideological similarities of that alibi to the "uplift" peddled by British colonial administrators decades ago.

But one respondent in particular was willing to linger in the discomfort of the moment, and go deeper into its implications: Jos, the wealthy descendant of one of Kenya's first influential colonial families. As I described in Chapter 1, Jos and I met in a café frequented by settler descendants, and he looked around as he spoke, dipping his voice to prevent his words from being overheard. As this transcript opens, he had been reflecting on what he calls a "sense of entitlement" among his peers:

Jos: I've really been thinking about that the last six months, 'cause of the . . . [he adopts a low, quiet voice] Tom Cholmondeley and, you know, you know, after he killed the second . . . terrible, the attitude to whites was just terrible. It's never been like that.

Janet: How did you experience it?

Jos: Oh God. You know . . . I heard it on the radio in the morning and then you get all the callers and [he adopts a low, angry voice] "Mrhrhrhr!" they're all like this. Then there were articles in the newspaper . . . I drove to get my paper and I pointed to the paperwoman [and she said] "He's one of *you*" or something. You know, the one who I'm always friendly with, you know, it was like that. And then, you know, I wouldn't read the papers in the coffee shop, I didn't even take it in; I'd just sit there with my head down, and we all kept our heads down, really, for a long time after that. Anyway. It was, it was a mass hysteria—through all the FM stations, all the newspapers, there were articles . . . one guy wrote and said: "One thing we resent most [are] these white people who live amongst us and think differently to us and just wish we weren't here and just would love all the animals and not us around." [Jos lowers his voice again, and looks at me significantly.] Which is *true!*

Dismayed, Jos ventriloquizes his detractors—the newspaper vendor saying "He's one of *you!*" and the callers to the radio station muttering "Mhrhrhr!" As he re-lives the moments in which he was forced to see himself in someone else's mirror, it seems clear that these experiences were shocking and transforming for him. He is able to make an astonishing concession about white Kenyans today: the black Kenyan suspicion that white Kenyans "just wish [blacks] weren't here," he says emphatically, is *"true."* Most of my white Kenyan contacts would deny feeling any such sentiment, protesting their commitment to the well-being of all Kenyans. But in characterizing this claim as "true," Jos is either making a claim about the white Kenyan unconscious or has thoroughly stepped into the perspective of a critical outsider, or both. Evidently, here is someone "imaginatively open," to invoke Crapanzano, to the complex reality around him, and apparently newly appreciative of black Kenyans' complaints.

This appreciation gives Jos a take on colonialism more complicated and layered than that of his defensive peers, and more overtly perspectivist. On the one hand, he says, aspects of "the old days" were better; "I was told things worked perfectly and the roads were good." Furthermore, he says in an amused voice, colonialism worked greatly to his own advantage:

> I personally . . . from my personal point of view, colonialism was *great*. You know, I lived a gilt-edged childhood, I went to the best schools, I came from a wealthy family. . . . But trying to get out of that perspective, and look at it from the perspective of an outsider looking at *any* colonialism . . . it's not a good thing. We basically *came* in, we subjugated the race, *told* them they were stupid, *treated* them like shit, and we *still* think it's a good thing. You know, 'cause that's essentially what you did in colo—okay, you built a nation-state around Kenya, and all the institutions and that was a *good* thing. In a way. 'Cause the modern Kenya was built on that. But for the indigenous population, who were sort of airbrushed out in a way, except as servants and subjugated beings, it can't have been much fun. You know, you weren't allowed in the restaurants, there was a color bar; "No dogs, Indians, and Jews, and blacks" [written] on walls. You could flog your servants; you could treat them like shit and nothing would happen . . . throw them out of their lands . . . yeah?

Jos goes on at length in this perspectivist vein, tacking between subject positions as he contrasts the benefits of building of a "modern country" and "prosperous nation-state" within which his own family was able to live in luxury, with the denigration of blacks under a "brutal regime." He concludes: "On one side I think it was crap, and on the other side, it was a good thing. You know." Even his response to whether or not feels he counts as "Kenyan" is layered with competing perspectives:

> I do . . . and I don't. I don't because I don't believe a lot of black Kenyans regard us as Kenyans. And that's true. You've met the taxi drivers and stuff and they'll say "You're a real Kenyan" and blablabla. But you read the articles after Cholmondeley and they'd say "They're guests in our country," they're this, they're that. Amongst the political intellectual classes who *are* the policy makers in the end.

Jos's account highlights a quintessential dilemma for contemporary white Kenyans. They say they wish to overcome the bigotries of the colonial era, but find themselves in a nation divided, with some citizens willing to embrace them as part of a diverse Kenya, but others indulging in keen bigotry of their own, cultivating ethno-tribalist antagonism and racial essentialism that paints whites as forever interlopers. Whites may hope for national unity that overlooks ethnic and racial differences, but in so doing, they set themselves apart in a way. For in Kenya's current political climate, practicing racial or ethnic "blindness" (should such a thing even be possible) is tantamount to being blind to the histories of inequality that forged the nation—and, some might say, is not a particularly Kenyan stance.

As for Cholmondeley, Jos doesn't give him much leeway. Like his white peers, but more so, Jos presents himself as more in touch with the Kenyan zeitgeist than Cholmondeley:

> The consciousness of the . . . of the people has grown so much over the last forty years, but [in] the last five years, it's blossomed so much, and I think [Cholmondeley] was *ssssoooo* out of touch. I mean, *I* could have told him, you don't go *shooting* African people. You just, they, it's not, it's not what you *do* anymore. You know, you could get away with it twenty years ago, thirty years ago, could pull a few strings, you knew Moi, you knew Kenyatta, you knew someone . . . *now,* it's—it's just completely changed . . . we don't have that same pull anymore. Cause the people now can say [high, indignant voice] "What the fuck are these white people having more advantages than us!"

On the subject of what fate Cholmondeley deserves, Jos again draws on multiple perspectives, declaring himself "ambivalent." On the one hand, he says, he feels compassion for Cholmondeley and his parents, "because I know that family." On the other hand, he says, he has a new awareness of how the case is perceived by others: "The fact is, you know, I have to try and look at from outside our community—and see it from a wider perspective." When you situate the Cholmondeley shootings in their historical and sociocultural context, he *looks* guilty . . . and so, in a way, do settler descendants.

"BUTCHER OF NAIVASHA" AND "SACRIFICIAL ANODE"

If Jos dwells in discomfort as he confronts anger against white Kenyans, only Tom Cholmondeley was faced with an accusation of guilt so serious that his life depended on refuting it. And only Cholmondeley found himself in a position of daily physical and spiritual punishment, replete with reminders of how loathed he had become, as he rubbed shoulders with Kenya's most downtrodden citizens.

There could hardly be a more dramatic reversal: from the Delamere family's elite colonial past to Cholmondeley's recent present. In Kamiti and in court Cholmondeley was caught in a system that had been created by British colonials and changed little. The judge and barristers still wear curled white wigs and don red or black robes. The court has no stenographer, so the judge (there is no jury) writes down every word of the proceedings by hand, further slowing a system that reportedly has a backlog of about a million trials. Inmates are often kept on remand for years—sometimes six, eight, fourteen, or more—before their cases are even heard. They have few rights, and their invisibility is pegged to their impoverishment.

The prison's infrastructure is also in dire need of repair, and conditions are notorious for their squalor and lack of clean water. Prisoners' families try to fend off malnutrition and illness by bringing fresh food, but guards often capriciously turn it back or throw it away. (The thermos of coffee I brought for Cholmondeley was handed back to me as I left the prison, and I heard someone behind me asking the guard in question: "Umekataa kwa nini?" [Why did you forbid it?]). Overcrowding can be epic—the prison holds at least three times the number of inmates that it was built for. Tensions run high within the prison walls, and brutal crackdowns are not unusual. In 2009, for instance, guards reportedly tortured one inmate to death for illicitly keeping a mobile phone; ironically the roundups and beatings that ensued were captured by other prisoners' mobile phones, the videos sent to Kenyan television stations.[30]

Cholmondeley's stay in Kamiti was hardly typical. His visitors were somewhat better able to furnish him with supplements and treats (chicken here, butter there), while his special status—and perhaps some under-the-table transactions from loved ones—meant he had a little more privacy than most, as well as a good mobile phone and a steady stream of reading material, which he stacked nearly to the ceiling along one wall of his cell. Still, he spent most of his days in a tiny, greasy, malodorous space beset by vermin. While his trial proceeded more swiftly than many, it still moved at times like a dinosaur stuck in a tar pit. It was evident that despite Kenya's reputation for corruption, his family's money provided no guarantee that he would survive the ordeal—indeed, those in his camp worried the judge might be facing steep pressures from above to convict him.

Back at the office table, I looked at the thin wire on Cholmondeley's glasses, which looked as if they might be about to slip off his face. I couldn't ask him about the shootings or the case; he wouldn't have answered, for legal reasons. Instead, I wondered rather generally what his experience had been like. Cholmondeley was frank. He described his repeated shocks in the months after the second shooting, as he read the newspapers and felt the brunt of a furious Kenyan public. He had been rocked back, he said, by the "preconceptions" of those who had called for his blood. He took offense at the journalists who had relied on what he called "trigger words" like "Happy Valley" and "Old Etonian" to mobilize sentiment against him. "Even the words 'colonial' and 'settler,'" he said,

> suggest something brutal, unimproved, unchanged. They have an aura of solidity about them. They get applied to governmental structure and practice and bring up the idea of something being allowed to ossify into something dysfunctional. . . . Those ossified structures are still here—hierarchy and ranks, the saluting and parading in the morning here in prison—it's old-fashioned, even militaristic and charming, but these are inadequacies resulting from the fact that nothing's really changed in forty years.

His words echoed what Sally Dudmesh had said to me impatiently over the phone: "If they run their life blaming colonialism for everything, they're going nowhere . . . they'll never progress." Kenyans' "self-loathing" about a stagnant structure, Cholmondeley suggested, was being projected onto him. Worse, he felt his core being had been misunderstood. Cholmondeley leaned forward, and his knees bumped the bottom of the table. "I get accused of being a vicious heartless white sod," he said, and I thought his voice might crack. "It makes you want to scream and tear at your clothes and cry: 'I'm not like that!'"

His life at stake, Cholmondeley was both legally and psychologically defensive. He railed against his accusers, saying he had been singled out by "reverse discrimination." He had been reading a lot in prison, including Jean-Paul Sartre's 1948 essay on negritude entitled *Orphée noir* (Black Orpheus), in which, as an antidote to colonial prejudice, he advocates an anti-racist racism (*racisme antiraciste*) that would ultimately bring the world closer to unity. Cholmondeley's voice rose as he argued that this "class of anti-racist racists [are] people who in their search for self-identity take on the worst traits of those they criticize." His sense of victimhood had been sharpened by a coincidence. While incarcerated for a year in the late 1970s without trial, reportedly on the orders of then Vice President Moi for his "anti-establishment" activities, the renowned Kikuyu author Ngugi wa Thiong'o had written a prison memoir, *Detained,* a screed against the brutality of European settler culture and the corruption and neocolonialism that followed Independence. Reading it in Kamiti, Cholmondeley became more or less convinced that he occupied the same cell as the famous anti-colonial writer had done: the last one on the left in the main block. With this striking similarity, Cholmondeley aligned himself with this canonical figure of Kenyan history. Was this, indirectly, a kind of claim to belong? Was he suggesting that if whites can be persecuted as blacks once were, perhaps they, too, are victims of a nation's growing pains as it wrestles with inclusion?

Perhaps so, but at some level Cholmondeley despairs of Kenya's prospects for racial integration. His elderly father awkwardly straddles Kenya and England, telling a documentary film-maker, "My tribe is a sort of, um, English. Although by nationality I'm Kenyan. But I know what my tribe is, so does every Kikuyu know what his tribe is. My tribe is English."[31] Yet Cholmondeley wished he didn't stand out so much, and Kenya's "tribal" distinctions evoked indignation in him. Several times in our conversation, Cholmondeley used a strategy much like Nicola's, adopting pompous voicing (italics below) to caricature the reviled white colonial:

> [There's been] a resurgence of [Kikuyu] ultra-nationalism . . . it's the crea-
> tion of a new unifying myth without the conception of multiculturalism.
> Since I'm someone from the *"hated white race,"* well, after January [2008,
> when Kenya exploded in politically sponsored ethnic violence], if there is
> such intergroup clashing, what hope do WE have of being integrated?

Like some of his peers, then, Cholmondeley holds the stereotype of Kenyan whites at arm's length, perhaps hoping to transcend the category. He recognizes, however, that Kenya's current fragmentation does not bode well for the happy incorporation of those tainted by colonial history.

Cholmondeley resists narratives of his own guilt, but he also had an unprecedented opportunity to better understand the experiences of Kenya's subaltern population. Over the years, he had had long conversations with fellow prisoners on wide-ranging subjects, including children (Cholmondeley has two young sons by his ex-wife, who moved them to England after the second scandal broke), land management, and agriculture. He had been surprised to connect well with one of the leaders of Mungiki, a controversial and sometimes violent politico-religious sect that is ideologically opposed to Westernization and Christianity. Cholmondeley called his Mungiki contact "a gentle, charismatic guy, very inspiring." As warders and inmates came and went from our vicinity in the office, I noted they and Cholmondeley exchanged wide smiles and friendly words. Cholmondeley told me he'd become something of an activist to improve conditions at Kamiti. He and Dudmesh raised funds for water pipes to provide the prisoners with a decent long-term water supply. He volunteered his assistance to inmates, including helping set up a blog for a project by another inmate called *Crime Si Poa* (Crime isn't cool).[32] By the time his trial came to a conclusion, Cholmondeley had obtained several computers for the prison and had begun to teach classes in computing and business. It felt like a version of the energetic developmentalist spirit I had seen in many white Kenyans, though Cholmondeley's efforts were clearly inspired by his newfound understanding of what it felt like to be utterly ground down.

Indeed, I was struck to find Cholmondeley showing a degree of sympathy for the vantage point of the neighbors who have looked over his fence with such resentment. At one point, for instance, he contrasted the perspectives of a hypothetical African neighbor and an aristocratic white, whom Cholmondeley again imitated in a deliberately snooty voice:

> People can't understand why [wildlife's] not okay for poaching. "But it's just a *swara*," they think; "it's just a wild animal." And that white idiots like to just preserve the animals to look at, like a Ferrari . . . all animals for them are *mnyama*—meat. Whereas we have a [he adopts a posh voice] *post-Words-worthian notion of a created wilderness; the beautiful aesthetic of the noble wilderness.*

The materialist white idiots with their aestheticized wilderness were coming to sound faintly absurd in the eyes of the hungry African neighbor. Cholmondeley went on: "It's pragmatism. If I was in that situation [of poverty and hunger], dare I say it, horribly, I'd be thinking along the same lines." (Why should such an admission be "horrible," I wondered? Because poaching is considered such egregious crimes by so many of his white Kenyan peers? Because to make this concession might, very indirectly, reflect some misgivings about his retaliation?) Along similar lines, Cholmondeley reflected on Kenya's ticking time bomb of inequity: "There is no middle ground between those with lots of land and those with only a tiny bit." He toyed with a radical solution, one that might have seemed suicidal from his vantage point outside of Kamiti: "We need something like our own French Revolution to create a proper middle class."

Cholmondeley had recently read David Anderson's 2004 book *Histories of the Hanged,* which details the execution of numerous Mau Mau leaders—many, in Kamiti itself—without due process. "To be candid," he says,

> I wanted to read it initially from a bigoted viewpoint; I wanted to look at it and say: [he adopts a tone of mock righteousness] "This is a bigoted account and it maligns my ancestors and it wasn't like that." But in fact it opened my eyes—it was very, very interesting on the court issues and to see how things really haven't moved on in that regard. In the end I had to say luckily I left my preconceptions behind and I found it a largely accurate and honest account. But I don't have to own it.

"What do you mean?" I asked.

"I don't have to feel guilty or responsible for it," he replied.

Cholmondeley's mind had been stretched by his experiences in Kamiti, but there were limits to how much guilt (legal, moral, collective, or psychological) he was willing to concede. He didn't particularly "accept the values of colonialism," he said, but felt it unfair to judge it using contemporary standards. He gestured in my direction: "Think back even in your own life, how convinced you were of what you did ten years ago and now you feel differently." Like other white Kenyans, he argued that "it would be a lot harder to demonize colonialism if the infrastructure of Kenya had moved on and didn't still look like the 1950s." He had little patience for hand-wringing over the colonial past, saying pragmatically: "Colonial history is part of what we are so let's get on with it and deal with it. Don't use it as an excuse for extra [ethnic] nationalism." And like so many white Kenyans, Cholmondeley articulated his wish that Kenya might move into a "globalized" future, in which "ethnic" divisions might yield to the "modern standard" of nationalism. Among other things, this would rule out incidents of "reverse discrimination" such as the one he felt so trapped in.

Yet the call for a liberal, inclusive, "global" society in which there is no differentiation—or animus—between groups can have a naïve element to it. Here, in fact, is a common site of white Kenyan structural oblivion, for when they wish that their conspicuous racial status might be neutralized, they appear to minimize both the colonial injustices that whiteness can evoke for some Kenyans, and the resultant economic gulf between so many whites and so many Africans today. Cholmondeley bristled at assumptions about his wealth in Kamiti, saying:

> I think [racial sentiment against whites is] a cover for class. For Europeans and some of the bigotry surrounding them. People always assume you're rich. In here people would come over to me when I was first in and say: "Give me some money." And I would say: "Why?" I'd say "Why don't YOU give ME a gift?" and you could see these guys wrestling with their preconceptions [his hands flurry around his head], but I held onto that, and some people got very annoyed at me but they eventually cottoned on.

Cholmondeley wishes to be inserted in a more empathic, reciprocal pattern of give-and-take; to him, the blunt demands of his fellow inmates feel vaguely dehumanizing, and he feels unfairly typified on grounds of race. Yet his fellow inmates know all too much about the intersection between class and race in Kenya—from colonialism until contemporary times. And they may have felt, not that it was rude of them to ask, but rather, that it was immoral of him not to give. An ethic of redistribution prevails across much of sub-Saharan Africa, and the haves are seen as morally obliged to give to the have-nots. Here, then, is another kind of collective guilt that many black Kenyans project onto settler descendants: in their ideology of possessive individualism, they are guilty of hoarding.

All in all I saw a contradiction in Cholmondeley, one related to but more profound than that in his peers. His public drama has shocked him into sensing the depth of enduring resentment against colonialism and former settler families. Unlike his peers, he has also cultivated empathy for the subjugated from first-hand experience in prison. On the other hand, Cholmondeley sees himself as unfairly maligned, a victim of "reverse racism." "I am the sacrificial anode for postcolonial Kenya," he tells me, likening himself to the metallic component affixed to the hull of a boat that attracts what is corrosive in seawater and disintegrates itself, thus protecting the boat's integrity.

After I left Kamiti, Cholmondeley contacted me a few times from a carefully concealed mobile phone in his cell. Every now and then he would send an update, whether admission to being "consumed with trepidation" about his trial, allusions to guards abusing inmates, or a light account of catching and roasting some "delicious" flying ants with other inmates. In spring of 2009, he must have been searching for his name on line when he pulled up the publicity page for a talk I had recently given at Stanford. The talk drew on similar material to this chapter, focusing on white Kenyans' mixed feelings as they processed popular resentment in the wake of Cholmondeley's scandals, and Cholmondeley's own mixture of empathy and defensiveness as he considered this anger. Although the talk cast him in a morally ambiguous light, he wrote: "I think it says so nicely what I have felt without being able to express it!" He instructed the moderator of his (now defunct) web site to post the talk for the public. I note this not to suggest that Cholmondeley would endorse my every interpretive move in this chapter, but to show that he was willing to see aspects of his contradictions and double-consciousness laid bare. And perhaps a more complex and layered account of his persona seemed preferable to the caricatures that had dogged him since his incarceration.

In the end, Judge Muga Apondi was the sole arbiter of Cholmondeley's legal fate. Two "lay assessors" (civilians, one man and one woman) had been assigned to follow the trial from the start and hand down their own conclusions, but the judge was under no obligation to cleave to their opinions. On May 5, 2009, the assessors declared their non-binding verdict: Cholmondeley was not guilty of murder. On May 7, Apondi told the court he rejected the defense's argument that the fatal shot came from anything other than Cholmondeley's Winchester rifle, yet Cholmondeley had not appeared to act with malice aforethought and had made desperate attempts to save Mr. Njoya's life after the shooting. Apondi thus acquitted Cholmondeley of murder, and—in a surprise move—declared him instead guilty of the lesser offense of manslaughter.[33]

While manslaughter can carry up to twenty years in prison in Kenya, the judge went easy on him during the sentencing the next week. After Cholmondeley's lawyer delicately clarified that the Delameres wished to look after Njoya's family's "spiritual and material needs," Apondi argued that Cholmondeley appeared "humbled" by his experience, continuing: "I hereby wish to impose a light sentence . . . to allow him to reflect on his life and change to an appropriate direction." Cholmondeley would serve eight months, beyond the three years already served on remand.

The spectators began to murmur loudly, and as Cholmondeley prepared to leave protestors shouted: "We want justice for Ole Sisina!" A group in the upper gallery held up large signs reading: "Butcher of Naivasha" and "2005–Sisina. 2006–Njoya. Who next?" A poll taken by a television station shortly after the verdict showed that 90 percent of respondents thought that Cholmondeley had gotten off lightly.[34] As Cholmondeley had predicted in our conversation, even if let off by the judge, "my name will be shit forever." Still, in the end, Cholmondeley served only five further months in Kamiti, receiving a standard sentence reduction for good behavior. On October 23, 2009, at about 5:00 A.M., he left the prison gates, and as the dawn rose, he was dropped off on a quiet road in the white Kenyan–dominated suburb of Karen where Sally Dudmesh lived.

A few months later, in an improbable summit between scions of Kenya's two most storied colonial families, Tom Cholmondeley and Richard Leakey met for the first time. While the Delameres had been serving as the primary architects of "white man's country" and all its inequities, the Leakey family had been piecing together the origins of humankind from fossil remains. Louis spoke fluent Kikuyu, and Richard had dived headlong into post-Independence Kenyan politics. In the 1950s, Richard told me, his family had had such a reputation as "nigger-lovers" among settlers that they were persona non grata as far as the Delameres were concerned.

I remember when I was a boy of about fifteen, hitch-hiking with another *mzungu* friend from Kitale to Nairobi ... [as we were] coming out of Nakuru this car slowed down and said, "You boys want a ride? Let's go to Nairobi." Turned out to be Cholmondeley's father. And, uh, he said, "Well, I'll be going to Nairobi later but you can come have lunch with us." So ... he asked the [other] boy who he was, which farm he was on ... and they find that [his family knew the Delameres]. And then he said [to me], "And who are you?" and I said who I was, and he said, "The Louis Leakey family? Well, I'm afraid I can't take you to the house for lunch, but you can get a ride from the driveway." So I hopped out and my pal went in for lunch. I mean, that was—I had a black skin. Of course.

Richard gave the Delamere family a wide berth after that. Still, he followed the details of the trail. The prosecution's case was weak, he felt, but he predicted the court would have to draw out the case for some years to avoid public outcry. The public, said Leakey, felt "we're not beating Tom; we're beating colonialism. . . . He'd almost been set up to be the whipping boy."

Now that he was free, Cholmondeley needed to figure out how to handle the predicament of the family's coveted land, and Leakey might have valuable counsel. Leakey reports the slightly surreal quality of the encounter. "I never thought I'd find myself in this house, with my name," he said to Cholmondeley, who replied, "I'm equally surprised to find somebody with your name in this house." Dudmesh floated the idea of turning the farming zones of the ranch into a conservation area, giving up the cattle herd so that the family could frame itself as more prominent stewards of Kenya's natural resources and wildlife. Leakey, however, knew from his tenure at the head of Kenya Wildlife Service in the early 1990s that the "conservationist" role could set Cholmondeley farther apart rather than helping him to fit in. "I said, *no*, you've got one of the best herds of cattle in the country! Do what you know how to do best. Farm it! We need farmers like you! Don't stop it! I mean, you can totally justify it as a son of Kenya, owning this land in a productive way. You knock the spots off these fellows in Laikipia. You shouldn't take all that land as conservation land."

But *can* Cholmondeley be counted as a "son of Kenya," by making "productive" use of the land? Wasn't this one of the original rationales the British Crown used to seize land from Africans and put it into the hands of whites? Productive ranching may be of service to Kenya, and Cholmondeley may even intend it as such, but as we have seen, good intentions don't go far in combatting perceptions of social inequality. This, indeed, is one of the dilemmas of structural oblivion for settler descendants; on the inside, they don't necessarily feel greedy, or racist, or wrong, but for those who feel victimized by their historical privileges, such objections lack credibility—and in fact, being part of an oppressive structure, present or past, is sometimes to be presumed bad to the core. Cholmondeley's critics, for instance, were quick to assume that he had killed in cold blood because as far as they were concerned, his family's history was so enmeshed with colonialism and all its cruelties that he might just as well have done it. White Kenyans would like the sovereign, liberal subject to be morally judged on the grounds of individual deeds and intentions, but against Kenya's historical, political, and cultural backdrop, the sons are held accountable for the sins of their fathers. Settler descendants thus find themselves in a no-man's land between the two poles of a binary opposition: on the one hand, the good intentions they proclaim, and hence the collective absolution they would like, and on the other, the collective guilt sometimes projected onto them, and hence the presumption of bad intentions.

When news of Cholmondeley's release was reported across Kenya, "Citizen TV" revisited the trial, the camera panning over Cholmondeley's face in court. In a display of British "stiff upper lip," which he had self-consciously alluded to in our conversation in Kamiti, he was composed and unreadable even when the verdict and sentence were being pronounced. The reporter Sheila Sendeyo voiced-over: "And now, as he starts a new life outside the prison walls, many are yet to understand the heart and mind of the man who managed to hide the anxiety of a possible death sentence from his face for years."[35] It was the first time I had heard curiosity expressed about how the man behind the caricature made sense of his experience, such suffering and loss had ensued from Cholmondeley's actions and such evil and guilt had been projected onto him.

4

Conflicted Intimacies

After her husband died in late 2001, Anna Trzebinski headed for the rugged Laikipia landscape, hoping its spare beauty would help her make sense of her solitude. The life of Tonio Trzebinski, a Kenyan-born artist of Polish and British descent, had resembled the grand, colorful gestures that splashed across his canvases. He traveled, partied, and surfed with well-to-do expats and elite white Kenyans of mingled European ancestry, and after several passionate years of marriage to Anna he had struck up an affair with a thirty-something Danish huntress. But in October he was mysteriously shot dead, his body found crumpled next to his white Alfa Romeo in the driveway of his lover's Nairobi home. The international media dug into the sensation—like the Cholmondeley scandals, Trzebinski's affair and unsolved murder became the subject of a *Vanity Fair* article. Meanwhile, Anna and her two young children were grief-stricken.

Anna Trzebinski grew up in the crucible of the Happy Valley set. Her mother, Dodo, had come from Germany to Kenya in the early 1970s with the infant Anna, but without a husband. In Kenya, Dodo married Michael Cunningham-Reid (d. 2014), a nephew of the late Lord Louis Mountbatten and stepson of Lord Delamere. Anna knows no other father than Cunningham-Reid, and says she doesn't remember any home besides Kenya. She grew tall, with long brown hair, confidence, and an abundance of creativity. With the family money, she attended public school and university in the United Kingdom, and made her name as an elite fashion designer. European celebrities such as Princess Caroline of Monaco and Kate Moss wear her work. She says she considers herself Kenyan, "white Kenyan," through and through.[1]

Anna herself told journalists that she was a little surprised when, as she worked through her grief during long walks in Laikipia, she fell for a semi-nomadic Samburu *moran* (warrior). Loyaban Lemarti was working as a tracker and guide for tourists, decked out in splendid style, with strands of colored beads crossing his chest and red and purple *kikoi* cloths dangling from his waist. He soon began to stroll with Anna as they chatted in a mixture of Kiswahili and English. Anna was struck, she says, "by his sense of self, total lack of ego. I could actually feel his strength, his sense of right and wrong. I immediately felt safe by his side. In 2005, they married, with Samburu symbolism; a bull was slaughtered, and Lemarti wore a lion skin. If there were tensions, Anna downplayed them: "His community have been so accepting of me. . . . I think it would have been harder if I'd married someone who was white but from a different religion or something like that."[2]

It's hard to know how Lemarti's community feel about incorporating Anna. But members of Tonio's family disapproved. Tonio's mother, the author Errol Trzebinski, was absent from the wedding and reportedly "very unhappy" about Anna's union to a "tribesman" who "cannot read or write." "He may be fun for the children," she said, "but I really don't think he is the right person to be a father to them."[3] Anna's father was more sanguine, insisting that unlike his stepfather Tom Delamere, who had "considered the black man a necessary evil," he had evolved some distance from old attitudes. "I've found out that the black man is a human being after all," said Cunningham-Reid in 2006, and, in a less colonial sounding gesture of good will, he deemed Lemarti a "very close friend."[4] Still, he conceded the marriage hadn't been accepted by everyone in the community of former settler families, where interracial marriage remains rare. Anna and Lemarti's union had been, he said euphemistically, "an experience."[5]

During my trips to Kenya I crossed paths with many white expatriates who struck up romantic relationships with Africans, sometimes moving heaven, earth, and one or the other partner to try to make a transnational marriage work. In recent decades, one German, French, British, or American woman after another has married a Maasai or Samburu man and settled in pastoralist territory.[6] I have met an aging Irish man puddle-eyed with adoration for his young Swahili girlfriend as he sketched the coastal home he hoped to build for them; a 22-year-old Englishwoman whose Luhya boyfriend was making arrangements to visit her at university in Britain; a San Francisco man hoping to bring one of my (male) Mijikenda research assistants over to California for good. There are difficult politics to many of these unions, but still, they happen.[7]

Among Kenyans from settler families, however, interracial marriages are less common. Richard Leakey, who has famously distanced himself from the settler descendent community and committed himself to Kenyan politics, says he finds some white Kenyans "pretty racist people deep down. They don't mix and they have pretty negative attitudes to their fellow Kenyans."[8] In conversation with me, he expressed bafflement about their resistance to interracial romance:

> I think forty-year-olds and younger [white Kenyans] probably had no choice but to go to schools with other races . . . they've had friends that were black, and as a result of that they've realized some of the prejudice that was bred into them may be a bit queer, a bit odd. And I think they do try to avoid it, but yet many of them, if they have a wedding, [it's] white boy marries white girl in Laikipia. They invite 300 people, and the only dark-skinned people are the waiters. . . . I cannot understand why they don't change.

Leakey's caricature rang true to me. I, too, encountered younger settler descendants decrying the racism of the "old colonial" generations and enthusiastically expounding on a harmonious, multicultural Kenya, but whose most intimate relationships were nevertheless with other whites. If settler descendants are looking for a way out of the charge that they are socially isolated or racist, why don't they publicly woo and marry black Africans more often?

Back in the United States, I engaged a black Kenyan intellectual who had also noticed the trend. He explained it in terms of a widespread Kenyan anxiety: "It's all about land. The whites don't want to divide up their land." But plenty of settler descendants are no longer major landowners and make their livings through other means, such as tourism or business. Money *is* at stake in settler descendants' ideas about love and marriage, but the concern isn't as simple as a wish to hoard land among their kind. Furthermore, elites rarely experience their own motives the way an economist or a Marxist analysis would characterize them; my respondents don't *feel* as if keeping property in the family underpins their marriages, in other words. And many of my respondents insisted (perhaps to impress me, but I think it goes beyond that) that they don't *feel* bigoted or racist. So how do white Kenyans interpret their aversions to interracial marriage?

The history of interracial relations in Kenya offers some backdrop, though it doesn't tell the full story. In the colonies generally, regulating who could have sex with whom was central to scoring racial boundaries—and these boundaries, in turn, reaffirmed Europeans' sense of control and superiority, as well as class and national differences.[9] Still, plenty of interracial sex took place in the early years of British settlement in Africa, particularly before European women were encouraged to come over. Indeed, for European men all over the global South, the forbidden other had an erotic allure—a force field scholars have deemed the "ethno-sexual frontier" or the "colonial contact zone."[10] Some settlers and administrators in Kenya regarded sex with African women as something of a "perk of empire,"[11] sometimes coercing African women into relations, sometimes compensating them. Some African women, in turn, made decent money from these sexual arrangements; each group took advantage of the other in their own way, and while African women often paid the greater price, many of these interactions resisted neat labels.[12]

But the longer-term unions were cause for concern among whites. Of course marriage was out of the question, and the social punishments could be acute for those who crossed racial boundaries. Children of interracial unions, for instance, were referred to as "half-caste" and ostracized in the settler community.[13] And early settlers feared the prospect of "degeneration," in which a sexual or marital relationship with an African might lead the European to adopt African dress, housing, and custom, and otherwise fall away from European standards and compromise white "prestige."[14] Nyamweru (2001: 184) describes an infamous European settler who lived on a farm outside of Gilgil with several Kikuyu women and their mixed-race children. The other local whites, she says, called him "Dirty Randall."

The colonial administration tried to keep this threat to white supremacy at bay. They deported European men with the most notorious connections to African women,[15] encouraged the growth of a female settler population, and promoted the use of male rather than female servants in the home. Unfortunately, male servants and female settlers meant further anxiety about the so-called "black peril"; fear that African males would rape their female European employers.[16] Some whites stoked the anxiety with the argument that licentious settler men were weakening the racial boundary, thus making white women vulnerable. One indignant settler, a Mrs. Fred Marutin, wrote in a 1914 letter to the *East African Standard:* "He who lays a plank across this gulf, and himself crosses it, leaves the plank then for the black man to cross in turn. Why should the black man respect your women when he finds that you do not respect and hold sacred his?"[17]

Over the next century, attitudes would change, but the colonial residue would linger. Devon, the elderly rancher from Laikipia, told me that "back in the day," settler men known to be sleeping with Africans were not allowed to set foot in the Rift Valley's Rumuruti Club. (This may have been Devon's exaggeration; if such a rule had been followed too meticulously, members might have been hard to come by.) As the Club fell on harder times and its membership began to decline, Devon said, Club officials eventually allowed such individuals to join, but on condition that they arrived solo. Over time, he says, their "consorts" could enter, but not their offspring; and finally the Club opened to their children as well. Still, says Devon, the stigma is hardly gone, and—as a number of my other respondents confirmed—older settler descendants in interracial relationships still tend to conceal them. Some aged white Kenyan men, for example, have taken on household employees or secretaries as their romantic companions, but they don't broadcast this publicly. Devon himself is sometimes named as the executor of his friends' wills, and he recently noted with surprise that two of them made large bequests to their "African wives." "Wives?" I checked. Devon replied: "Who can know?"

The social geography of interracial distance is reflected in the colonial-era derogatory phrases "going native" or "going bush." Some white Kenyans still use the latter phrase to refer to one of their own sleeping with or marrying an African. One of my respondents born in the late 1950s defined "going bush" tentatively as: "Going, going a bit stupid because they've gone out with an African"—though he insisted that he, himself, would never use the phrase. A more elderly Kenyan defined it by invoking another old colonial phrase: "You know, [it's] letting the side down." The "sides" to which he refers can be mapped not only onto race, but also space. Civilized, "white" space has been rationally ordered and made productive in a European model, in contrast to the uncultivated African "bush," which in colonial models was seen as primal, chaotic, and potentially polluting.

Undiluted racism still creeps through the undergrowth among some white Kenyans. Nicola introduced me to a septuagenarian at a golf club, for instance, who asked about my project, then made a bid for me to represent his generation in a positive light. Unlike his parents, he said, he really liked "the African." "And if you meet any who don't, Jenny," he said, getting my name wrong, "then it's really time for them to go. No point in staying on if one doesn't appreciate things here." Once he had moved down the links, Nicola glowered at the back of his red-and-orange-striped shirt. He was, she said, a "complete old-school racist" who refers to the club staff as "monkeys" and "velcro-heads" when they're out of earshot. "Things may be changing, but he hasn't exactly caught up with the times," she said flatly.

For some, catching up with the times has meant looking back on their own childhood attitudes with consternation. Jonathan, for instance, came of age in the 1950s on a farm outside of Kitale. At the time, he believed Africans were different at every level of existence: "You *felt* growing up that there was an *inherent* difference in physiology, and psychology, and sentiment." From his point of view, the difference was pitiable. "Like, the idea of snogging a woman," he marveled. "I'd never even seen an African kiss, and I thought, 'Gosh, these poor people, they're being deprived of the joys of the snog! I think it was because one grew up in such a segregated way." Even playing on the farm with African children did not quite demystify them:

> They would go home to bed completely separately from where we went home to bed, and I remember thinking gosh I feel sorry for them because they can't possibly *dream* things that I dream. They can't possibly . . . because they went to bed in that little round hut over there and probably slept on a skin on the floor and didn't have a bed and so didn't snuggle down. So therefore they *couldn't* be dreaming the same things I was dreaming about. And, and you know, I was feeling really sorry for the poor African because he does—you know he can't enjoy these things! Huh! So there was a very clear distinction.

Jonathan's first experiences of integration included the opening of his preparatory school to African and Indian entrants after Independence. By the 1970s, elite private schools such as Banda, Hillcrest, and Nairobi Academy were accepting multiracial (albeit still very privileged) students, and some of my respondents' parents made a point of sending their children to schools with a racial quota system to be sure they would be exposed to diversity. Jos, the urbanite I've discussed in earlier chapters, looks back with chagrin at how little empathy the white students had for newcomers: "How difficult it must have been for the first African and Asian students at my school . . . we weren't particularly rude to them, but they were like one or two in 180, and we really had very little idea." Jonathan, too, didn't pay the African or South Asian students much mind. It wasn't until he attended university overseas and found himself avoiding European students and befriending instead an

African and an Indian that he came into a sense of common humanity. "I think that's when I really began to realize that actually we all function in the same way. They *do* actually snog, for one." Jonathan now sees the storyline of deep biological differences between races as a colonial fiction.

Whites' racial ideologies had to respond, one way or another, to the social shifts that transpired with Independence. As schools shook off their tight racial exclusion, the registration and pass requirements that had curtailed the movements of Africans were lifted, as was the petty segregation that had separated whites, Africans, and Asians from one another in hospitals, railway carriages, and the like.[18] Africans gained greater access to higher education, political office, the judiciary system, land, and innumerable professional opportunities. These days Kenyans of African, Asian, and European descent rub shoulders in law offices, factories, farms, dairies, import-export businesses, and banks. The grown children of former settlers knock back a whisky in a boardroom with Luo and Sikh power-brokers, and chat amiably about business with the Kikuyu manager of a store in their coffee-shop franchise. Racial boundaries are sometimes traversed in small an unexpected ways, as in the case of an elderly coastal white woman who began to enter her Giriama gardener in the local Horticultural Show ("It was *radical*," says one of her neighbors). The once-exclusive social clubs across Kenya have become multiracial, though they remain places for aspirants to see and be seen. Karen Club, for instance, which is still strikingly white, occasionally sees former Prime Minister Raila Odinga in the bar after a game of squash. Watching a polo match one day with a small group of white Kenyans, I realized that my companions and I were sharing bleachers, beer, and idle conversation about horses with Gideon Moi, son of the former Kenyan president. (Moi junior is notoriously suspected of looting the Kenyan government to the tune of U.S.$500 million; but if the encounter dismayed me for that reason, it was routine for my acquaintances.)

Though mixed-race individuals were historically rejected from settler society, matters are shifting somewhat in Kenya's younger generations. The terminology for those of mixed black and white parentage has changed; while a few elderly informants used the phrase "half-caste," for instance, those of younger generations noted its degrading connotations. Some mixed-race young people prefer the more even-handed phrase "point-fives" (meaning, one half). Clem, who favors the expression *nusu nusu* (Kiswahili for "half half"), sometimes has a drink after hours with a safari guide of Indian descent and the guide's friend, who seems racially unclassifiable to Clem: "These are now our friends, who are grown into the community. And now you . . . [amused voice] you don't know—what *is* he, black or white, now! Huh! And that is happening *a lot.* I've got quite a *few* friends like that. Who, actually, I have to say I treat *just* like anyone else in my life. It's . . . um . . . no problem."

Such integration is fine, suggests Clem, but his phrasing suggests nevertheless that whites push through some puzzlement as the received binary opposition—black versus white—is challenged in their midst. And certainly the socializing of black African, Asian, or mixed-race Kenyans with white ones is greatly facilitated when they share a class and educational background. Tom Cholmondeley, who moves in moneyed and cosmopolitan circles, informed me that he has a number of "mixed-race" friends around his age, but pointed out that they had traveled to Europe for secondary school or university before returning to Kenya. There are exceptions to this emphasis on class and education as grounds for friendship—such as the Laikipia-based safari guide Richard Bonham who not only grew up playing with the children of plantation laborers on his mother's coffee farm (as did other settler children), but also, as an adult, prefers eating with his African porters while on safari. Bonham is proud to have been dubbed a "white Maasai" by his Maasai neighbors, but he resists the calls for land redistribution by Maasai activists and when he married, it was to another white Kenyan.[19]

Indeed, many settler descendants I met cleave to their cultural comfort zones, and this, in conjunction with their geographic choices, often amounts to self-segregation. Most Nairobi-based whites from former settler families opt to live in the white enclaves of Karen and neighboring Langata to the southwest of the city center.[20] Some of them speak wistfully about the divide. The young businesswoman Naomi, for instance, lives in a largely white neighborhood, but insists it's not for lack of curiosity on her part. In a way, she wishes she could insert herself into more racially mixed social life the way expatriate arrivals tend to. "If I was a visitor," she says, "I'd probably choose to live in urban Westlands or the Lavington area, and I would choose a very mixed group of people to hang out with." But it's a national thing, she rationalizes, to cluster along ethnic lines: "I'm a *Kenyan,* so I live the other side of town. I'm rooted here and I find I mix more with the people this side of town. Whether [or not] I find them to be the most interesting. Actually, I probably *don't.*"[21] Jonathan's reasoning is similar, explaining the segregation in terms of benign cultural insularity. Whites happily

work and "aspire" together with Africans, he tells me, invoking a popular European model of nationalism where people are loosely glued
together by effort and shared dreams for the nation's future.[22] "But I
think when you actually socialize—you know, really let your hair
down," he continues, "you *naturally* do it with the people you feel most
comfortable with."

For Jonathan, in fact, the social distances that remain are unconscious, and "sort of tribal." Whites don't avoid Africans because they
don't belong in Kenya; quite the contrary. In Jonathan's reasoning, they
are merely one among many self-segregating tribes: "A Kikuyu would be
far happier socializing with fellow Kikuyu. We would feel far happier
socializing with fellow whities. But we would like to regard ourselves as
successfully integrated in all those other respects!"[23] Paradoxically, these
implications that white Kenyans are a "tribe"—a phrase I heard from
several other white Kenyans, too—seems a strategic means of fitting in,
for if they are just another of Kenya's forty-plus "tribes," they are equally
entitled to be part of the nation, and to pursue their own interests and
social circles. As Clem put it to me, "People stay with their own cultures.
It's the same even within the black culture, there's tribal divisions.
They're the *same*, the Kikuyus, the Luos, they're doing exactly the same
as us." The line of reasoning is ironic, given how many told me they
wished Kenya would do away with the ethno-tribal divisions that have
wracked the nation with violence and framed them as foreigners. In
these conversations, however, Naomi, Jonathan, and Clem actually align
themselves with a mild version of tribalism that, when they draw upon
it themselves, might seem to help them fit in as part of the Kenyan social
landscape and justify their lifestyles, with whites being no more exclusionary than anyone else. And in so doing, they also concede that their
attested ideal of a wholly unified and integrated Kenya is perhaps not, at
the level of social intimacy, precisely what they want, any more than
Kikuyu or Kalenjin who favor their own kind.

One can see their segregated socializing at play across Kenya. At a
yoga class in Karen taught by a cosmopolitan man of mixed racial origins, I see perhaps twenty white faces, two that look Asian, and one
African. At a cattle auction in Laikipia, African farmers stroll the
grounds together and stop to admire livestock in a corral, while families
of European descent cluster together on another side of the fence in
broad-brimmed hats against the sun, the men wearing shirts with button-down collars and the women handing out snacks to children. Back
in Mombasa, on her sunny veranda, the elderly settler Grace frames it

in terms of levels of affinity. "It's true to say one's attitude has changed [since childhood]," she says. "I mean, I really like African people!" Yet she feels a little sheepish that liberal ideologies haven't changed her social life. "I *know* lots of Africans," she says, then stammers: "I've never entertained . . . it's . . . I'm quite ashamed of that actually, but the fact is that I haven't, I don't have any African friends." Trying to capture the quality of segregated integration among white Kenyans, Naomi sums it up: "You mix, but you don't end up *really* mixing."

This, then, is the backdrop to my respondents' discomfort with interracial romance. For some, the aversion is brutal and archaic. One disgruntled barfly in his sixties, a notoriously angry man who referred to a restaurant staff member as "the missing link," told me with malicious glee of his conversation with a female friend: if she dated an African, he told her, he would never speak to her again. But his white Kenyan peers widely discussed him as a troubled, off-putting man, embittered by his personal setbacks, and a *kaburu*—a bigot in the old, South African colonial style. He was perceived, in other words, precisely the way most white Kenyans don't wish to be seen. Hence most of my respondents, particularly those with university education or cosmopolitan experience, are careful not to frame the topic in racial terms, perhaps especially around me. Instead, cautionary tales about "cultural difference" abound. Grace tells me about a young European man who "married an African girl." She's relieved that her own children didn't follow suit, "because I do think the culture thing—and it's on both sides, it's not just on the white side either—it's very hard, and it's even hard for the children." Jonathan has a white Kenyan friend "whose daughter is stepping out with an unusually well-heeled, cultured Kikuyu" (note that here "cultured" appears to refer to "high" or modern culture), and his friend, Jonathan said, is still mired in colonial notions of a racial hierarchy, and "*cannot* get his head around it." Jonathan and his wife have had searching conversations about it, and conclude they'd be fine if their own daughter forged an interracial union, as long as she found someone culturally similar. "If there was a huge gap culturally, then it wouldn't matter if they were black, brown, red or white, says Jonathan." Still, he's not optimistic a reasonable match can be found, "because, yeah, culturally we are quite different."

The replacement of biological racism by subtler forms of aversion has been described by theorists like Franz Fanon (1956) and Étienne Balibar (1988 [1991]). In post–World War II Europe, they observed, as biological racisms began to wane, cultural differences became the grounds for exclusion. In the guise of liberalism, they argue, this so-called cultural racism presumes the inferiority of non-Western societies, and touts "development" as the leveling mechanism that will curtail poverty and bring global equality to all races.[24] The settler descendants' assumption that Africans need to "come up to the level" of their white romantic partners if the union is to work seems a variation on this theme. Clem, for instance, explains the perils of an intercultural romance. He has a good friend, a European expatriate named Maurice, who fell for a Kikuyu woman, Dorothy. They lived together for about ten years, and then Dorothy got pregnant and pressured Maurice to marry her. Four years later, says Clem, she left him, but it may have been for the best. He elaborated: "Culturally, they're so different . . . she was very Kikuyu, very sort of . . . uh, what's the word . . . uh, not 'tribal', but . . . uhh-hmm, local Kikuyu."[25] He looked at me tentatively, groping for an ideo-logically correct way to say it: "She wasn't very Westernized?" Ulti-mately, their families just "couldn't mix," he says, and they lived separate lives for so long that the relationship failed. Clem chose his words care-fully, framing their breakup in terms of cultural difference while dancing away from the potentially loaded word "tribal," but his remark still assumes their success would have hinged on Dorothy Westernizing rather than Maurice Africanizing, as it were. And when the business-woman Naomi tells me that white Kenyans "won't have such a cultural divide" as long as the Kenyan state provides financial opportunities for its youth, she presumes that upward mobility will help more Africans to become more like Westerners. Subtle judgments such as these come as well from settler descendants like Eleanor, who castigates the old-fash-ioned bigotry of some of her peers and says with a sensible air: "Talk to someone on your level, it doesn't matter what else is there." Abhorrence of miscegenation, then, is being rephrased in terms of subtler cultural and class-based aversions.

White Kenyans allude repeatedly to "cultural differences," but this baggy phrase masks a more pointed ideology when it comes to romantic love. To white Kenyans, romantic love should be an emotionally heartfelt affair forged from the connection of like souls. Ideally, this companionate union is founded in emotions separate from economic needs and aspira-tions. According to Jennifer Cole and Lynn Thomas, Westerners have tended to assume that in contrast, African societies treat romantic "love" (if they even have a concept of it) as sexual and financially motivated, with marriage often a pragmatic matter arranged by one's elder kin and secured through a bride price (the exchange of cattle, for instance).[26]

Westerners have also posited radically different expectations as regards fidelity and parenthood.[27] In point of fact, say Cole and Thomas, one can't draw such neat lines between "African" and "European" experiences of love; not only does this framework overlook affection experienced by Africans, but African societies are also diverse, modern styles of love and family life have influenced urban middle-class Africans, and plenty of Western romantic unions are motivated partly by finances.[28] But the stereotypes are powerful and simple. Settler descendants idealize a love between evenly matched romantic companions and fear that Africans prioritize practical gains over emotional ones.

The middle-aged businessman Colin, for instance, tells me most of his white Kenyan peers "don't like to be seen with a Kenyan lady, a little beauty, because automatically people will assume that she's being paid or she's after his money—everything but genuine care." Such interracial intimacies, he implies, are inappropriate; "genuine care" ought to be divorced from materiality. Several of my respondents suggested that white isolation stems from fear of being financially targeted—in spite of the growing African middle and upper classes. A woman from a farming family, Olivia, scoffs at the geriatric German, British, and American men who come to Kenya and take younger African lovers. "It's appealing to African women here to have an old *mzungu* man look after them," she says, "because generally he has the money, he wants to have a child with them, he will give them *everything* they want, and he will just be the adoring, *doting* husband." She chuckles as she describes how the young settler-descendant set gossips about these unions. "Probably quote derogatory," she concedes, "but anyway, that's just us."

Olivia has an inkling that their aversions go beyond concern about these whites being "used," and into another, more visceral realm of race and taboo. But this dimension is not easy for them to articulate. Clem, for instance, told me cheerfully in an early encounter of ours that interracial dating was on the rise and increasingly accepted in the settler-descendant community. He may not have remembered that conversation, for several weeks later after a few drinks in a bar he remarked that such relationships are "a real problem, because of the cultural issue." "What if there's a woman who has a similar upbringing to you, with a similar educational background?" I probed. He hesitated, squirmed in his seat, and replied with an awkward laugh: "Then there's the *sub*-cultural problem. Of bias within our own community." Several white Kenyans in their twenties told me that they personally would not have a problem with interracial dating, but they would worry what their parents would think.

"If I'd come home when I was fifteen with an African boyfriend, my dad would have hit the roof," one young woman said. "Because that's just not what you do."

Colin, single in his forties, described the internalized stigma: "Well, the Kenyan-born whites, they've got a fixation that it's not done, and they've got a problem—and I'm talking about myself, too—whether it's snobbishness or hypocritical stupidity or lowering yourself to a level that in the distant past was not acceptable, I don't know." In Colin's formulation, we see hints that the aversions at stake are not only racial and cultural, but also class-based. Historically, settler prestige was grounded partly in the rejection of even "low-level," impoverished whites, so the "snobbishness" he refers to may include his community's historical aversion even to (for instance) poor Afrikaners.

The popular stereotype of the African romantic partner milking a white benefactor for financial gain would certainly trigger images of the "wrong" socioeconomic tier of society. In our conversation, though, he frames race as the point-blank indicator of problematic difference. He is tempted—he would be "delighted," in fact, to spend a night, a week, or a month with a "Kenyan lady," but only on condition it happened "somewhere else where I would not be seen." A few old settlers, he says, are having a wonderful time fathering children with black Kenyan women, "and to hell with society." But most white Kenyans will feel it's "not the right thing."

Colin himself frames this "fixation" as a "problem." Contemporary waves of liberal humanism and idealizing discourses about the multicultural nation have presumably caught up with him and waft uncomfortably over his resistance to public displays of interracial romance. Indeed, the feelings Colin describes can disturb other whites who collude in them. When I brought the topic of interracial romance up with the young wildlife expert Trevor, he laughed uneasily, looking straight ahead as he drove his Land Rover across the game reserve we were exploring. In an earlier conversation Trevor had been at pains to describe to me his family's efforts to assist the surrounding community and involve them in their ranch's "community-based conservation" (see chapter 2). He had railed against the "Zimbabwe mentality" that kept some white landholders in Laikipia from making concessions to their black Kenyan neighbors, and insisted that his own attitude, by contrast, was "we're all Kenyan, what's the difference?" But in matters of romance, he cleared his throat before he replied. "Well, I guess that's where we're still a bit colonial." Even when white Kenyans can frame their own bias *as* bias, it is hard for them to shake; atavistic and irrational, a gremlin of racist history in the corners of their souls.

So what becomes of the few visible pairings between Africans and white Kenyans from former settler families? A Kenya-born, Ivy League–educated Kalenjin man in his twenties whom I know dated a white Kenyan woman but found it too uncomfortable to deal with the quiet disapproval of her extended family, so ended the romance. And Charlotte, a middle-aged white Kenyan entrepreneur, lives with her younger Kikuyu boyfriend John in a coastal town, but at the expense of her reputation among her peers. John is a high-school graduate who works in the tourism industry, though not at Charlotte's income level. The couple dote on their dogs and cats, and share meals, movies, domestic responsibilities and heartfelt conversations about their families, even if there are times when Charlotte expresses concern at John's solo trips to the local nightclub. But far more frustrating for Charlotte is the perception of her white Kenyan peers. James, another white Kenyan and a family friend of Charlotte's, told me privately he and others were concerned that John was using Charlotte for financial gain. They all questioned Charlotte's judgment in letting John move in with her. No wonder the couple do most of their socializing among the more accepting—and more racially intermarried—community of Italian expatriates.

One interracial romance turned so tragic that it came, for some settler descendants, to seem like a morality play. A photographer from an old white Kenyan family, Charlie Grieves-Cook, was in a long-term romantic involvement with a top black Kenyan model named Diana Sifuna when her apartment was stormed by armed intruders looking for "the *mzungu*," reportedly to steal his car. Grieves-Cook tried to hide by dangling from the balcony railings, but fell to his death. Although the London *Telegraph* described Sifuna's Langata apartment block as "upmarket,"[29] one of Grieves-Cook's friends spoke of her living "in a dodgy area."[30] The event triggered whites' anxieties about being targeted, and his death, for some, seemed like a warning about the perils of crossing into another zone—geographic, class, and racial.

When I asked Jos, who secretly has such critical feelings about the colonial past, why white Kenyans don't intermarry the way expats do, he leaned in with knit eyebrows. "I, I, I don't object to it," he stammered, "because I'm doing it myself, but I feel you're breaking a taboo. In other people's minds, it's slightly like breaking a taboo." Jos had developed romantic feelings for a Kikuyu woman. His voice wobbled a little. "You're, you're taking yourself away from the community," he explained. Did he hide his relationship? "No," he denied, but "my life is in such . . . um, compartments . . . um, I, I just keep that in one compartment and . . . " His voice trailed off, and he made a soft "tsk" sound. Then he sat back and drew breath: "Because, you see, I grew up amongst those views. And they are *so inbred* that still now I'm trying to break out of those prejudices. Your personality is soooo conditioned, it's not actually the real you, I believe anyway. I would *like* to break down those things and just become without any prejudices, like a normal Englishman."

A "normal Englishman," Jos feels, could integrate himself, living an interracial relationship in full view—an idealization, to be sure, but a telling one. England, his narrative goes, has moved ahead morally, while its former colonial community remains stuck. Jos is so uncomfortable with his internalized prejudice he has sought therapy to reconcile his upbringing with the longing of his heart. Therapy, in other words, to deal with the colonial legacy within.

Couples like Anna and Lemarti have pushed against the heavy weight of prejudice and skepticism. But after they got married they attempted an end-run of sorts around some of the doubters. They founded a luxury tourist camp in Laikipia on land rented from a Samburu group.[31] Rather than denying their differences, "Lemarti's Camp" glories in them, suggesting a fantastic fusion of Samburu (and Maasai) connections to the land with a taste for fashionable comforts. Guests take private charter flights from Nairobi and find themselves sleeping like pampered colonials in platform tents of cedar and canvas, illuminated by kerosene lamps at night. Lodge workers pour warm baths in outdoor tin tubs, prepare gourmet food, and speak good English. In the common areas, open to the breeze and birdsong, ethno-chic chaise longues sit atop hide rugs and exquisite textiles. Fine whisky, glossy books, and beaded Maasai walking sticks rest on tables carved from the wood of wrecked dhows and inlaid with ivory, bone, and shells. Some of the décor is made in Anna's Nairobi workshop, where she and a group of Maasai women also manufacture her fashions, attaching bone handles to purses, black-and-white guinea-fowl feathers to shawls, and pastoralist beadwork to suede safari jackets. She uses "authentic indigenous designs" of "my native Africa," and deems herself fascinated by anything "made by a human hand that carries the cultural values of generations."[32]

Though Anna deems herself an "African native," the lodge's publicity materials play up Lemarti's cultural background as the most special asset the lodge has to offer.[33] Lemarti and his Maasai friend Boniface, the two primary camp hosts, are pictured on the web site in brilliant pastoralist regalia, smiling at each other while appearing to bump spears. They are "nomads," reads the copy, "whose lifestyle and peaceful co-existence with the natural environment has changed little over time."[34] The cultural tourist is promised a very special experience: "You will walk amongst wildlife with warriors armed only with traditional weapons, our sharp senses and generations of knowledge. For a few magical days you will inhabit another world; our world." Each guest is paired with a personal warrior guide, who will accompany him or her through the Laikipia terrain. The guides teach children customary games and beadwork, help them paint their faces warrior-style, and, armed with spears, take them out to find dried bones and wildlife, including packs of African wild dogs. Guests who venture into a nearby village may be feted with song and dance and have livestock sacrificed in their honor.[35] And in publicity for the lodge, Anna repeatedly invokes the fig tree in the center of camp, which she says elders have deemed sacred, and which confers a blessing on all who stay there.

The web site is at pains to establish that Lemarti and the other guides know how to make guests comfortable, speaking English and understanding modern audiences (they have hosted television shows together, it notes). But it does not dilute the Samburu image further by mentioning, for instance, that Lemarti likes to dance in clubs in Paris,[36] or that he can sometimes be found wearing jeans at Anna's elegant house in Karen, Nairobi's upmarket suburb. In media interviews, Anna repeatedly contrasts a pure Africa with spoiled modernity. She is "so sad," she says, "that so many Kenyans do not value and keep alive their traditional cultures," and she finds the pace of modernization "terrifying."[37] Fortunately, she says, she is lucky enough "to live with people who are still so pure."[38] Lemarti has become, in their union, the public symbol of such purity, while Anna is the modern looking on, beset by nostalgia—not quite the "imperialist nostalgia" described by Renato Rosaldo (1993), but nevertheless a sentiment that fetishizes the possibility of a static "tradition" that the conditions of cultural contact have made impossible.[39]

Though Anna's marriage is an exception to the rule in the former settler community, it has precedents, as I have noted, among white travelers who seek romantic liaisons with people of color, sometimes even imaginatively "becoming" the other in an exhilarating display of cosmopolitanism.[40] In Kenya, this dynamic was famously documented by the Swiss-born Corinne Hoffman, whose four-year marriage to a Samburu man in the late 1980s made her, she says, a "white Maasai."[41]

European travelers since the 1990s have been in the throes of "*moran mania,*" expecting to be mesmerized by Samburu or Maasai warriors on their trips to East Africa, according to the ethnographer George Paul Meiu.[42] (*Morans,* in turn, stand to profit from representing themselves as "ethno-commodities," like so many other African groups in recent decades.[43] In particular, they exert maximal appeal if they play to the stereotype of themselves as sexually available warriors, even though they risk moral opprobrium from some in their own communities by doing so.[44]) In cultivating a marriage with Lemarti, then, Anna more closely resembles a European tourist than a settler descendent, but her kinship bonds with Samburu perhaps have special significance for a white Kenyan from a community anxious to prove it belongs. One wonders whether her marriage has a symbolically redemptive quality, serving as a cultural and racial reconciliation of sorts.[45]

In fact, although Kenya's settlers were loath to marry Africans, and most kept African society at arm's length, a select and striking few did stake their belonging on a particular kind of cultural intimacy. Three notable figures in particular owed their fame and sociocultural capital in part to being semi-incorporated into tribal peoples but tacking back into the world of white privilege. Notwithstanding that he appropriated an enormous tract of their ancestral land in the Rift Valley and helped broker their displacement, the third Baron Delamere famously deemed himself a "friend of the Maasai" and professed himself a great admirer of their noble, dignified aesthetic. His perceived connection with them would help build his reputation among whites as the unofficial leader of their settler community. Karen Blixen, whom many settlers saw as unnaturally respectful of blacks, rhapsodizes in her memoirs about her connection with an impoverished African boy whom she rescued from illness and employed as her cook. The world-famous paleontologist Louis Leakey, too, broke with settler convention, becoming semi-acculturated among Kikiyu as a child in the early 1900s, accepted by some as a member of their "tribe," and one of the only white voices to insist that Kikuyu customs were worth preserving.[46] In the process, all of them got to feel as though they belonged to Kenya and Kenya to them.[47]

None of this is meant to reduce Anna's and Lemarti's bond to mere strategy. It surely took bravery for Anna to follow her heart, going against the grain of her family's opinion and rocking the wider white Kenyan community. Meanwhile, critics cannot object that Lemarti is exploiting Anna's wealth, for his cultural background and his very otherness have become commodities for them both.[48] Nor can old-fashioned whites quite complain that Anna has "gone bush," for in her interface with wealthy Western clients, she's become a *purveyor* of "bush" as nostalgia for precolonial purity. "Anna's panache and style," comments one reviewer, "have married with her husband's authentic connection to the land to make it a special experience."[49] Here, then, is one idiosyncratic resolution to the dilemmas of interracial marriage for a white Kenyan: turning one's merger into a luxury brand.

AN INTIMATE ECONOMY: DOMESTIC STAFF

White Kenyans are concerned about how they are symbolically tied to Kenya, as Kenyans, and most have a block against getting there through marital kinship. But another type of close bond is available to them, through relationships with their domestic staff. Like many whites from settler families in Africa, many of my respondents have genuine affection for at least some of their workers who have been an intimate part of their lives, some since birth. The bond might be called one of "fictive kinship." In anthropology, the phrase describes any stipulated relatedness, and while it doesn't demote such ties (after all, the imagination plays a role even in our blood and marital forms of kinship), in this case I do mean to draw attention to a fictional element of the relationship in question.[50] For although settler descendants feel romantic love should not be staked on financial dependency, they have built what they feel is a kin-like relationship with some staff members upon just such a foundation. Their descriptions of these relationships, furthermore, mostly ignore the ways in which these bonds are economically structured. And while my research doesn't focus on the experience of domestic staff, I did collect enough data on this matter to say that staff members do not universally share their employers' understandings of family ties.

Domestic servitude has blurred the lines between work and family in many cultural and historical contexts, and white Kenyans are not alone in projecting fictive kinship onto their domestic staff. Karen Hansen, for instance, describes colonial families in Zambia who claimed to have kin-like relationships with their domestic servants, though Hansen herself sees much inequity in the dynamic.[51] Scholars of slavery in the American South, such as Micki McElya, note that slave owners tended to depict the "mammies" who took care of white children as loyal "members of the family," held to their positions through paternalistic relationships of mutual affection rather than economic or legal forces; yet slaves ate all their meals in the kitchen and had the rights of an object rather than an equal.[52] From the strictures of slavery to the more benign architecture of marriage across many cultures, economic bonds seem common to many kin-like arrangements. But among white Kenyans, the financial exigencies that anchor their domestic staff to them seem relatively hidden from their consciousness, since they prefer to foreground what they feel to be familial relationships of affection, which many assume is mutual—sometimes to the point of sacrifice or risk.

In the late 1990s while I was studying religion and ethnicity among Swahili and Giriama of the Kenya coast, I came to know an elderly woman, Delia, the daughter of an old settler family, now living south of Mombasa. Delia had a reputation in the white Kenyan coastal community as kind and generous, and she invited me for a fish lunch here and there to learn about my fieldwork. Before we ate, Delia would flurry around vociferating about her struggles to pay her telephone and electricity bills. Another headache: the cost of repairs to her decrepit "Arab style" ceiling whose mangrove beams, chewed to pieces by termites, constantly threatened to crash down upon the occupants. Nevertheless, she had diligently salaried the same two domestic staff members for decades. The most vivid figure was a Chonyi man named Samuel, and to her credit, Delia had abandoned the pernicious colonial habit of calling even geriatric male domestic workers "boy"; Samuel was her "staff." Samuel brought plates of freshly cut mango for breakfast and chicken and rice for dinner, taking care of household chores in between—dishes, laundry, dusting, throw-pillow arranging, and daily rites such as opening the curtains in the morning, putting the mosquito nets up, and polishing the Swahili brass and copper plates that adorned the niches in Delia's whitewashed walls. Hudson, an aging Kamba man from the Machakos area, took care of the grounds in an unhurried, methodical style. The garden thrived in his care, sporting a tamarind tree, at least four species of palm, white jasmine vines, fragrant yellow frangipani, and the ever-present bougainvillea. As evening fell, Hudson was also responsible for locking the wrought-iron gate at the foot of the driveway (the threat of armed robbery was real), and securing the large, ornately carved Swahili doors at the front of the house.

Delia and her staff were able to bump along in fragmented Kiswahili communications several times a day to discuss the household chores and plan for the arrival of her guests, but otherwise, the men didn't have much of a social life. Samuel had family a few kilometers away and was able to visit them on weekends, but Hudson seemed entirely cut off from society. He barely tolerated the ways of the coastal people, she told me (he was prone to derogatory remarks about Chonyi hygiene), and he almost never spoke unless it was to reply to a friendly question with a monosyllable. He rarely left the compound, and he saved just enough to make the long bus journey to Machakos every few months—when a family emergency struck, he borrowed from his employer to go there on short notice. But Delia took pride in looking after the welfare of both men. Once Hudson grew very ill and she lumbered him in her car to a private clinic, where he was diagnosed with malaria and tuberculosis. Hudson would have trouble following the detailed timetable of his medications; after all, I noticed, he signed for his wages by inking his thumb with a ballpoint pen and pressing it into Delia's accounts book. So Delia drew him a color-coded chart with moons and suns to indicate the times of day when he should take each. About Samuel's many requests for "extras"—bus fare, settling a medical bill for his daughter—she would press her hand to her forehead in concern for her own cash flow. But it was clear she felt bound to respond to their troubles with assistance.

Once Delia went out of town for a couple of weeks and asked me to pay her staff on Fridays. Like many domestic staff workers, Samuel and Hudson lived in single-room quarters in the garden behind the house, with cement walls and a corrugated tin roof and a long-drop outhouse standing a few feet behind the dwellings. Each room had a grimy mosquito net over a cot, a couple of hangers on a clothesline, and a camp stove on upturned cement blocks that served as a bedside table. Accounts book in hand, I noted that Delia paid them Ksh 4,000 a month each. This, it turns out, was generous. The average monthly wage paid to domestic staff by white Kenyans on the coast in the late 1990s was, by my reckoning, roughly Ksh 3,000, or U.S.$40. Such wages met the minimum requirement of Kenya's labor laws and provided enough for basics—food, second-hand clothing, a little beyond that—but they couldn't possibly cover contingencies such medical bills and children's school fees. I did some math and thought rather munificently that if it were up to me, I'd pay domestic staff at least three times that amount.

Later, I came to understand that my sentiments on this matter are widely shared by newly arrived expatriates of European and American extraction—and that such feelings are also widely disparaged by settler descendants. Yet the same white Kenyan employers insist they are fond of their staff and consider themselves responsible for their well-being. I puzzled over this tension before I came to understand its historical backdrop, and the contemporary structure of feeling that upholds it.

One can trace the roots of white Kenyan authority to an earlier, more brutal era of master-servant relationships. In elite Victorian households, the have-nots—chambermaids, butlers, footmen, and so forth—were thought to be a different "sort" of people, relegated to a life behind the scenes, and treated with varying combinations of paternalism and abuse.[53] In early Kenya Colony, it wasn't only adventure-seeking aristocrats but other new arrivals, too, such as former soldiers with little to their name but the land given them by the Crown, who could afford servants at very low wages. The colonial tax system and the Crown's seizure of land drove many Africans to seek whatever menial labor was available, and Kenya's so-called Master and Servant laws were skewed in favor of European employers—more so than in England by the early twentieth century. Flogging (particularly in earlier decades) and jail were common punishments for misdemeanors and desertions, and when fines were meted out laborers often wound up in jail anyway because they couldn't afford to pay. Some employers routinely withheld part of a laborer's monthly wages to ensure that their employees stayed on.[54]

Europeans leaned heavily on their servants, but sharing domestic spaces with Africans fed settler anxieties about rebellion, rape, and pollution from a supposedly lower human order.[55] Employers were suspicious of African hygiene, and tried to bend their servants to comply with European expectations of domestic order and cleanliness. Meanwhile, to maintain prestige in the eyes of their staff, settlers sometimes tried not to let the servants see them doing work and adopted an "aloof and inscrutable manner," the historian Dane Kennedy says. The putative "loyalty" of the servant was code for "absolute submission to the will of his master . . . an archetypal symbol of the colonial relationship at its best."[56]

And then, there were the emotional contradictions—for these troubling hierarchies co-existed with deeply felt sentiments. Colonial historians have of late taken pains to explore the "tender ties" that sometimes found a way to lace even brutal colonial hierarchies, and in the Kenyan case it is easy to find affectionate references to servants in settler memoirs.[57] The historian Christine Nicholls, who grew up in a settler family and experienced pre-Independence dynamics directly, sees it this way: "Whites could be kindly and considerate to individual workers in their houses and on their farms, and loyalty and strong affection developed between many whites and individual Africans, on both sides . . . yet such relationships were intrinsically doomed because they were based on paternalism."[58]

The inconsistencies and tensions could be startling. Inhumane flog-gings for minor infractions would be meted out in one household, and heartfelt care for ailing staff in the next. But even the kindliest employers relegated their servants to such a child-like role that, as noted above, even an elderly man in the kitchen would be referred to as "boy"—a pattern that rankled so deeply, Kenyans continue to cite it as a classic example of the depredations of colonialism (as did Barack Obama in his July 2015 trip to Kenya, discussing his grandfather's humiliating employment in a British household). Sometimes, settlers enjoyed "sacrificing" for their African dependents, especially administering medical aid directly to bleeding wounds or febrile foreheads, Brett Shadle notes. They groused about workers' lack of gratitude, but their acts of charity, like all unre-paid gifts, helped to secure the hierarchy between the needy and their benefactors.[59]

Today the average white Kenyan home (based on those I saw in Nai-robi, Naivasha, Laikipia, and Coast Province) has about three to five domestic staff members, working as cooks, cleaners, gardeners, nannies, and watchmen. Some commute to work by *matatu* (minibus), bicycle, or foot, while others live on their employers' land, usually in Spartan single-room dwellings at a remove from the main house. Historically, settlers usually employed men in the home, to avoid the sexual temptations posed by female employees, and because fewer women came out to seek domestic labor. Domestic servitude now seems prevalent among single mothers, who sometimes bring their children to live with them, but some white Kenyans still prefer that staff family members remain invisible to them. One elderly woman on the coast, for instance, instructs her (male) servants not to bring their wives or children to her home because, she says, "I just don't want a village in my backyard."

Domestic staff (and "staff" is the word white Kenyans prefer today, skirting the decadent connotations of the term "servant") thus spend most of their time tending to their employer's family rather than their own, and moving quietly to clean large homes that range from simply appointed, if breezy and comfortable, to outright luxurious, including swimming pools, multi-car garages, and guest wings. Some white Ken-yan décor evokes Europe, with gilt-framed oil paintings, imported antiques, wrapped leather chairs, and wooden wall paneling. Still, many touches also index the African setting: thatch over an open porch; whitewashed walls; impala horns mounted on the living room wall; soapstone candlesticks from Kisii; colorful Tinga Tinga paintings of wildlife; and gossamer mosquito nets sweeping down over four-poster beds. Having dusted and straightened the interiors, staff may shift outside to hand-wash laundry in brightly colored plastic tubs. Among their responsibilities is keeping their own uniforms clean. The garb varies from home to home, but many men sport a shirt with a button-down collar while women often wear a monochromatic short-sleeved dress with white trim on the sleeves and collar, a white apron, and a kerchief covering their hair.

One can see these uniforms and the splendor of the homes of affluent white, Asian, and African families in a recently published photo essay on Kenyan domestic servants by the photographer Guillaume Bonn, born in Madagascar as a third-generation member of a French colonial family.[60] In his images we see staff standing at the edge of a garden party awaiting requests for drinks, doing laundry in the back of the house, and arranging crisp blue and white throw pillows on an enormous bed. But Bonn's essay, entitled "Silent Lives," also obscures a kind of intimacy imprinted on the psyches of some of my respondents. Most white Kenyans were tended by African nannies (ayahs) when growing up, and some from older generations were wet-nursed—a practice that the British aristocracy and some African societies happened to have in common (though for very different ideological reasons).[61] A few of my interlocutors felt this had made a deep impact on them, most particularly Charlotte, who says she doesn't look on herself as being "a white." "I've been born and brought up here," she says. "I was brought up on a black woman's milk, but, you know, her milk is the same my mother's milk. Just because the skin's black why should I treat her differently to the way I treat my mum?" Charlotte went on to have an interracial relationship as an adult, but even those who would never cross that social boundary remember the kin-like care of household employees. One middle-aged woman from a storied aristocratic family, Eleanor, described an intimate bond, sealed with bodily fluids: "Some of the people that worked for us who came from the dry country would *spit* on us as a blessing you know, and [my mother] would *not* allow us to flinch, we had to take to being spat upon. And those people treated us like *their* children. You know we were beautifully looked after. There was never a feeling that they didn't care a *lot* about us."

Children had the most unmediated intimacy with domestic staff, and hadn't yet come to grips with the lines that separated them—hence one anecdote I heard about a boy from a settler family who, during the Mau Mau era, asked the family's Kikuyu cook if he could be scarified in the next Kikuyu age-grade initiation ceremony. He was denied by the cook himself, who rightly foresaw a political disaster with his adult employers. Nicola also remembers her 1960s childhood as a time before the stark racial lines had sunk in: "It's strange, but I don't remember ever that it mattered what color anybody was." When she was about six and her parents were out, she said, she would go "hang out with our gardener," who was in his teens. She taught him how to read; "I couldn't understand why he couldn't read and I could." As she grew up, she says wistfully, indoctrination into racial categories had its way, and she realized people were "actually sort of *made* to be different." In a similar narrative arc, an elderly man from an elite colonial family tells me of hanging around "at the back of the house," where the kitchen washing-up took place and the domestic staff lived. He felt like he was part of this "club," this "big community round the back," until he was sent to an all-white boarding school and the idea of a divinely ordered racial hierarchy was inculcated into him—one he now questions.

These realizations are hardly unique to contemporary white Kenyans. Tamara Schefer has explored the stories told about their nonwhite caregivers as children by white South Africans, whom the past few decades have starkly confronted with the depredations of apartheid. She detects nostalgia, guilt, and shame in their adult realizations of how oppressed they must have been, and how oblivious to this many of them were themselves at the time.[62] My Kenyan interlocutors didn't express shame per se, but they were nostalgic for an intimacy that they now realize couldn't stand the test of adult social life.

In fact, when there was genuine depth of feeling among settlers for their staff, all sides were keenly aware of the racial hierarchies involved. Francine, who moved from Kenya to Britain in her twenties shortly after Independence, ruminates about her peculiar sense of being "friends," but within a terrible social asymmetry: "For years and years [when my family lived in Nairobi] I used to visit our old cook on the coast. We were *genuine, proper friends*. Couldn't write to him or anything but *every* time we went to Mombasa I would see him. I thought of him as a genuine friend. . . . when Africans were looked on as a group they were looked at as uncivilized, but the individual friendships went on."

Even since Independence, structural asymmetries cannot always be breached by feeling. The ethnographer Katja Uuusihakala (1999) describes a man from a settler family, "Douglas," who after many years abroad returned to Kenya in 1992, where he chanced to meet Matthew, the son of one of his father's domestic servants, who had grown up to become a bank manager. Douglas and Matthew shared a tearful embrace, then Douglas committed the faux pas of inviting Matthew to his cousin Derek's house. Derek, also a settler descendant, refused to let Matthew and his wife dine in the house, making them stay on the veranda for tea. Douglas was left disturbed by the contradiction between his strong feelings of affection for Matthew and the reminder that his family's identity was founded on racial inequities internalized by his white Kenyan kin.

In light of such a legacy, what are the varied ways in which my respondents relate to the domestic staff in their homes today? I witnessed a range of emotional attitudes, varying from person to person and day to day. Some employers can be prickly; I recall, for instance, an elderly woman who seemed to stiffen whenever her staff members entered the room, appearing to resent their repeated queries about how she wanted them to carry out their tasks. Yet she expected them to have mastered the details; at one lunch event when a young man brought out a dish of creamed chicken and rice, she snapped: "What's the *matter* with you, John? Bring the fork for the chicken! *No,* not that one! Come on!" Another woman on the coast was so notorious for verbally abusing her staff that rumors circulated among my Giriama friends that she might be a witch. In a few cases I heard about, interactions are volatile, begetting what Shireen Ally calls a "dialectic of attachment and denigration"; a to-ing and fro-ing between intimacy and estrangement, care and angry reprimand, familiar in master-servant relationships in colonial and apartheid-era South Africa.[63] Grace, an elderly woman, sums up the contradictory impulses among her peer group, as she sees it: "We're very *kali* [fierce, stern], but really we're very kind." But while barked commands and reproaches are the tools of some, many settler descendants aim for a more affable relationship, striving for kindliness. Some contrast themselves against the most elite of white employers; Nicola, for instance, adopted a mock, hyper-aristocratic accent as she voiced the worst of the settler families: "I think there *is* that Happy Valley set. They really do exist . . . I mean I know of people who talk of, you know, of *'the staahff'* badly. And it's not something I would ever do or appreciate, either." Jonathan agrees that "lording it over" servants is unacceptably disrespectful.

In my perception, and though there are exceptions, it's the younger white Kenyans who came of age around Independence or later who are least inclined to berate staff, and more likely to inquire after staff members' families, josh staff members about their romantic interests, and discuss local events such as a strike, a robbery, or Kenyan athletes with them in colloquial Kiswahili. A few settler descendants on the coast communicate in sufficient depth with their staff that they call upon them as go-betweens with shamans in their community, as I describe later. This readier flow of communication is not, however, imagined by either side as ordinary socializing. The fact that some whites still feel they must keep up the impression of prestige was made clear to me by Clem, who reflected one evening that he just "can't bring himself to be drunk in front of the staff."

Regardless of how *kali* they can be, many of my respondents also repeatedly proclaimed their care for staff members. To them, the paternalism so richly described by historians feels like a moral responsibility.[64] Cressida, the mother of one of my white Kenyan contacts in Nairobi, feels "maternal" about her domestic staff, her son says, for instance. "She makes a huge, huge contribution to their children's education," he told me, "so big that she doesn't even tell Dad." She reserves special concern for the night guard, Kipanga, who sits for hours through the night in a hut a little larger than a telephone booth at the foot of the driveway. By law, Kipanga isn't allowed to carry a firearm, but he does have a bow and arrow with a poison tip to threaten intruders. Incongruously, he has also been employed by the family long enough to grow hard of hearing and to fall asleep on the job. Every night, before she goes to bed, Cressida walks down the driveway to bring him a cup of coffee and two bananas. She could just shake him awake, but she wants to save him face, so instead she heaves the massive wrought-iron gate next to the guard house shut with a resounding clang. Her son grouses with amusement: "So we have to be woken up every night for the sake of not embarrassing our night watchman!"

Yet I was still bothered by the tension between these expressions of concern and the remuneration of staff members. Many settler descendants I met paid their domestic staff at or around Kenya's bare-bones minimum wage; as of 2015, this comes to about Ksh 10,500 per month for house staff, nannies, and gardeners in cities or municipalities, and just over Ksh 6,000/month in all other areas.[65] These figures may allow an individual to scrape by, but typically they do not allow for saving, domestic consumption, or the comfortable support of a family—and they are roughly half to a third as much as that paid by many expatriates.[66] Why would this be the case? Historically, wage fixing had both economic and ideological rationales. In the 1920s, settler farmers deliberately held down the wages of farm workers and domestic staff to avoid competition among themselves and curtail labor mobility between farms, the historian David Anderson notes.[67] Christine Nicholls quotes a colonial health officer writing in 1955 as representing of a common settler view of the time: "The African labourer is regarded by the European farmer as being lazy, irresponsible, and unreliable and there is certainly some excuse for this opinion as his output of work is low no matter what wages he receives. It is therefore uneconomical to pay good wages."[68]

This insulting rationale for low pay was not shared by my respondents, but other arguments were. A prevalent line is that higher wages would "spoil" the staff and put pressure on the neighbors to pay more as well, thus souring social relations among employers; a tacit agreement among former settler families, then, appears to keep wages low. Another more magnanimous, and popular, argument is that lower wages serve the social good because they allow employers to hire more staff, who would otherwise be unemployed. "I'm sure they'd rather have a small wage than no wages at all," says one. And several rationalized that low wages are better for staff because they prevent them from spending money in naïve or self-destructive ways. Nicola is self-conscious about appearing "colonial" about this, but defends her argument:

> Now, this is going to sound really bad, but what they do is, they come in as expats and they say "My *God,* they're paying their staff peanuts; it's absolutely terrible. Blablabla." You know, "You old colonial whatevers." And then they'll triple their salaries. Which is fine, but do you know what? These people live for today. If you give them ten thousand shillings for today, they will spend it. . . . Like if they buy land, [they'll be] kicked off because it was all conned, it was not rightfully for sale. And what's so sad is, you've just, like that, basically put some guy out of his means. . . . how long then is that expat there—two years? Then they're gone. . . . To *me,* I see it as unfair. . . . you've actually just now put them in somewhere which is *unrealistic.*

Nicola's reasoning resembles the widespread arguments that aid to Africa, in the form of monetary handouts, tends to be squandered without inculcating long-term structural change. Looked at another way, of course, if white Kenyans collectively paid their staff higher wages they would become part of a long-term structural change, particularly for those in their employ for decades at a time. After all, unlike expatriates, most white Kenyans are not planning to leave any time soon—many of them *are* "the long term" for their staff.

But even their conscious rationales for low wages do not, I think, exhaust their underlying motives, because there's another wrinkle to the economic relationship between staff and white Kenyan employers. For many, minimum wage is too low to constitute a living wage, which means that staff depend on employers for further necessities. Some employers, as a matter of course, supplement wages with a large sack of maize meal *(posho)* each month, which provides staff with a major staple. But staff still come up short for medical and dental emergencies, education for their children, travel needs, and community expectations, such as supporting bereaved families or contributing to a wedding feast. The typical pattern, then, is for staff to approach their white Kenyan employers with a request, and for their employers to mete out "extras" or "loans" when it suits them. My respondents report bailing staff out of innumerable personal dilemmas and crises, fulfilling what one informant calls her "pastoral requirements" toward servants.

Through this economic arrangement, employers become inserted into the dramas and rites of passage of their staff members' extended families, often across generations. The relationships thus established are both intimate and hierarchical. We see the dynamic at play as Eleanor describes her gardener's request for funds for his grandfather's funeral:

> The other day the gardener came to me. He says: "My grandfather's died and we have to, my mother has to arrange the funeral." And [the gardener is] trying to lay away some money to buy a farm. He *just* gave me 5,000 shillings to keep in the attic. Then his grandfather dies and he's expected to fork out for the family a couple of goats *and* get home, so he says I'm going to need 2,000 bob [shillings] . . . And he just said to me straight out: "But you've got to contribute something." . . . I *could* have said: "Well, I've got your 5,000 bob, take it out of that." But I just thought: he has this aspiration [to buy the farm]. . . . So this isn't the moment I'm going to say no to him. So I gave him a little money.[69]

Eleanor's story is a common one. Staff members ask for leave at short notice—or simply vanish—to attend the funerals of family or community members and request funds to pay for their transportation or a contribution to the funerary feast. Employers expect this to happen, though their sympathy is proportional to their sense of the event's relevance. Those living on the coast, for instance, complain about the disappearance of Mijikenda staff members to attend massive and costly multi-day funeral ceremonies, sometimes for people staff knew only distantly. Upon their return, employers gripe, some employees have contracted malaria after spending so many nights in the open and need to be nursed back to health. But inconvenience is shunted to the background when the situation is urgent or tragic. Sometimes the children of staff fall seriously ill and have to be rushed to hospital, or worse. When tragedy strikes, many employers will pay hospital bills, morgue fees, and funeral expenses or help in other ways. One white Kenyan friend told me of how when a staff member's young son was killed in an accident, his own family had to transport the body tied to a surfboard on top of the family car, an image that still rattled him.

Writing at the turn of the millennium, the anthropologist Blair Rutherford describes a related dynamic in Zimbabwe, where white farmers long treated their farm workers paternalistically, taking pride in bringing "modernity" into the latter's lives through what Rutherford terms "domestic government" (Rutherford 2001). In colonial Rhodesia, whites supplied food to their workers rather than paying them a living wage, regarding this as a matter of looking after their workers, who, they said, lacked the discipline to "budget." Although the Zimbabwean government subsequently legislated a minimum wage, the general pattern of "control and authority" among white employers persisted into the postcolonial era, especially since farmers controlled their workers' access to housing and credit.[70] Rutherford focuses on economic and spatial relationships rather than fictive kinship per se, but he notes that farmers and workers alike sometimes used the trope of "family" to capture the organization of the farm.[71]

The paternalism in employer-staff relationships helps white Kenyans sustain a narrative of fictive kinship by inserting employers into the dramas and rites of passage of their staff's extended kin networks, often across generations, I suggest. Their patterns of ad hoc payments structure the employer-employee relation like a patron-client one; an unequal exchange relationship in which the subordinate will probably never be able to reciprocate fully—particularly when the assistance is given as a "loan" that both parties suspect will never be repaid.[72] This arrangement is familiar to many staff members, given that patron-client relationships have been historically prevalent in many parts of sub-Saharan Africa. Confirming some white Kenyan intuitions, furthermore, patron-client relationships often overlap with a sense of kin-like rights and obligations. Perhaps for this reason, employees do not necessarily beg for help; sometimes they simply *expect* that their employers, who assume responsibility for their basic needs, will comply. But if there are expectations of help on one end, white Kenyans don't forget that they retain the power to adjudicate the situation ("this isn't the moment I'm going to say no to him," says Eleanor, indicating that she could say no if she saw fit). If they do agree to help, they get a chance to feel virtuous. And having received funds in the spirit of a sympathetic rescue rather than an impersonal monthly wage, the staff member's dependency increases, and so too may her or his loyalty, whether performed, heartfelt, or both.

There are clearly reasons, then, for employers to prefer to earmark "extra" handouts for family needs rather than letting staff spend money freely. A paycheck is impersonal, but a gift or a personal loan is social glue, especially a gift considered necessary because of a dramatic rupture in someone's life. Clem, the Nairobi-based safari guide in his forties, reports such a dynamic with his own domestic staff. (Clem is a bachelor; in married couples it's usually the woman who has the most contact with domestic staff, and is most likely to engage in the affective-economic dynamics I describe here.) Clem pays his staff partly in bags of maize meal, and complains habitually in an affectionate but paternalistic tone about how they keep running into one medical crisis after another, "especially with their children." While he is irritated by their recurrent requests for loans he knows they can't repay, he can tick off the issues in engrossing detail—a case of cerebral malaria in an eight-year-old; three trips to the clinic; two simultaneous medications, one hard to procure; a mother distraught to the point of pathos. The paltriness of their servants' pay thus involves white Kenyans, directly and indirectly, in the biological needs, dramatic life-and-death dramas, and extended kin networks of their staff. These patterns unite employer and employee in a paternalistic relationship and establish quasi kin-relations between employer and staff members' extended families, perhaps especially from the white point of view.

Whites report this as emotionally exhausting, but such weariness, I suspect, is part of what makes them feel connected to Kenya. Some interlocutors noted it was a relief to go abroad, because it's easier to use appliances to clean one's home, and they don't have to deal with what they call the "emotional rent" of their servants. Clem tells me when he goes on a casual camping safari with friends, he prefers not to bring staff along. In that way, he can be entirely free of worries about how they are doing. Beneath these gripes, though, one senses that white Kenyans want to be involved, however indirectly, in the messy realities, ritual transitions, and family tragedies of the ordinary black Kenyans from whom they otherwise live at such a remove. They feel for their staff, and feeling needed, useful, and emotionally embedded in this way may create a sense of belonging to the Kenyan people and, in turn, to the nation.

White Kenyans also cite their dynamics with their domestic staff as evidence that they understand Africans better than other groups. African and Asian employers, who, white Kenyans delicately say, are rather more likely to physically abuse, deprive, or cast off their domestic staff, are one such foil. This, not coincidentally, dovetails with white Kenyan tropes of black Kenyan leaders as corrupt and self-serving, and with long-standing settler stereotypes of rapacious Indian merchants. In both of these well-worn narratives, those from settler families (and indeed colonialism itself) come across as more socially responsible.[73]

Expatriates who "parachute through" are the other main foil used to justify white Kenyans' treatment of their domestic staff. My own experience of house-sitting for a well-to-do friend, in which I found myself racing to make the bed and empty the trashcan before the housekeeper arrived, probably approximates the liberal guilt of some of these "two-year wonders." The low-wage workers who make our middle-class lives in the West so comfortable are usually invisible to us, toiling in overseas factories, for instance, and I found it discomfiting to watch someone else washing my undergarments by hand in the back yard. "Just let them do their job," was the white Kenyan response; "they are glad to have the work and it'll throw them off if you try to do it for them." One white Kenyan woman explained that expatriates are awkward with servants because they weren't brought up with them, whereas for her, "you don't think about it; it's second nature." This ease, she says, isn't about dehumanizing them, but about a hierarchy that appears to her free of guilt or resentment: "There's certainly no question of your not treating them like a fellow human being. It's just that you have an easy master-servant relationship." Emily, a Nairobi resident in her sixties whose family has farmed and done business in Kenya for the past century, suggested that the whole dynamic is based on deep mutual understanding:

> I am very fond of my staff. I think I understand some of the pressures that they're under, from their families, from their home environment, from their aspirations for their children. And we *hope* that we pay them quite generously, but nothing like an expat pays them. Because they do pay them much more than the people who live here. But when it comes to the *crunch*—say, when my house servant's son is in college, she couldn't possibly afford to pay for that, so I help. I believe people who've lived here for longer, even though they may not be so generous on a monthly basis, *they know* they are the backstop and if things go wrong . . . the thing is if they come to you, how can you say no? *You* who have cars and clothes, whereas life for them is . . . is actually the next thing to impossible. So they know you're not going to say no of course you're not going to say no. . . . they share your house. They know everything about you.

Although it may overgeneralize about the generosity of white Kenyan employers, Emily's statement explains the sense in which she feels different from expats. White Kenyans may pay their servants less, but their holistic economic relationship with their staff is more intimate, compassionate, and empathic, she feels. Nevertheless, listening to her, I couldn't help thinking again that it's the low pay itself that creates the need for this "backstop" to begin with.

There may be logical gaps in white Kenyans' rationale for what they pay servants, but there also clear emotional rewards, and some of my informants insist that the emotional connections flow both ways, invoking the theme of "the loyal servant" that dates to the colonial era (and, indeed, can be found elsewhere, as in the American South, where former masters would recount how their faithful slaves had protected homesteads against marauding Union soldiers).[74] One man tells me his elderly domestic servant Charo, with his family since he was a teenager, would "sooner die" than not work for them. Others, too, cited instances where their servants risked their own safety to keep them from harm's way. Says Nicola: "They're incredibly loyal people. You know they protect your things. And you. They *do!* And they really care for you. It's amazing. It's a bit like my driver. You know my driver, he never . . . in all that nonsense that went on [during the violent clashes of late 2007 and early 2008, many of which happened near Nicola's home], he sort of, he looked after me. There was no way he wouldn't get me home."

Being with the same family for many years can also give a servant a kind of seniority in the household. The gruff Laikipia rancher Devon describes the aura surrounding his household cook:

> He's been with the family so long it's not true [in other words: for so long you can hardly believe it]. And my kids subconsciously are politer to him than they are to me. You know: he is Wanjiru. And Wanjiru is someone special. . . . What that special is, nobody knows. And there are two old men on the farm, one's me and the other is Wanjiru. Now Wanjiru's grandsons treat me like my children treat Wanjiru, it's a funny sort of thing.

Wanjiru's time depth in Devon's household gives him license to have a say in its social order, rather like a family patriarch:

> I've taken a girlfriend home, and Wanjiru has let me know [grave, slow] she's *not* the sort of woman you bring here! . . . His tenure of service is such that he's entitled to have an opinion! I went on one occasion to some friend's house. There was this girl . . . very pretty, and very shapely. Anyway I met her and [brought her home] and she, you know, turned up with a good quarter

of each bosom sticking out of the front of her t-shirt. And the cook was [he enunciates in a strict voice] *not* amused!

Apparently Wanjiru approved of Devon's other friend, a widow closer to Devon's age, whom Wanjiru "treats as the lady of the house when she's visiting." "I *listen* to his opinions," Devon says, "because I know he's more astute than I am." In this narrative, Wanjiru upholds the family's very propriety, dignity, and class stature, knowing what is good and right for Devon better than he himself does. His machinations around Devon's romantic life suggest to Devon that Wanjiru knows who would be up to quality as his potential kin. Although Wanjiru's opinions suggest his pride of place in the home, surely, too, they uphold the expected hierarchy as well, furnishing the ultimate luxury for the man of the house; a servant who prizes and guards his master's reputation as if it were his own.

Logistically, economically, ideologically, and emotionally, then, some white Kenyans profess themselves entangled with domestic staff members in kin-like relationships. These extend through staff members' individual lifespans, and vertically and horizontally across staff members' own kinship networks. The multi-generational ties are important to my interlocutors, who play up the fact that their employees have been "part of the family" or "in the family" for a long time, sometimes across several generations. They would press stories of a cook, gardener, or houseman who had been "passed" or "handed" down from parents to children over the decades on me. To them, the generational braiding of lives may feel like a kind of redemptive hybridity, one they are unlikely to achieve through intermarriage. It might not be far-fetched to suggest, in fact, that these claims of fictive kinship are also claims at some subterranean level of what might be called "fictive autochthony." White Kenyans will never have the primordial time depth on the land of "first comers,"[75] but to boast about the depth and breadth of one's fictive kinship ties in Kenya is to assert roots, even if shallow ones.

And what do employees say about white Kenyan employers from former settler families? How do they perceive them, and do they feel they have a "family" relationship?[76] A full treatment of these questions requires a different kind of research study from my own. However, seeking at least a provisional sense of staff perspectives, I enlisted a Giriama research assistant to conduct ten interviews in Kiswahili or Kigiriama with Kenyans (one Kamba, three Luo, and six Giriama individuals) who have worked at length in the homes of former settler families. Nearly all of them said their employers were organized, punctual, and highly rule-governed (sometimes "strict") in their expectations. A few contrasted their *mzungu* (white) employers with elite African and Asian employers, and—in keeping with white Kenyans' own stereotypes— indicated they preferred to work for whites because they felt they were less likely to be physically or financially abused.[77] But the pay from white Kenyans, they agreed, is low, and while several noted that their employers had an "urge to help" with soft loans and emergency money, some indicated they had to make a strong case "with evidence and facts," as one man put it, to extract such assistance. When they received aid, employees appreciated the sense of a social safety net, remarking that there are advantages to being employed by the same family over the long term.

But when asked if they felt like part of their employer's family, their responses complicated white Kenyans' understanding. (Kiswahili has several words for "family": *jamii* and *jamaa* refer loosely to many kinds of kin and communal relationships; *familia,* the term my research assistant used, is a direct translation of the English word and has similar connotations.) Only one respondent, now retired, offered an unqualified assent: "I surely felt part of their family. They really took care of me." Another noted that it "depends on the person you're working for," and said that in her best employment situation, "my employer tried so much to make me feel like part of the family, but when the rest of their friends were there I had to keep my distance." The rest of the respondents demurred entirely. "No, from day one the relationship remained official," said one. "No," said another, "never. They never share conversation or meals with you." Said a third: "They have a way of treating you so nicely when they mean it, but you will never feel like part of their family." She added that white Kenyans perceive potential African partners, female or male, as "gold-diggers," saying keenly in Giriama: "Kamazhala mwana mwiru bule [They do not give birth to black babies]." With this observation, she brings us bluntly back to that limit of most white Kenyans I spoke to; namely, romantic commitments to Africans. For although white Kenyans cement what they say are family alliances with their servants though an engine of financial dependency, most reject marriage with black Kenyans in part because, in European ideologies, romantic kinship alliances are meant to be free of material motives and material asymmetry—ideally, anyway, if not in fact (Cole and Thomas 2009). In light of the daunting hierarchy between them, and the feeling that they are held at arm's length this way, it is not clear that all employees can embrace the same bonds of kinship that white employers imagine.

White Kenyans' own narratives about staff also offer clues to the limits of their intimacy. Grace, for instance, recounts a story about a former domestic staff member that could be read as a sign of the man's lack of emotional attachment to the family, though she interprets it in the opposite way: "My old Kikuyu [servant] . . . never stole a thing, not a thing, not a thing, and we had him for twenty odd years. When we were leaving, he started to steal. And that is because—and I was so *hurt,* and then I really realized it was because he felt that his loyalty to us was gone because we were abandoning him . . . he really was so much part of the family, and it was *such* a shock to him."

Grace understands her staff member's thievery not in terms of pragmatics or economics—with the family's departure, the threat of termination was no longer a deterrent from stealing—but rather in terms of the special kin-like bond between employer and servant, which she believes he felt had been violated. For Grace, the betrayal initially presented a puzzle: how could the rights and obligations of kinship be so suddenly ruptured? They probably could not, of course, unless they did not feel entirely kin-like for all players to begin with.[78] Grace's own language, furthermore, betrays the fact that she locates her former servant somewhere between kin and a possession: "When we had him, he became part of the family—the children still talk about him, and they had him right up until we sold our house."

In Devon's narrative, too, we see a boundary to Wanjiru's entitlements, evident in an event that Devon facetiously called "one of the most horrible things I've ever seen in my life." Devon's son married a Jewish-American woman who failed to grasp the complex force field of intimacy and distance that shapes Kenyan master-servant relationships. The daughter in law, he says, "actually kissed my cook goodbye on one occasion when she was out here. Poor cook nearly died. *I* nearly died. I know the cook was *mortified.* He was *speechless* for the rest of the day. *I* was *speechless* for the rest of the day." Wanjiru, it seems, is "with the family" but not wholly "of" the family—and Wanjiru himself (according to Devon, anyway) appears to recognize these limits.

Settler descendants want to belong. They don't want to be seen as colonial racists or as spoiled and unhelpful elites. Many say they embrace a multicultural Kenya, and younger white Kenyans in particular seem to strive for affable, mutual connections with black Kenyans. But in this longing, there are still strains of distance, denial, and structural oblivion.

They wish to integrate, but most balk at interracial romance; they would love to see the country united, but concede the temptation to self-segregate along "cultural" lines; they want to be loved by their domestic staff, but they secure affection through a structure of economic dependency, sometimes obscured by their own good feelings. In claiming that they are "family," my interlocutors may hope to put down their roots in the place they love, but the types of intimacy they establish with black Kenyans still seem limited. Although their intimate patronage of domestic staff, for instance, does integrate whites into Kenyan life in a fashion, particularly since staff members are culturally familiar with the dependencies that arise from patron-client relationships,[79] their patronage rests on a symbolically problematic hierarchy that can exacerbate the ongoing resentment of whites' socioeconomic superiority. To hearken back to Christine Nicholl's words, these relationships might be said to be "doomed" in a sense because of their paternalism, particularly in the post-Independence era, when whites wish to be embraced. Furthermore, arguably, settler descendants' insistence on an economic structure that keeps staff members coming back cap in hand may slow staff participation in the financial independence aligned with the "development" so many white Kenyans say they champion.

A conversation with Jonathan and his British-born wife, Corinna, summarizes some of the dynamics I aspire to capture here, and the intimation of possible change. Speaking about white Kenyan servant relationships, Jonathan says: "We chug along on a road that is most comfortable to all involved." Their relationship with their staff, he explains, goes back many years, and is one of "*total* commitment to their welfare. Which is reciprocated by a total commitment to *our* welfare from them." If his staff need anything, he says, they'll come to him to ask. But, he says, "If we were to ask them to come sit down and have a cup of tea with us it would be *totally* unnatural and uncomfortable."

Corinna broke in abruptly: "But that's 'cause we've never done it. I mean, there are people who start off that way, who want their driver to sit with them, have lunch with them. Expatriates." Jonathan looked a little taken aback, and opined, "And it results in a very uneasy sort of . . . "

Corinna interrupted again. "Well, not necessarily. Because," she said, turning to Jonathan with a loving but firm tone: "You're very set in your ways, but there are people who do it differently."

5

Linguistic Atonement

When the filing of the second charge of murder against Tom Cholmondeley dominated the headlines after 2006 (see chapter 3), his reputation as a killer of indigent Africans was so toxic that most settler descendants tried to distance themselves from him. Yet he also had a nucleus of supporters who rallied to defend his character. The *New York Times,* for instance, reported that although some people living near his ranch branded him hot-tempered, Cholmondeley's "white friends" described him as "much different: charming, genuine, a good listener, a father involved with his two sons, the type of rancher to speak Swahili to his workers and look them in the eye."[1] Taking the claim further, a couple of friends of his informed me eagerly that he was "studying Kikuyu" while on remand—an overstatement, as Cholmondeley himself would later inform me, but a telling rumor given that the deceased man in the second case, Robert Njoya, was himself Kikuyu. These claims drew on an assumption that circulates widely among today's settler descendants; namely, that there is a link between their competence in African languages and their ability to treat Africans humanely.

We have seen why white Kenyans today might feel insecure about how welcome they are in Kenya. Many families that stayed after Independence insist they love the country, but in the past decade they have suffered from bad publicity, which repeatedly evoked the evils of colonialism. Some, in Laikipia, have been asked (unsuccessfully) to do penance in the form of land redistribution; Cholmondeley's incarceration, meanwhile,

felt a bit like a punishment for settler history. And there are psychological and social barriers to settler descendants' full integration, including
their own mixed feelings. They struggle to feel like cultural citizens,
particularly when their race suggests their lack of autochthony; their
privilege means that most don't relate to the difficulties of the "man on
the street"; and their patterns of socializing and marrying, for most,
include a noticeable degree of self-segregation. The comments surrounding Cholmondeley and his language, then, are not merely characterizations of a man in an exceptional bind. They speak to sweeping matters
of national belonging among white elites in contemporary Kenya. In
fact, white Kenyan aspirations and anxieties are at the heart of what
they say about language—particularly Kiswahili, Kenya's national language and lingua franca. (*Ki-* is a Bantu prefix indicating a language
variety: "Swahili" and "Kiswahili" designate the same language; "Swahili" is the anglicized name for it.)

A key component of nationalism among settler descendants is a shift
from colonial disparagement of Kiswahili to a more congenial attitude
toward it, particularly among younger generations.[2] Public interracial
romance is still frowned on in the settler descendant community, and
the use of African languages seems to offer a safe symbolic version of
social intimacy. Many of my younger white Kenyan respondents talk
about Kiswahili with an attitude I call "linguistic atonement"; a stance
of enthusiastic feeling about African languages, pitched as if to mitigate
a history of colonial discrimination. Part of linguistic atonement is the
hope that Kiswahili might help them achieve a sort of "connection," a
mutual sympathy of sorts, with Kenya's majority, while signaling their
eagerness to be part of the nation. Some add that Kiswahili feels good
to speak, opening expressive possibilities of warmth, candor, and philosophical equanimity that, in their account, are more sealed off to them
when they are in a more European (for some, "English") mode of personhood. For some settler descendants, then, linguistic atonement
amounts to a symbolic and emotional corrective to the condescension
of their predecessors. But while their linguistic attitudes seem to reach
for reconciliation—the mending of pathological colonial relationships—
I also suggest that these amends are limited. Linguistic hierarchies
remain, tenacious, not only among white Kenyans but among *all* Kenyans, and in their talk about language varieties, my respondents again
seem hampered by structural oblivion, largely unaware of the ways in
which their own language ideologies continue to support a structure
that privileges them.

Before I pursue this argument further, it is vital to offer a bit of history about colonialism and language in Kenya. When Cholmondeley's friends touted his African language abilities, they were suggesting he didn't have the attitudes one would expect from someone with an uber-colonial heritage. As a rule of thumb, colonial settlers all over Africa were disdainful of the languages they encountered there.[3] For those in East Africa, for example, it didn't matter that Kiswahili had a venerable history. The language (really, a cluster of related language varieties) is based largely on Bantu grammar and a vocabulary derived from Bantu, Arabic, and other Indian Ocean languages. For centuries it had been the vernacular for many denizens of the East African coast, and it had extensive literary, poetic, and Islamic traditions. The language had also been carried into the interior by Arab trade routes, and pidgin forms of it had become a widespread lingua franca. But despite Kiswahili's cosmopolitan past, negative associations with the language were rife among newcomers. Mungai Mutonya and Timothy Parsons summarize attitudes in the 1930s: "colonial settlers (both British and Asian) and military officers considered Kiswahili to be a low prestige language necessary only for facilitating basic communication with their African subordinates."[4] Wilfred Whiteley, who spent time in Kenya and Tanganyika in the 1940s in the British Army and went back in the 1950s to do linguistic research, also notes that Europeans in East Africa saw Kiswahili as inferior to "proper" language, having, some suggested, neither literature nor "grammar."[5]

Around the 1930s, colonial officials in East Africa decided to fix a "standard" Kiswahili for administrative purposes, based on the dialect spoken on Zanzibar Island, an economic hub at the time.[6] Officials training for colonial service, then, studied this rigid and formal grammar and vocabulary at Oxford or Cambridge before heading over for their postings—where they often found their constituents didn't speak this version of Kiswahili anyway. Many early missionaries also used Kiswahili because it was associated with another Abrahamic religion, Islam, which they felt was at least a shade closer to Christianity than "paganism." Others preferred to preach in local tongues to reach hearts and minds.[7] Some colonials thus learned Kiswahili and other vernaculars with impressive facility—well enough to preach, to command and organize large numbers of workers, and, in the Mau Mau era, to direct the home guard or interrogate insurgents.[8] But despite its utility, Kiswahili remained "a means of reaching down to people, rather than of enabling them to reach up to the administration."[9] Some officials, furthermore, doubted that ordinary Africans had the "intellectual capabilities" to grasp the grammatical complexities of the standard version.[10] Ironically, though colonials themselves had fixed the standard version, many Europeans in Kenya persuaded themselves they could disregard it—partly because so few Kenyans spoke it to begin with, and partly out of sheer condescension.

Many settlers spoke a simplified "secondary pidgin" version of the pidgin Kiswahili used by upcountry people.[11] However, many others barely attempted to learn even the most rudimentary versions of this language, which colonials and their subjects alike called "kitchen Kiswahili," since whites used it mostly to communicate with domestic staff.[12] It was also known as "Kisettla," referencing the sociopolitical role rather than the ethnicity of the speakers. Unlike other African languages, it was used uni-directionally (perhaps the only other such designation was "Kihindi," the cluster of pidgin strategies used by Asian employers with their own staff). This version of Kiswahili was not merely nonstandard (after all, plenty of upcountry Africans were fluent in nonstandard Kiswahili) but "broken," revealing the speaker's discomfort and uncertainty in using it.[13] In his summary of dozens of British settlers' memoirs, Dane Kennedy describes them as "rife with stories of servants who bungled jobs because they failed to comprehend their masters' instruction [in Kiswahili]—and often received a beating in recompense."[14] Meanwhile, the colonial administration did not encourage Africans to learn English, despite a good deal of African enthusiasm to do so, out of anxiety that learning English suggested ambition above one's rank.[15] (The same dynamic apparently obtained in colonial Rhodesia and to some extent in postcolonial Zimbabwe, where farm workers who spoke English to white managers were seen as "uppity.")[16]

Settlers did sometimes lace their writings, and presumably their speech, with the occasional Kiswahili word. In his reading of settler writings from the early twentieth century, Brett Shadle finds settlers favoring certain Kiswahili borrowings, especially *shamba* ("farm"), *toto* (an attenuated version of "child"), especially "kitchen *toto*" (a child or young person working as a servant in the kitchen), *panga* ("knife"), *ayah* ("nanny"), *bwana* ("Mr." or "Sir"), *bibi* ("Ms." or "Madam"), *dogo* (an attenuated version of "small"), *kubwa* ("large," also attenuated), and *baya* ("bad," also attenuated). In most cases, he reports, adjectives were used ungrammatically, without matching the relevant noun class. Shadle speculates that when used in writing for European audiences, such borrowings were a means of "claiming exoticism," but when used in East African newspapers, they may have functioned "to emphasize their sense of being a colonial people."[17] Kiswahili has long been used by whites, then, as a marker of locality and perhaps belonging, but the broader context of its use in the colonial era must be understood. It was a language used to mark one's presence in East Africa, to be sure, but it was also a language primarily of domination.

The use of Kiswahili for command and control is plain in *Up-Country Swahili Exercises: For the Settler, Miner, Merchant and Their Wives, and for All Who Deal with Up-Country Natives Without Interpreters* (1936) by F. H. Le Breton, a practically minded upcountry resident.[18] Like language textbooks we see today, the book includes translation exercises for the student. What strikes the contemporary reader is the casual disparagement in these passages, which seem designed to remind arrivistes of the attitude they should strike when speaking to "the natives." Take the following exercises, which ventriloquize directives settlers would issue to their servants:

> Take those shoes off the bed . . . Clean my boots at once! . . . You must fasten every button . . . Bring three cups . . . Bring food immediately.
>
> You have got the knife, boy? No sir, you have. No! I have not got it!
>
> Boy, get my bath water ready and don't put in as much hot water as you did yesterday. I like it hot but not too hot.
>
> Boy, my razor is spoilt. It will not cut even a little. I know you have used it to shave your head, and my scissors likewise, they are still dirty with your black hairs.[19]

The racial hierarchy in these examples fairly leaps from the page, down to the classic evocation of the polluting other, as well as the settler's insistence, even in these hypothetical conversations, upon having the last word. But condescension was evident not only in *what* was said but also *how* it was said; in the very structure of the way the language was used. Although Le Breton purports merely to capture the simplifications of upcountry language, for example, he also emphasizes that settlers need not exert themselves to learn "the intricacies of correct Swahili."[20] In keeping with this, scholarly descriptions of Kisettla explain that settlers tended to anglicize grammatical sequencing; to disregard obligatory subject affixes and replace them with personal pronouns; to radically simplify noun classes and their agreements; to shift adverbial forms to adjectival ones; and to simplify verb tenses, relative pronouns, and object markers by omitting morphemes in this agglutinative language.[21] So, for instance, while coastal or standard Kiswahili would use prefixes and infixes for a sentence such as "Nilimpatia chakula" (I got food for him), Kisettla would simplify verbs, leave out morphemes, and use free-standing pronouns to get the idea across: "Mimi napata yeye chakula" (I/me -get him food). Kisettla also tended to negativize verbs with the term for "no," *hapana*. Instead of "Sitaanguka" (I will not fall), Kisettla would use "Mimi hapana anguka," which can be roughly glossed as "Me no -fall."[22] To any ear accustomed to standard Swahili, these sound appallingly clunky. Le Breton was right, of course: many upcountry Kenyans already cut corners in Kiswahili, particularly when it comes to noun classes and infixes,[23] but when one considers Kisettla's grammatical and lexical anglicizations—to the point of a hybrid sentence like "Tia *[-put] scones* ndani *[in] oven and* lete chai *[-bring tea] pot*"[24]—one can see why the linguist Dell Hymes referred to Kisettla as "the most aberrant variety of Swahili pidgins."[25] Most important for my purposes is that Kisettla embodied, in the phrasing of the Kenyan linguist John Mugane, "a state of mind"; a willfully belittling stance.[26] Settlers' nonstandard versions of Kiswahili, then, weren't typically a means of fitting in with upcountry Kenyans. Their choppiness and lack of fluency showed a certain indifference to the language and its speakers.

The depredations of Kisettla were the subject of a tongue-in-cheek 1930s pamphlet penned by one settler who, probably not wanting to incur the wrath of his peers, refused to be identified by anything but his initials, "J. W." He sums up the differences between Kisettla and standard Kiswahili with the following distinction: "KiSettla or *mimi kupiga wewe* [lit., 'I to-hit you'] Swahili is believed to be derived from KiSwahili or *watu wale wawili walipokuja* [lit., 'when those two people came'] Swahili."[27] In these droll labels, the first language variety is wielded in the service of brute physical domination, while the second comes across as a medium of neutral conversation. These hierarchies are reflected in the care given to grammar in each case; Kisettla transparently disregards verb conjugations, whereas "Kiswahili Swahili" not only conjugates verbs but (unlike Kisettla generally) shows careful concordance with one of Kiswahili's sixteen noun classes. While the four repetitions of the prefix *wa-* are technically correct, they must have across as unnecessarily flowery and mildly amusing to the settler readers so used to driving home their messages without syntactic fanfare.

J. W. goes on to advise the new settler in his communications with Africans: "Never hesitate; you are the Big Noise. It's wonderful how the missing word will spring to your lips. . . . If you are not at first understood, shout. If the native addressed still refuses to comprehend, it is mere contumacy and, for the sake of your superior intelligence, should be treated as such. Remember, it is his own language that you are condescending to speak to him."[28]

The "Big Noise"—domineering talk personified—did not need to be concerned with the grammatical structures of Kiswahili. If the linguistic hash that resulted failed to communicate, mere volume would pound home the message. Examining the Kiswahili pidgin spoken in the East African military, Mungai Mutonya and T. H. Parsons conclude, too, that "conversations between colonial authorities and African auxiliaries were authoritarian, limited, and often garbled."[29] For many settlers and authorities, then, Kiswahili was something one condescended, rather than aspired, to speak.

A recent conversation with Richard Leakey reveals that the offenses of Kisettla are still on the radar of Kenya's political elite. Leakey, who has spent nearly half his life embedded in Kenyan politics, remarks: "In the circles I'm in, a lot of the leadership of Kenya [government], when you're letting your hair down and making a joke about something you will often mimic the settler Swahili. Many Africans will parody and make a point of criticism by reverting to settler Swahili. When they're discussing something in a pejorative way, they don't like someone's attitude, they make a joke using exactly those sorts of phrases."

Leakey couldn't come up with an example, but when I suggested "Lete tatu *bottles* na hapana *take the tops off [Bring bottles three and no take the tops off]*," he was emphatic: "*Exactly.* I've heard it many times, these parodies of settlers." The group that most clearly represents Kenya's triumph over British sovereignty still remembers (and has reappropriated) the condescension in settler language. No wonder it was so important for Cholmondeley's friends to clarify that he not only speaks Kiswahili but also, simultaneously, "looks his workers in the eye."

SINCE INDEPENDENCE: NATIONALISM AND "CONNECTED" PERSONHOOD

Today, most settler descendants I spoke to aged about fifty and younger no longer blare with confidence as the Big Noise. As we have seen in preceding chapters, white families in Kenya have had to amend their relationship with black Kenyans over the decades. They have (mostly) come to grips with the handover of political power to African elites, and they now work alongside an accomplished and educated African and Asian middle class. They say they mean well, they wish to belong to and contribute to Kenya, and they wish to connect more with Africans, but such connections are vexed by layers of complexity and ambiguity. They don't look autochthonous in Kenya, their families were on the "wrong" side of Kenyan history, their marriage patterns and dinner parties remain largely white, and in light of some recent objections to their privilege as settler descendants, they sometimes doubt that they are fully accepted as cultural citizens. Many experience some version of moral double consciousness, in which they both defend their entitlement to belong and wonder whether they are so entitled.

Language can be a useful symbolic tool for a white person hoping to belong to an African nation. In the 1990s, for instance, one middle-aged white Zimbabwean man, anxious about his future citizenship in the country, told J. L. Fisher "I've been desperately trying to learn Shona, to know what people are saying around me . . . it's ridiculous that we were taught Afrikaans at school."[30] Contemporary reports about white Zimbabwean farmers exiled from their land sometimes note that the farmer speaks "fluent Shona," with the subtext that their wish to belong in Zimbabwe is sincere.[31] Such reports seem an effort to counterbalance white Zimbabweans' linguistic history, in which many settlers did not learn Zimbabwean languages or their (immigrant) workers' vernaculars, but instead sometimes addressed farmworkers in chiLapalapa, a command language that emerged from South African farms and mines.[32]

In South Africa, language politics among whites have been largely dominated by white Afrikaans-speakers' anxiety that their language has been marginalized by English and putatively contaminated by the nonstandard versions spoken by "Coloureds."[33] But some whites who grew up in South Africa, such as an elderly man described by Fisher who moved from South Africa to Zimbabwe, have come to value black African languages. He alludes nostalgically to "squatting down with the old men, talking in Ndau [a Shona dialect]", and says that when he travels to Australia, he misses isiXhosa so much he talks to himself in the tongue. "My heart bleeds for Africa," he adds, and adamantly, repeatedly refers to himself as a "white African."[34] Indeed, self-professed liberal whites in South Africa treat fluency in a Bantu language as a signal of important social contact with black South Africans, and—more important—an index of feeling. For this reason, Helen Zille, current premier of the Western Cape province and former leader of South Africa's opposition party, the Democratic Alliance, speaks isiXhosa, and has famously urged all white members of her party to learn an indigenous African language. Zille told a BBC journalist, "Of course it's not enough . . . [but] what we have to do is show people across lines of ethnicity and race that we really care for each other."[35] Meanwhile, youtube home videos of white toddlers speaking isiXhosa elicit mingled responses from native isiXhosa and isiZulu speakers, ranging from cynical ("Must we now we celebrate just because a son of racist can speak Xhosa?") to enthusiastic (e.g., "I like him," and even "That's our next president").[36] Though African responses to these white efforts may be mixed, it does seem that many white citizens across Africa consider speaking African languages important to their performance of belonging.[37]

For a person like Richard Leakey, too, who sets himself apart from settler descendants, language signifies the depth of his involvement in Kenyan society. To a journalist, Leakey touts his daughters as "real Kenyans" by noting that they attended a government school as part of a tiny white minority, and adding that they "speak perfect Swahili."[38] In conversation with me, Leakey elaborated the importance of language in his life, underscoring that he sees himself as an exception: "In my case and my brother's [his brother Phillip has also served as a member of Parliament], I speak Kiswahili I would think two-thirds of my time every day. In business, at home, with big people, little people, [as] head of the civil service, secretary of the cabinet . . . I would generally address the president in our discussions in Swahili. It's easier to communicate and make nuanced jokes in Swahili, which we're both more comfortable in. But so few white Kenyans would do this. And yet they *want* to."

Leakey is right; they do want to, but precious few would use the language for two-thirds of the day. That said, he may be downplaying the extent to which some settler descendants have cultivated the language in recent decades. It's true that there are some younger whites who don't speak it well, but those I spoke to tell me they are embarrassed about this (especially in the face of two-year wonders who have studied the language extensively). And many born since Independence speak standard, near-standard, or nonstandard Kiswahili pretty comfortably, and some, quite fluently indeed. I've heard younger white Kenyans having extended conversations in Kiswahili with the hostess at a restaurant in Nairobi, a car mechanic in Thika, and assistants working for a conservation-related beach cleanup, without the clumsy improvisations or anglicizations documented among early settlers. Typically, I witnessed these interchanges when my recording device was off, but occasionally I jotted translations into my field notes to capture the inter-active dynamics. On one occasion, for example, a thirty-something safari guide I shall call James here[39] approached the front desk of a social club and leaned against its varnished surface to greet a younger staff member with "Mambo, *boss*—vipi? (Hey, boss man, what's up?)," to which the reply was "Fiti," a Swahilization of the English word "fit," slang for "I'm well, I'm sound." "Lete stori! [Tell me something!]," James said in playful slang, but before the younger man could reply he turned and addressed the oldest staff member, an assistant manager, in nearly effortless Kiswahili. My field notes capture James's affability: "So, listen, *mzee* [a respect term designating an older or esteemed man], last time I came in there was this German couple—did you see them? They had so much mud on their headlights nobody could see them when they pulled their car out at night, and then they almost hit my dog and they didn't even stop or turn back—and then they just roared out of the gate. Did you hear about it? Who are those guys? Have they been coming around here much? I think I need to have a talk with them."

The assistant manager responded politely to James' indignation, and told him whatever he knew about the expatriate couple. James didn't cleave to high formality in his Kiswahili (he deleted a few infixes and fudged some noun classes), but aside from groping momentarily as he referred to the vehicle's headlights ("zile, zileee . . . taa za gari"), he seemed perfectly comfortable in the medium, and didn't resort to angli-cizations, except for "boss" and *stori,* which are borrowings Kenyans routinely use anyway. I noticed similar patterns when my recording device picked up white Kenyans speaking Kiswahili during my sit-down conversations with them. For instance, during a discussion with Mar-cus, a second-generation white Kenyan born in the mid 1950s and now working in the coffee industry, he broke off several times to address his driver:

I was at university in South Africa. Hang on; lemme speak to this guy. Uh, Peter? [Marcus says Peter's name the East African way—"Peetah," as opposed to a more British pronunciation, "Peetu(r)h"—and then begins to speaks in Kiswahili very rapidly.] *Hiyo gari nimeona imefika lakini ni mtu nimekubali kuongea na mimi* [I saw the car arrived, but there's a person I've agreed to converse with]. [Marcus gestures toward me.]—*Ile rafiki yangu* [This one's my friend]. [Peter and I exchange greetings in Swahili.] Um, so, *wakati atapigia halafu tunaweza fanya ile pran yetu. Kwa hivyo ngojea ile dereva hapa hapa, na wakati anarudi, mwambie anatoka barabara* [unintel-ligible] *Kikuyu. Na hawa wanajua hiyo gari yako* [Um, so, when he calls, then we can take care of our plan [*pran* sounds like a Kikuyu pronunciation of this loan word]. So wait for that driver here, and when he comes back, tell him he should go to the main road [unintelligible] Kikuyu. And they'll recognize your car]. Where were we?

Marcus speaks Kiswahili faster than he speaks English, and while there are nonstandard formulations in his phrasing, this is very comfortable and familiar use of the language. Granted, he is still using it to give orders to an employee, but his speed and facility suggest some settler descendants have come a long way from the "me no fall" Kiswahili of some of their forebears.

Many of my respondents also engage in rapid code-switching, sprinkling their English with Kiswahili words or phrases, such as this white Kenyan café owner in her fifties, addressing her employee: "Judy, *tafadhali* [please] can I have a, a um a tuna? *Stima amerudi?* [Has the electricity come back on?]"(Note that the speaker marks *stima*, electricity, with the wrong noun class, using the indexical verb prefix *a* instead of *i*, but correctly uses the present perfect tense *-me-*.) A young entrepreneur to a shopkeeper, discussing a leather bag: "Yes, I'd love to have a look at the red one, soooo, *nitarudi Jumatano kuangalia* [I'll be back Wednesday to have a look]." Some use Kiswahili for opening and closing routines; a safari guide answering a mobile phone call from one of his employees, for instance, says: "Hullo? Hullo? *Habari yako? Ndio* [How are you? Yes]. Okay I'm not there at the moment; I'm planning ahead to go to town so I won't be there until at least 2:30, 3. Okay. Okay. *Sawa, tutaonana* [Okay, see you later]." In conversation with one another white Kenyans may insert Kiswahili terms here and there: "Shall we go get some *chakula* [food]," or "That *kali* [harsh, fierce] woman will never keep her friends." Some use more rarified, playful vocabulary, such as the middle-aged white Kenyan woman speaking on the telephone in English to a white CEO about her horses and saying: "Flash is a bit *goigoi* [lazy] because—Flash is being *goigoi* with his feet." These examples are terribly ordinary, and in themselves they don't much differentiate white Kenyans from other cosmopolitan Kenyans who code-switch—indeed, that is part of my point.[40] These examples may move between English and Kiswahili, as Kisettla did, but many of them do not seem designed to pull rank so much as express solidarity and identity. Kiswahili has become folded nonchalantly into white Kenyan identity in new ways since the era of Kisettla, even as many younger white Kenyans have aspired to be folded into Kenya's own identity.[41]

What prompted this general shift from an aversion to Kiswahili (on the part of many settlers, anyway) to an embrace of it? To contextualize this change, it is important to note how large English looms in Kenya. By around the 1920s the colonial administration expressed its long-standing concern that Africans who learned English well would refuse menial labor.[42] After World War II, however, they succumbed to a new anxiety that Kiswahili might be used to stoke African nationalist movements. Their policies, then, shifted to promote English while expunging Kiswahili from most school and bureaucratic contexts. In the years after Kenya's independence in 1963, African nationalists embraced both languages; Kiswahili was decreed the national language in 1974, and English remained important as part of "the wider demand for equality of opportunity."[43] Kiswahili became a required subject through secondary school starting in the early 1980s, and although public servants are allowed to serve in English or Kiswahili (both of them counting as "official languages"), Kiswahili still plays the role of the lower code, for English is also required in school *and* stands as the language of higher education, white-collar work, and political prestige.[44] In a colonial holdover now reinforced by global linguistic politics, high court proceedings and parliamentary deliberations are conducted primarily in English, most national newspapers are written in the language, and anyone dealing with international commerce, politics, technology, or academia must know it well.[45] English has also been incorporated into many Kenyans' lives and identities; it is extremely common in urban settings such as Nairobi, and some elite families with inter-ethnic marriages use it as a first language at home.[46] The varieties of English spoken by the many ethnic and regional groups in Kenya have distinct subnational forms of pronunciation and their own grammatical idioms and idiosyncrasies.[47]

In Kenya's linguistic landscape, then, English is the paramount language of education, wealth, and cosmopolitanism,[48] while Kiswahili is seen by most as a lingua franca with a nationalist flavor. Roughly 65 percent of Kenya's population speaks some variety of Kiswahili, primarily as a second or third language, since the coastal Swahili people who speak it as a first language are a small minority.[49] Mastery of standard Kiswahili is a sign of education, but more typically, speakers learn non-standard versions of the tongue through inter-ethnic communication. Young urban Kenyans often use a rapidly shifting Kiswahili-English (and indeed multilingual) hybrid form known as "Sheng"—a growing locus of creativity, if an unsettling one for older generations.[50] Although nonstandard Kiswahili is common, and often well received, some black Kenyans express embarrassment about using nonstandard dialects, and the Kenyan press has sometimes castigated upcountry people for their "bad" Kiswahili.[51] A Nairobi-based lawyer who speaks flawless English told me she and her friends felt that "improving" their Kiswahili would be a mark of Afrocentric and national pride.

Regardless of how it's spoken, Kiswahili can provide a means of transcending the potential ethnic obligations or tensions aroused by the so-called tribal vernaculars.[52] Kenya is home to dozens of these, including Kikuyu, Kijaluo, Maa, and Kigiriama (exactly how many depends on how they are counted). Such "mother tongues" are widely spoken— some speakers, indeed, are monolingual—but in institutional contexts, ethnically linked languages are marginalized, treated as parochial and potentially divisive.[53] In light of Kenya's periodic flare-ups in which politicians pit ethnic groups against one another, Kiswahili has become especially important for indexing nationalist neutrality.[54] Still, when one considers Kenya's commercial, political, and educational landscape, English is the language of highest prestige.

There's an irony, then, in the language politics among white Kenyans vis-à-vis other Kenyans. At the same time that English language education has become more prevalent among and important to the Kenyan middle class as they seek upward mobility (sometimes on a global stage), competence in Kiswahili has become more important to white Kenyans as they grapple with moral double consciousness and seek a means to signal their belonging to Kenya. And they are right to think that Kiswahili is crucial to the way other Kenyans judge them. My conversations with black Kenyans about white Kenyan linguistic competence revealed a breadth of perspectives, often pegged to their wider opinions of white Kenyans, but language recurrently seems important to perceived national allegiance. One restaurant worker from the coast, who has had positive interactions with white Kenyan patrons, claims that "Most of the white Kenyans speak better Kiswahili than our own leaders"—a compliment to white Kenyans, at the expense of Kenyan politicians, who are often the targets of public cynicism. Another individual, who works in a social club frequented by settler descendants in Nairobi, has a mixed view, saying: "Some are very good in Kiswahili, and some not." A third respondent, from Taita-Taveta, indicates the Kiswahili she has heard from former settler families is "not very good," while adding that her white Kenyan employers did not treat her with any particular warmth. Perceptions of white Kenyan Kiswahili abilities vary, but what endures is the judgment that speaking Kiswahili comfortably—not necessarily the standard, but some version of the language—is of social, even moral, importance to cultural citizenship. As I discuss below, some black Kenyans feel patronized when whites address them in Kiswahili, but nevertheless, they would likely agree that the ability to speak the language is an important marker of being Kenyan.

Witness the public attitudes toward a young member of an established white Kenyan family, Jason Dunford, who competed in the 2008 and 2012 Olympics as a member of Kenya's swimming team (as mentioned in chapter 1), posting a new record in 2008 for the 100-meter butterfly. Dunford's relatives told me of his pride in appearing for Kenya on an international stage, but Kenyan bloggers on one sports-related web site were surprised that a white man could have represented their nation in the Olympics and cynical about the subject. Wrote one skeptic: "I bet he doesn't speak a word of Swahili . . . ok maybe one or two but not fluent."[55] In fact, Dunford was a Swahili minor at Stanford University at the time—a fact that probably confirms both that he was not fluent in the standard form (though he must have picked up some Kiswahili during his Kenyan childhood) *and* that he was invested in learning it well. But the bloggers' remarks signal that white Kenyans' race codes them as interlopers, and they need any linguistic advantages they can get to establish their legitimacy as part of the nation. No wonder younger white Kenyans have gone from seeing Kiswahili as a language of command, to prizing command of the language.[56]

If good Kenyan citizens are meant to show affiliation to the national unit through language, this places the most elderly of white Kenyans in an awkward position if they never learned Kiswahili well. These men and women came of age in the crucible of colonial racism, but now they're mindful of the stigma attaching to the colonial past, perhaps especially in my presence. Some elderly white Kenyans expressed embarrassment about their language abilities, conceding that the younger generations are far more comfortable with—in the words of several elderly informants—"the African," and correspondingly more adept with African languages. But although they considered themselves too far gone, too set in their ways, to have gained any additional fluency themselves, I was tantalized to encounter the same rationalization of their linguistic limitations in two elderly former settlers of British descent (to whom I spoke independently of one another). According to them, Britons have difficulty learning Kiswahili simply because British and African languages and cultures are so intrinsically different. By contrast, they both said, certain other Europeans, particularly the Italian expatriates who populate the Kenya coast, learn Kiswahili more easily, because both their cultures and their languages are similar. In a classic maneuver familiar to scholars of language ideology, language here is treated as iconic of (resembling) various qualities of the speakers.[57] Not coincidentally, many white Kenyans regard Italians as especially permeable to African influence, and not usually in a flattering way; they construe Italians as more emotive, more dramatic, and more corrupt; more willing to engage in the kind of bargaining that characterizes local commerce; more willing to entertain interracial romance; and more susceptible to occult practices and witchcraft than themselves. To some elderly white Kenyans, then, their limitations in Kiswahili did not emerge primarily from a racist social and political arrangement, but rather from a dispositional and cultural chasm between Briton and African, and a corresponding one between English and Kiswahili. They aren't personally to blame for Kisettla, in this view, and neither are colonial politics.

Younger white Kenyans, of course, are jumpy about being aligned with old colonial narratives. Some even fret that the very way they speak English could mark them as disdainful and self-segregated. Their accents aren't identical from one person to the next—their families have different class backgrounds; some have traces of influence from continental Europe; some have spent more time in Britain than others; some have more white South African friendships than others; and so forth. Thomas Hoffmann nonetheless found the accents of a sample of white Kenyan adults and children from multigenerational families in Nairobi and Gilgil to be strongly grounded in RP, or "Received Pronunciation," spoken primarily by the upper class in the south of England. These Kenyans' pronunciation of words such as "cloth" reflected a particularly archaic, "conservative" version of RP, which he suggests was inherited from the upper-class settlers of a century ago. Hoffmann interprets this linguistic pattern in terms of the enduring forms of self-segregation I discuss in the preceding chapter.[58] These white Kenyans' speech reflects their extensive schooling, socializing, dating, and intermarriage with others of European extraction, notwithstanding their black African caretakers and playmates when young and colleagues when grown.[59]

And in the wake of the Cholmondeley scandals, when all settler descendants seemed at risk of being convicted of being colonial fossils, white Kenyan English accents were used against them.[60] Journalists in particular, clustering around Cholmondeley's social set when looking for anecdotes and quotes, charged that settler descendants speak in an aristocratic British accent (often considered by outsiders as the "most British" of British accents) that supposedly directly mirrors their social distance from Kenyans of other backgrounds. Jonathan Clayton, reporting about racial tension and the Cholmondeley incident in the *Times,* writes that "most [settler descendants] still speak in loud upper-class accents." Volume, of course, isn't a property of accents, but Clayton was probably trying to point to what he perceived as arrogance.[61] And the journalist Rob Crilly depicts Tom Cholmondeley as speaking with a "cut-glass English accent,"[62] evoking the precise, crystalline tones of the elite, and perhaps the notion that British aristocrats were once the only ones who could afford cut glass.

Sociolinguists have argued that it isn't fair to assume that an accent reflects deeper qualities or allegiances, but scholars also recognize that there's nothing like social tension to bring out such assumptions. No wonder some of my white Kenyan interlocutors tell me English can be an awkward medium when they're trying to fit in. Mike, a tourism operator now in his twenties, was the only white student at his school when his parents moved to a remote rural area, and has a painful memory of the other students "taking the mickey out of me" by making fun of his British accent when he pronounced their teacher's name. "I guess it made me realize that we're sort of a minority here," he says. For Mike the stakes weren't terribly high, but for Tom Cholmondeley every symbol that made him stand out during his incarceration seemed a threat to his survival. No doubt this was in the back of Cholmondeley's mind when he told me, "I have such strong pronunciation that it instantly marks me as a stereotype . . . I often wish my English [pronunciation] was as neutral as my Kiswahili to avoid prejudice." While Cholmondeley's situation was extreme, his statement about language nonetheless distills a more general anxiety on the part of his peers.

So how, then, to dust away one's colonial residue, besides simply speaking Kiswahili? One can ostentatiously celebrate the language, too. In my presence, some younger white Kenyans born since Independence rhapsodize about Kiswahili, as if sheer enthusiasm might atone for colonial disparagement. A young white Kenyan scientist, for instance, told me that after several years of education abroad, "[My Kiswahili's] a bit rusty; I've been away. It's getting rusty, but I just need to get back six months and it'll get back again. I love it; it's a beautiful language." Such aesthetic evaluations seem an overcompensation for the past, reaching the opposite extreme of popular colonial opinions of Bantu languages—and indeed, as linguistic anthropologists have noted, shifts in language attitudes often mirror shifts in social alignments.[63] These remarks about loving the language aren't simply made in passing; some white Kenyans put in a real investment of time, as when they opt to sit for Kiswahili O levels or A levels at school.[64] A number of my interlocutors who hadn't studied Kiswahili in school told me they were embarrassed about their "grammatical mistakes," showing respect for the standard form that so many settlers had pooh-poohed a century earlier. Neatly matching Kiswahili's noun classes with the appropriate prefixes in one's adjectives and verbs shows respect, not only for the language, but also for one's interlocutor; it is both formal and polite. Even so, it can be a mark of pride to be comfortable with the widely spoken nonstandard versions of the language, which (among other things) neglect aspects of the noun class structure but still use verb tenses, locatives, and the language's agglutinative structure more deftly than Kisettla did. In fact, as long as one's nonstandard Kiswahili sounds convincing rather than "broken," a speaker can symbolically align with other Kenyans who speak it similarly, marking themselves as insiders rather than Western naïfs who learned the standard form's rigidities at a foreign university.[65] I haven't heard settler descendants using the informal Sheng dialect that got started among youth in Nairobi's urban core, but some young informants told me they had peers with some facility with it—a mark of pride for them.[66] And honorifics sometimes reflect this wish to connect through language. The settler descendants I met tended to be careful to address elder Kenyan males as *Mzee,* a term of respect—and I occasionally heard younger white men address younger black Kenyan men as *ndugu,* a respectful term roughly translating as "brother" (in the broad sense).

For these respondents, Kiswahili is central to their sense of national belonging. It is "especially important" for white Kenyans to speak Kiswahili, "as a way of overcoming negative stereotypes about white Kenyans and as a way of being considered a more genuine citizen of Kenya," Olivia, a Laikipia-based wildlife specialist, told me. "When I start speaking Kiswahili to them, they'll often say: 'Kweli, we ni moja wetu' [Truly, you're one of us].'"

Such a remark does paradoxical work, marking Olivia as an insider, but still an outsider of sorts, since the very fact that it can be articulated and understood presumes her difference. Still, Olivia takes this slightly divisive compliment as a step in the right direction—a step toward being accepted as "more genuine." The middle-aged businessman Gordon agreed, saying, "It would be embarrassing to speak a language of your country of birth poorly" He added: "It symbolizes a full empathy with the country and its people." A farm manager in his fifties who speaks Kikuyu is "very proud of the fact that he speaks Swahili with a Kikuyu accent," says his daughter; "He considers himself a Kikuyu." Evidently, this man sees his linguistic ability as a mark of Kenyan authenticity, to the point of helping him to assume membership in a nonwhite ethnic group (whether only in his own mind). However, several white Kenyans noted that although a few words of local vernaculars can be helpful, speaking African languages other than Kiswahili can risk sending "the wrong signal" in light of Kenya's ethnic tensions. Some of them have forbidden the use of such vernaculars in the workplace, asserting they believe in Kiswahili as a "unifying force." This unification, they hope, will include them. One white Kenyan woman in her twenties, Fiona, expresses this vague ideal in an e-mail to me: "Perhaps in the past English was something that separated 'us' from 'them'. Now it is something that unites 'them' with 'us,' even as Kiswahili has in the reverse united 'us' with 'them.'"

The aspiration to fit in and symbolically level the playing field prompts younger white Kenyans to hold up their elders as a linguistic and social foil. As I've noted, some settlers and officials in the colonial era actually did learn Kiswahili and other African languages with relative fluency, but I found this fact largely buried in my young interlocutors' eagerness to contrast the new era with the old one. In response to my question about how younger generations differ in how they relate to "Kenya and Africans," for instance, one thirty-something woman, Ava, turned instantly to language in order to highlight the contrast:

> Well, [my] mum and my father's Swahili is a joke. They don't, they're crap, it's a joke, I mean it's terrible. It's an *embarrassment,* actually, to me. But that's *fine,* that's them then, you know, they weren't allowed it . . . but it doesn't mean they're not Kenyan. It's their Swahili's really bad. I'm *really* lucky my Swahili's really good. 'Cause I've worked at the coast and I think it's a beautiful language and it's my language of connecting.[67]

Olivia tells me she teases her mother for the thick British accent evident in her Kiswahili, and for using what she calls "Swahilified English phrases, like 'Funga *gate*-i' [Shut the gate] or 'Lete moja *green cups*' [Bring one (of the?) green cups]." Marcus portrays his parents as blithe participants in colonial language attitudes when they came over from Europe in their late twenties. To him, their poor grasp of Kiswahili was twinned with their social distance from Africans: "They spoke appallingly, with no empathy and a jolly British accent," he says, with obviously affection for them, but a slightly critical edge as he notes how much more engaged his own purchase on the language has been. The environmental anthropologist Megan Styles found similar narratives when she interviewed flower-farm owners from settler families in the Naivasha area. Her informants, she says, preempted criticism of their "old colonial ways" by "pok[ing] fun at their parents' and grandparents' 'Kitchen Swahili,' [and] . . . aristocratic airs."⁶⁸ Some critiques of the colonial era, however, are not as gentle. Jonathan, who grew up near Kitale, spoke wistfully about the racial divide he felt as a child, telling me that he had become fluent in the Kalenjin and Kiswahili languages through contact with African playmates on his family's farm, but when he arrived at school in the 1950s, the languages were literally beaten out of him by his teachers because of rules forbidding them in his school. He was only later able to pick up Kiswahili again, communicating with his workers in it as a farm owner. In his narrative, African languages were an organic part of his natal environment, and the old colonial order had to use violence to curtail this natural cultural and linguistic mixing.

My respondents, of course, were born and/or raised in Kenya—giving them a potential linguistic advantage compared to the generation of their family (however far back it was) that first arrived in East Africa. Although making an effort to learn Kiswahili as an adult may be an index of good intentions or good will, speaking an African language from childhood gives some of my interlocutors a more powerful symbolic weapon against charges that they are interlopers, since it implies a more long-standing, possibly lineage-related connection to the place (related to the efforts to construct fictive autochthony I discuss in chapter 4). In making this case, my interlocutors contrast themselves to the European and American expatriates they sardonically call "two-year wonders," who often arrive to work with an NGO or some other "do-good" organization (as my respondents refer to them). Many settler descendants I spoke to regard two-year wonders as having a naïve and superficial grasp of all things Kenyan, and this includes language. Although occasionally white Kenyans say they have been put to shame by expats who speak excellent Kiswahili, I have also heard younger white Kenyans making snide remarks about their starchy use of the standard form and lack of fluency in local idioms. By contrast, in narrating their life stories to me, some white Kenyans emphasized their childhood facility with African languages, as if this long familiarity marked their penetration by the place, entwining the two ontologically.

Quite a few in their fifties and younger told me that their childhood exposure to Kiswahili was an important part of their life histories, as if to index a kind of autochthony, as well as their social intimacy with African children. Some told me of learning Kiswahili and/or local vernaculars from children who lived nearby, or from their ayahs (nannies) and the domestic staff at their homes. In such narratives, this symbolic authenticity is often bound up with their other defenses of their entitlement to belong in Kenya—the labor they have put into the land, the fictive kin relations they have with domestic staff, and so forth.

Some white Kenyans invoke their linguistic fluency in front of a wider audience; there is, after all, money to be made from international tourists who see white Kenyan guides in the wildlife industry as embodying a genuine African essence. The luxury safari outfit run by the Carr-Hartley family, for instance, notes on its web site that brothers Robert and William are: "fourth generation Kenyans from a family that has always been connected with wildlife. The Carr-Hartley brothers both rode a rhino before a horse and both speak several Native dialects, more comfortable with Swahili than perhaps their mother tongue, English."[69]

The site goes on to explain the brothers have "Africa and its wild places entrenched in their very souls." African languages, here, are enlisted in a broad kind of belonging that extends, vaguely, to intimacy with wildlife. In a related vein, when the BBC nature presenter Saba Douglas-Hamilton—born of an Italian mother from a settler family and a British expatriate environmentalist father—gave an interview to Britain's *Sunday Times* in 2009, she not only detailed her plans for giving birth outdoors to align herself with Kenya's wildlife, but also pointedly noted that her "first language was Kiswahili" because most of her playmates were local Kenyans.[70] (Saba's first name means "seven" in Kiswahili, while her sister's, "Dudu," means "bug"; family lore has it that they were named by "local Maasai tribesmen," a narrative suggesting that her parents, too, wished to embed their family in the place through language.)

Of course, white Kenyan attraction to Kiswahili isn't merely about gaining international clients or belonging through a tenuous kind of autochthony. Quite a number of my respondents indicated that the language is important in how they relate to other Kenyans, and even has an important bearing on the kind of people they feel they can be. (I discuss below the varied reactions on the part of black Kenyans to these efforts.) Several settler descendants who speak Kiswahili well told me it helps them to "connect" with Kenya's majority—and that there is a deep, intrinsic link between the language and a particular way of being in the world. Although most settler descendants, like their colonial predecessors, haven't nourished much ethnographic curiosity about African life except at an aesthetic or folkloric level, they do have a gestalt ideology that "Kenyan culture" tends to be more convivial, relaxed, and ready to defuse tensions with humor than European or British culture. Hence, while a mish-mash of English and Kiswahili can index a cosmopolitan nationalism for white Kenyans (just as it does for many Kenyans), some hope that through Kiswahili they may be able to adopt a casual mode of personhood that facilitates communication and connection. James, the safari guide, associates Kiswahili with an easygoing, on-the-street sociality, explaining that this stance is part of belonging to Kenya:

> The way I live my life and because I speak Kiswahili—and I'm fluent . . . I've always liked, I really enjoy speaking to people, and this is one of the pleasures of Kenya. They are very nice people. They're good fun, they're accommodating, they're nice people . . . it's really a pleasure to see them and you speak to them, you say hello . . . I always liked to interact with people, in the market you joke, you walk through [town], you know . . . I say hi, I mean, you know . . . even some of the beggars recognize me. You know what I mean?

James's allusion to speaking with everyone in town, including "some of the beggars," suggests an impulse to use Kiswahili to create the impression, however fleetingly, that the class- and race-based playing field has been leveled and Kenyans of all backgrounds can connect with mutual pleasure. Note that James's use of "they" and "them" subtly reinscribes the distance between his own group and that of black Kenyans (a linguistic tic that I can't resist mentioning has been observed among settler descendants by Richard Leakey as well and that irritates him profoundly). Nevertheless, in James's account, we see his hope that the language facilitates a friendly sociality that just might counteract racial and class-based hierarchies. The businessman Gordon, in his fifties, also associates Kiswahili with a more direct, less inhibited speech style than he experiences with "Europeans": "I have a very strong communication with people of Kenya. I find them wonderfully uninhibited, wonderfully easy to talk to, total strangers and set up a conversation that you couldn't do with a European. It's weird. It's straight into direct conversation; just shoot the shit right away. I speak fluent Swahili so that helps."

In Gordon's rendering, Kiswahili helps give his communications with "people of Kenya"—by whom he presumably means black Kenyans—an uncanny immediacy; direct and almost magical access to a candid channel of talk. The young wildlife expert Trevor, too, explained that being able to "have a chat" in Kiswahili was integral to an easy camaraderie with other Kenyans, bound up with demonstrating common frames of reference and origins: "an understanding of Kenya and where you're from, backgrounds and that sort of thing." In a discussion of how white Kenyans can "get things done" in the country in ways that foreigners cannot, Trevor adds: "I think it comes down just to an understanding, and patience, and knowing their language, and . . . not being dogged about it, if that makes sense, and [not] wanting something to happen today. And, and an understanding that yeah, it might take a week, it might take two weeks."

In this account, knowing the language is part of a bundle of attitudes that white Kenyans can adopt to align themselves with customary African pacing. I also noticed white Kenyans code-switching from English into Kiswahili to invoke aphorisms that suggest an unhurried tempo or an amenable attitude, such as "Haraka haraka haina baraka [(Haste, haste has no blessing]" or "Bahati ya Mungu" [It's God's will/fated by God]," uttered by one respondent after a tree fell in her yard and crushed part of her car.[71] Shadle also found early twentieth-century settlers using the expression "Shauri la Mungu"[(It's God's will]" in their writings, but doing so as a kind of reported speech to capture what they perceived of Africans' "fatalism, their unwillingness to take control of their own lives and futures."[72] The difference between his finding and my own is that I found settler descendants using phrases like this to adopt such stances and align themselves with them, rather than criticize them.

Occasionally, white Kenyans use the language to signal they are part of a common struggle against arbitrary abuses of power within the Kenyan infrastructure and political system. I have heard them, for instance, make offhand remarks about corrupt politicians using Kiswahili, and most would certainly use a local phrase (such as "tkk" or "Toa kitu kidogo [Give a little thing]") to allude to the common practice of bribery in Kenya. I witnessed an especially vivid example of the link between Kiswahili and a register of ironic complaint while visiting Cholmondeley in Kamiti prison. Cholmondeley used English to check in with a prison warden about his repeated requests to be allowed to use a laptop provided by his family; when the warden offered a noncommittal response, Cholmondeley switched into Kiswahili, saying, "Mara ya tano, bwana! Mara ya tano! [It's the fifth time, man! The fifth time!]," with an air of humorous frustration that struck me as familiar in local discussions of the maddening qualities of red tape in Kenya. Using Kiswahili, he thus bowed out of the "cut-glass" English accent he frets about and seemed to appeal for empathy by taking himself down a notch. Whether in the incarceration Cholmondeley faced or the milder efforts to fit in by more ordinary white Kenyans, their linguistic atonement aspires to find a zone of contact and partial likeness between themselves and other Kenyans.

While my interlocutors did not come right out and say that they preferred the persona they inhabited through Kiswahili, they did sometimes make a wry remark about how Europe—most especially England—tends to breed emotional repressions that include, in the words of several, the proverbial "stiff upper lip." In their current social climate, this kind of reserve risks coming across as stilted, and some white Kenyans even frame it as unhealthy by contrast with the warmth they say they detect in African Kenyans. "I do think we—our parents' generation—could be a little formal," says James. "They didn't mean to be, but it was just the way things were." James invokes a theme I heard from many: that his exposure to England left him cold, for not only was it "dull," but "the people there are just so unfriendly, it makes the air even chillier." By contrast, he says, talking to black Kenyans makes him feel "a lot more relaxed." A variation on this theme of longing appeared in colonial discourse—for example, in the idealized notions of the noble savage and the innocent native. As the anthropologist Renato Rosaldo has noted, imperial agents sometimes fixated on these supposedly Edenic modes of personhood that colonialism itself set out to alter in its "civilizing mission."[73] Among younger white Kenyans, however, I detect a shade of envy in which they are critical of the emotional limitations in their own heritage. I sometimes wondered whether the tart critiques of colonialism in Kenya have made some of them ambivalent about their own pedigree and perhaps even their power. Chatting in Kiswahili seems to make them feel more laid back, more integrated, and even more emotionally healthy.

LINGUISTIC HIERARCHY, STRUCTURAL OBLIVION, AND THE PRIVILEGE OF MOTION

Speaking Kiswahili probably does help some white Kenyans gain a modicum of acceptance from some people they interact with (though not always—see below), but linguistic enthusiasm can't erase the structures of power set up in the colonial era and now reinforced by global dynam-ics. One legacy is a persistent hierarchy of languages that goes largely unquestioned by white Kenyans—indeed, it is taken for granted by many Kenyans of all races. If Leakey and his brother use Kiswahili in all con-texts, high and low, among the working class and the wealthiest politi-cians, for most white Kenyans, English is the higher language, used for education, the office, and among the professional class. Naomi, a young professional, says she uses English with "other white Kenyans, my indig-enous Kenyan colleagues, or Kenyan Asians, though I also use the occa-sional word in Kiswahili to them. But I always greet my house staff in Kiswahili, as I do with any other stranger on the street." There are ideo-logical divisions, then, that divide their language use between classes, formality, and even feeling. Jonathan says: "Generally, [I use English] in a technical context if the other person is quite educated . . . [and] Kiswa-hili for more fluid and intuitive communication." One of Cholmonde-ley's friends says: "Kiswahili is a far more emotionally direct language and allows a much closer feeling quickly, and character insights. [It's] useful for Aspergics"—in other words, for those who have difficulty parsing indirect social and emotional signals. A safari guide told me he enjoys speaking Kiswahili because it's "a very explicit language"—a statement ambiguously stretched between the possibility of the kind of transparency just mentioned, and the possibility of profanity. "And," he adds, it's "fun to communicate in."[74] My contacts recurrently say they use the language primarily for what they call "chatter with my staff," "joking," "shooting the shit," or "banter" with "white, black, or brown friends." Many told me they used Kiswahili for "slang." Most white Kenyan Kiswahili actually *doesn't* fit sociolinguistic definitions of slang, which refers to innovative words and phrases with a rapid turnover,[75] but I suspect my interlocutors use the term invoke the informal, even cheeky register they enjoy in Kiswahili. Their use of Kiswahili for infor-mality is so habitual, the linguistic division of labor can go unnoticed. The hotelier Gordon, for instance, told me how much he prided himself on using Kiswahili when he chatted with employees, but as we talked, it dawned on him that he always delivered his formal, written speeches to them in English. "I never thought about that until now," he muses.

Settler descendants, then, appreciate the informality they associate with Kiswahili, but they also yoke Kiswahili to the heart and English to the head. This equation draws upon a classic colonial ideology: things African are informal, more about feeling, while things European are rational and consequential. In the narratives I collected, furthermore, my respondents don't recognize that these qualities emerge from the way the languages are embedded in historically constructed hierarchies, rather than being intrinsic to the languages. In fact, like any language, Kiswahili has infinite potential. Coastal Kenyans who speak Kiswahili as a first language, for instance, prize linguistic indirection and complexity, lacing their utterances with formality, innuendo, and respectful honorifics. Kiswahili in Tanzania, to the south, has a very different standing, too; the language has been central to nation-building efforts, and state planners have institutionalized its use in everything from governance to higher education. There is nothing essential in the language, in other words, to preclude it from functioning as a language of power, intellectual discourse, and formality, as Richard Leakey seems to recognize well. However, most white Kenyans essentialize Kiswahili as less intellectually sophisticated than English, a judgment that implicitly reflects on black Kenyans who speak it.[76]

Meanwhile, English with all its prestige remains white Kenyans' primary language of identification. The Carr-Hartley brothers cited above, for instance, are doubtless very comfortable speaking Kiswahili, but in my observations of white Kenyans, even those fluent in the language don't use it as the main language when speaking among themselves or in their own homes; it simply feels wrong to them unless it is used, as they put it to me, "for the occasional slang term." Hence, one of my informants, who in her fifties was already taken aback by her elderly father's marriage to an "African who couldn't speak English," told me of her aversion to their "incredibly awkward teas" in which family members were "forced to speak Swahili" in order to be mutually understood. Kiswahili plays an important role in white Kenyan identity, but English remains central to their sense of intellectual authority and kin relations.

There are important class implications to all of this as well. Black Kenyans recognize the national and global prestige of English, of course, and while Kiswahili can certainly be heard in the halls of power, some African elites eschew Kiswahili because of its subordinate connotations; as one attorney put it "Swahili is for the *wananchi* [native-born citizens, in this case with connotations of peasantry or lower status], but not for me."[77] One of my acquaintances, a highly educated, well-to-do man born to a Kikuyu father and an English expatriate mother told me that he had nearly failed his Kiswahili exams in school and now avoided the language as much as he could—even though his poor Kiswahili sometimes led to him being called a *mzungu* (white). He was hard pressed to explain why he was not attracted to Kiswahili (less, indeed, than settler descendants), but it seemed a way of leaving behind identification with Kenyans of lesser status. Meanwhile, high-prestige Kenyans (whether of European, African, or Asian descent) frequently speak English with their colleagues of rank, and are far more likely to use Kiswahili with domestic staff, vendors, and employees with relatively less formal education. This pattern was easily observable among my own informants, as in the case of Marcus, the coffee company executive described above, who interrupted our conversation to speak to a white-collar African colleague in English, but used Kiswahili to give instructions to his driver. And while English can be learned by anyone, settler descendants who speak English as a first language have the advantage of being most tightly associated with the language most connected to wealth, development, and Westernization.

The power dynamics I have outlined also mean that at least some urban, well-educated black Kenyans I know find it patronizing when whites initiate conversations in Kiswahili rather than English. As a café owner on the outskirts of Nairobi phrased his objection, "Do they think I never went to school? Kenya is a modern country."[78] I have heard the same sentiment repeated by black Kenyan scholars and businessmen. Although my own efforts in Kiswahili over the years were welcomed by many rural Kenyans, I soon learned that many black Kenyans with good English preferred that I converse in that language. Some white Kenyans don't appear to recognize this, but others remark on it. "It's a matter of pride," says Gordon; "Some people have a chip about us speaking Kiswahili and think it's condescending." A white conservation scientist concurred: "I know one Kenyan African woman . . . who feels that when white people speak to her in Kiswahili they're talking down to her, so I'm aware of that sensitivity." And the white businessman Simon observed that speaking English to "well educated" Kenyans made them "feel on a par . . . as if [they have] a better education than the man next door." In some cases, white Kenyans say, they wind up in stilted English conversations that could have gone more smoothly if they had simply taken place in Kiswahili. There can be tensions, then, between white Kenyans' impulse to connect and the ways their efforts in Kiswahili are received by some—but white Kenyans insisted to me that they did not mean to denigrate their black interlocutors.

Settler descendants' use of Kiswahili is layered with conscious efforts at interracial leveling and connection and a mostly unconscious colonial residue of linguistic ranking and class- and race-based distance. This is perhaps most evident in the linguistic division of labor they describe, in allocating Kiswahili to the "heart" and casual talk, and English to the "head." Because younger white Kenyans are so aware of their positive feelings about Kiswahili, but—in my conversations, anyway—relatively unaware of their role in an enduring linguistic hierarchy that continues to benefit them, I deem their language attitudes an instance of structural oblivion; that is, another example of overlooking their complicity in their own privilege. Yet this failure feels innocent to them; the young white Kenyan speaks Kiswahili to be friendly and "Kenyan" rather than to reinforce a hegemonic hierarchy.[79]

Indeed, looked at one way, settler descendants' linguistic practices perpetuate a classic European condescension toward things marked as African. On the other hand, it is striking that at least some of my interlocutors implied that the personhood they inhabit in English has limitations they bridle against. Kiswahili may not be a code of formality or power, but for white Kenyans (in their ideology, and thus in their subjective reality) it seems to possess expressive stances they value: emotional candor and transparency; instant connection with others through "banter"; the cool, witty, socially fluent persona who communicates through "slang"; even the philosophical cast of mind, once so maddening to their colonial predecessors, in which one does not live by clock time alone, or dismisses hardships as "God's will." Perhaps, then, even as white Kenyans collude in a linguistic landscape that gives English more intellectual cachet than Kiswahili, they are also using Kiswahili to give themselves a certain kind of relief. Part of the pleasure of bilingualism is that it allows them to move between the authority of English and the felt authenticity—both nationalist and emotional—of Kiswahili. This kind of authenticity may seem especially desirable in a rapidly globalizing world where liberal humanists applaud the ability to forge "connections" between different kinds of people and different social strata. Arguably, in fact, their very ease of motion between contexts—what the sociologist Shamus Khan has called a "radical egalitarianism" of tastes among those with privilege—is a sort of currency for white Kenyans, in a place and an era where aristocracy has lost its luster.[80] Maybe it is their movement between the authority of English and the felt authenticity of Kiswahili that lets them feel both "white," in the sense of holding on to a privilege-granting category, and nationally "Kenyan," while marking themselves with the prestige of global cosmopolitanism.

What isn't clear, though, is whether their efforts at linguistic atonement are enough for them to redeem their cultural citizenship. Speaking African languages can help some settler descendants feel like they have forged intimate connections with black Kenyans, but linguistic connection needn't beget the bodily and social intimacies such as intermarriage or group socializing that most of my respondents have tended to avoid (see chapter 4). And while white Kenyan language practices aspire to atone for colonial desecrations and provide whites with liberating potential through an apparently freeing linguistic register, they tacitly keep European authority in place through the symbolic and pragmatic hierarchy I have discussed. Kiswahili is needed and subordinated, valued and devalorized, a subtle instrument of white privilege. And for all of the positive aspects of white efforts at linguistic atonement, it attempts reconciliation without making reparations inasmuch as it does not so much reapportion advantages as carve out a fresh way of inhabiting elite identity.

6

The Occult

The Nairobi blogger "Lost White Kenyan Chick" kept up a stream of commentary in early 2008, when the nation was being shredded by horrifying violence. To outsiders it looked as if so-called ancient tribal hatred had reared its ugly head again after a close presidential election in late 2007. To those in the know, it was clear the election had been rigged in favor of the incumbent president, and politicians were pitting ethnic groups against one another in a cycle of revenge. Lost White Kenyan Chick joined the chorus of objections, writing in dismay: "It is absolutely shocking what these leaders have done to our fellow Kenyans. We are one tribe . . . KENYAN!"

A few days later, Lost White Kenyan Chick shifted to a lighter tone with an entry titled: "A small chuckle for you amongst all the chaos." Apparently some people in Mombasa had taken advantage of the instability to loot stores, but suddenly they were returning the goods—food, television sets, and so forth—for fear of supernatural reprisals. Giriama friends on the coast told me of rumors that to curtail the thievery, someone had recited an Arabic spell. Lost White Kenyan Chick went on: "If stolen things are not returned those looters who stole them will have a spell cast on them and they will go mad and be unable to pee!! So can you believe, once word had got around of the threat of this prayer being said, loads of things have already been returned . . . I really must get into this 'black magic' thing—it sounds damn useful. I'll be reading up and let you know how it works out. I do wish someone would put a spell on those big boys fighting it out for the presidency."

We have seen younger white Kenyans hoping to remedy what Vincent Crapanzano has called the "psychological apartheid" of Africa's colonial era[1] by expressing solidarity with the Kenyan people, making rhetorical efforts to distance themselves from "old colonials," and, in some cases, embracing the Kiswahili language. However partial their efforts, however compromised by structural oblivion, we have seen some of them frame themselves as cosmopolitans willing to align themselves with Africans in ways their colonial forebears were not.[2] But the African occult seems to be a sticking point. Lost White Kenyan Chick, for instance, is fiercely loyal to her suffering "fellow Kenyans," but reverts to parody when it comes to what she calls "black magic." Like her, plenty of white Kenyans have steered clear of witchcraft, spirit beliefs, and indigenous rituals, seeing the occult as superstitious and irrational. Others, though—especially those who have spent a lot of time on the coast—have found themselves embroiled in it in spite of themselves. And some of them are spooked, if not horrified, by these encounters.

Before he took over his family's safari business and moved upcountry, for instance, a third-generation settler descendant in his late thirties whom I shall call James[3] lived in Mombasa, operating the boats that take tourists out to catch marlin, sharks, and other deep-sea species. Some of his domestic staff and co-workers were Swahili and Mijikenda people (including members of the largest Mijikenda group, the Giriama), and from them James heard a good deal about spirits, rituals, and witchery among coastal communities. At times, these occult forces became too real for comfort.

One evening, as we were talking about my research on Giriama spirit mediums, James was moved to tell me about something that had happened in his home by the beach. As he lay one night on the brink of sleep, James suddenly found himself pinned to his mattress as if by an invisible force.[4] He recalled: "I felt such an—I felt so oppressed. There would be movements, you know, like, if you can explain, movements in the dark. I don't know how to explain it . . . I thought there was someone in the room. I don't know what. To the extent that I even said in Swahili: 'Wewe toka!' [Get away, you!]. And I was doing that, *and*, I could hardly move! . . . Now, I'm—I don't know how long it was, just—I was shit-scared."

James kept the lights on all night in terror: "I thought I was losing the plot." The next morning he asked his domestic staff members, most of them Giriama men, whether they'd noticed "anything different" lately.

The staff told him knowingly there had been a malevolent spirit hanging around the place for several weeks. The cook, Katana, said he had been paralyzed in his own bed in a downstairs room on the very same night. Thoroughly frightened, James knew what he had to do. "I told Katana: '*Bas* [Okay]. Here's some money.' I said: 'You guys go, I want you to go to a *mganga* [diviner/spirit medium], to your *mganga,* yeah.'"

According to the diviner, whom James never met face to face, the spirit was linked to James's tenant, a mysterious European woman renting one of the rooms in the house. The spirit visitations ended soon after the tenant moved out. But the whole affair made James jittery. By the end of his discussion with me, he needed to establish some distance from what had taken place:

> I know that [the Giriama people] are very entwined with the *mganga*, uh, whether good or bad or whatever, it's very much part of their lives and it—a lot of it is mind, you know? Definitely most of it is mind . . . the mind can play the most amazing games . . . all these guys who live on this coast are all deep into this stuff. And they have their *sheitani* [spirits], bad *sheitani*, the good *sheitani* . . . at night they have these demons who walk the beaches, you've heard all of that, you've heard it, actually. I tend to take most of— normal common stuff that you hear with a little bit of—pinch of salt . . . since it's been so much set in their nature, it's, it's part of their lives, and it's effective. It is effective . . . You see what happened when Katana—he always goes and sees his *mganga*. It's like going to see your psychiatrist I suppose.[5]

As he talks through his experience with the occult, James tries to hold it at bay. Spirit beliefs and the use of ritual practitioners, he says, are "set in [Giriama] nature"—suggesting they remain at arm's length from those of European descent like himself. Spirit visitations, it turns out, may just be mind games; talk about spirits should be taken with "a pinch of salt"; and Katana's visits to his *mganga* are "effective" because of their psychiatric power, not their supernatural force. But I couldn't help noticing that James's return to skepticism was only partial. With phrases like "most of it is mind," James left room for a crack in the dam of rationalism. "Most" of it is mind . . . but what about the rest of it?

James's encounter with the occult struck a chord with me. As a graduate student doing research on coastal religion, I, too, had once felt the presence of spirits. Back then, as the months went by, my experiences became more and more uncanny. Clocks stopped, locks stuck, and lights extinguished at unsettling moments, not long after my Giriama friends warned me the spirits might be in pursuit of me. When diviners summoned their helping spirits to tell my fortune, they told me I had a liver problem—and I did (benign, but still). They were able to guess who was jealous of my research assistant, and they knew what kind of item I had misplaced that morning (an umbrella). One especially charismatic *mganga* seemed able to read a word I had memorized simply by scrutinizing my eyes. As these encounters gathered steam, I surprised myself by wondering whether these forces might be real.

Later, after I discovered that the word-reading *mganga* had actually fooled me with a simple magic trick, I returned abruptly to the detached, secular, analytic stance I had arrived with. I decided to chalk all those events up to coincidence, and I could see my suggestibility in hindsight. Still, the arc of my experience proved that a Westerner could flip-flop between a state of disbelief and belief more readily than I would have guessed. For me, it was a relief to return to a state of disenchantment, for, as I put it later, "our pact as anthropologists is to go 'there' without ever quite leaving 'here.'"[6] But I knew I was going home to the United States once my fieldwork was over. What is it like for white Kenyans such as James, who grew up with talk of witchcraft and spirits flowing through the air? How do they deal with the unnerving qualities of the occult, when they say they want to belong to Kenyan society, but like their colonial forebears they want to transcend the stigma of "superstition"? What crises of consciousness might this tension precipitate?

The occult is most alive for settler descendants who have spent time in coastal areas such as Mombasa, Watamu, Kilifi, and Malindi. Their sunny white-sand beaches, palm trees, and blue waters had special appeal for European families who sold their upcountry lands at Independence, for retired settlers, and for anyone looking for a laid-back seaside environment. Some whites live in their beach houses for only part of the year before heading back upcountry, but all of them are familiar with the prominent ethnic groups in Coast Province. Mijikenda people, Giriama in particular, often work as staff in white homes or petty laborers in white-owned businesses. In my conversations with white Kenyans, I repeatedly heard that well-rehearsed line: the coastal region was especially "rife with witchcraft" and spirit beliefs, and occult practices were slowing Kenya's path to modernity. And yet, as I got to know my interlocutors, I noticed a pattern of confessionals. When a spouse was out of earshot, or when the breeze was blowing enough that they could speak softly and not be heard by their friends at the next table, they would tell me of their secret thoughts about or encounters with the occult. Some, it turned out, had enlisted the help of *waganga* to deal with unruly staff. Others had sought occult assistance for personal healing, or even to bewitch other whites, blurring the boundary between white identity and a kind of magic once thought to be the exclusive terrain of Africans. As they spoke, it was clear these forces seemed all too close to many of them.

Kenya is home to dozens of ethnic groups with different occult practices. Among coastal Giriama, positive magic, known as *uganga* (in both the Giriama and Swahili languages), involves spirit mediumship and healing rites that call on spirits, ancestors, and the creator-god Mulungu to address physical ailments or bewitchment. Ritual devices include incantations, libations of palm wine poured onto the ground, animal sacrifice (from chickens to cows), washing with and ingesting sacred herbs, and effigies of problem-spirits that can be tossed into the bush, crushed underfoot, or scuffed away. Chicken blood is a common means of luring evil spirits out of the body, while talismans can protect; these are made with rarities such as bits of sea creatures, lion's fur, sacred herbs collected from the forest, or scraps of the Quran (the Giriama's neighbors are the Muslim Swahili, and Islam is thought to be a repository of potency even by non-Muslims).[7] Practitioners can also use charms (*fingo*) and other paraphernalia to prevent wrongdoing such as thievery. But malicious witchcraft (*uchawi* in Kiswahili; *utsai* in the Giriama language) is considered so dreadful that I could only learn about it through hearsay, for to practice it—even to have intimate knowledge of it—is to risk being exiled or murdered. Using incantations, botanics, and paraphernalia, a witch can make the victim's luck (their "star") fall, or throw a blood-sucking spirit at them to drive them mad or drag their fortunes down. Any bad luck, insanity, illness, or death can thus fall under suspicion of witchcraft, which is effectively human malice transformed into an invisible, invasive force. One of the most common restorative rites among Giriama is called the *kuhundula,* or the unbinding of the "knots" of witchery.

It can be awkward these days for anthropologists to talk about the occult. Historically, witchcraft has been used as an excuse to demean and subordinate Africans, and as anthropologist Adam Ashforth notes, dwelling on it risks appearing "[willing] to compromise the fruits of victory over racism and oppression."[8] In a scholarly context, it also feels to some like an "old" topic, since many Africanists now focus their studies, not on putative "traditions," but rather on contemporary dynamics of globalization and modernity. Adding to the complexity, many black Kenyans are themselves conflicted about the occult. Most have encountered the idea that occult ways are backward and prefer to identify with and work towards a modern Kenya.[9] And yet the occult is still a vivid part of their lives. Where there is greed, jealousy, or awe—in politics, capitalist accumulation, and new technologies such as cell phones—there are often rumors about occult forces and witchcraft.[10] And when bad things happen to ordinary people, positive occult powers offer hope of recourse. The supernatural is thus framed by many Africans as outmoded, yet it is still highly relevant.

Just as black Kenyans find the occult anxiety-provoking, so, too, do settler descendants. But the context for white fear is different. The official colonial line was that the occult is superstitious poppycock at its root, but African metaphysics held more fascination for whites than official ideologies suggested; then as now, the occult seeped into whites' awareness in surprising and discomfiting ways. And today, settler descendants still feel a tension between their apparent susceptibility to these African ideas and their simultaneous need to express a kind of immunity to them. Some try to contain the occult as a concept, framing it, as they spoke to me, as separate from their "core" European-influenced sense of rationality and self-determination, which they see as important to bringing Kenya into a "developed" future. At the same time, though, contradictions abound. Often it isn't clear whether white Kenyans think psychology is the main culprit in witchcraft, or that witchly forces themselves are real. And trying to pin them down what they "believe" is a futile errand, since—as I shall show—belief itself makes them feel vulnerable to these forces so antithetical to who they want to be. Ironically, this particular anxiety actually makes them more (rather than less) similar to many black Kenyans.

COLONIAL ERASURES

Occult practices have a long history of unnerving whites in Africa. In his procolonial screed penned in the mid-1950s, for instance, the settler-administrator Christopher Wilson ticks off innumerable African "superstitions" without context or understanding, and lavishes attention on the horrors of animal sacrifice (a goat seems to lose its life on every other page). Africans, he concludes, "surrender [themselves] helplessly to the irrational and fanciful imaginations of superstition and magic," tossing away "all hope of intellectual advance" while succumbing to the authority of so-called witchdoctors.[11] The colonial state agreed, seeing the containment of witchcraft as an urgent priority; it is terribly hard, after all, to govern a society if witches are thought to have more power than colonial officers. British colonial officials across East Africa denigrated occult beliefs as spurious and backward, but also recognized the sheer power of the beliefs themselves among Africans, and watched with dismay as their colonized subjects projected great power onto supernatural practitioners, including prophets and those practicing harmful magic.[12]

In 1909, the Kenyan colonial government passed its first Ordinance forbidding witchcraft practices. The Ordinance was reissued in 1925 after two rounds of revision that criminalized witchcraft accusations while expanding the involvement of local authorities—chiefs, headmen, and the like—in its prosecution. Crackdowns could be draconian, focused on extinguishing not only practices but also beliefs. This dynamic came to a head in the early 1930s during the so-called WaKamba Witch Trials, in which the Supreme Court of Kenya sentenced sixty Kamba men to death—not for practicing witchery themselves, but for killing a neighbor woman they believed to have practiced witchcraft.[13] On the coast, colonial officials curtailed the Mijikenda *ngoma* dances led by spirit mediums and healers, finding them unnerving and fearing, too, that they might be a guise for large political gatherings.[14] Practices such as spirit possession and prophecy were so stigmatized that officials often deemed them a kind of "madness."[15]

Of course, such talk about the African occult was based on failures of understanding, and one such failure was semantic. Colonial vocabulary simplified local cosmologies, disregarding the subtleties of *uganga* (positive magic, in Kiswahili, often including divination and healing) and *uchawi* (negative magic), including the fact that these may be carried out by the same person.[16] Bureaucratic language sometimes conflated magical harm, spirit possession, healing, poisoning, oathing, prophesying, and other occult forces.[17] The consequences have been legal and far-reaching; the 1925 Witchcraft Ordinance, for instance, which is still part of Kenyan law today, deems "possession of charms" to be a legal offense, but "charm" is a vague notion, which has sometimes been used to encompass the ritual tools for positive magic.[18]

Colonial aversion to the occult came to a head during the Mau Mau insurgency in the 1950s. Many Mau Mau fighters took or were forced to take oaths of allegiance believed to have supernatural binding force, in order to secure political allegiance and fortitude against colonial rule. Settlers and administrators alike were horrified by the content of these rituals—incantations, animal sacrifice, drinking blood, eating raw flesh, and so forth—and framed them as bestial, pagan, and savage. One member of the Kenya Regiment who fought against Mau Mau rebels embellishes the "vile acts" accompanying oath-taking, and claims "virtually all" participants hiding in the forests outside of Nairobi would have taken oaths involving "sexual shenanigans with women, animals both live and dead, and finally with catamite boys, who, because of the acts involved, also had to be expendable."[19] Most alarming for colonials was the prospect that the population would fear the oaths enough to cleave to the rebel cause. In language now notorious, colonial officials set out to ritualistically "cleanse" the oath-takers—sometimes with terrible and widespread violence—so as to "rehabilitate" them.[20] Ironically, the same historical moment brought the colonial administration into its greatest proximity with the occult, since officials decided to outsource some of the de-oathing procedures to local ritual experts, bureaucratizing these supernatural means.[21]

While the colonial state exerted its legal opposition, churches across Kenya—Anglican, Presbyterian, Catholic, Quaker, Methodist, Lutheran, and others—preached their moral disapproval. Whatever the internal contradictions of the missionary process,[22] Christianity was always portrayed as consistent with modern rationality and distinct from the magical thinking of the colonized. To believe that minor spirits, ancestors, or curses can affect one's fate, to see agency in inanimate objects, or to try to harness such forces oneself was to indulge in heathenistic behavior.[23] In this view, the occult was part of a culture of wasted energy and paranoia antithetical to development and salvation.

Was there any discrepancy between official colonial discourse and more privately held sentiments and fears? We might expect so, given that scholars have repeatedly described a push-pull of repugnance toward and desire for the Other in colonial experience.[24] The anthropologist Peter Pels finds that in late colonial Tanganyika, "the denial of witchcraft by missionaries went along with a much more murky practice," and missionaries may have experienced more fascination with and more "moving towards" African lifeways than they were prepared to admit publicly.[25] Pels also suggests colonial-era novelists and ethnographers were anxious about witchcraft, not only because it embodies the "irrationality" that colonialism wished to expunge, but also because, at some level, colonials suspected that it might be a real force.[26]

In Kenya, there were glimmers of the same among administrators. The historian Richard Waller, for instance, notes that colonial legislators in Kenya were publicly obliged to deny the validity of witchcraft, but the archive suggests that their true opinions "probably varied widely." A provincial commissioner in 1928, for instance, called witchcraft "farcical," yet a district commissioner around the same time said that he "[couldn't] help believing that there is some supernatural power we know nothing of."[27] Presumably settlers also had a range of responses to the occult. Some must have dismissed it blithely, while others would have responded like a very elderly former settler to whom I spoke in 2004, who could barely get a word out to express her feelings about witchery, her shoulders shuddering inside her floral blouse as she made a visceral sound: "Hrrrrr." At least some, then, found that the creepiness they associated with the occult had persuasive power.

"SUPERSTITION" AND SETTLER DESCENDANTS

As the historian Katherine Luongo has observed, colonialism in Kenya set two worldviews in opposition: African cosmology versus European-style bureaucracy. Despite their fiercely pitched battle over the past century, both live on in contemporary Kenya with as much energy as ever. Colonial legislation did little to deter occult practices, and while some Kenyans claim that witchcraft has been on the decline because of Christianity, others suggest that it has merely been driven partly underground.[28] In fact, Kenya's High Court has been kept busy by occult accusations, especially since the 1925 Witchcraft Ordinance is still on the books. It isn't unusual for politicians to accuse their opponents of using witchcraft against them, and voters are sometimes illegally pressured through occult means such as oathing. Looking at these case files, Luongo concludes that today's judiciary "has read witchcraft as an ineluctable element of Kenyan life, and as such has devoted less . . . energy to eradicating it and more to negotiating it."[29] Meanwhile, the state continues to surveil and limit even the positive practices of *uganga*.[30]

Despite politicians' involvement in the occult, Kenyan elites publicly frame it as an obstacle to progress. The coastal areas are singled out as particularly vulnerable. In the Malindi Municipal Council's Strategic Plan report of 2004, for instance, a group of Arab, Asian, Swahili, Mijikenda, and European contributors asserted that "entrenched community values on witchcraft [are] considered retrogressive to growth and thus bound to negatively influence institutional development."[31] And in a 2009 article in Kenya's *Daily Nation* entitled "Witch's Hand Seen in Coast Poverty," a provincial commissioner attributes the Coast Province's economic failures to "backward practices like witchcraft."[32] Publicly, many Kenyan politicians and laypeople frame Kenya as a "Christian country."

When settler descendants criticize occult practices, what are their motives today? Shades of Christian judgment, of course, underpin the history of colonial opposition to the occult. Yet many white Kenyans no longer attend services, suggesting their religious enthusiasm has attenuated. Elderly informants tell me that under African church leaders, who favor vigorous song, dance, and a call-and-response style of oration, Anglican churches in Kenya no longer ceremonially invoke England the way they once did. "I just can't get used to all the cacophony," says one. Several settler descendants told me they had explored other cosmologies such as Buddhism, while a few young people framed their religiosity in spiritual rather than institutional terms, saying they see God in the natural beauty of the Kenyan landscape and wildlife, and require no church to feel worshipful. Evidently, white Kenyans in younger generations are less wedded than their forebears to a strict notion of religious identity, and some have a cosmopolitan interest in non-Western religious customs.

Though the settler descendants I spoke to aren't hemmed into a devout life, they still feel cultural pressure to avoid the occult. In the colonial era, of course, settlers engaged in various forms of self-policing to differentiate themselves from Africans and prove, even to themselves, that whites carried the banners of self-control, rationality, and civilization.[33] Today, while they don't publicly use the language of racial superiority, settler descendants do believe—like many black Kenyan elites—in the cultural superiority of modernity compared to the occult, which they frame as parochial and backward. At pains to belong to the independent nation, whites also insist they are part of the vanguard of Kenya's development—and rationality is part of that equation. "We're just level-headed types," said one to me; "We've lasted this long here because we keep our heads, and we care what happens here. I don't think it's an exaggeration to say we're an asset as the nation keeps moving forward."

As white Kenyans nominate themselves as an elite group that can be of use in moving Kenya "forward," they have as their foil the well-worn claim that "many Africans are still very superstitious." They recognize the sizable urban black Kenyan elite, of course, but some white Kenyans were adamant in conversation with me that rural blacks in particular hadn't caught up with modernity. When I asked Letty, a retiree living in Malindi, about the prevalence of occult practices among the Giriama, she tried to choose her words tactfully, but still invoked a classic colonial formulation: "[W]ith the Giriamas and people like that, they have not, they're so, they live so much in their still very tribal . . . they're still in that respect very um, backwards [is] not the right word; they haven't um, ah, matured or been educated enough, mixed in with another society. They're still a very close knit tribe down here. Very close knit." Letty implied that the occult should fade out with the rise of "education" and exposure to other (presumably more "modern") social groups. We can infer from her model, then, that cosmopolitan whites aren't supposed to traffic in African occult ways.

While some white Kenyans were blunt in their condemnation of occult beliefs, others had been influenced by global strains of liberal humanism and cultural relativism that softened their tone. In speaking about *uganga,* for instance, James was quick to assure me that he accepted it: "[I]t's part of their culture. I can understand that . . . I understand it. And I will not *ever* criticize them or say [*unintelligible*] how can they believe in that. Because they *believe* in it, it's part of their culture." Such professed relativism was not exclusive to younger people; even Agnes, in her late sixties, asserted that "I respect their beliefs." Yet these speakers continued to identify mystical thinking as the domain of Africans, not whites, and in spite of their expressions of tolerance, they couldn't help implying that it would be best if Africans left it behind. "It's tied in to these people's lives very much and their tradition and their culture," James said. "It's become very central to it. . . . It's difficult for them to shake it off." In their expressions of personal indifference, furthermore, they sometimes seemed to protest too much. Agnes asserted repeatedly that "basically it doesn't interest me. . . . Things that interest me, I do inquire about, but this has never interested me. . . . I've got my feet planted firmly on the ground." And although James had several long conversations with me about his occult experiences, he reminded me from time to time that he was neither curious nor credulous: "I, you know, I'm not someone who, I actually tend to take things a lot with a pinch of salt. . . . I'm not interested in looking into the sort of occult or all that. For me I think it's just below—I don't, it doesn't interest me." Other respondents, too, repeatedly insisted upon their "common sense" and self-possession, saying: "You have to make your own decisions in life" and "You can't let yourself be steered by something else."

A favorite storyline, then, is that whites see the folly of magic and witchcraft while many Africans do not. In a variation on this theme, some white Kenyans enlist occult help cynically in order to scare their workers straight. One man in his seventies, Pieter (born in Kenya of Swedish descent, but speaking with a British English accent), insisted he knew little about local magic, but related a familiar scenario of using the occult defensively to police employees:

> The only witchcraft I know about is the type of witchcraft where we white people take advantage of witchcraft. I haven't done it myself, but I have many friends who have. What they do is, if they have trouble in a household, or if they have trouble on a farm, and the trouble won't go away, and they try to resolve it one way or another, even if they bring in the police or whatever and the trouble goes on and on and on. What you do is you go far away from your farm and you get a hold of a *mganga,* and this *mganga,* [if] he agrees to your price and everything, he will come to your farm and he will perform this witchcraft.[34]

Rather like the colonial administration that appointed occult practitioners to "cleanse" oath-takers in the Mau Mau era, white Kenyan employers may pay local experts to perform ostentatious rituals, setting out charms, lines of charred sacred herbs, chicken blood, and so forth, to signal that thievery and other malfeasance will be supernaturally punished. Similarly, an elderly retiree tells me the Malindi Golf Club was once subject to so much petty thievery, she hired a couple of *waganga* to come and "do their mumbo-jumbo" to frighten the thief. With this dismissive phrase, she makes clear that she rubbishes any actual supernatural reality behind it.

But while many white Kenyans suggest that they are too level-headed to think the occult has real force, some of their narratives betray bewilderment about its mechanisms. I heard many stories, for instance, of domestic staff who fall ill out of the blue, convinced that they are cursed. The employer typically solicits the help of a medical doctor who finds that "there's nothing physically wrong with them"—or the staff member is so sure of his own doom he refuses medical care altogether. These tales culminate in the total loss of hope and a rapid physical decline. Agnes describes the behavior of her cook in his final days: "It was as if he turned his face to the wall. . . . He just refused to take his medicine. Two days later he died." In her memoir *Out of Africa,* Karen Blixen describes the death of a man named Kitosch who had been badly beaten by his colonial master for riding a mare without permission. During the ensuing trial, two colonial doctors testified that Kitosch had successfully willed himself to die. Blixen deems the tale a "beautiful" account of the "fugitiveness" and will power of "wild things."[35] Later Ngugi wa Thiong'o would deplore Blixen's stance, which exonerates a brutal colonial act of murder.[36] While the circumstances of Agnes's tale are utterly different, she shares one aspect of Blixen's stance: wonderment that Africans appear able to will themselves to die. And for Agnes, the wonderment is compounded by the bafflement—even frustration—that anyone could be so gullible as to kill themselves through what appears to be sheer belief.[37] But here is the thin end of the wedge of ambiguity in white Kenyan narratives. For as often as my interlocutors implied that belief itself was the culprit, merely a psychosomatic mechanism by which credulous Africans could make themselves sick, they just as often kept open the unsettling possibility that occult forces might have a real hand in it.

THE ANXIETY OF SUSCEPTIBILITY

Whites, then, do sometimes consider the possibility that they themselves could be targeted by these forces. The elderly widow Lucy, for instance, told me of a settler friend she grew up with who fired a servant and suddenly developed strange spots on her body, dying almost immediately. She was, explained Lucy with wonder and horror, "a very sophisticated woman! Not a—you know—whatever! And she just believed it was witchcraft! And she died! . . . Who'd done it? [It was] one her servants who she'd got rid of. . . . .She came to see me seven days before she died. And she was all right!"

Lucy's unease stemmed partly from the fact that her "sophisticated friend" had believed so strongly in witchcraft. She was shocked by this, because educated Europeans are not meant to fear it. Yet there were shades of the same anxiety in Lucy herself. She was so aghast that her seemingly healthy, otherwise rational friend could die so suddenly that she seemed to be entertaining the possibility that witchcraft might be real. Perhaps the disgruntled employee had hit his mark.

In some of these narratives, white Kenyans seem to fear what anthropologists have widely recognized: namely, that the magic of subordinated groups can serve as a kind of resistance against powerful ones.[38] My interlocutors didn't frame the dynamic exactly like this, of course, but some were clearly nervous that doing wrong to Africans could invite supernatural reprisal. One middle-aged coastal resident, Stephen, told me of disquieting advice he had received from white Kenyan friends who had moved to the coast before him: "Everybody's been saying to me don't ever go against the Giriama because they'll put witchcraft on you." Even the oldest former settlers, those most reluctant to associate themselves with local magic, admitted that mysterious bewitchments in their community have planted a seed of fear in them.

Some of these jitters revolve around one of Kenya's most heated historical issues: entitlement to land. Grace, for instance, related a striking anecdote about bewitchment in the era just around Independence. A British friend of hers had worked as the registrar of land titles out of Mombasa, and was charged with sorting out title deeds along the entire Kenya coast. He traveled north to the Swahili-dominated town of Mambrui, and when he returned, he came down with an illness and "this awful rash." Grace continued:

> [H]e was really obsessed by the fact that he had had, you know, something—some sort of spell put on him, because he went from one bad moment to the next. So he went on leave and he'd only got six months of his contract left, and he'd applied not to come back . . . [he] felt he'd been bewitched because he knew where, you know, [the land was]. They didn't know about aerial photographs, and things, and he'd had old aerial photographs and [he] was silly enough to joke about it, when they said, "How do you [know all of this about our land]," you know, it was something to do with that . . . And in a way I guess he walked into it by saying: "Aha, you see, we have our powers, too," or *something* like that, I imagine. . . . Because he did think it was a joke to begin with! But they didn't take it as a joke.

In this account, the registrar's arrogance was his downfall. In likening his aerial photographs to a dark, otherworldly power, he had thought he was mocking the occult, but in doing so he became its target. According to Grace, the man sank into despair over the subsequent months. In a desperate bid to "try to get over all of this," he even got married, but, she says, "It didn't work." He was institutionalized for mental illness, and eventually took his own life. Grace herself is terrified of local magic, telling me she wants nothing to do with it. She explains that when she lost her diamond ring, "somebody suggested that I go to a witchdoctor because I would find out *immediately* who had taken it. I said: 'I'd rather lose the diamond ring' . . . I'm scared of it . . . I'm scared of it. Simple as that . . . I mean, I just absolutely would not want—if *they* want help that way, and feel it helps them, then I understand, it's their culture, but I personally, um, I wouldn't I wouldn't touch it. I'm too frightened of it."

Grace's statement of cultural relativism ("if *they* want help that way . . . then I understand") goes beyond mere tolerance to worry that the occult forces could be real ("I'm too frightened of it"). Seen in this light, her narrative about the registrar is a cautionary tale in which harmful magic keeps colonial hubris in check. Yes, title deeds and technology have given Europeans certain kinds of control, but dismissing African "powers" as impotent is tempting fate.

The link between witchcraft and land appears in other white narratives on the coast. A number of whites told me that locales with famous

Mijikenda or Swahili shrines were suspected to be bewitched, and that some settler descendants agreed with the rumors that the villages of Mambrui and Takaungu, a centuries-old Arab slave-trading port on the Kenya coast, are haunted. Grace, for instance, describes both sites as "spooky places," adding, "I'm not the only *mzungu* who has felt it." In a separate conversation, James echoed her, saying that Takaungu was "a very spooky place . . . I go there and I get goose pimples." Another white Kenyan living in Mombasa described seeing some "gorgeous real estate" at Takaungu, but added: "I saw those black magic items hanging in the trees . . . it made me leery . . . I decided I didn't want to live there." While coastal residents have accused Arabs and Swahili of slavery and land-grabbing, they also remember European offenses, ranging from the centuries-old Portuguese invasions to the British colonial displacement of Giriama from the Sabaki river area.[39] Might settler descendants' anxiety about Takaungu represent a half-buried fear of reprisal? Nobody made the connection explicit, but these hauntings are enough to drive some away from this site of African suffering.

Very occasionally, whites express fear that witchery could be used to interfere with their financial well-being. Stephen, a middle-aged man who grew up on a settler farm in the Rift Valley and now runs a small business in Kilifi, finds himself in direct competition with some Swahili, Arab, and Kikuyu who run shops in the same arcade: "An African, if he sees somebody else who's got the same business as him doing better than he is, will immediately run to a *mganga*. To get medicine, to go against them, to push their business down. And that's happened. To *me*. And sure enough, I've lost a little bit of business, but not to the extent of having, of being forced to close down. Nearly did once."

Stephen goes on to tell me that the Swahili man who owns the arcade complex uses evil jinn (Islamic spirits) to bewitch his tenants. "One by one, all his renters are going down in business." On the face of it, this would seem a way for a landlord to shoot himself in the foot, but in Stephen's reckoning, it's more important for this man to flex his jealousy through supernatural means than to be economically effective. And Stephen himself has been spooked by the forces at hand.

CROSSING THE BOUNDARY: WHITE KENYANS ENLISTING THE OCCULT

A few white Kenyans have adopted occult means for their own ends. Some use positive magic in an effort to restore their health or fortune. I first encountered this dynamic when I was in the midst of my dissertation research and I received a phone call from a woman from an old settler family. "It's about Jamie [her son, a university student in Britain]," she said. "He's on holiday and he heard you were doing this work with the witchdoctors." She paused. "He needs a sort of reference from you." Jamie sounded a little hesitant on the phone, but earnest. He told me he had been vacationing in Latin America and had purchased a drum from a craftsman in a rural area. Riding back to the city on the bus, he had encountered a bedraggled man who—for reasons Jamie couldn't fully explain—stared at Jamie maliciously while making odd hand gestures toward the drum. Jamie couldn't stop thinking about it. He fell ill with an intestinal problem over the next few weeks, and became convinced that the man had bewitched his drum and through it, him. Now back in Kenya, he decided to enlist the help of the *waganga* he had heard so much about, and he wanted me to broker the deal. I had been doing fieldwork on coastal religion for months, so Jamie knew I would have contacts.

In keeping with Giriama custom, Jamie's healing process began with a *mburuga,* or divination session, led by a female spirit medium named Mudzo in her mud-and-wattle dwelling near Rabai. As Jamie sat cross-legged in front of her, Mudzo indicated that he should place two hundred shillings (worth a little more than U.S.$3.00) on the dirt-packed floor between them. It was much more than she would normally charge, but it is standard practice among diviners to ask more of those who have it. She lit incense, inhaling the curling smoke deeply, and incanted to summon her Arabic helping spirits. Some minutes later they arrived; Mudzo's toes began to twitch, she coughed, and she began to utter a string of nonsensical syllables in a high-pitched monotone. Later, Mudzo translated for us: the spirits confirmed that Jamie and his drum had been bewitched and prescribed the ritual form to remedy it.

Several days later a healing specialist named Kalume worked with two female assistants to effect the cure—the *kuhundula,* or untying of the knots of witchery—in a well-swept clearing beneath some trees. While Jamie's mother stood by in a long denim skirt and a crisp oxford shirt with rolled up sleeves, Kalume instructed Jamie to disrobe and climb into a shallow grave with his drum; a symbolic death, to set the stage for his rebirth and healing. Jamie kept his boxers on for modesty's sake, but gamely stepped into the rectangular pit prepared for him in the earth. Kalume covered him with a white cloth and pieces of pounded maize, appealing to the spirits and the Giriama godhead, Mulungu, to remove the "bad omens" Jamie had brought back with him. He held a small chicken by the feet, cut its throat, and sprinkled the blood over the cloth to entice any bewitching spirits out. The assistants gave Jamie a ritual bath in water infused with sacred herbs, and instructed him to continue these ablutions daily at home. When I called a few days later to ask how he was faring, Jamie's mother was amused, telling me that he was "walking around with bits of green clinging to him." Jamie kept his account light-hearted too, saying that he was glad he'd "chanced his arm [a casual Britishism meaning to take a chance] with the witchdoctor" and he thought he might feel a little bit better, but he wasn't sure.

Jamie didn't go back for more, but some settler descendants do. Naomi, for example, the businesswoman in her thirties mentioned in earlier chapters, has used the assistance of *waganga* for several years, ever since she had a terrifying near-death experience. Naomi had been running a non-profit research project in a small village on the south coast, where she was the only white, overseeing several black staff members. One of her employees had behaved irresponsibly, but unfortunately, he was also the son of an important public figure, so when she "sacked him," she grew "quite afraid" of the social consequences. A couple of months later Naomi was walking alone near the water when she was run down by a hippopotamus and badly mauled. She hovered between life and death for several weeks. While she was in the hospital, some of her staff told her they had found an arrangement of bones on her property, a sign that someone—probably the former employee— had bewitched her. In deep alarm, Naomi had her staff put her in touch with a local *mganga* to undo the witchery, and she recovered her health, slowly but fully.

In recent years, Naomi has continued to use the help of a *mganga*. Another white Kenyan friend, someone from upcountry around her age, told her: "If you ever need someone to help you, to protect you, I know a guy." "His name is Nelson," she said, and I realized she was the only settler descendant I had spoken to who actually named a *mganga,* showing a level of familiarity with a ritual practitioner almost unimaginable among colonial-era settlers. When one of her staff members stole a vital piece of equipment, Naomi brought Nelson to the coast and recovered the equipment through a combination of supernatural appeals and ordinary searching. On other occasions, Naomi calls upon Nelson for assistance when she feels that her affairs are going awry in an "unnatural" way.

These uses of magic run against the grain of white Kenyans' rational ideals, but they also show that the occult has become part of the circuitry of culture for at least some of them. This can pose a challenge to their sense of identity. Frederick, a coastal wildlife specialist in his fifties, told me of his involvement in negative magic, but left me uncertain as to where he stood. A white friend, he said, wanted somebody in his office to be transferred out of Kenya to a branch in another country, and Frederick had gone with him to a specialist:

> The person involved came along with a photograph of the person who should be transferred, and we went to see the witchdoctor, and uh, [he] wanted a black chicken, wanted it slaughtered on the spot, and [the] person actually didn't want the chicken killed, so the witchdoctor said okay, I won't kill it right now but we'll make it go to sleep. So. Held the chicken and stroked its head, chicken played dead. . . . And he did his, uuh, bit of talk and extra money changed hands, and at the end of the month, [the] person was transferred. But not the person that *should* have been transferred, but the person who *wanted* them to be transferred. [Frederick laughs] So it kind of backfired.

In Frederick's laughter and the uncertainties of his account, he seems to distance himself from the event. It isn't clear, for instance, why the ritual "backfired" (was the magic thwarted by the half-hearted treatment of the chicken? Or was the ritual failure proof that there were no real occult forces at play to begin with?). Frederick had been party to a witchcraft rite, but in his account of it, he kept it at some remove.

Of all my interlocutors, Stephen used the help of *waganga* the most dramatically. In other aspects of his life, too, he has done much to cross old colonial boundaries. When I met him, he was cohabiting with a Kikuyu woman ("I've gone bush," he said sardonically), and was proud, he told me, that he does not share the racist attitudes he attributed to many white Kenyans. His white Kenyan peers regard Stephen as vulnerable and somewhat unhinged. After learning more about the depth of his involvement in *uganga,* I began to see why he would unnerve his European peers.

By Stephen's account, he first began to entertain the possibility of witchcraft while horseback riding with a colleague of his, a German expatriate married to a Swahili man. Stephen has three horses, his pride and joy, and his favorite steed, Malaika, had been repeatedly felled by illness and accidents. "My German friend said to me at that point: 'Stephen this is not normal . . . maybe someone is putting witchcraft [on your horse].' And I said, 'Sabine, that only happens to people who believe in it. It doesn't happen to—' and she said, 'No no, not necessarily.' . . . She said, 'If I were you I'd go and see this *mganga* somewhere *way* up in the hills—a Giriama—on your way to Malindi.'"

In Stephen's initial refusal, we see again the idea that it is belief in witchcraft, not witchcraft itself, that afflicts people. But he caved to his European friend's urging and went to visit the diviner she recommended. He was awestruck when, during the divination ceremony, the diviner seemed to make a bottle embedded in the soil before her rise up from the ground without any natural explanation. He was astonished by her accuracy; she knew without his having to tell her that he was having trouble with a "large animal" that kept falling ill. Finally, the diviner described the employees at Stephen's stable, and instructed him to fire one of them, a Giriama worker who she said was jealous of an upcountry worker: "[The diviner said:] 'Get rid of that short one. He's the one that's causing your problems.' . . . I said 'no, I can't do that. You have to tell me how you know this.' So she said: 'He came with a beetle and ground [up] the beetle and put it amongst the hay. And he did witchcraft on that horse because he doesn't want the upcountry man to be in charge of the horses; he wants to be the boss of the horses' . . . She knew everything. She knew *everything*." Stephen went straight home and pinned the accused employee against a tree with his arm:

> And I said to him in Swahili: "*Kumbe* [Oh, wow], it's you who's been doing all this to my horse, eh? Is it true you've been the one that's damaging my horse? Because I'm going to do *exactly* to you what you've done to my horse, in fact, I've already organized it." Frightened him like that . . . "I've just come from a *mganga* and I know: you're the one who's been doing this. That's right." . . . He knew immediately. Without me having to tell him. I said, "You're the one who's been doing this," and he started shaking.

On a later occasion, Stephen returned to the *mganga* to discern which of his staff members had killed a valued pet of his. Once again, Stephen went straight home and fired him.

This man who had once thought that witchcraft was a problem of belief rather than a real force eventually became tangled in a web of black magic involving his first cousin, Alger. It started when Alger borrowed some money and failed to pay it back. When Stephen tried to collect, things got ugly fast; Alger accused Stephen of spending too much on his "black girlfriend" while shutting out his family. Ramping up the conflict, Alger hired ritual specialists to put a spell on Stephen, but his plans were foiled by one of his own employees, John, a Giriama and a born-again Christian. John wasn't getting paid by Alger, so he decided to sound the alarm by writing a letter to one of Stephen's friends: "[Instead of paying me, Alger] used the money to go to witch-doctors to force Stephen's girlfriend Dorothy to part ways with him or kill her completely. . . . So Alger went to the witchdoctor . . . he wants to finish Dorothy and Stephen's relationship so that he can live happily again. But because of my strong faith in Christianity . . . I could not keep quiet while all the plans of evil were going on."

John appended several lists in Alger's handwriting of "wishes" he had given to the *waganga*. In one of these, Alger writes that he suspects Stephen of hiring witchdoctors of his own to bewitch Alger and Alger's children: "It seems they are winning. We have to do all we can to stop them from harming us." In another, Alger enumerates fourteen desiderata, including that he be able to "sell all my things," that he win a "court case in Nairobi," that his bills be paid, and that his family be "kept safe from any more evil." The last item on the list: "For Stephen to be very very upset when we leave town, and for his whore to leave him."

Stephen freely shared all of these documents with me, as well as copies of his own letters to his cousin. In one of these, he refers to Alger's belief in witchdoctors as "pathetic," and repeatedly urges him that he is wasting his money on quacks and that he must turn to God:

> Alger, unless you help yourself you are going to end up in worse problems than you are already in because of your obsession with witch doctors, my advise [sic] to you is to stop seeing these people who are only doing to you what you are doing to me, milking your money for nothing in return. Start going to church and ask God for forgiveness for all the wrong you have done to others and to ask God for help . . . hopefully we will meet one day in heaven if you ask God for forgiveness.

These exchanges are rife with simultaneous attraction and aversion to the occult. Although Stephen has been using occult means for years, in the last letter, he plays the role of a good Christian who can see through the quackery of local superstition. Also ironic, of course, is that Alger's nefarious use of Giriama witchcraft is brought up short by a Giriama man who has internalized the "Christian values" once considered the domain of Europeans. For Stephen, the line between cultural worlds has become blurred, but the world of witchery is simply too threatening to be assimilated to his identity. He attempts to redraw the line by aligning himself with Christianity. Perhaps he was terrified of what Alger's witchery could achieve, and perhaps he had begun to spook even himself with his own use of the occult.

John's Christian disapproval raises the question of what other black Kenyans on the coast make of whites who use the occult. Many of my Giriama friends and contacts knew of whites using the services of *waganga*.

Some saw it as a measure of growing African prestige. Said one healing expert: "Our *dawa* [medicine] is now recognized around the world." Said another: "We're in an era of change, and whites are curious. They see that we Africans have a kind of technology they should explore. As long as they aren't breaking the law of the land and remain respectful, they can do as they wish." Some laypeople told me *waganga* were enthusiastic about attracting white clients through word of mouth, because they could charge whites so much. A few, however, told me of their suspicion that whites might be poaching the few supernatural advantages Africans have for their own benefit. Said an older man: "Our *waganga* should focus on tending the house of Mbodze and Matsezi," the ancestral Giriama couple; working with other ethnicities seemed to him a betrayal of sorts. Some Giriama wondered whether African methods would even work for those of European descent. A few *waganga,* for instance, noted that while Mulungu, the Giriama godhead, might be willing to help whites, the *koma,* or Giriama ancestors, definitely would not. In the words of one, "Mulungu is merciful and will fix anyone, but the ancestors won't help a white person. Each and every sub-tribe of Mijikenda have their own ancestral posts of remembrance, and these hold the ancestral spirits. If whites don't keep these posts of remembrance, there's no way they can be helped by any ancestors."

Some of these conversations implied that whites are very common visitors to *waganga*—but this is presumably because most of the whites mentioned in these discussions were tourists, visiting students, and expatriates, often Italians. It's easy for curious visitors to find brokers to lead them to *waganga,* for there are many "beach boys" and other figures who hang around tourist areas to offer various kinds of assistance and services for a fee. Once they have satisfied their curiosity, adventure-seekers can lay claim to an "authentic African experience."

The stakes are different, however, for settler descendants. On the one hand, they fervently wish to belong to Kenyan society and be counted as Kenyan. On the other hand, they harbor the residue of colonial ideologies of European cognitive superiority, whether or not they want to, and frame themselves as elite, level-headed instruments of Kenya's development. Any whiff of local superstition runs against the grain of such an image. (To put their dilemma another way, and pulling together some other strands of this book: it seems that just when settler descendants want to be counted as "Kenyan," the colonial unconscious rears its head; and just when they want to remain "European" in their rationality, they turn out to be more influenced by their African cultural surroundings than they are necessarily comfortable with.) Since they feel they aren't supposed to get involved with the occult, but some of them do anyway, their discussions of it are conflicted and ambivalent. As part of this ambivalence, white Kenyans keep circling anxiously back to the notion of "belief"—a notion more complicated and troubling than I had realized.

THE ANXIETY OF "BELIEF"

"Belief" arises so often in discussions of witchcraft and magic because the concept is central to Judeo-Christian-Islamic religions, even though plenty of smaller-scale religious traditions have found ways to be less concerned with it.[40] Post-Enlightenment Western ideologies generally treat "belief" as the commitment to the truth of a certain idea, ideally based on some kind of persuasive evidence. A rational person, furthermore, is expected to have internally consistent belief states, rather than erratic or clashing ones.[41] But when white Kenyans discuss the occult, belief doesn't seem such a clear-cut, either-or mental state. When I remarked to Stephen how many white Kenyans seemed to fear African religious forces, he replied: "Well, of course they do; they're here, in the thick of a great band of witchcraft that runs up and down the coast. Trying not to believe is like going to a bar and trying to just drink water." At first I thought Stephen was referring to the impressionability that can make belief drift as one changes context,[42] but in a separate conversation weeks later, when Stephen and I knew each other much better, he reframed things: "The Giriama have bats who can follow you and put a spell on you to believe," he insisted. "Once you're out of range they can't get to you anymore, so you stop believing it." In this formulation, the supernatural forces in question are real, but they only work in a particular territory. One's belief in these forces waxes and wanes relative to one's distance from that space. Looked at this way, belief is hardly about rational decision-making on the basis of evidence. Instead, human minds can be changed by occult forces themselves.

Bats putting spells on people—Stephen is stretching white Kenyan identity considerably to encompass this idea. A more guarded confessional came from the elderly woman Letty when I asked her where she stood on the question of the occult. Her blue eyes fixed the table between us and she shrugged helplessly as she spoke: "Honestly, there is something in us that half *believes* or *wants* to believe, but we know we *shouldn't* believe in this sort of thing . . . because that's the way we're brought up that you're not *supposed* to believe in things like that." In Letty's model, upbringing is the source of desirable personal identity for settler descendants, establishing a kind of ideal core self with a clear sense of what one "should" believe.[43] But the African surround provides pernicious messages that destabilize the ideal core self, giving rise to something like half-belief, or perhaps half-buried temptation to believe.

The dilemma Letty describes is particularly keen for some younger white Kenyans who consider their affinity with their black Kenyan neighbors, however vague this feeling may be, to help justify their belonging. Their narratives are fraught with ambiguity as they flirt with the possibility that the occult might be real and their uncomfortable sense that this standpoint threatens the controlled, rational person they want to be. Several of my interlocutors caught themselves in contradictions. James, for instance, interrupted himself in the midst of a stream-of consciousness monologue about the occult: "I believe it is the mind. . . . I do I think that most of it is the mind. . . . I believe a lot of it is the mind, *but,* and now I'm sort of contradicting myself, there is still a lot out there that no one really knows about how it works. And so it it's difficult to gauge."

Stephen, too, catches the tension in his own narrative. During one of our conversations, he suggested that witchcraft isn't real; it's only when a person is spooked by it that they can make themselves sick, psychosomatically. But here is what he said in the next breath when he remembers what had happened to his horse Malaika: "Actually, I think I'm going to contradict myself now, because that [bewitchment] happened to an animal. I mean an animal doesn't have the right to believe or not to believe. The witchcraft actually [he taps his desk for emphasis] went against my animal."

In some other narratives, speakers seemed to tack between confessing their fear of the occult and disavowing belief in it, with no apparent sense of contradiction. Listening to them, I sometimes found myself frustrated by their lack of resolution: did they believe in occult forces, or not? In time, I realized this tension couldn't be resolved, for standard notions of "belief" aren't really up for the job of capturing the complexity of their positions. But certainly the possibility that they *might* believe is terrifying for some of them, and I heard some creative linguistic strategies to handle this threat. Spatial and physical metaphors are especially handy for holding the occult at bay. Evoking a kind of permeation of African bodies by occult beliefs and practices, white Kenyans on the coast repeatedly told me that Giriama were "steeped" or "mired" in witchcraft.[44] White Kenyans say they avoid this permeation by keeping their distance; "I don't delve into these things," as several of them put it.

But while statements like these could be taken as a lack of interest, a closer look at their turns of phrase suggests they are busy keeping fear—and fearful forces—at bay. When speaking with James about his spirit encounter, for instance, I asked, "What did you make of it all?" The awkwardness of his reply betrayed his anxiety:

> *James:* I don't know, I mean, don't ask *me*. It's just one of those things. I mean I really can't sort of go on find[ing] explanation for these things but I am definitely [he pauses] . . . will say that I am slight—yeah, I've been exposed to these things so I ca—I have to admit that I am slightly, I do, I [pause] from a distance [pause] feel [he pauses yet again, and we both start to chuckle] that there's something there.
>
> *Janet:* Why is it that . . . you phrased it that way?
>
> *James:* Um . . . 'cause I don't really want to be—I don't want to delve into it. Yeah? I do believe from a *distance* there's something there.

As James spoke, he groped for clarity and grew increasingly rattled, until we both began to laugh at his awkward speech. But his lack of fluency wasn't careless; instead, it seemed to reflect the exquisite care he took to avoid making any straightforward or enthusiastic statement of belief. Even when he seemed on the brink of admitting something like belief ("I am definitely . . . "), something held him back. After much hesitation, he concluded that "from a distance there's something there." Getting too close to the occult, even verbally, is a frightening prospect.

Other white Kenyans, too, struggle to locate their center of gravity somewhere in the murky terrain between the skepticism that modern rationalists are supposed to nourish and the concession that occult forces may be real. Take Agnes, who admits to being "quite colonial" in her attitudes but does not dismiss the occult out of hand:

> *Agnes:* It might be all hocus-pocus, or it might indeed work. And it obviously—although, I personally don't believe in it, there are those who do. And for those who do, it is obviously a potent weapon or a potent cure. Whichever way it's going to be.
>
> *Janet:* . . . What do you mean when you say "I don't believe it"? Do you mean: I think it's impossible that any sort of supernatural something could be going on? Or what do you—
>
> *Agnes:* [interrupting me] No no no no. I I I grant that [she clears her throat] supernatural things do happen. But [she enunciates each word distinctly] I personally cannot believe *in* the supernatural.

Agnes began with an ambiguous statement: "It might be all hocus-pocus, or it might indeed work," but she "personally doesn't believe in it." When I pressed her to clarify what she means, she ultimately granted the existence of "supernatural things." Yet it seemed crucial for her to insist that she "personally cannot believe *in* the supernatural." On the face of it, this might seem a contradiction; according to common Western ideologies, one is supposed either to believe something exists or not. But Agnes drew a distinction between acknowledging that a force existed and "believing in" that force; perhaps for her "believing in" is about commitment, faith, and identity.[45] For Agnes, the occult may be real, but she refuses to incorporate it into her sense of who she is.

Frederick, who told the equivocal story about the chicken "playing dead," tried to hold the occult at arm's length—not only with linguistic ambiguities, but also with the help of other supernatural forces. He told me of a ritual his staff commissioned at their workplace to bring in more clients so that they could keep their jobs. More clients eventually came, but Frederick added uncertainly: "So whether it was lucky or what, I don't know. But anyway it *did* work." He continued with another series of equivocations: "But I know that the local people themselves I mean, amongst the Giriamas and some of the upcountry people really believe very strongly. . . . And if they are bewitched, they're *bewitched*, and that's it. You can't do anything about it. So they *really* believe in them. [He pauses for about two seconds.] I believe that—in it on a fact for *them*." I was unsure how to interpret this. "You believe in it how?" I asked. Frederick responded:

> For *them*. Yeah . . . the Giriamas amongst themselves they're often um, well, for instance one of my staff, they said he was uh, uh bewitched because he didn't share meat which I had given to him amongst his community. So he was bewitched and uh [Frederick switches to a lower voice] maybe he was even poisoned, indirectly. [Frederick returns to his regular register] And he died! Three days later! So, if they believe, this is what happens. So I believe that they amongst themselves believe it. But I don't believe, or [long pause] I wouldn't get myself involved in anything of their spirits and such because actually I think I have maybe my *own* stronger power.

At first Frederick said he believes in the power of witchcraft, but only "for them." Then, describing the bewitchment of one of his staff members, he speculated that the man's death might have been through "indirect" poisoning—whatever that could be. Next he asserted that he didn't believe, but after a long pause, he said that he had "his *own* stronger power," suggesting that occult forces are real for him and he needs to guard against them. When I asked for clarification about the nature of this power, he informed me that "it's a Christian thing."

Although few of the interlocutors I describe in this chapter were devoutly religious, Frederick wasn't the only settler descendant who seemed relieved at the idea that Christianity could supernaturally trump the occult. Stephen told me that his business defied the bewitchment of his landlord because he prioritized Christianity: "I strongly believe that [my surviving in business] is because I'm not brought up to believe in *maganga*rism *[sic]*.[46] That I do *really believe in God* and I *really do pray* with Jesus. I honestly believe that Jesus has more strength than the witchcraft."

Stephen's announcement once again invokes the importance of belief statements themselves. The very act of stating what one does and does not believe—regardless of what one does, experiences, or feels—is important to the performance of white Kenyan identity. Agnes's vehement assertion that she, "personally, cannot believe *in* the supernatural," too, and Frederick's evasive statement that "I believe in it . . . for *them*" suggest that unambiguous belief statements about the African occult are to be avoided. Stephen revealed the same aversion in our first conversation, when I initially raised the topic of *uganga:*

> *Janet:* So one thing I want to know is since you've lived on the coast for so long, what do you know about *uganga?* There's a huge amount; it's much bigger than I can—
>
> *Stephen:* [Interrupting me] I don't believe in it. But these people have been brought up with *maganga*rism right from the word go, and it's rather like being brought up on mother's milk or goat's milk, you know.

Stephen emphatically asserted that he didn't believe in *uganga* and naturalized it to "these people" (black Kenyans), using a biological metaphor. Yet later that same day he told me about hiring diviners to hire and fire staff members. Consistency did not seem to be Stephen's priority. Instead, it was most important for him not to make any point-blank statement of belief in the occult. Among settler descendants, such professions of belief are danced around, choked upon, fearfully alluded to, yet scrupulously avoided, as if their very utterance were a deep betrayal of who the speaker hopes to be.

Noticing these evasions again and again, I couldn't help thinking that belief statements themselves have taken on a talismanic quality. Admitting belief in the occult, it seems, can make a person vulnerable to unde-

sirable social consequences and fearsome forces. Both of these possibilities were highlighted in a discussion I had with Priscilla, a
second-generation Kenyan with Italian roots, whose friends were mostly
of British descent. When I asked what she "knew" about *uganga* or
uchawi, she replied: "I know that it's extremely common. I know that
it—absolutely common, and it does exist, for sure." I pressed her,
revealing my own fixation on belief states: "Do you believe in it, or do
you just believe that they believe in it?" Priscilla responds with emphatic
gesticulations that reflected her level of fear, at one point even putting
up a wall with her hands as if fending off invisible demons:

> Let's put it this way, that with [my staff] I would never admit to them that I
> could believe in it. Because, when they try to involve me in this kind of thing . . .
> my reaction is: I'm a *mzungu* and I do not believe in this kind of thing . . .
> because I don't want them to think you can become vulnerable. Because the
> moment that they think you [pause]—you never know. You know? You never
> know. . . . We don't have the power to, to control this kind of magic forces,
> whatever you want to call them.

If her staff members knew that Priscilla believed in *uganga,* she would
incur both a loss of face and a kind of threat. If they know she is vulnerable, she implies, they might actually use terrifying magic against her.[47]
At the end of this conversation, Priscilla achieved clarity about one
thing: "We Westerners are . . . *pretending* to be rational. Rationalize
everything."

In a 1981 article entitled "How Man Makes God in West Africa,"
the anthropologist Karin Barber argues that for Yoruba, the prestige
and efficacy of the Orisa gods rise and fall depending upon the attention
of their human devotees, without whom they fade into insignificance.[48]
Yoruba recognize the importance of human attention in making supernatural forces potent. In a similar vein, I found in my fieldwork among
Giriama that "belief" itself is sometimes treated as if it can invite or
strengthen the occult. When I asked Giriama men why they were less
likely to be spirit-possessed than Giriama women, I heard again and
again the paradoxical answer: "We men don't believe in spirits, so they
don't bother us as much."[49] Adam Ashforth locates a similar dynamic
among black South Africans in Soweto, who fear that evil forces might
be the cause of their hardships. Many seek supernatural help from specialists, but assert, in the words of one, that witchcraft "partly exists . . .
but me, I don't believe."[50] The startling similarities among settler
descendants and Africans from various parts of the continent suggest a

broad and loosely shared cultural field of fear that belief itself—and, I would add, even talk *about* one's belief—risks making the occult more real.[51] And while it was common for colonials to jab at "superstitious Africans" for conflating the word with the world, it seems that in their very efforts to distance themselves from the occult, settler descendants do just this.

Is it possible that in all this cultural intermingling, hierarchies of difference will ultimately be loosened? One doesn't want to be naïvely optimistic, but Naomi's perspective on the occult offers a clue to the possibilities. She uses the help of *waganga,* taking their supernatural powers as real, but treating them as consistent with Western modes of help. "I firmly believe," she announces, that "a lot of these *waganga* are very clever psychologists and psychiatrists." When I replied there could be a tension between treating the occult as real and treating it as mere psychiatry, she proposed a compromise: perhaps, she said, the strength of a person's belief can psychosomatically magnify the supernatural effects of magic. As for her *mganga,* Nelson, she uses his help, but retains her self-determination:

> Sometimes Nelson has called me out of the blue. I find it uncanny, just uncanny, that he so often catches me at a moment when difficult things are facing me. But it's very important to me that he not control my life. I don't want to be unable to act without consulting him first. It's like having a psychiatrist; it's not good for people to have to consult their psychiatrists before they do anything. I need to be the one steering my life. . . . I don't want to *dwell* in this stuff.

Finally, Naomi added something that startled me. She told me Nelson's powers had helped her with her workplace dilemmas, then added with a pragmatic air: "It's a way of having someone on your side. You're running an organization, see? And you need all the help you can get. It's a management tool." I was used to hearing white Kenyans talk about the occult as primitive superstition, and suddenly it sounded like a modern corporate facilitator. Could this be the wave of the future, among white Kenyans—an Africanized version of their enthusiasm for pragmatism and progress?

That may be unlikely, but still, there's no question that white identity in Kenya has changed over the past century. Even the hint of cultural relativism among some settler descendants as they talk about the occult is worlds away from the contempt most settlers had for African lifeways. That said, most still hold tightly to the idea that the West brought and will continue to bring improvements to Africa, and that they are uniquely positioned to facilitate this flow. For most, the occult remains a major limit to their willingness to accept or assimilate to some of the lifeways around them. Moving forward, their conundrum will remain: Can they hold on to such a notion of cultural supremacy but still be embraced as fully Kenyan?

Conclusion

White Kenyans have a slang term for whites in Africa they perceive as especially retrograde: *kaburu*. The word refers to an unreconstructed type, possibly Afrikaner, definitely low in intellect and high in racism. In the decades after Kenya's independence, settler descendants circulated schoolyard jokes hinging on a character named van der Merwe, a fictive Afrikaner who embodies the *kaburu* spirit. Here, Olivia relates a typical van der Merwe joke from her childhood:

> Van de Merwe is assigned to measure the height of a pole. He tries shimmying up to measure but fails to get to the top; he tries this, he tries that, all to no avail. Eventually an African asks him why he doesn't take the pole down, measure it, and then put it back up. Van der Merwe thinks a moment and then says: "That's stupid, you bloody *kaffir* [a racially offensive slur]. I've got to measure the height of the pole, not its length!"[1]

The *kaburu* foil, the Afrikaner-style colonialist, represents everything that the Kenyan settler—especially after Independence—supposedly is not. The *kaburu* is disrespectful to Africans, logistically incompetent, and morally backward. He follows the creed that, as Olivia puts it, "White people *rule;* it doesn't really matter where or how; they just *do.*"

The middle-class and well-to-do settler descendants I encountered in Kenya, between bars and beachfront gatherings, social clubs and offices, Land Rovers and tented safari camps, enjoy and defend their lifestyle, but they're aware they can't afford a rigid creed of white supremacy. They know they are a privileged community under scrutiny. And at critical junctures such as the Cholmondeley trial or the Maasai protests over white-owned land in Laikipia, they become re-racialized; singled out as problematic by virtue of their racial community's colonial history.

This book has probed the moral double consciousness occasioned by these critiques, and explored the techniques some white Kenyans use to respond to the discomforts of seeing themselves being seen. For many I spoke to, defensive expressions of nationalism seem an effort to try to establish their belonging in Kenya. And as part of this nationalism, settler descendants, time and again, draw distinctions between *types* of whites in Africa. We have seen their stereotypes of two-year-wonder expatriates, those do-gooders who, say my respondents, think they understand how to help, but really just meddle in the workings of a nation they don't fathom. (Perhaps even worse, to settler descendants, are the expats who adopt mannerisms they associate with "Kenya cowboys," sometimes drawing on a template they've pieced together from novels and Hollywood productions.) But their most morally significant foils hail from other former colonies, especially South Africa and Zimbabwe (formerly Rhodesia), where white-run regimes were famous for brutal extremes of segregation and discrimination. At Kenya's independence, some settlers who couldn't stomach living under black rule headed south to those same nations, leaving some whites who stayed on in Kenya feeling almost progressive by contrast. Here, for instance, is Trevor, describing how his stint at secondary school in 1990s South Africa clarified why he belongs in Kenya:

> That sort of cemented more than anything why I was Kenyan. Because there's obviously that whole apartheid time in South Africa and I got in around the time it truly opened up. And just that sort of feeling of black and white and boundaries and everything down there, you could feel the tension straight away. You know, you walk in a street in Kenya and chaps [are] really friendly. You get down there and there's complete change of attitude. And that sort of that made me feel, well, we're lucky where we are.

An older white Kenyan from an agricultural family, Eleanor, makes similar claims, insisting white Kenyans must not be conflated with white South Africans:

> [Also] I think South Africa is definitely a different kettle of fish. I don't feel at home there because the race tension there is unreal. In England [where Eleanor went to university] people were like: "You *South African!*" and it was all one mush. I couldn't understand it then because I'd never been there and experienced that . . . but when I went to South Africa I was like, "Ho ho,

now I see what the problem is." But Kenya is so far from that. Maybe because [of] what actually happened in apartheid. And I just don't think the whole tension has ever been here.

Marcus, the coffee-industry manager, makes a similar claim:

You can drive around parts of South Africa, and you know the way they talk to the indigenous [sic] is unacceptable . . . the Afrikaners [are] very racialist types . . . the one single reason I would not move to South Africa is the black-white relationship. It's just so uneasy. Security is *so* bad. You will be shot because of who you are, not what you have [on the basis of race rather than class, in other words]. You're very unlucky [that is, it would be very unusual] here to be shot for who you are.

For other white Kenyans, Zimbabwe is a major foil. Naomi, the businesswoman who insists that black and white Kenyans live in "intertwined worlds," told me, "I remember we went for a [sporting event] down to Zimbabwe in 1980 and I was *shocked* . . . I felt it was quite a culturally divided country. It was more racist, I don't know, more black and white. I mean people come here and think it's black and white but it *isn't* black and white."

Even the United States is not immune from such comparison. One young woman whose family had lived in America for a couple of years said:

When we went to the States I found the mentality there—the racism was unbelievable, and me coming from here, everyone was like, "Gasp! You terrible person; you're so racist!" And I was just like: "What?" I was so shocked. We had this African American delivery guy, UPS, used to come every day and when we left he said, "You people are the only ones who treated me on the same level as everyone else." And Mum was like: "*Us? We* get criticized [for being] *racist!*"

My respondents suggested that Kenya is special not only for having relatively fewer racial tensions, but also, they say, for having a different kind of colonial history. Some settler descendants draw up a contrast between different modes of colonial governance to suggest that British colonialism wasn't so bad after all. The businessman Simon frames it as having been quite benign by suggesting that settler colonialism and colonial exploitation are mutually exclusive: "You know the Brits they came, didn't want to cause any harm, settled, whereas in the other African countries [with] diamonds, copper—a lot of European countries came in, got what they could, and gapped it [took off]. But people from outside came to Kenya to *settle,* to make a living here, as opposed to exploit."

Gordon, the Nairobi hotelier, suggested that other colonial powers showed malice, in contrast to the British. "Okay, the British did some terrible things but not as terrible as the Portuguese and the Belgian and the French. And [the British] were quite good colonizers. And they *left* quite a very good working infrastructure whereas the Portuguese pulled everything down to their last teaspoon when they left." And Evelyn, from a long-standing, aristocratic farming family, insisted that by contrast with the Belgians in Central Africa, the British came to Africa with a helpful, future-oriented mentality: "If you read [Adam Hochschild's book] *King Leopold's Ghost* [about colonialism in Belgian Congo][2] . . . *their* method of colonization was very different to the British method and they really only went there to extract and not to build. And I think people came here to build. I really do. I think that they wanted to build the country and they wanted to take it forward."

Clearly, settler descendants in Kenya have been unsettled by objections to British colonialism, particularly when those objections rub off on their families, framing them as exploiters. While they aren't wrong when they point out the atrocities Europeans perpetrated elsewhere in Africa, it isn't difficult to find structural oblivion in the ways they rhetorically frame the situation at home. Troubling aspects of colonialism in Kenya—the seizures of African land, the systems of squatting and taxation that exploited African labor, and the mass incarcerations and human-rights abuses during the Mau Mau era, for example—are swept under the rug to help these speakers sustain a sense of legitimacy in the nation.

But these narratives shouldn't be reduced merely to their structuring of oblivion. These speakers are also insisting that there's more than one way to be a white person in Africa. Indeed, whites all over Africa make intra-racial distinctions among themselves, underscoring the social constructedness of racial categories. While historically these lines tended to be based on geographic origin (e.g., "Boer" vs Anglo-Saxon vs southern European) and class, today, the starkest lines often take political stance into consideration; in today's South Africa, for instance, progressive white citizens are at pains to distance themselves from the apartheid regime and its racism, as well as the "Boer nationalists" who continue to make separatist gestures.[3] In Zimbabwe, white Euro-American expatriates who arrived in the 1980s and 1990s have been eager to distinguish themselves from white supremacist former Rhodesians.[4] In recent years, some younger whites have come to describe themselves as "new-breed Zimbabweans," to juxtapose their attitudes against those of their elders.[5] And in Tanzania, the geographer Richard Schroeder says, a discourse differentiating "good whites" from "bad whites" has emerged in recent years, particularly as leftist white expatriates (most of whom came in sympathy with the state's liberation and socialist causes) criticize a wave of "rough" and "abrasive" South African immigrants and investors for reproducing apartheid racial relations in Tanzania. A member of an old American missionary family feels the South African arrivistes don't even count as "white": "*Makaburu* [the plural of *kaburu*] are not white. No one considers them to be *wazungu* (i.e., like European or North American whites); they are *Makaburu*."[6]

In this final example of internal white differentiation, we come full circle to the *kaburu* figure. Looking closely at the historical roles this stereotype has played in Kenya, we can see that the political rationale for rejecting the *kaburu* persona has made a 180° turn. A hundred years ago, British settlers found Afrikaners in Kenya distasteful because, says the historian Brett Shadle, they were too lowly. The crude ways of the barefoot, undereducated Boers who had migrated north during and after the Anglo-Boer war and lived on under-resourced farms near Eldoret blurred the lines between white and African, and embarrassed the cause of British settler "prestige." In other words, the *kaburu* figure posed a threat to white supremacy.[7] Yet in the years since Independence, imagined *kaburu* figures have been considered bad by white Kenyans precisely because they embody white supremacy (and a particularly crude and inept variety at that). In the shifting of *kaburu* narratives, then, we see settler descendants shift from a mentality of white supremacy to an anxiety that they might be accused of it.

WHITENESSES

If there is no one way to be white, this recognition should trouble any simplistic understanding of that elusive term, "whiteness." Scholars have used the term, in an extensive literature that began in the United States and has expanded globally, to highlight and examine the advantages that have historically accrued to whites. Some focus on "whiteness" as a set of meanings and potencies imputed to white people—as in Ira Bashkow's (2006) exploration of Orokaiva people in Papua New Guinea, who project wealth, ease of motion, and a lack of social obligations onto "whitemen." Similar projections take place in Kenya and elsewhere in sub-Saharan Africa, in cases where whites are assumed to be rich and technologically advanced—where certain versions of modernity, in other words, are sometimes "raced" as white. But the most common scholarly discussions of "whiteness" use the term to designate a "historical systemic structural race-based superiority."[8] Definitions like this helpfully clarify that white privilege and racial domination can be sustained even when whites don't feel themselves to be racist (as well as, of course, when they do). In many studies, then, "whiteness" is centrally understood in terms of systems, structures, efforts, and subjectivities that retain white control and white privilege.[9]

Certainly this has been part of my focus, too. In my discussions of subjectivity among settler descendants in Kenya, I have argued that structural oblivion—comprised of erasures and ideologies—is one mechanism by which this group of whites legitimate their privileges. Through denials, amnesia, selective narratives, and self-sustaining ideologies, many of the settler descendants I spoke to uphold the notion that Kenyan whites' ways of life and ideas of the good are morally ideal and helpful to Kenya, and don't often recognize when these ways of life and ideas are emergent from colonial mentalities, Western hegemony, or white privilege. It is hard for my respondents to see that so many of their value systems are Eurocentric, in part because they see their preferences as best for Kenya.

So, for instance, most of my white Kenyan interlocutors consider it commonsensical that capitalist economic growth, "development," and possessive individualism, rather than small-scale reciprocity, are the best economic arrangements for all. Many believe that first rights to land come from using the land "productively," and that pastoralism is intrinsically destructive or shoddy. They favor a model of civic (liberal) nationalism, such that one's highest allegiance should be to the nation-state rather than to an ethnic group, clan, or other small-scale unit of identification. They believe culpability should be judged at the individual level rather than the collective level, and that individuals' intentions should weigh heavily in this adjudication—a formulation that favors their colonial predecessors (if and when they considered themselves "well-meaning") and absolves current generations from redress for any sins of their ancestors. They share "modern" ideas about romantic love and companionate marriage and downplay the role of material transactions in kinship attachments (in spite of the fact that they glue together their kin-like relationships with domestic staff by keeping them materially dependent). They feel English is the language best suited for formal, intellectual, and technical discussions, while Kiswahili is more connected to informality and emotion. They prioritize rationalism over mysticism, and deem occult superstition backward (in spite of the fact that some of them draw on the occult). In these taken-for-granted priorities and values, they overlap with many cosmopolitan and well-to-do black Kenyans, at the same time that they do not honor or particularly understand some of the very different priorities, values, and indeed resentments that circulate among many others. Settler descendants may see their norms as having no racial basis, yet such norms tend to benefit whites overall. In this regard, then, part of my study has indeed explored the aspects of whiteness concerned with keeping the upper hand.

And yet, like other scholars, I find it helpful to think about whiteness in terms of internal diversity—in terms of whitenesses, to use Melissa Steyn's term—rather than framing it as unvarying and essential.[10] As noted, whites in Africa make internal distinctions among themselves, as do whites elsewhere; John Hartigan (1999) and M. F. Jacobson (1999), among others, have demonstrated that in the United States, whites make intra-racial distinctions on the basis of geographic origin, class, locality, political styles, and other considerations. But beyond such forms of differentiation, a quick comparison between whites in the United States and in sub-Saharan Africa suggests a profound difference: whereas whites in the United States enjoy the luxury of a less marked racial identity than persons of color, whites in Africa are a conspicuous minority who realize they stand out, whether because powerful, resented, or both. Furthermore, what it's like to be white in Kenya has also changed considerably since Independence, particularly since the colonial heritage has been reframed as a form of pillage based on unjust racism. Arguably, the varying discomforts and responses that ensue— including the unsettling condition of moral double consciousness, the anxiety about belonging, the defiant denials, and the unhappy admissions—are not incidental to my respondents' whiteness; we should consider these enfolded, in all their plurality, as part of it.

Thus, for instance, certain stances and longings are part of a distinctly white Kenyan repertoire: the expression of nostalgia for their African playmates, a wish to "connect" with their domestic staff and workaday Kenyans, enthusiasm for Kiswahili (as, perhaps, a surrogate of sorts for more embodied interracial intimacies that still make them uncomfortable), and insistence they care about the nation and its people. When settler descendants have crises of conscience, like Jos, who sees his own wealth as emergent from a caste-based colonial system, or like the few Laikipia farmers who concede that Maasai activists have a viable point, they are not leaving whiteness behind, but coming to inhabit a new variation on the theme of privileged experience. And when they deny that colonial history is relevant to how they should be judged today, they are embodying a defensive white subjectivity that parries a contemporary, globally circulating, conversation about restitution and redress. For although colonial whites in Kenya long faced criticism from government administrators and liberal interest groups in Britain, today settler descendants find that the critical voices are more powerful than ever; not only are some of the old myths justifying the colonial endeavor rejected, but whites also fear they may be asked to pay for it in one way or another. Theirs is a new generation of white stories that are always responding, in varied, uneven ways, to criticisms leveled at older versions of whiteness.

Other scholars of whites in postcolonial Africa, too, are exploring a range of white reactions to their displacement from political power. To be sure, in an objection to the slide of their privileges, plenty of whites have fought to retain their socioeconomic status and cried, "Reverse racism!"[11] Among some white farmers in Zimbabwe who have faced violent dispossession from their land, there has been a resurgence of racist rhetoric and hardening of antipathies.[12] Among some Afrikaners in South Africa, there has been a push for new forms of separatism and white supremacy.[13] But some white citizens have turned in different directions. Their shifts in footing include questioning older narratives of white superiority; soul-searching and remorse; and fresh realizations about the depth of and reasons for anger toward whites.[14] In South Africa and Zimbabwe, some whites have applauded and worked toward progressive structural changes in spite of their personal risks of becoming marginalized or isolated.[15] A controversial personal essay by South African philosopher Samantha Vice recently concluded that an attitude of guilt, shame, and self-work is the only morally appropriate stance for a white South African, and that even progressive whites should not be involved in political process, for "because of the brute facts of birth," she writes, "few white people, however well-meaning and morally conscientious, will escape the habits of white privilege."[16] Vice's words were met with mingled applause and criticism by South Africans of all shades, but she certainly generated conversation. Looking at such examples, we can see that "whiteness" among African citizens is plural, shifting, and sometimes painful. To quote the title of Melissa Steyn's seminal 2001 book on white South Africans after apartheid, "whiteness just isn't what it used to be."

In Kenya, dramatic events such as the Cholmondeley trial, activism such as that of Laikipia-based Maasai, and broad, global movements of inclusion such as Community Based Conservation have prodded some (even if not all) white Kenyans into less insularity and more self-awareness. Perhaps one harbinger of change is represented by the artist Sam Hopkins, whose mother is the granddaughter of the settler-hotelier Abraham Block. Hopkins's personal history is hybrid; his father is English, and the family lived in Kenya for only part of each year until he moved back to Kenya full-time as a young adult. He feels at home in Kenya, but frets, he says, about whether, or how much, he belongs. His creative projects have involved many black Kenyans, both members of the educated elite and residents of the massive Nairobi slum Mathare, where Hopkins collaborated on programs for the "Slum TV" media organization he helped found. Moving between the elites and the dispossessed, Hopkins is reflective about the advantages and temptations that come with being white. As we discussed how he was able to secure legal permits for a project, he told me, "I'm very aware that [my identity] is double-edged . . . I want to be treated like an ordinary Kenyan, but it would be tough to give up those privileges."

True to this spirit of reflection, in a 2010 project, Hopkins assembled a series of close-up photographs of dead insects against the glowing aquamarine water in his parents' swimming pool. In the accompanying text, Hopkins writes that as a child he felt compelled to rescue these insects as they drowned, an exercise even then he saw as "fairly pointless," particularly in light of the "far more serious things . . . concerning death and suffering in Kenya." He meditates on the "absurdity" of having so much water to drink and swim in in a country with so much poverty, and sees his work on privilege as "ironic" even as it "acknowledges a certain complicity with the situation."[17] Hopkins is not transcending whiteness (I wager, in fact, he would see that as impossible); rather, in conceding his moral double consciousness, and in striving to see structural oblivion with clear eyes but realizing he can't entirely shake off his role in the structure, he is embodying a new way of being white.

Hopkins's approach to his position in Kenya is marked by his unusually intellectual and artistic mind-set. Gordon's experiences of being a white Kenyan are more typical of the accounts I heard from some of my respondents. He cites, for example, his role in a community project with a group of Maasai, designed to set an example that would teach them to curb their environmental damage. Seeking to show the Maasai how to use arid land more sustainably, he and his colleagues bought a plot of overgrazed land from the pastoralists, dug a borehole, installed a solar pump, and used the water to irrigate trees. During the ethnoterritorial violence of early 2008, however, the Maasai returned, arguing that they had sold their land too cheaply, and threatening to burn the young trees if the land wasn't returned. Gordon was disenchanted.

> We said: "Have we done something wrong? We thought we were working with these guys!" This is the sort of culture where one generation sells [land, and] that money isn't invested and gets frittered away. Then the next generation comes along saying, "I think our dad used to own all this! Look how good it looks now that someone has planted it!" So it's a very emotive, *very* emotive issue. I mean, when it comes to the idea [that] whites should redistribute their land, the first thing you'd say is I *really* disagree with it. But then, it runs too deep, the feelings and the culture and the tribal law. So I think there *has* to be some form of redistribution. You're sitting on a hundred thousand acres. I'm sure you can sit on ninety-five and be just as happy. Can you give five thousand to the people on your perimeter who are desperate?

Gordon works his way through several subject positions in this narrative. At first, he and his colleagues are optimistically teaching Maasai how to use the land, in the vanguard of conservation and development that settler descendants have preferred to occupy. Next, they are brought up short, finding that the Maasai haven't appreciated their example as they'd hoped; instead, they claim that the whites acquired the land unjustly. In conversation with me, Gordon accuses them of irresponsible budgeting and capricious ethnoterritorialism, and there are inklings of structural oblivion to his objections; it's hard for him to understand the reasoning of a group that has been historically so marginalized. At the same time, however, we see an element of double consciousness; he has been forced to recognize the depth and difference of feeling on the other side. In alluding to "tribal law," for instance, he gives a nod to the fact that there may be more than one way to adjudicate landownership. And although he "*really* disagrees with" land redistribution, this opinion has been unsettled as he considers the Maasai standpoint. Some minimal redistribution, he concedes, might be necessary in Kenya's social context—indeed, the way he framed it in his final, rhetorical question to me, it comes to sound reasonable and moral.

All of the themes in Gordon's narrative—his role as steward, his surprise when stewardship is seen as insufficient to compensate for his privileges, and his mingled responses to this double consciousness— resonate with what I heard from other white Kenyans. In modeling the range of whitenesses today, we should include both the comforts of being white and the discomforts of living in a world where whites are increasingly asked to reckon with criticism and different worldviews.

A WHITE TRIBE?

Part of this reckoning, it seems, is facing the question of whether white Kenyans should construe themselves as a distinctive ethnic or "tribal" group, or downplay their distinctiveness from other Kenyans. Certainly, as in colonial times, there have been the occasional whites who find themselves aligned and semi-identified with a particular ethnotribal group. There is the safari guide who prefers the company of his Maasai workers, or the farmer who grew up speaking fluent Kalenjin thanks to his boyhood friends. Back in the day, of course, there was Louis Leakey, who grew up speaking Kikuyu with his childhood playmates, reportedly learning to walk with a Kikuyu gait (a legendary quality some of my Kikuyu contacts still talk about), and receiving an honorary Kikuyu name. But note that Louis's son Richard adamantly refuses to affiliate himself with any particular group, in large part because he feels Kenyan politics urgently need less ethnotribal favoritism and bigotry. Similarly, alarmed by Kenya's postelection ethnic violence in 2008, the blogger Lost White Kenyan Chick wrote emphatically "we are one tribe . . . KENYAN!" This, certainly, is the kind of nationalism most of my respondents felt would be ideal; a sense of belonging to Kenya and to one another irrespective of race or ethnicity. The sentiment reflects positive changes, as settler descendants have attempted to renounce the overtly racist worldview that would have held them back from any such alignments in an earlier era. It also reflects a degree of self-interest, given how perilous ethnoterritorial sentiment and violence can be to national stability and, potentially, to them. In this spirit, some settler descendants favor Kiswahili, precisely because it is the national language and a lingua franca, and ban other languages from the workplace. And certainly this civic nationalism, if it dominated Kenya, would favor white Kenyans' ability to feel that they belong. The problem with this stance is that it is vulnerable to the accusation that white Kenyans fail to understand the weight of historical inequality the way that so many Kenyans do. Although plenty of Kenyans would love to see a peaceful and unified Kenya, plenty of others feel that without some ethnotribally (and possibly racially) based restitution, social justice has been discounted.

Yet at other moments, some settler descendants appeared to buy into their own ethnotribal distinctiveness, even if in only a mild or semi-sardonic fashion. The matter particularly came up in our discussion about their habits of socializing, as we talked about their tendency to self-segregate geographically and romantically. In such cases, reversion to the narrative that "it's a tribal thing" seems a way of suggesting that since ethnotribal self-segregation is a common pattern in Kenya, whites' tendency to socialize primarily with other whites makes them more rather than less Kenyan, just one tribe among many. Yet—as my respondents are aware—such categorical thinking runs the risk of tipping over into a vision of Kenya in which the issue is not merely finding one's comfort zone, but, in some hands, endorsing bigotry. It is an awkward dance they do. Looked at cynically, one might argue that when tribalism helps white Kenyans feel they fit in, it is convenient to claim it; when tribalism threatens to exclude them while destabilizing the national infrastructure they rely on, they disdain it as backward.

WHITE AFRICANS?

If "whiteness" among Kenya's settler descendants is plural, and the matter of whether they wish to be considered a "white tribe" is ambiguous, so, too, is the question of whether they can be deemed "Africans." "African" is not the sort of identity marker that a person can readily claim for themselves (like "gay" or "straight," for instance), nor is it legally conferred on someone by the state, like a national identity (though, as I have explained, even with a passport, not all Kenyan citizens may be perceived as equally "Kenyan"). Rather, "African" is a judgment call, and a contested one at that. Sometimes the term is used as a vague cultural descriptor, as in phrases like "African dance," "African food," or "African religion." When white Kenyans describe a practice as "very African," it usually means they do not identify with it as theirs. They may be accustomed to it, even fond of it, but then again, they may not be. As we have seen, there are limits to how much settler descendants are willing to assimilate cultural arrangements and modes of thought that they mark as "African."

When "African" is used to characterize a person, furthermore, the default use of the term in Kenya and elsewhere alludes to a person born and brought up in Africa, *and* having phenotypically evident genetic roots there. The typical use of the term, in other words, is both cultured and raced, which means that if a person who isn't black wishes to claim "African" status, they need to mark it—hence the title of Louis Leakey's 1937 autobiography, *White African*. In those days, such an identification was highly unusual. With his keen interest in Kikuyu lifeways, Leakey was considered a misfit by other whites in Kenya, whom he angered by proclaiming that it could never be a "white man's country." Most of the elderly former settlers I spoke to would not deem themselves "African." Nor, indeed, would some middle-aged and younger settler descendants. Some feel it would be provocative to use an appellation with its racial connotations, and some find it ill-suited to their sense of self. Frederick, for instance, the fifty-something coastal resident who runs a small nature park with many Giriama staff, tells me, "I don't *think* of myself as, as an African. Thirty years ago when my staff would say we'll give you a Giriama name, and this or that—[I said] *no,* don't . . . I'm not a Giriama, and I'm a *mzungu* [white person] who's brought up here and I don't associate myself with other races or colors or creeds." Being white is a paramount element of Frederick's identity; Africanness, which he sets in contrast to whiteness, is patently not.

Yet many white Kenyan respondents tried to play down their racial difference in conversation with me. Trevor, for instance, the Laikipia wildlife expert from a well-to-do family, aligned himself with the Kenyan everyman, racially and ethnically ambiguous but firmly rooted in the nation: "[I'm] no different to any other Kenyan, I don't think, a true Kenyan who's been born [and] brought up here . . . everything you've ever known is Kenyan . . . I'm no different to a guy in Nairobi, a guy in Malindi, [who's] been brought up here. And I've *never,* never looked at it as 'Well, you're, you're a European being brought up in Africa.' That's never even crossed my mind."

Trevor's use of the phrase "true Kenyan" (and "a guy in Nairobi, a guy in Malindi") may be code for "black Kenyan"; this, anyway, would jibe with the fact that settler descendants sometimes steer away from racial terminology. Claims like Trevor's embody settler descendants' wish to belong, while rhetorically minimizing their differences.

Others I spoke to, in fact, fervently wished to be counted as African, "just like any other tribe in Kenya," as one middle-aged settler descendant put it to me. Take the words of Jonathan, the Naivasha farmer who objected that he wasn't allowed to check "indigenous" when he went to renew his national Identity card: "I'm *not* a European! You know, you can call me, I'm a [slightly mocking tone] 'whitey,' but I'm not a European. Because I'm not, um, I've never had anything to *do* with Europe! You know, I'm a *white African!* Those four years [at university abroad], all I could think of was getting back to my *beloved* country. If I walk into a shop in England I won't know what to do with myself!"

In other independent sub-Saharan African nations, the desire to be called African has been on the rise among white citizens, as part of their bid to belong. Some whites from Zimbabwe and South Africa are among them.[18] Some Afrikaners have insisted for generations that they are African, a sense intensified by the fact that their language, Afrikaans, is spoken only in South Africa and Namibia, and because many cannot even pinpoint relations or friends in Europe, their ancestors having arrived several centuries ago.[19] Of course, for some whites, claiming African status doubtless has a strategic element; it is convenient to belong when one wishes to stake a claim to land, jobs, or other entitlements. But for some, says Melissa Steyn, the appellation indicates "an important shift in subjectivity, of identifying with the current nation-building project."[20] Some whites, then, use the term out of solidarity and pride, as part of a shared agenda of redefining African nations in the eyes of the world. At a recent meeting for a nongovernmental organization with U.S. donors, Richard Leakey tells me, board members were discussing whether the money should be channeled through the United States, because it's safer, or controlled entirely on the African side. "The Americans were saying 'Africa's not safe,'" Leakey related, but the board member from a wealthy old white South African family retorted: "Listen, we are an emerging continent and we Africans want a place at the table. Do not put us down."

Whatever their motives in claiming to be African, settler descendants meet with a mixed reception. In Zimbabwe, politicians' rejection of white belonging has been profound. According to J. L. Fisher, politicians and policy-makers have increasingly argued that Zimbabwe's resources are for its "indigenous," a concept defined on grounds of genealogy, history, and "culture," and a concept that has led many to conclude whites "do not belong in Zimbabwe because their cultural origins, and therefore their place, are elsewhere . . . fixed in perpetual otherness."[21] Some critics have noted that whites' efforts to be deemed African are suspicious, arriving precisely at the historical moment when it would be convenient for them to blend in and symbolically efface the privilege that offends so many.[22] In a widely discussed 2010 op-ed in South Africa's *Mail & Guardian,* Sentletse Diakanyo suggests that when South Africans of European descent try to "reclassify" themselves as African, it runs contrary to the widely accepted assumption that "African" is a racial designator, and insultingly erases a history of race-based oppression. "When white Afrikaner supremacists had signs saying 'Europeans' and 'Non-Europeans' to enforce segregation between Africans and Europeans," he writes, "there was never any ambiguity around the term 'European'."[23] Indeed, in South Africa, as Richard Schroeder points out, whites under apartheid enjoyed the perks of being white, while "'Africans,' by contrast, were natives, Bantus, 'kaffirs,' people without rights and privileges who belonged elsewhere, people who were hardly people at all."[24] For these reasons, one of Melissa Steyn's white South African respondents makes a case that "Africanness" is something a white person "has to earn," through self-education and efforts to redress white privileges.[25]

In one of Sam Hopkins's early art projects, he asked black Kenyan sign painters to "paint what they see" on his identification card. After they followed suit, he said, "Now, paint me as an African." Some of them repainted him as a black man, while others objected: "But you *are* African!" Still, Hopkins may have been considered an exceptional case, being more integrated and sympathetic than some settler descendants. We have seen in my earlier chapters that some black Kenyans express skepticism—partly class-based but partly race-based—that white Kenyans count as fully part of the nation. Presumably, the descriptor "African" is harder still to earn.

Settler descendants would love to be judged on their own terms, based on their individual efforts and intentions, yet the colonial past, and the structurally entrenched white privilege that lingers on, keep rising up to interfere. They are wrestling with the incoherence of a consciousness founded on colonialism that is confronted with the imperative to renounce it. They struggle with the simultaneity of wishing to "connect" with black Kenyans, and their lingering residues of felt superiority and aversion to certain African lifeways. All of this disconcerting doubleness, all of these very contradictions, are part of being a white Kenyan. Some of their uneasiness was summed up at the end of one conversation at a restaurant in Nanyuki. My informants and I talked about this and that— their anxiety about Maasai activists, their financial support of a new orphanage, their efforts to curtail abuse against donkeys. As I walked away from our table, one of them launched a parting shot. Raising her voice, she said in a jocular tone, "We're not bad people!" I laughed, and she laughed back. Then her companion chipped in, "But we are privileged. We are." The first woman looked mischievous. I can't remember exactly how she phrased it, but this is how I remember it: "Once you figure out how both of those are true at once, you have your book."

Notes

1. See, e.g., McGreal 2006 and the comments section at http://kumekucha .blogspot.com/2008/09/getting-away-with-murder-cholmondeley.html.

2. Shadle 2015.

3. Drawing on 1989 census data, Katja Uusihakala (1999: 29–30) estimates that in 1999 there were probably about 20,000 in Kenya's *mzungu* (white) community. However, note that the 1989 census counted only 3,184 "Kenyan Europeans" (most of them presumably settler descendants); other categories of whites include those who arrived (or whose families arrived) after Kenya's independence in 1963, some of whom would have applied for citizenship, and the tens of thousands of white expatriates living in Kenya temporarily. For details of the exodus of white Kenyans and the influx of white expatriates in the 1960s, including a decline of the original settler population during that period from roughly 55,000 in 1962 to 10,000–15,000 in 1969, see Hoffman 2011: 6.

4. I have not found any ideal or comfortable designator for referring to Kenyans of African descent. "Afro-Kenyan" or "African Kenyan," which I have used in some publications, have the advantage of downplaying racial phenotype in favor of geographic origins, but they also raise questions of whether white or Indian Kenyans can be considered "African" and perhaps invoke the loaded suggestion of Afrocentrism. (To some readers, too, "Afro" signifies a hair style.) "Indigenous Kenyan" is problematic because in Kenya, as elsewhere, the descriptor "indigenous" is sometimes reserved for underrepresented groups such as pastoralists and hunter-gatherers. "Black Kenyan" is less than ideal because it is explicitly racial, but Kenyans do very occasionally use the phrase *Waafrica weusi* (black Africans), so the term "black" is not completely alien, even if it is almost never used to describe "Kenyans." Most of the time I use the phrase "black Kenyan," and occasionally "African Kenyan." In a few instances,

as when discussing the colonial era, when the principal form of nationality was British subject status and almost no whites in Kenya would have claimed they were Kenyan or African, I simply use the designator "African." As I explain in n. 5 below, I use the phrase "white Kenyan" because "European Kenyan" does not sit right with respondents who say they do not consider themselves the slightest bit European.

5. The phrase "white Kenyans," which I use (along with "settler descendants") because it is more neutral and less ungainly than other options, is used by some white Kenyans themselves, usually when they need to distinguish their group from black African and Asian Kenyans. Some, however, flinch at an appellation that conspicuously foregrounds their race. Several of my respondents insisted they were "Kenyan, pure and simple," on the principle that their race should be left unmarked and their sense of national belonging foregrounded, but given that I focus on so many contexts in which my respondents *are* racially marked, I can't abide by their wishes. A few of my respondents alluded to their own group as "the white tribe" of Kenya, glossing whites as simply one of many ethnic groups belonging in Kenya, rather than interlopers— a rhetorical move I discuss further in the Conclusion. (For examples of this locution among Kenyan-born white authors, see Hartley 2009; Nicholls 2005.) Although most African Kenyans allude to whites as *wazungu* (sing. *mzungu*), most (though not all) white Kenyans avoid this term, for two reasons that I can discern: (1) because to utter the term is to "other" oneself, and (2) because the term conflates citizens and expatriates, and white Kenyans consider themselves to have a far better claim to belong in Kenya than temporary white visitors from elsewhere. The phrase "European Kenyans" doesn't sit quite right either; several of my respondents insisted that they should not be deemed "European" in any way, because they do not feel at home in Europe. Occasionally, my interlocutors would use a hyphenated descriptor such as "Kenyan-English," but I cannot adopt this because a number of those I quote are of mixed European descent (even if the majority have at least some British roots). Note that when I use the phrase "white Kenyans," I am referring to surviving settlers and their descendants, rather than to whites naturalized after Independence.

6. See Ong 1996; Rosaldo 1994.

7. See, e.g., http://jamhurimagazine.com/index.php/sports/3566-jason-dunford-carrying-of-kenyan-flag.html; www.theeastafrican.co.ke/OpEd/comment/Dunford+had+every+right+to+carry+Kenya+flag+/-/434750/1477280/-/40w4a2/-/index.html>; www.the-star.co.ke/news/article-89665/im-proud-rainbow-nation-kenya-has-proved-it-can-be; www.letsrun.com/forum/flat_read.php?thread=4711737&page=1; and many messages from African Kenyans of support for Dunford's carrying the flag, www.facebook.com/kenya.swimmer/posts/10151160029305152. I should note that, like other anthropologists, I reject the notion that the "racial" differences reified in public discourse are biologically important. The genetic variation within categories such as "black" and "white" is more extensive than the genetic variation between them (see, e.g., Marks 1995). However, even though racial classification and the social meanings of the term "race" vary enormously across time and social space, racial ideas are of tremendous social importance.

8. Belonging has become a prominent theme for whites across sub-Saharan Africa lately, emblematized in the title of David McDermott Hughes's 2010 ethnography, *Whiteness in Zimbabwe: Race, Landscape, and the Problem of Belonging*.

9. After I first invoked the concept of double consciousness in early talks about my material on white Kenyans (see, e.g., McIntosh 2009c), I came to have misgivings about it, for several reasons. The radical imbalance of power between white Kenyans and African Americans was an obvious one, and I wasn't sure I could bend the concept of double consciousness to whites and still keep that in sight. Another is that, historically, in Kenya and elsewhere, white privilege has been partly comprised of the luxury of *not* having to think about how others see one; of *not* being disturbed by double consciousness, so that one can enjoy the comfort of structural oblivion. When white Kenyans see themselves being seen, it is mostly because a half-century's worth of political protest and the global rise of liberal humanist values are penetrating their structural oblivion and shifting their subjectivity, even if only partially and in fragmented and fleeting fashion. For African Americans in Du Bois's era and beyond, on the other hand, double consciousness was not optional; rather, it was a daily humiliation that involved a perpetually split sense of self and low self-esteem. A further dissimilarity is that double consciousness among African Americans occasioned not only the lacerations of self-esteem described by Du Bois, but also a kind of holistic code-switching, in which black Americans had to follow white rules and accommodate white standards of social comportment if they were to have any credibility in a white-dominated society. These stringent requirements exceed anything that is asked of white Kenyans today. However, when I later discovered Linda Martín Alcoff's (1998) essay invoking (and encouraging) double consciousness in white identity crises in the United States, as well as Brett Shadle's (2015) use of the term to discuss settler culture in Kenya, I returned to my conviction that the concept might be broadened to accommodate different power dynamics than those described by Du Bois. It has come to feel apt and helpful in characterizing the ways in which white Kenyans shift between moral self-assurance and anxiety precipitated by their critics, even as I recognize that the term must always be critically understood.

10. Du Bois 1996 [1903]: 8.

11. See also Medina 2013.

12. Du Bois 1996 [1903]: 8.

13. Cf. Johannes Fabian 2000 and Ann Stoler 2009.

14. Memmi 1991 [1957]: 53.

15. Lonsdale and Berman 1992; Cooper and Stoler 1997; Stoler 2002, 2009. See also Pels 1997.

16. Stoler (2009: 258) sees so much self-deception in colonialism that she suggests "the ability to know and not know, to believe yet not believe in" on the part of elites in imperial contexts "begs for" more analysis.

17. Shadle 2015: 20.

18. This general political shift is discussed as well by Celia Nyamweru (2001), who describes arriving in 1965 Kenya as an American graduate student to find European settlers still openly proclaiming their dislike for Africans, but

by the 1990s found Kenya to be "racially harmonious" and segregated primarily by wealth (174, 186–89). That said, her focus as her essay proceeds seems to shift from Kenyan-born whites to expatriates and mixed-race offspring (many of black Kenyan fathers who met white partners overseas), as well as Asian Kenyans. She does not closely trace the shifting attitudes among former settlers and their progeny.

19. Alcoff 1998: 24.

20. A word is in order about the terms "tribe" and "ethnicity," each with its own connotations, and about my use of the term "ethnotribal." In that both tend to presume a degree of common ancestry and shared "culture," however loosely construed, the terms "tribe" and "ethnicity" overlap, but "tribe" has connotations of primitivism and insularity that "ethnicity" does not. Many anthropologists consider the term "tribe" hopelessly tainted by its history of pejorative and essentialist uses in colonial contexts, whereas "ethnicity" is more neutral and more agnostic about whether the common ancestry in question is actual or mythical. Furthermore, like my colleagues in anthropology, I regard ethnic identity to be dependent upon social and semiotic construction; on ongoing work to reify, mythologize, and sometimes enforce group boundaries. The helpful and underused term "ethnotribal" is simultaneously etic (capturing the analyst's standpoint) and emic (capturing the standpoint of cultural insiders), for the first half of the term treats group identities as constructed, while the second half recognizes the primordialist standpoint, and preferred terminology, of cultural players on the ground.

21. See, e.g., Haugerud 1995: 40.

22. Branch 2011, Haugerud 1995.

23. Lynch 2011.

24. McIntosh 2009.

25. See Geschiere 2009; Geschiere and Nyamnjoh 2000.

26. Bhabha 1994: 86, 89; see also Fanon 1952 and Memmi 1957 [1991].

27. Steyn 2012: 10.

28. Comaroff and Comaroff 1991.

29. Cooper 1980.

30. Nader 1972. Though Nader focused primarily on bureaucracies, other anthropologists have been inspired to expand the study of those in power to include scientists, Western tourists, Wall Street financiers, and many other elites.

31. Harding 1991.

32. Blee 2008: 6–7. Blee also notes she had been prepared to hate her informants, and was surprised and somewhat dismayed to find them more intelligent than she had thought, and to realize that—excluding their ideologies of race and politics—they had more opinions in common with her than she had expected. Such revelations prompted her to rethink her assumptions about the framework motivating their racism. See as well James Dawes's *Evil Men* (2013), in which he explores the complexity of cruelty on the part of convicted war criminals from the Second Sino-Japanese War.

33. Rosaldo 2000.

34. See esp. Stoler 2009.

35. Crapanzano 1985.

36. Terence Ranger (1998: 256) argues that it is common, in colonial studies, for whites to be "distorted by the burden of power," making it that much harder to see them as "human beings . . . with a fully human capacity for heroism and villainy and mediocrity." Alasdair Pennycook (1998: 29) contends that a less caricatural view of colonials helps us understand their relevance to the contemporary world: "[b]y seeing the complexity of colonial relations, we are also more able to see how colonialism is more closely linked to the complexities of current relationships."

37. On white South Africans, see esp. Crapanzano 1985; Goodwin and Schiff 1995; Nuttal and Coetzee 1998; Steyn 2001, 2012; and Schroeder 2012, which examines the migration of white South Africans who are making economic inroads in Tanzania. As the material on this population of approximately four million whites expands, some has come to emphasize internal differences, such as class and political diversity. On white Zimbabweans, see Rutherford 2001; D. M. Hughes 2010; Fisher 2011; Kalaora 2011; and Pilossof 2012 (with bibliography of additional literature). White Kenyans have not been much studied by ethnographers; exceptions include Uusihakala 1999 and Fox 2012.

38. McIntosh 2009a.

39. For a candid discussion of some pros and cons of this aspect of ethnographic methodology and ethics, see Neyfakh 2015.

40. See, e.g., Ralph 2014.

41. Melissa Steyn (2001) similarly reports that despite the differences among her white South African interlocutors, she nevertheless found important shared narratives. See as well Shadle 2015, arguing that early twentieth-century European settlers came to share certain worldviews, in spite of their diversity of origins (and, indeed, the disparate colonies where they settled).

42. Antonius Robben (1996) conducted interviews among victims and perpetrators of Argentina's "dirty war." He found that some Argentinian generals lavished such gentlemanly kindness and charm upon him that he was occasionally led astray from his critical and analytical purposes.

43. Being in the presence of those I found most objectionable was awkward, to say the least; they usually knew I would disagree with them, yet if I spoke my mind fully and passionately, I could alienate these important research participants. Similarly, Richard Schroeder (2012: x), who conducted ethnography among South African whites in Tanzania, describes his discomfort around bigoted informants. He eloquently discusses the dilemmas of complicity for the ethnographer who has to "maintain a sometimes uncomfortable silence in order to effectively observe, record, and ultimately understand" objectionable behavior.

44. I thank Elizabeth Ferry for this helpful chiasmus.

45. Cole 2002.

46. Coombes, Hughes, and Karega-Munene 2014

47. Miller 1971.

48. See L. Hughes 2005; Kennedy 1987: 130; Lonsdale 1992; Meinertzhagen 1957: 51.

49. Land policy is described in detail in Sorrenson 1968 and Kanogo 1987. For a discussion of the spiritual depth of investment many Kenyans felt and still feel in their land, see Shipton 2009.

50. Bennett 1963: 14; Wolff 1975: 66.

51. Kennedy 1987: 42.

52. Shadle 2015.

53. On formerly more fluid models of group identity in Kenya, see, e.g., Lynch 2011; Waller 1985a.

54. For examples of how ethnic stereotypes live on among settler descendants, see white employers' discussion of their various employees described in Fox 2012.

55. Kanogo 1987.

56. I take the phrase from historian Dane Kennedy (1987: 46).

57. In 1919, e.g., a major soldier settlement scheme with a view to Kenya's economic development, as well as strengthening the hand of the white minority, involved over two million acres of land and nearly 700 new settlers, some of whom had previously served in British India; many were ex-officers (Duder 1993).

58. Ibid.; see also Kennedy 1987: 43, 56–57.

59. Duder 1993: 71.

60. Shadle 2015: 17.

61. Duder 1993: 71; Nicholls 2005: 197; Shadle 2015: 6. See as well W. Jackson 2013 on the marginalization of indigent and mentally ill whites by the settler community and the colonial administration.

62. See Gregory 1971. The relationship between whites and Asians in Kenya, then and now, is worthy of another book altogether (for a history of Indians in Kenya, see Aiyar 2015). Settler descendants do interact with Asian Kenyans in the workplace, social clubs, and public spaces, and in some cases cultivate friendships with them. However, the socialization has its limits, just as it does with black Kenyans, and Kenyans of European and Asian descent tend to be quite endogamous. My analysis focuses more narrowly on whites' engagements with black Kenyans for several reasons. First, the "denial and belonging" referenced in my title point to settler descendants' anxieties about belonging in Kenya, especially anxieties stemming from critiques of their community's treatment of black Kenyans. In attempting to belong, furthermore, these whites must reckon centrally with black Kenyans rather than Asian Kenyans, who aren't certain of their entitlement to belong either. In a way, then, Asian Kenyans share some dilemmas with settler descendants, but these surely play out in ways particular to their community (and whatever their special dilemmas are, they are not of central interest to most of my respondents).

63. Shadle 2015: 4.

64. D. Anderson 2000.

65. Kennedy 1987: 105.

66. Shadle 2015.

67. Kennedy 1987: 105.

68. wa Thiong'o 1981: 613, 616, 618. See also Shadle's (2012) description of the ironies of early twentieth-century settlers beating "natives" in order to "teach" them not to be cruel to (i.e., to beat) animals.

69. Shadle 2015.

70. For divisions within colonial officialdom between eugenicist notions of intrinsic African inferiority and environmentalist theories of supposed African "backwardness," see Campbell 2007. It should as well be noted that many colonials imagined that "civilization" could come to "the African," but only over the *longue durée*—hundreds of years, perhaps—because Africans were supposedly so culturally backward and so inherently obdurate. In this view, rushing to take on the trappings of civilization could even be dangerous for Africans. Social and individual dysfunction among Africans under colonialism, then, was sometimes explained as the result of civilizing too quickly (see, e.g., Vaughan 1991).

71. Shadle 2015: 37.

72. See Hodgson 2001 for a rich discussion of early rhetoric of development among colonial officials in Tanganyika.

73. Nicholls 2005: 244. A glimmer of progressivism, to give one example, emanated from the politically active settler Olga Watkins, who in the early 1940s urged that Africans be allowed to serve as members of the Legislative Council. Another exceptional settler, Elspeth Huxley's mother, Nellie Grant, suggested that an "educated African" be permitted to deliver an address to the Njoro Settlers' Association (ibid.: 234).

74. D. Anderson 2005; Elkins 2005.

75. Cooper 2005: 54.

76. For a detailed account of Kenyatta's political involvements leading up to his indictment, and his trial, see D. Anderson 2005.

77. See Styles 2011.

78. The phenomenon of Afrikaner "poor whites" has historical roots in the scorched earth policies pursued by the British during the Second Anglo-Boer war (1899–1902), which stripped tens of thousands of Boers of their livelihoods and killed at least 20,000, many of them women and children, in concentration camps. The Afrikaner population gained from subsequent apartheid policies, but lost privilege after apartheid's end, with some families falling back into poverty.

79. W. Jackson 2013.

80. www.ukentv.com/1/post/2012/05/the-white-kenyanis-just-like-you.html.

81. See n. 4 above. The term *mzungu* is widely used to designate those with white skin, and it instantly racializes and others its targets. It also conflates expatriates with white citizens, something white Kenyans particularly resent.

82. Geschiere 2009; Geschiere and Njamnjoh 2000.

83. See Fisher 2011: 32, 136; D. Hughes 2010; Pilossoff 2012; Rutherford 2001.

84. www.facebook.com/NTVKenya/posts/407732929274768?comment _id=4605886&offset=0&total_comments=132.

85. Cf. white Zimbabweans' sensitivity to being deemed "settlers"; the term implies to them that they cannot be "part of Africa." Some whites have countenanced the criticism, arguing that their fellow whites would need to both admire and assimilate into African culture(s) in order to legitimately fit in (Fisher 2010: 169). In another interview with the same journalist, Bell emphasizes: "I was

born in Mombasa, at Mama Ngina Drive to Mr and Mrs Ginger Bell." In Bell's words, one might even detect a blend of *jus soli* (rights of the soil) and *jus sanguinis* (rights of blood) arguments, even if his blood is still not of the most (folk) widely accepted racial "type." See http://mashariazgitonga.blogspot.com /2013/10/after-court-win-i-may-now-sell-land-to.html and /www.business dailyafrica.com/Butcher-s-son-who-took-on-Moi-and-won-/-/539546/1477548 /-/item/2/-/10pcsln/-/index.html.

86. Styles 2011: 305. I should add that white Kenyan discourse about their "two-year wonder" expat social foils often rhetorically erases the existence of a group that lies between the short-term expatriate and the settler descendant. There are whites in Kenya who arrived after Independence, but who have been in country long enough to apply for citizenship, and some of who have established a decades-long commitment to it (see, e.g., Nyamweru 2001).

87. www.worldaffairsjournal.org/article/almost-out-africa-white-tribes.

88. Ibid.; and see, too, http://archive.spectator.co.uk/article/16th-november-2002/38/white-man-in-kenya.

89. This is a dilemma shared en masse by the some four million white South Africans, particularly since the Truth and Reconciliation Commission forced a very public outing of some of the worst atrocities of the apartheid regime. See, e.g., Nuttall and Coetzee 1998.

90. Fisher 2011: 60ff.

91. Styles 2011: 316.

92. Nancy Scheper-Hughes (2005: 474) mentions seeing white South Africans use air quotes around contested terms.

93. Bennun 2003: 134; Hiltzik 1991: 232; I. Williams 2005: 16.

94. See as well Honey 1999: 324. For detailed description of a (now defunct) tourism experience, orchestrated by one settler descendant family, in which Maasai were represented as if frozen in time, see E. M. Bruner 2001. The family hired Maasai to appear and dance without interacting with the tourists. Before emerging for their performances, the Maasai were urged to remove their wristwatches, refrain from speaking English, and wear only "traditional" clothing. After observing the spectacle, tourists would enjoy tea and crumpets on immaculately groomed lawns. The operation was shut down in the 1980s because some tourists objected to its colonial overtones.

95. www.bwsafaris.com.

96. Similarly, in her history of whites in Kenya, Christine Nicholls (born in Kenya of British descent and since relocated to the United Kingdom) refers to the Happy Valley set as an "un-representative coterie [who] have attracted all too much attention" (Nicholls 2005: xiv).

97. See as well Nicholls 2005; Trzebinski 1985.

98. Wilson 1952: 13. Wilson arrived in East Africa in 1911 as a member of the Colonial Medical Service and went on to a career as a member of Kenya's Legislative Council, serving on several administrative committees, including as a "member for native interests." To be sure, a few administrators had produced writings critical of colonialism, such as Norman Leys and W. McGregor Ross, both of whom came to question white settlement on moral and economic

grounds (Leys 1924; McGregor Ross 1968 [1927]). Their books did not, however, seem to have been read by my respondents.

99. Nicholls 2005: xiii.

100. Duder 1991: 432.

101. See, e.g., Markham 1942; Huxley 1959; and Karen Blixen's memoir *Out of Africa* (1937), published under the pen name Isak Dinesen. Although Danish, Blixen thoroughly entwined her life with Kenya's British aristocrats in the early twentieth century.

102. See Huxley's *White Man's Country: Lord Delamere and the Making of Kenya* (1953 [1935]), which touts Delamere's development of large-scale farming in Kenya, and her semi-autobiographical *The Flame Trees of Thika* (1959), about growing up in a tenacious coffee-farming family. Most historians see Huxley as a defender of the settlers, but she did sometimes recognize their ethnocentrism (Nicholls 2005: 153), and, as time went by, agreed that Kenya should move toward independence (Nicholls 2003). It should be added that her fictional imagining in her novel *Red Strangers* (1939) of how Kikuyu might have perceived white lifeways, including their critical views of the seeming illogic and cruelty of a money economy, is an unusual example of literary perspectivism in a settler.

103. For a bibliography of nostalgic memoirs by settler women, see Lorcin 2012. Elderly former settlers recently compiled a volume entitled *Childhood Memories of Colonial East Africa* (Considine and Rawlins 2008), and former members of the Colonial Service in East Africa produced a collection called *I Remember It Well* (Le Breton 2010). Further reminiscences from settlers and administrators include Knowles 2008, Parker and Bleazard 2001, and Cuthbert and Cuthbert 2007. The magazine *Old Africa* (www.oldafricamagazine.com) publishes brief submissions from people—mostly of European descent—who grew up in colonial East Africa. A white Kenyan contact told me of a rumor that the editors had initially solicited submissions from whites only, but had agreed after some arm-twisting to include writers of African and Asian descent. However, the latter submissions are few and far between and are rarely critical of colonial policies. The magazine's mission has expanded into publishing a series of monograph-length memoirs and biographies about, e.g., settler farming, whites' anxious memories of the Mau Mau era, and missionary endeavors.

104. Lonsdale 1990: 398.

105. D. Anderson 2005: 4, and see Elkins 2005 on the abuse of detainees. Further sources on the Mau Mau include (but are certainly not limited to) Barnett and Njama 1968, Bennett 2012, Branch 2009, Kariuki 1975 [1963], Lonsdale 1990, and Odhiambo and Lonsdale 2003.

106. Coombes, Hughes, and Karega-Munene 2014: 2. This bid for recognition culminated in the unveiling of a prominent statue of Mau Mau Field Marshall Dedan Kimathi Wachiuri in Nairobi in 2007.

107. Elkins 2005: xiv.

108. Many British journalists and public intellectuals, some of them conservative and struggling to wrap their minds around the extent of colonial misbehavior, lambasted Elkins as a mere proponent of angry propaganda (see, e.g., www .guardian.co.uk/theguardian/2008/apr/07/opendoor; www.independent.co.uk

/opinion/commentators/niall-ferguson-home-truths-about-famine-war-and-genocide-482314.html; www.telegraph.co.uk/culture/books/3634984/They-died-cursing-the-British.html; www.telegraph.co.uk/culture/books/3634566/The-dark-side-of-the-Empire.html). However, as Branch (2009: xv) notes, "respected figures within the fields of imperial and African history have fiercely criticized Elkins's arguments" as well. Within Kenya, the Luo historian Bethwell Ogot (2005), e.g., has argued that Elkins pits African heroes against British villains, underplaying the brutal behavior of Mau Mau fighters. The Rutgers historian Susan Carruthers, among others, finds Elkins's representations of settlers and administrators "cartoonish grotesques" (2005: 492). See as well Blacker 2007 on challenges to Elkins's numeric data, and Branch 2009 and Hughes 2011 for further critiques of how Elkins's volume has been used by some Kenyan actors to promote a distorted version of Kenya's history. Elkins has issued a defense of some of her claims (Elkins 2011), and regardless of other criticisms of her book, her accounts of horrendous state-sanctioned torture were empirically borne out by the discovery of a concealed colonial archive in the United Kingdom in 2012 (see D. Anderson 2013).

109. Branch 2009: xv. When the volume was launched in Nairobi in 2005, then Vice President Moody Awori, who was also the chair of the recently recognized Mau Mau War Veterans' Association, spoke at the reception. See as well Hughes's (2011) description of Mau Mau veterans using Elkins's text as support for state-backed revisionist histories (favorable to them, but disturbingly narrow) that would extend from Kenya's museums to classroom textbooks.

110. See Branch 2009; Coombes, Hughes, and Karega-Munene 2014: 230–31; Hughes 2011.

111. With raised eyebrows, Bernard Porter notes settlers' tendency to social amnesia about the Mau Mau era, focusing on Niall Ferguson, author of a controversial "panegyric" to colonialism entitled *Empire: How Britain Made the Modern World* (2002), who lived in Kenya as a boy. Porter draws special attention to one of Ferguson's memories of his return to Kenya just three years after Independence, while still young. Ferguson writes: "scarcely anything had changed [since colonial days]. We had our bungalow, our maid, our smattering of Swahili—and our sense of unshakeable security. It was a magical time, which indelibly impressed on my consciousness the sight of the hunting cheetah, the sound of Kikuyu women singing, the smell of the first rains and the taste of ripe mango. I suspect my mother was never happier." Yet less than a decade earlier, Porter notes, the Mau Mau rebellion and the British response to it had shaken the nation, and while the little boy may be excused for being unaware of that in the 1960s, "by the time he came to write his book, some knowledge of it should have percolated through " (Porter 2005).

112. As already indicated, a large majority of those I interviewed in conducting this fieldwork would not have been directly involved in the crackdown on the Mau Mau, for most were too young or, when elderly, women. However, I do know that three men I spoke to had had or likely had had some involvement, and certainly their involvement may have been murderous. I would remain in the dark about their Mau Mau stories, because they preferred not to

speak to me about this highly charged topic. Since my aim was never to explore first-hand accounts of the Mau Mau conflict, I decided not to push the issue. At any rate, my Kikuyu interlocutor's essentialization of white Kenyans as "murderers" and his corresponding implication that his father's involvement wouldn't have included killing of loyalists, e.g., were in keeping with the spirit of revisionist histories. See Hughes 2011.

113. D. L. Smith 2005: 246–48. See also Carothers 1954; Leakey 1954.

114. D. L. Smith 2005: 230. Smith sounds a recurrent theme in my white Kenyan informants' accounts: that colonials had wanted to see black Kenyans evolve and modernize ("We wanted the best [for them]," he writes [p. 297]), but Independence catastrophically interrupted progress in this respect.

115. www.nation.co.ke/lifestyle/lifestyle/Blomfield-Hate-him-or-love-him-/-/1214/1334954/-/11onceq/-/index.html.

116. www.nation.co.ke/oped/Letters/Honour-too-those-who-helped-to-defeat-Mau-Mau-rebellion/-/440806/1876562/-/gupltpz/-/index.html.

117. www.nation.co.ke/oped/Letters/Colonists-brought-Kenya-into-being/-/440806/1891412/-/6c3kgv/-/index.html.

118. "We should celebrate much of our past rather than apologize for it," Brown went on to say. British colonialism, he implied, had done the colonized world a favor by promulgating "British values" such as liberty, tolerance, and civic virtue (Brogan 2005). "The truth is, Britain has never even faced up to the dark side of its imperial history, let alone begun to apologize," the historian Richard Drayton wrote in response (2005).

119. www.bbc.co.uk/news/uk-22790037.

120. D. Anderson 2013.

CHAPTER 2

1. Various groups speaking Maa and deeming themselves "Maasai" have assimilated over the years, and many who self-identify as Maasai are not pastoralists. Neither ethnic identification nor linguistic affiliation are historically rigid, and what it means to "be Maasai" is continually in flux (see Carrier 2011; Spear and Waller 1993). Contemporary census methods do not do well by pastoralist peoples, and the Maasai in Laikipia are very hard to count. I have heard estimates ranging from 4,000 to 40,000. The number of whites descended from settler families who are now Laikipia landowners and the percentage of the land there that they own are also hard to pin down with precision. Sources sometimes conflate newer European and American arrivals with whites who have family roots in Kenya, and the parceling out of subdivisions and other land transactions sometimes take place below the radar of the Ministry of Lands (Letai 2011b). Kantai (2008a: 60) pegs the number of "white settler families" in Laikipia in 2004 at thirty-seven, and while his wording is ambiguous, it is plain that either most or all of those families have roots in the colonial era. Writing for the British paper *The Telegraph* in 2004, David Blair stated that twenty-seven white-owned ranches covered almost half of the land in the district. In late 2012, Mathew Lempurkel, the Laikipia County ODM (Orange Democratic Movement) branch chairman, claimed that "more than 60% of

land in Laikipia is owned by white settlers" and pledged to right the historical injustices against pastoralists (Waweru 2012). An "AfricaFiles" web site names some of the white Kenyan families linked to Laikipia and claims that twenty "foreigners," including those of British descent, own 74 percent of the land there (www.africafiles.org/printableversion.asp?id=6723). For more on recent land transactions in Laikipia, see Letai 2011a, 2011b.

2. For richer discussion of the influence of colonial land policy on contemporary Kenyan land politics, see, e.g., Kanyinga 2009. For discussion of white Kenyans' rhetorical bids for a limited sort of autochthony, see McIntosh 2015.

3. D. M. Hughes 2010; see Trzebinski 1985 for a description of some early settler struggles with agriculture and animal husbandry.

4. For more on the EAWL, see van Tol 2013.

5. EAWL 1975 [1962]: 92–93.

6. Ibid.: 2

7. See, e.g., Shipton 2009.

8. For an expanded look at colliding ideologies surrounding land, particularly among Luo people in Kenya, see ibid.

9. Cronon 1983.

10. Berman and Lonsdale 1992: 35; Clayton and Savage 1974.

11. Locke 1690, *Second Treatise on Government*, chap. 5, § 32, www.gutenberg.org/files/7370/7370-h/7370-h.htm. And see Tully 1980. Katja Uusihakala has argued that settlers staked tremendous self-image on their "knowledge of the land and . . . ability to improve and to utilize it" (Uusihakala 1999: 37–38).

12. Tully 1994; see also Cronon 1983.

13. L. Hughes 2006a: 26.

14. Schroeder 1999; Adams and McShane 1997.

15. See also D. M. Hughes 2010: 51.

16. Berman and Lonsdale 1992: 20.

17. L. Hughes 2006a: 3–4.

18. Pastoralism was seen as "a way of life that kept Africans idle, unnervingly on the move, and impervious to the benefits and constraints of colonialism," according to Berman and Lonsdale (1992: 35), threatening white control in Kenya. See Hodgson 2001 for a detailed account of similar ideologies in colonial Tanzania.

19. Hodgson 2001: 84, 6.

20. L. Hughes 2006a: 157; D. Anderson 1984.

21. Neumann 1992.

22. L. Hughes 2005, 2006a.

23. Maasai dispossession is "mired in myth and myth-making, contestations of history . . . arguments over the meaning of land ownership, 'rational' land use, stewardship of wildlife resources and different concepts of justice" (L. Hughes 2006: xvi).

24. Ibid.: 172.

25. Ibid.: 43.

26. Ibid.: 19–20, 49, 51–55, 71, 81.

27. Ibid.: 50. According to Lotte Hughes (personal communication, November 10, 2013), it is likely more people than this were moved overall by the time

the moves were completed in 1913. It is difficult to calculate the total number of people moved, in part because some were moved prematurely in 1910, and others were counted as having begun moving south in summer/autumn of 1911, but that move was suspended due to weather, and it's not clear how many made it through to the Southern Reserve. When the British held a census of Maasai still remaining on Laikipia in later 1911, Hughes says, there were still 4,000 there, plus 160,600 cattle and 1.06 million sheep.

28. Ibid.: 44, 50; see also Tignor 1972.

29. L. Hughes 2005: 208.

30. See Schroeder 1999.

31. D. Anderson 1984.

32. L. Hughes 2006a: 137.

33. Ibid.: 151.

34. Quoted in Ndaskoi 2006: 35. See also DePuy 2011: 37ff.

35. See Glover and Gwynne 1961; Tignor 1972; Hodgson 2001: 106; see also L. Hughes 2006a: 105, 118ff.

36. DePuy 2011: 48.

37. Ibid.: 35–36.

38. L. Hughes 2006a: 118.

39. Ibid.: 56.

40. Ibid. Similarly, collective Maasai mythology romanticizes the Laikipia area to the point of idealization. "Its sweetness," Lotte Hughes writes, is "constantly compared to the bitterness of the south" (ibid.: 105). Her extensive review of the veterinary, epidemiological, biological, and ecological evidence on cattle health in the Northern vs. Southern Reserves reveals a complex story. Maasai cattle may have had resistance to illnesses that deteriorated when the move exposed them to other strains and other contingencies, such as concentration of cattle. All in all, it does seem that cattle were more susceptible to disease after the 1911–13 move (ibid: 118ff.). At the same time, Hughes indicates, "The dangers of sharply demarcating an ecologically harmonious 'before' and disharmonious 'after' colonial intervention in Africa are . . . very real" (ibid.: 107).

41. Wadhams 2009; "British Military Inquiry Rejects Kenya Rape Claims," *Guardian,* December 14, 2006, www.guardian.co.uk/world/2006/dec/14/military .kenya; "Rape Victim's Case Against British Soldiers Closed," *Standard Digital,* November 4, 2011.

42. In the 1913 case, Maasai plaintiffs claimed that the Maasai signatories to the 1911 agreement had lacked the authority to enter into it, that it violated the 1904 agreement, and that it did not benefit the Maasai. Maasai illiteracy proved a major disadvantage in their ability to establish their version of events (L. Hughes 2006a: 6–7). Over the years Maasai periodically accused Britain of neglecting their needs while favoring Kenya's other ethnic groups (L. Hughes 2005).

43. See L. Hughes 2005: 211; Munei and Galaty 2010.

44. L. Hughes 2005; 2006a: 25–26. Activists then and since have also confused settler leases with the notion that the Maasai Agreements involved timebound leases, which they did not (L. Hughes, personal communication, November 10, 2013).

45. L. Hughes 2005: 221.

46. This compensation, said the petition, "should be in the form of lands and territories equal in quality, size and legal status to those taken away from [Maasai] wrongfully. It should also include monies to mitigate their social-cultural welfare such as education, livestock management and markets, amenities and infrastructure. The compensation should be just, prompt and fair to benefit all the population of MAA people" (quoted in Kantai 2007: 112).

47. L. Hughes 2005: 221; see also Ndaskoi 2006.

48. Lacey 2004.

49. "Government Forces Subject Laikipia Maasai to Human Rights Abuses." *Cultural Survival,* September 17, 2004, www.culturalsurvival.org/news/michael -tiampati/government-forces-subject-laikipia-maasai-human-rights-abuses.

50. Quoted in Kantai 2007: 113.

51. Ndaskoi 2006.

52. Lacey 2004.

53. See Kantai 2007: 110; 2008b.

54. Kantai 2007.

55. For some summary of the Ndug'u Report, see Southall 2005. For details about some of these power-brokers and their holdings in Laikipia, see "Who Owns Kenya?" http://butdoisay.wordpress.com/2008/01/31/who-owns-kenya -by-the-masai-warrior.

56. It has been established that colonial authorities in Kenya strove to destroy or hide their most damning archival records concerning the crackdown on Mau Mau insurgents (D. Anderson 2013).

57. D. M. Hughes 2005: 14.

58. Thomson 1885: 407; Eliot 1905: 3, quoted in L. Hughes 2006a: 24.

59. Berman and Lonsdale 1992: 23; Hughes 2006a: 35.

60. L. Hughes 2006a: 24.

61. Southall 2005, www.worldbank.org.en/country/Kenya.

62. From "Bolshevik"; in British English, the term connotes combativeness and obstreperousness.

63. The theme that the British administration handed out only "empty lands" can be seen in other settler family origin stories as well, as in this family's narrative of their receipt of lands in the highlands: www.borana.co.ke/about /history.html#.VlsIN3arTIU.

64. See, e.g., Igoe 2004, chap. 2 and n. 85.

65. Whorf 1956.

66. Cohn 1987.

67. Eliot 1933: 642.

68. See as well L. Hughes 2006b.

69. Hartley 2004.

70. L. Hughes 2006b, which see too for dissenting views of Maasai among early travelers and administrators that were forgotten or never much disseminated among settlers.

71. See, e.g., Waller 1985b.

72. Maasai did have a fearsome reputation among many in East Africa as cattle raiders who sometimes killed to purloin others' herds, and the young

moran warrior class were regarded even by Maasai elders as hot-headed and sometimes impulsively violent. Intimidation was sometimes part of their strategy of expansion by which they secured access to key grazing grounds (Sindiga 1984: 26). At the same time, however, Maasai had a history of symbiotic trade arrangements with neighboring agriculturalists (ibid.). When Commissioner Eliot considered the possibility of creating native reserves, e.g., it was evident that the Maasai needed more protection from the settlers than vice versa. He wrote in 1903: "the stupidity of the Masai or the brutality of Europeans may render [intermingling] impossible" (L. Hughes 2006a: 28). Eliot's deputy also suggested that the Maasai would not use violence against Europeans "so long as we treat them fairly and do not deprive them of their best and favorite grazing grounds" (ibid). A military intelligence report in the same year also suggested that Maasai were "unlikely to turn violent" (ibid.: 30).

73. Interviewing settler descendants who own flower farms in Naivasha, Styles (2011: 65–66) encountered a good deal of resentment, too, and portrayals of Maasai as interlopers, since they hadn't been "permanently" settled there. A third-generation white Kenyan in his late forties said: "These Maasai here came in 1982. They never lived here permanently before then. . . . They came because of the flower farms and they make a bloody fortune selling the livestock that they water in the lake and graze for free on *my* land."

74. See, e.g., Galaty 1992; Neumann 1997; Waller 1985a.

75. Coulson 2010: 1.

76. Cronon 1983.

77. Hartley 2005. It is notable that Hartley uses the contested phrase "Kenya cowboy" so admiringly, when several of my other settler descendant respondents were at pains to distance themselves from the stereotypes that sometimes attach to it. These associations include (depending on who one's speaking to) being hard-drinking, reckless, womanizing, entitled, and uneducated—as well as somewhat less damning qualities (nature-loving, free-ranging, self-sufficient, and the like).

78. Hartley 2007.

79. L. Hughes 2006b; Tidrick 1980. Some admired the Maasai for qualities they saw as aristocratic, flattering themselves and these tribesmen with a shared dignity (Tidrick 1980).

80. Hodgson 2001, 2011; L. Hughes 2006b. This imagery both appeals to tourists (Bruner 2001) and nourishes the idea that "a 'traditional' idyll . . . has been shattered by modernization" (L. Hughes 2006a: 4; see also Kantai 2007: 119 and Hodgson 2011: 44 on "nostalgic reassertion" of ethnicity among Maasai). In Kenya and Tanzania, many Maasai have come to embrace the predicate "indigenous" in a strategic bid for rights to resources before audiences in the UN, the African Commission, and beyond (Hodgson 2011). See also Styles (2011: 67), who writes, "[C]ontemporary Maasai oral histories are likewise discursive constructs designed to fit the current political climate."

81. www.maasaierc.org/the-maasai-people.

82. See, e.g., Shipton 2009.

83. On its 2003 web site, which is now defunct (www.maasaierc.org /maasailegacy.html), MERC rhetoric goes on to seamlessly merge Maasai land

use with Western conservationist fantasies, quoting almost in the next breath Romain Gary's novel *The Roots of Heaven,* set in equatorial Africa in the mid twentieth century, which centers on a Frenchman attempting to save elephants from extinction by poachers and big-game hunters: "It is not possible for a free man to catch a glimpse of the great elephant herds roaming the vast spaces of Africa without taking an oath to do whatever is necessary to preserve forever this living splendor." The effect of combining Maasai bids for land with this extract is striking, for it rhetorically aligns the "freedom" (whether actual or longed-for) of three very different kinds of actors: elephants, "free men" (implicitly, based on the source of the quotation, Europeans), and Maasai pastoralists. The conflation is ironic, given that settler descendants today celebrate their own freedoms of mobility while denigrating the pastoralist mode of ranging freely.

84. Arham 1985; Brockington and Homewood 1999; Collet 1987; Goldman 2003; Igoe 2004; Parkipuny and Berger 1993; Sindiga 1984. For historical comparison to Native American equilibrium with wildlife, see Cronon 1983.

85. Adams and McShane 1997; Glover and Gwynne 1961; Hazzah 2006; L. Hughes 2006a; Sindiga 1984. Glover and Gwynne (1961),e.g., found that the arid land in the south resulted in a regressive ecological cycle, in which herds eroded the soil. Summarizing numerous studies, L. Hughes (2006a: 171–72) concludes that the overgrazing and overstocking of which Maasai have been accused "were a direct result of increased confinement, overcrowding in certain areas, curtailment of seasonal migration, an almost continuous state of quarantine, and early restrictions on cattle trading, although another contributory factor was improved veterinary services, when they eventually came, which led to larger stockholdings." Degradation, in other words, was an outcome of colonial interference in Maasai cultural ecology, rather than intrinsic to Maasai lifeways. "The lessons of the colonial era are clear: extensive alteration of traditional Maasai animal husbandry and cultural ecology led to severe land degradation," Isaac Sindiga (1984: 31) says. Meanwhile, Leela Hazzah (2006: 29) argues that the more precarious living situation of Maasai has meant that their tolerance for losing cattle to predation has gone down, while their resentment against lions and other wildlife has risen. That said, pastoralists historically have been more tolerant than agriculturalists in sub-Sharan Africa; these attitudes have been reflected in a recent comparative study in Laikipia by Michelle E. Gadd, http://primate.rutgers.edu/pfscp/Gadd_05Laikipia.pdf (see also Lindsay 1987). And, of course, Maasai involved in conservation for the sake of tourism, such as those at Il Ngwesi in Laikipia, have adapted to conserving big game for profit.

86. Hodgson 2001: 59, 85; see also Waller 1985a.

87. See Akama 1996; Honey 1999: 330.

88. Ironically, Maasai had ecological knowledge of how to use Rift Valley land that could have come in handy for early settlers who tried cattle-herding. They avoided certain pastures in Nakuru and Njoro, e.g., because they (unlike settlers) knew them to be mineral-deficient, and at one point they advised Galbraith Cole on how to save his sheep from tick-borne diseases by moving them to other pastures (L. Hughes 2006a: 157).

89. See, e.g., Goldman 2003: 17–18; Honey 1999: 319; Styles 2011.

90. For discussions of theories of landscape, including landscape as cultural meanings and cultural process, see Hirsch and O'Hanlon 1995.

91. A sense of profound connection to land is widespread among whites in Africa who are faced with the prospect of losing it. This has been particularly evident among whites in Zimbabwe and Southern Africa. To offer but one example, the writings of Doris Lessing about Southern Rhodesia, where she lived between the ages of five and thirty, also bespeak a deep attachment to the land. As she once wrote of her own shock at returning and learning that she had been declared a "Prohibited Immigrant" there, "you cannot be forbidden the land you grew up in, so says the web of sensations, memories, experience, that binds you to that landscape" (Lessing 1992: 11).

92. An observation by the late Maasai Justice Moijo ole Keiwua about Commissioner Charles Eliot in the early twentieth-century begins to get at the contradictions: "[He] cannot in fairness call the Maasai wanderers. Between the Maasai on their land, and the British who had wandered all the way from little England, who was a wanderer?" (Keiwua 2002).

93. Dinesen 1937: 3.

94. Quoted from Considine and Rawlins 2008: John Cowan, pp. 9–10; Adam Edmonson, p. 63; Ruth Rabb, née Block, p. 55; Joan Jolley née Stephen, p. 95; Alda Dugono née Guizzon, p. 7; Caroline Adams, née Hartley, pp. 222–23; John Wroe, p. 185; Beryl Screen, previously Lloyd, p. 46; Catherine Hart, née Hook, p. 180. Note that the speakers also imply that they felt safer when they were younger. The sentiment seems linked to nostalgia for childhood innocence, but in some of these idealistic accounts the country is represented as innocent as well, relatively free of both crime and racial tension. Such a narrative underscores the popular white Kenyan theme that the country was on a better path in the hands of the British.

95. Tanya Saunders, "About the Author" (2007), www.wildernessdiary.com/tanya-trevor-saunders.

96. D. Hughes 2010: 24.

97. Steinhart 2006.

98. Dinesen 1937.

99. See Steinhart 2006 for the historical backdrop to this shift. Suzuki 2007 astutely discusses an analogous conceptual shift in Zimbabwe, where whites reframed animals from "wild" animals to be hunted to "game" subject to management and administration, a maneuver that both situates whites as compassionate caretakers and allows them to package and sell images of animals as touristic attractions, from which their safari companies profit.

100. See, e.g., Schroeder 1999.

101. Berkes 2007: 15189.

102. Honey 1999: 310.

103. Igoe 2004; see also Brosius, Tsing, and Zerner 2005.

104. Honey 1999: 301–3.

105. See Western 2000 for an exposition of his conservation philosophy.

106. Lewa Wildlife Conservancy, www.lewa.org.

107. Ol Donyo Lodge's Maasailand Preservation Trust (www.eyesonafrica.net/african-safari-kenya/ol-donyo-lodge.htm), run by the settler descendant

and safari guide Richard Bonham, is a case in point. Another example is Loi-saba Lodge, owned by several white Kenyans, which bills itself as "a fully inte-grated local community project," employs staff from surrounding Samburu and Maasai communities, and draws on income from tourism to raise money for the communities' schools, clinics, and other expenses (www.africansafaris.co.ke /loisabalodge.html).

108. A wave of scholarship coming out of Tanzania, Kenya, and other sites of African ecotourism finds that in spite of good intentions, many CBC initiatives continue to marginalize local knowledge claims and secure Western economic and cultural hegemony. CBC risks simplifying the desires of the surrounding com-munities, and in some cases fetishizing a view of Maasai as "custodians" of wild-life, while overlooking the fact that, as Goldman 2003: 20 puts it, wildlife has become "the animal of the government" for many of them (see as well Akama 1996; Brockington and Homewood 1999; Igod 2004; Neumann 1998; and for broader, multinational critiques, see Agrawal and Gibson 1999; Berkes 2007).

109. Honey 1999: 325; see also Akama 1996.

110. Phombeah 2004.

111. See Shadle 2012 for a lengthy discussion of settlers' frustrations with African (mis)treatment of animals. In the early twentieth century, settlers some-times whipped Africans who were found being cruel to animals, believing it to be an effective means of inculcating empathy into them.

112. It is an important development—even if subtle—that some white Ken-yans now try to wrap their minds around alternative perspectives on wildlife with some degree of cultural relativism and structural understanding. Whites (whether in Africa or out of it) have long recognized that many African pasto-ralists, peasants, and members of the middle class do not share the Western aesthetic and conservationist zeal for wildlife. While the reasons for this have been well-rehearsed by scholars, it should as well be noted that this lack of interest can be overstated, and there is a vibrant group of African conservation professionals today. Plenty of conservationists have not been kind about this difference, seeing it as a mark of primitive psychology, "ignorance," or "irra-tionality" (Neumann 1992: 88). Some white Kenyans I spoke to, however, showed an embryonic understanding that different vantage points emerge, not from essential inferiority or obtuseness, but from different structural situations. Yes, African pastoralists and peasants do not "treasure" wildlife as white Ken-yans do (in the words of one), but there are reasonable explanations for this. See Akama (1996) for a discussion of rural peasants' and middle-class Kenyans' socioeconomic and cultural reasons for viewing wildlife more apprehensively than enthusiastically. On the other hand, see Garland 2006 for a detailed dis-cussion of the investments of African wildlife professionals.

CHAPTER 3

1. Shipton 2009.

2. There's a famous debate in anthropology about whether or not we can identify societies dominated by shame (the prospect of public humiliation) ver-sus those focused on psychological guilt (superego and conscience). Although

there may be no neat dividing line, Western societies often emphasize the importance of self-recrimination and private feelings of penitence.

3. L. Hughes 2006.

4. The fourth Baron Delamere married Diana Broughton, whose former lover Joss Erroll had been murdered under mysterious circumstances. That drama was re-enacted in the 1987 film *White Mischief*, set in 1941.

5. Steinhart 2006.

6. *Last White Man Standing* (2010), Plus Pictures/Day Zero Productions for BBC-DR-DFI-ITVS.

7. See Fox 2012 on "security" concerns and among white Kenyans in Nairobi, and their founding of private security firms.

8. www.nytimes.com/2006/09/05/world/africa/05kenya.html?pagewanted =print&_r=0.

9. Seal 2008.

10. Musila 2008: 159.

11. Seal 2008.

12. Hammer 2006.

13. William ole Ntimama, Maasai member of Parliament; see www .dailymail.co.uk/news/article-406577/Murderous-world-gun-toting-Happy-Valley-set.html.

14. "Gun Killing That Divides the Rift Valley," *Observer*, May 8, 2005.

15. Seal 2008.

16. Planz 2006.

17. "Getting Away with Murder: Cholmondeley Style," *Kumekucha*, September 17, 2008, http://kumekucha.blogspot.com/2008/09/getting-away-with -murder-cholmondeley.html.

18. "Murder Most Foul," *Jamaapoa*, May 20, 2006, http://jamaapoa .blogspot.com/2006/05/murder-most-foul.html.

19. delamere-court-case-kenya.blogspot.com/2007/12/bloody-rift-3-source-mens-vogue.html; aaj.tv/2006/05/angry-kenyans-demand-expulsion-of-white-settlers.

20. See also Mark Seal's (2008) discussion of the outcry and rumored "assassination squads."

21. See Steinhart 2006 on the complex history of white colonial attitudes toward wildlife. For decades, colonial hunters were deeply implicated in the destruction of Kenya's wildlife and evinced both mixed feelings and contradictory policies about conservation.

22. Cole utters this phrase in the 2010 documentary about the Cholmondeley trial, *Last White Man Standing*.

23. Crapanzano 1985: xxii.

24. Hughes 2006: 32.

25. See, e.g., Krog 1998; Pilossof 2012; Steyn 2001; Vice 2010.

26. Fabian [1983] 2002.

27. See, e.g., McGreal 2006.

28. See, e.g., Cooper 2002.

29. White Kenyans draw heavily upon the liberal teleologies of "development" discourse widespread among many NGO workers (and elsewhere).

30. "Kenya Jail Beating to Be Probed," *BBC News,* November 19, 2008, http://news.bbc.co.uk/2/hi/africa/7737168.stm.

31. In the documentary *Last White Man Standing.*

32. www.nation.co.ke/news/-/1056/676640/-/view/printVersion/-/a23miq/-/index.html.

33. "Kenyans Outraged at Light Sentence for Killing of African Man by White Settler Heir," *Pan-African News Wire,* May 14, 2009, http://panafricannews .blogspot.com/2009/05/kenyans-outraged-at-light-sentence-for.html.

34. *Last White Man Standing.*

35. "Cholmondeley a Free Man" (October 23, 2009), www.youtube.com /watch?v=JzuFfMHKC80.

CHAPTER 4

1. I did not speak to Anna Trzebinski or Loyaban Lemarti personally, though I do know some of their social contacts and relatives. My account of their love affair (and its symbolism) derives from the many publicly available journalistic accounts of their marriage, some of them linked to on the Lemarti's Camp web site (www.lemartiscamp.com; see the "Press" tab).

2. Selva 2005.

3. Ibid.

4. McGreal 2006.

5. Ibid.

6. George Paul Meiu, personal communication, March 2012. See also Meiu 2011.

7. Nyamweru 2001 describes the rise of interracial marriages as stemming partly from young Kenyan men traveling to the United States and Europe and striking up relationships there; many offspring of such unions have returned to live amongst Kenya's prosperous, multiracial middle class. Nyamweru contends that typically, such individuals have become "fully integrated into African ethnic groups" (185).

8. McGreal 2006.

9. For the most influential scholarly discussion of "carnal knowledge and imperial power," based on archival research in the colonial East Indies, see Stoler 2002. On similar dynamics in sub-Saharan Africa, see also Hansen 1989; Kennedy 1987; Pape 1990; Shadle 2015.

10. I take the first phrase from Nagel 2003 and the second from Pratt 1992.

11. Shadle 2015: 86; see as well Nyamweru 2001.

12. With the influx of soldier-settlers after World War I, African women, girls, and boys were subject to sexual exploitation (Best 1979: 26; Trzebinski 1986: 31; see also Pape 1990 on such dynamics in colonial Zimbabwe). Letters, memoirs, and diaries of early settlers also imply numerous short- and long-term encounters with sex workers. That said, African sex workers were not always mere victims— White 1990 indicates that some in early colonial Nairobi profited substantially. And cf. also Brennan 2004 on sex workers in the Dominican Republic.

13. Nicholls 2005: 195 writes that "[m]embers of mixed marriages and their offspring—the 1931 census recorded 205 'half-castes'—were ostracised and

therefore kept very much to themselves." "Mixing" with those of Asian descent, similarly, was anathema to settler culture (Shadle 2015). The taboos surrounding interracial marriage were pernicious enough to stick even as colonial sovereignty was beginning to crumble in the years leading up to Independence (Nicholls 2005: 249), and clearly, as I indicate, for more than four decades beyond that.

14. Kennedy 1987: 173, 176; see also Shadle 2015.

15. Kennedy 1987: 177.

16. Pape 1990; Kennedy 1987; Shadle (2015). In point of fact, sexual assaults were actually extremely rare (Nicholls 2005: 178; Shadle 2015: 134). But anxiety about the "black peril" resulted, among other things, in the arming of women and the insistence that male domestic servants be symbolically infantilized.

17. Shadle 2015: 104.

18. Kennedy 1987.

19. See www.travelandleisure.com/articles/profile-meet-richard-bonham-safari-legend.

20. For detailed history and analysis of racial segregation in Nairobi, see K'Akumu and Olima 2007.

21. Studying the floriculture industry in Naivasha, Megan Styles found that Dutch expatriates, who readily intermarried with Africans, characterized the descendants of British settler families as "very closed," by contrast with their own more "liberal-minded" approach to social life (Styles 2011: 323).

22. Jonathan's understanding of what holds Kenyans together resonates with aspects of Ernest Renan's (1882: 19) formulation of modern nationalism: "To have common glories in the past and to have a common will in the present; to have performed great deeds together, to wish to perform still more--these are the essential conditions for being a people." Jonathan, like my other white Kenyan respondents, hopes fervently to work together with other Kenyans to help the nation achieve future greatness. Yet for many other Kenyans, the nation's most salient "common glory in the past" was battling the colonial presence, a dynamic that works against the full inclusion of white Kenyans.

23. There are many ways to understand white Kenyans' self-segregation, and the young white Kenyan Max suggests an interpretation that moves beyond the notion that this is simply white prejudice rationalized in terms of their Kenyan national citizenship. After working for an NGO job in one of Nairobi's underprivileged communities and being robbed several times, Max told me, he began to rethink the matter: "After these incidents I felt less comfortable being in [a black-dominated neighborhood] and I began to understand why the white community excludes itself, because they're scared. And maybe they feel like targets. So it works *both* ways, integration works *both* ways, and that's probably very politically incorrect to say, but I think black Kenyan society's hard to break into." Max seems to feel that whites may justifiably be scared; because of vast income disparities, they are likely to be the targets of thieves. He suggests, too, that not all black Kenyans would welcome whites in their midst, and though he doesn't elaborate why, he hints that class and racial resentment are the issues.

24. In the colonial era, a version of this message was framed as the "civilizing mission" brought to the biologically stunted black masses; today it is the "developmental imperative" brought to the culturally mired black masses. Cultural racism, theorists argue, tends to be blind to the deleterious impact of colonialism and oblivious to non-Western understandings of global justice (see Gilroy 1991; Wylie 2001). Put in my terms, cultural racism suffers from structural oblivion.

25. Two of the examples I have just given involve Kikuyu partnering with whites. Kikuyu have long had a vexed relationship with settler families and their descendants. Early settlers notoriously displaced and disenfranchised Kikuyu when they claimed the "White Highlands." Since the vast majority of Mau Mau fighters attempting to reclaim land and rights were Kikuyu, and since a handful of settlers were apparently betrayed by their Kikuyu domestic workers' collusion with Mau Mau operators, sometimes with fatal results, the ethnotribal group became tainted among whites with a reputation for brutality and untrustworthiness (see D. Anderson 2005). At the same time, however, Kikuyu's proximity to settler culture and Nairobi meant they were among the first to take up Western education, Christianity, and opportunities for upward mobility. The first ruler in postcolonial Kenya, Jomo Kenyatta, was also Kikuyu, and some Kikuyu benefited disproportionately from his era of power. Today, Kikuyu are numerically dominant among black Kenyan elites, and so among the most likely to qualify as "cultured," to use Jonathan's phrase. Yet the history I describe has also resulted in an enduring white Kenyan stereotype that Kikuyu can be devious, even Machiavellian (see, e.g., Fox 2012).

26. Cole and Thomas 2009. See also Shadle 2015 on related attitudes among early colonials in Kenya.

27. Western fatherhood, for instance, increasingly demands close engagement with one's children.

28. Cole and Thomas 2009: 6–10.

29. www.telegraph.co.uk/news/worldnews/africaandindianocean/kenya /9131725/Kenyan-model-questioned-after-former-British-public-schoolboy-boyfriend-falls-to-death.html.

30. www.independent.co.uk/news/world/africa/briton-dies-in-kenya-balcony-fall-7546537.html.

31. The land comes from the Koija group ranch, which belongs to approximately 1,500 Samburu. See Cademartori 2011.

32. ke.linkedin.com/in/anna-trzebinski-585b9130, annatrzebinski.com /alifeofmychoice.

33. Initially, Anna and Lemarti had planned to call Lemarti's Camp "Rites of Passage," but they changed the name later. See Di Giovanni 2007.

34. http://lemartiscamp.com.

35. Lucia van der Post, "Kings of All We Survey." *Tatler Travel Guide 2012*, www.lemartiscamp.com/reviews/editorials.

36. DiGiovanni 2007

37. Kenya fashion: Anna Trzebinski, www.indagare.com/passions/10 /departments/173/6657 (accessed 2013, but URL found defunct in late 2015).

38. www.facebook.com/anna.trzebinski/info?tab=page_info.

39. In Rosaldo's definition of imperial nostalgia, colonizers mourned the passing or transformation of the native lifeways that colonialism itself (paradoxically) had destroyed or imperiled, and these sentiments hid racist brutality and white domination. Anna is mourning a cultural loss precipitated by colonialism and modernity, to be sure, but could hardly be accused of championing brutal racial domination, particularly given her commitment to raising a family with Lemarti. Some might detect in her words a faint family resemblance to an old colonial concern that rapid modernization might be detrimental to Africans (cf. Shadle 2015; Shaw 1995; Vaughan 1991). However, Anna's expression doesn't seem begotten of that particular essentialism (she does not, in other words, seem to think Africans can't handle modernization), but rather expresses a wistful and highly aestheticized appreciation of indigenous lifeways.

40. For a discussion of eroticized pastoralist warrior-figures, as well as the commodification of unpredictable ethnic encounters, in East African sex tourism, see Meiu 2011. On belonging through interracial intimacy, see Hubinette and Arvanitakis 2012: 703, who contend that "through intimate relations with people of color" we see the "construction of a white anti-racist cosmopolitanism" that helps white people to feel at home with people and places of the non-Western world.

41. C. Hoffmann [2005] 2007; and see too Meiu 2011.

42. Meiu 2009, 2011.

43. The notion of ethno-commodification is explored in depth in Comaroff and Comaroff 2009.

44. For a discussion of the social perils risked by Samburu who participate in these liaisons, see Meiu 2009.

45. Hubinette and Arvanitakis 2012.

46. See Shaw 1995 for further details of Leakey's relationship with Kikuyu.

47. And all of them, it should be added, enacted a mid-twentieth century mode of cosmopolitan privilege that has been described, in its twenty-first-century guise, by the sociologist Shamus Khan (2010). In this mode, elites get status not by barricading themselves away from the rest of society, but rather by moving seamlessly between registers of high and low. Their very ease of motion between social strata and contexts comes to feel like a mark of prestige.

48. The lodge is estimated to bring approximately U.S.$80,000 per year to the community, through direct employment, ground rent, and a surcharge that goes to community members. See Roberts 2011.

49. Van der Post, "Kings of All We Survey" (cited n. 35 above).

50. In the mid-twentieth century, anthropologists first coined the term "fictive kinship" to capture the many "family" ties across cultures that are based on solidarity and feeling rather than blood relations or marriage. The phrase has since been problematized, because some have taken it to imply these kinship relations are somehow less real than those based on biology (cf. Carsten 2000; Schneider 1984; Weston 1991).

51. Hansen 1989. See also Ehrenreich and Hochschild 2004.

52. Southern "faithful slave" narratives imagined that slaves were "removed from market forces and economic exigency," and in these white narratives, master-slave relationships were "more like a familiar relationship between

father and child based on a set of mutual obligations and responsibilities as well as affection" (McElya 2007: 5; see also Auslander 2011). Often, slave owners claimed to have a lifetime responsibility for the well-being of their slaves, including providing medicine, housing, and so forth, and imagined that the enslaved nourished a heartfelt loyalty to them in return. On domestic workers and fictive kinship, see also Hondagneu-Sotelo 2001; Wallace-Sanders 2008.

53. Dawes 1974 argues that the Victorian aristocracy presumed that the have-nots were part of the divine order of things, a notion that justified relegating them to a largely invisible life behind the scenes. Tucked away in attics, basements, and back staircases, servants were often kept in penury, and sometimes worked to the bone under appalling conditions. To be sure, interest in one's servants' welfare was considered a virtue, and household management books indicated that servants should be shown the kindliness one would give to "children" (13). This pattern of class differentiation would have infused the attitudes toward servants among some of Kenya's early colonials, particularly the many with roots in the British aristocracy.

54. See D. Anderson 2000: 484, 470. As the years went on, more Africans became aware of the provisions of the law and began to bring abuses to court, but still, some servants suffered fatal or near-fatal beatings when their masters meted out "rough justice," irrespective of the letter of the law (472). The court, furthermore, would hand down a flogging for particularly severe offenses. Although the 1930s and 1940s brought the rise of labor unions (Cooper 1987), the punitive sanctions against workers remained on the books until the 1950s. All in all, the disparity between labor laws in the United Kingdom and Kenya reflected a racist paternalism.

55. Scholars of colonialism have characterized such "micro-level" concerns as both emergent from and stoking the macropolitical colonial order (see Kennedy 1987; Hansen 1989, Stoler 2002).

56. Kennedy 1987: 153–54. See also Shadle 2015 on white enactments of prestige in front of their servants.

57. On these "tense and tender ties"—the affections and intimacies that coexisted with troubling hierarchies in colonial contexts—see Stoler 2001, 2002.

58. Nicholls 2005: 247.

59. Shadle 2015: 41–42.

60. J. L. Anderson 2013.

61. The aristocracy felt that breast-feeding was deleterious to a noblewoman's body, and sometimes outsourced the job to the working class. African women in some communities, on the other hand, would nurse one another's babies as a form of nutritional support, particularly for women who could not nourish their babies themselves.

62. Shefer 2012. In the American South, childhood intimacies between black and white children were eroded as they gradually learned the etiquette of their social stratification (see Rittenhouse 2006).

63. Ally 2011: 1.

64. See esp. Shadle 2015.

65. Statistics available at www.africapay.org/kenya/home/salary/minimum -wages.

66. That said, if my white Kenyan interlocutors are to be believed in the matter, it may also be higher than the average wage paid by elite Africans and Asians to domestic staff.

67. D. Anderson 2000: 476.

68. Nicholls 2005: 246.

69. It is worth noting that white Kenyan handouts to staff are not infrequently given "under the table"—typically, concealed by women from their husbands. Since these transactions take place in an informal economy rather than an official one, it has the additional effect of marking the relationship with staff as grounded more in affect and social relationships than in purely economic transactions.

70. Rutherford 2001: 88–89, 95, 97–98, 101.

71. Ibid., 98.

72. Cf. Scott 1972. For further structural analogues, see discussion of the Hacienda form of debt peonage in Latin America in Wolf and Mintz 1957.

73. Apparently Kenyan colonials also considered themselves more compassionate employers than Asians, but early twentieth-century legal records do not obviously reflect this (D. Anderson 2000: 482).

74. Brett Shadle, personal communication, March 2015.

75. Geschiere 2009 deems this ultimate status "Ur-belonging."

76. Such relationships have clearly been emotionally salient to many Africans, as attested, e.g., by Dangarembga 1988 (in Zimbabwe) and Oyono [1956] 2012, depicting life as a "houseboy" in colonial Cameroon.

77. Indeed, the former Kenyan civil servant and whistle-blower on corruption John Githongo penned a controversial op-ed in 2000 entitled "Why Maids Prefer White Masters," in which he argues that domestic servants are routinely subject to "humiliation and abuse at the hands of their fellow Africans." He does not mention Asian employers, but indicates that expatriate white employers are preferable to "local Kenyan *wazungu*" (white Kenyans, in other words), who are seen as having a more "colonial mentality." Githongo's critics charged that he is in the pockets of the British. See Githongo 2000 and http://eastafrican1 .blogspot.com/2007/01/why-john-githongo-prefers-to-be-maid.html.

78. After the death of Guillame Bonn's grandfather, his Malagasy domestic, Juliette, who had worked for him for fifty years, left abruptly, stopping neither for compensation nor good-byes. The family was taken aback, but Bonn interprets her actions as an eloquent assertion of power; "she needed neither us nor our money" (Jon Lee Anderson, "Silent Lives," *New Yorker,* March 5, 2013, www.newyorker .com/online/blogs/photobooth/2013/03/silent-lives.html#slide_ss_0=1).

79. Cf. Haugerud 1995.

CHAPTER 5

1. Gettleman 2006.

2. The relationships between Kenyans of Asian descent and Kiswahili are also historically interesting and complex, and include a distinctive pidgin variety of Kiswahili, but this topic would merit a separate exploration beyond the scope of this work.

3. See Errington 2008: 27–28; Irvine and Gal 2000; Gilmour 2006.

4. Mutonya and Parsons 2004: 114.

5. Whiteley 1969: 8.

6. The body that carried this out was called the "Inter-territorial Language Committee."

7. There were, nevertheless, ongoing debates among missionaries concerning which language was best for evangelism. Some felt that local vernaculars would reach the heart more effectively. See Whiteley 1969: 11.

8. Caroline Elkins, personal communication, January 28, 2013. Elkins's preference is to emphasize settlers' and administrators' competence in Kiswahili, especially in light of their involvement in the 1950s in the incarceration and interrogation of Mau Mau detainees. Some whites, too, served in "pseudo-gangs" as part of the counterinsurgency against Mau Mau, disguising themselves in blackface and making their way into the forest with loyalist Kikuyu and others; this would have required good Kiswahili abilities. Elkins has suggested that my informants may have lied about the relative linguistic incompetence of their colonial predecessors as a cover-up, of sorts, for their involvement in the crackdown on Mau Mau. My own reading of the evidence, however, is that while some officials and settlers in the first half of the twentieth century knew Kiswahili and other East African vernaculars well, many did not bother to cultivate African languages. Furthermore, regardless of the variation in settlers' and administrators' linguistic competence, my interlocutors' emphasis on colonial linguistic incompetence, which can also be found in the white Kenyan narratives collected by Megan Styles (2011) in Naivasha, is *ideologically* important. The image of the bumbling colonial is a useful foil in younger white Kenyan narratives of their own superior linguistic competence and Kenyan nationalism. My focus is not on pinning down with precision exactly who spoke Kiswahili well or poorly in the past, then, but rather, primarily, on stories settler descendants tell about themselves and how eager they are to be seen as distinct from "old colonials."

9. Whiteley 1969: 61.

10. Mutonya and Parsons 2004: 115.

11. Vitale 1980: 47.

12. Kennedy 1987: 157; Buxton 1928: 42; Leys 1924: 49; see also Hymes 1971: 519.

13. cf. Duran 1979: 141.

14. Kennedy 1987: 158.

15. See Kennedy 1987: 156, 158–59. In the early colonial era, many settlers were deeply uncomfortable when Africans took on the habits and accoutrements of colonials, seeing this transition as hubristic. Those Africans who attended school and learned English were sometimes perceived as having merely a "veneer" of European culture atop a deeply, essentially African core (Kennedy 1987: 163).

16. See, e.g., Rutherford 2001: 124.

17. Brett Shadle, personal communication, January 9, 2015.

18. Le Breton 1936.

19. Examples from ibid., pp. 33, 38, 47, and 51 respectively.

20. Le Breton 1936: 3. Thanks to the linguist Anthony Vitale 1980 for pointing out this tension.

21. Whiteley 1969; Vitale 1980. Given that settler efforts were based on disregard for rules and, in domestic contexts, anyway, the barest imperative of getting by, the term "Kisettla" should probably be taken to index not a stable language variety, but rather a family resemblance between improvisational linguistic strategies that varied across space and time.

22. See Vitale 1980: 57. It is regrettable that Vitale does not clarify when or where he collected his own linguistic data, or the ages of his informants. Since his article was published in 1980, his material must have been observed or elicited in the 1970s or earlier. Some of it, then, probably postdates Kenya's independence, but presumably his informants came of age and learned their Kisettla during the colonial era.

23. Duran 1979; Wouter-Kusters 2003; Myers-Scotton 1979

24. Vitale 1980: 62.

25. Hymes 1971: 519.

26. John Mugane, personal communication, January 28, 2013.

27. J.W. [1932?]; this was evidently first published in the *East African Standard* and later circulated as a separate pamphlet, presumably because of its popularity.

28. Ibid.: 6.

29. Mutonya and Parsons 2004: 125.

30. Fisher 2011: 116.

31. See, e.g., www.csmonitor.com/2000/0517/p1s3.html and http://denfordmagora.blogspot.com/2010/01/white-farmers-under-siege-right-now-in.html. Rory Pilossof, a white Zimbabwean scholar, tells me that in his study of white Zimbabwean farmers (Pilossof 2012), he found that "being able to speak Shona was so often used as a defense of a particular farmer/person, and often with an amazement that that person could have been 'attacked' or targeted in the land reform." He adds that a number of his white friends and acquaintances are now studying Shona, a postcolonial form of engagement he sees as similar to what I describe among white Kenyans (Rory Pilossof, personal communication, September 23, 2014).

32. Rutherford 2001: 124.

33. See van der Waal 2012.

34. Fisher 2011: 152.

35. https://youtu.be/jXvfm2BbLvY.

36. https://youtu.be/4jfoWHDAGBg. A second video along similar lines, featuring a toddler whose housekeeper has taught him isiXhosa and cheerfully quizzes him in that language, can be found at https://youtu.be/Td4SjzfC1yI. The opening text of the latter video frames the toddler as "amazing." Some online commentators, many of them black South Africans, seem approving, but several point out that no one should be "amazed" by a white child picking up an African language.

37. Language ideologies among white Kenyans are distinct to their nation's history and should not be taken as neat reflections of white language ideology elsewhere in sub-Saharan Africa. Demographic and political differences point to

the likelihood of different dynamics from one place to another. Not only are post-apartheid politics younger in South Africa, for instance, but also white South Africans make up nearly 10 percent of their country's population and are divided into Afrikaans and English speakers, with both languages being widely spoken by people of color as well. Nevertheless, it does seem that when white South Africans or white Zimbabweans learn indigenous languages, as opposed to having absorbed them from, e.g., their nannies, they are sometimes attempting to send a signal of sympathy or allegiance. It would be of great interest to see a sustained exploration of whites' language ideologies in Zimbabwe, particularly in the wake of the evictions of white farmers from their land, the rise of a poor white class, and the exodus of so many from the country.

38. www.guardian.co.uk/world/2006/oct/26/kenya.chrismcgreal.

39. In other publications (2006, 2009b), I call him "Richard," but I use "James" to identify him in this book to avoid any confusion with Richard Leakey.

40. See Myers-Scotton 1993 on code-switching between English and Kiswahili among Nairobi University students seeking to present themselves as both cosmopolitan and local.

41. Kiswahili is also a factor in the identity of some former Kenyan settlers who relocated after Independence. A woman who was fifteen when her family left Kenya, and who loves to attend the U.K. reunions of her former British school there, told me shortly after one of them:

> We have a sort of *language* we speak; I've just been speaking it at lunchtime with these people. It's a mixture of English and Swahili words and we just, it was the language we all spoke to each other when we were growing up, because we had *much* more to do with the Africans than our parents ever did. Growing up there we actually *did* play with them although our parents didn't *like* us playing with them. So we developed this sort of closeness to the African which people like [my parents] didn't have. And we were *deeply* traumatized by having to come to this country, and have never settled any of us. And that's why we cling together in these reunions. And we feel like a people without a country, completely *stateless*.

42. Nabea 2009: 123.

43. Mazrui and Mazrui 1998: 144, 145.

44. Ogechi 2003.

45. See ibid. and Michieka 2005. Debates about the roles of English and Kiswahili in Kenya have been ongoing since Independence. It has long been argued that English has in effect colonized Kenyan minds with hegemonic European sensibilities (see, e.g., wa Thiong'o 1986), and Kiswahili's role in political contexts such as parliamentary discussion has waxed and waned (see Mazrui and Mazrui 1995). Nationalist movements to advance Kiswahili's official status have been thwarted on grounds that many politicians speak better English than they do Kiswahili, and the language has wound up continuing to serve relatively "lower-status functions" (Githoria 2008: 25).

46. Nabea 2009.

47. See, e.g., Schmeid 1991, 2006.

48. Harries 1976: 159; Nabea 2009.

49. Wouter-Kusters 2003.

50. See Githoria 2002. In fact, Sheng has multilingual influences beyond English and Kiswahili, but its complexities are beyond the scope of this discussion.

51. Harries 1976: 162.

52. Githiora 2008; Myers-Scotton 1993.

53. See Ogechi 2003.

54. It should be noted again that Kiswahili is the first language of the Muslim Swahili peoples of the Kenya coast. However, Swahili people were not centrally implicated in the 2007–8 wave of ethno-political violence, which was more focused around political and territorial conflicts between upcountry people such as Kikuyu and Luo. Furthermore, Kiswahili is the first language of only a small fraction of the Kenyans speak it. Hence, all in all, Kiswahili retains its connotations of relative political neutrality.

55. See LetsRun.com forums at www.letsrun.com/forum/flat_read.php?thread=2013555.

56. With apologies to Bernard Cohn (2008).

57. On language essentialisms, see Irvine and Gal 2000; McIntosh 2005.

58. Hoffmann 2010. One white Kenyan writer told me that "the colonial accent isn't so much plummy as it is archaic," with softened vowels that evoke "England forty years ago." Hoffmann also found that white Kenyans' pronunciation is variably influenced by their life trajectories. He indicates in a footnote (p. x) that he was told that the so-called Kenya cowboys have their own distinct accent. I heard this too. A couple of white Kenyans, for instance, insisted that their "Kenya cowboy" peers—the more rugged, outdoorsy set—tend to have more "pinched"—or raised—vowels, suggesting some white South African influence. All such claims may be true in various cases; white Kenyan varieties of English have probably branched off and taken different trajectories, like tributaries of a river.

59. Nevertheless, when speaking to black African interlocutors white Kenyans sometimes shift their accent and articulation, speaking a little more slowly, decoupling contractions, and pronouncing words in ways that approximate Kenyan English phonology. Sometimes white Kenyans adopt Kenyan English grammatical formations such as doubling an adjective or adverb—"small small" or "slowly slowly"—for emphasis. At other times, they adopt Kenyan English idioms. Locutions I heard from white Kenyans, particularly when speaking to black Kenyans, but sometimes to other white Kenyans as well, included: "You have been lost" (i.e., "I haven't seen you for a while"); "Even me, I'm not sure" (i.e., "I'm not sure either"); "Help me with a glass" (i.e., "May I have a glass"); "I'll pick you at seven" (i.e., "I'll pick you up at seven"); and redundancies such as "Me, I like it when they open early."

60. See Irvine and Gal 2000 for a discussion of "iconization" in language ideology.

61. Clayton 2005.

62. Rob Crilly, "Aristocrat Accused of Murder Tries to Shift Blame to Friend," *Irish Times*, July 9, 2008, www.irishtimes.com/newspaper/world/2008/0709/1215537641497.html.

63. There is not only an emotional hypercorrection but a semiotic logic here; shifts in language attitudes often broadly follow shifts in social alignments (see Irvine and Gal 2000; Schieffelin et al. 1998).

64. Kiswahili is a required subject in government-funded primary and secondary schools, but an optional one in most of the private schools typically attended by whites. During the colonial era, the British curriculum did not usually include the language, and some schools actually forbade its use on school grounds, seeing it as a potential political threat. In 1952, for instance, state officials were intimidated by labor movements in Kenya and other forms of rebellion that coordinated resistance across ethnolinguistic groups through the medium of Kiswahili. Officials recommended expunging Kiswahili from school contexts and bureaucratic contexts except in coastal regions where it was the vernacular. In some pre-Independence schools attended by whites, Kiswahili was forbidden for primary school students, but was offered as an "extra," fee-paying subject in secondary school. After Independence, the emphasis on English remained for a few years, but in the 1980s Kiswahili became a mandatory subject taught in all of Kenya's state-funded schools. Today, in state schools, the first four years of primary school are taught in the vernacular, with both English and Kiswahili taught as subjects. Beyond the primary level, English is now the medium of instruction except for those pursuing Kiswahili studies at the university level. Still, in post-Independence private schools catering to Kenya's elite, Kiswahili is optional or not even available. A number of younger informants told me that their schools did not offer it as a subject in the 1970s or 1980s, and several noted that in elite schools, white, black, and Asian students mostly spoke English outside of the classroom.

65. This shared experience of a relatively low-status cultural practice, one that has no prestige but that symbolically unites members of a community nevertheless, seems an example of "cultural intimacy" (Herzfeld 1997).

66. Despite the greater enthusiasm about Kiswahili on the part of young white Kenyans, and their overall superior ability compared to their predecessors, one does occasionally come across a younger white who has gotten away with learning the language poorly because English has become so widespread in Kenya.

67. Although younger white Kenyans pride themselves on being more engaged with Kiswahili than their forebears, they tend to speak kindly of colonial linguistic attitudes and to regard the linguistic shortcomings of the older generation in this respect as products of their time and social moment.

68. See Styles 2011: 308–9. Styles's white Kenyan informants took pride in expertise that "had accreted over generations" and yoked it to their ability to speak Kiswahili, she says, citing the example of a young woman who justified her involvement in floriculture in contrast to expatriates she saw as culturally naïve by saying, "I knew the language and I knew the people" (310).

69. See http://carrhartley.com/about-us/our-people.

70. Robinson 2009.

71. Such uses of Kiswahili play a similar role to the appropriations of Spanish by anglophone Americans explored by Jane Hill, who writes: "Mock Spanish works to create a particular kind of 'American' identity, a desirable collo-

quial persona that is informal and easy going, with an all-important sense of humor and a hint—not too much, but just the right non-threatening amount— of cosmopolitanism, acquaintance with another language and culture" (Hill 2008: 128–29).

72. Shadle, personal communication, January 9, 2015.

73. Rosaldo 1993.

74. There is a certain irony to white Kenyans' insistence that Kiswahili is "fun" relative to English, given that young Giriama on Kenya's coast, in their text-messaging, anyway, regard English as the language of fun and play, rather than Kiswahili or their first language, Kigiriama (McIntosh 2010). Nevertheless, English is the language of transnational commerce and upward mobility for all groups.

75. Sociolinguists generally count word- or phrase-level substitutions that lower the tone of formality and tend to have fairly high turnover in a speech community as "slang" (see, e.g., Eble 1996).

76. A similar (though not identical) dynamic can be found among anglophone Americans who use parodic "mock" Spanish, semiotically linking the language—and, Jane Hill (2008) argues, its native speakers—to pejorative, offensive topics and registers, but sometimes gaining some cachet for themselves in the process. To be sure, the younger white Kenyans I spoke to aspire to more interracial interactions and connections than many anglophone users of mock Spanish, giving them a more ambivalent relationship to Kiswahili than the former tend to have to Spanish.

77. Quoted in Harries 1976: 159.

78. An American anthropologist colleague also reports having been told that his use of Kiswahili is "dangerous," in the sense that it threatens a kind of linguistic sanctuary for private information (Dillon Mahoney, personal communication, March 1, 2013).

79. Some kind of structural oblivion is shared as well by many well-meaning Western visitors to Kenya, but my white Kenyan interlocutors' sense of being directly implicated in colonial history motivates their keenly felt wish to connect and, in some cases, atone. I should clarify that despite the dilemmas I point out here, I do not mean to discourage any European or American who might have been planning to engage with and learn Kiswahili. However, I would encourage sensitivity to the history and ideological dynamics I discuss. Although it cannot clearly prescribe what to do in any given linguistic situation, such awareness contributes to rectifying the "oblivion" in "structural oblivion" and may encourage dialogue about it.

80. See Khan 2010: 16, which draws on fieldwork in an elite preparatory school in New England to argue that contemporary elites in the United States no longer sustain their privilege through self-segregation. Quite the contrary; today, Khan says, it is "ease of motion" between social strata and registers that makes the mark of privilege: "The elites I have observed are not . . . barricading themselves behind the armory. Instead, they are learning how to acknowledge . . . distinctions when necessary while also composing themselves as if such distinctions did not exist. The hierarchy is everywhere . . . but with the right skills the hierarchy seems to disappear" (71). If easy motion between social registers is a

strategy of privilege, this might help to explain some of the similarities between white Kenyan language practices and the Anglo American appropriations of Spanish documented in Hill 2008.

CHAPTER 6

1. See Crapanzano 1985: xxii. Crapanzano was writing specifically about South Africa in the 1980s, focusing on the mentality of the white South Africans he interviewed.

2. Hannerz 1996 describes a cosmopolitan orientation as "a willingness to engage with the Other . . . an intellectual and aesthetic stance of openness toward divergent cultural experiences."

3. As noted in chap. 5 n. 40 above, I call this respondent "Richard" in other publications, but since this book also cites Richard Leakey, I use "James" here to avoid confusion.

4. See Hufford 1982 for a lengthy discussion of cross-cultural accounts of so-called sleep paralysis and the imputed presence of supernatural beings while in such states.

5. When it comes to the topic of the occult, my effect on my respondents' words may have been especially complicated. They knew I had studied African religion, so perhaps some were less shy about confessing their interactions with it to me. On the other hand, since I'm from the West, they assumed we share an understanding about the value of rational personhood, effective management, and what one of my interlocutors called a "clear head." I know, too, that they assumed my politics to be generally left-leaning, which probably inspired some care in choosing their words about the occult. My interlocutors' narratives are always shaped by my presence and their ideas about who I am, what I want to hear, and how they want to come across.

6. McIntosh 2004:75.

7. See McIntosh 2009.

8. Ashforth 2000; 2005: 113. I should add that probing the influence of African cosmology upon white experience is a little out of step with the direction of much scholarship these days. When anthropologists study "globalization," for instance, they tend to focus upon the flow of influence—economic, political, religious, and so on—from "the West" to "the Rest," and the complex ways in which such influences are received. The movement of ideas from subordinate to dominant groups has been treated as a less politically urgent matter. See Comaroff and Comaroff 2012 for an exception in their extended discussion of "theory from the South," or "how Euroamerica is evolving toward Africa."

9. On a similar dynamic in South Africa, see too Ashforth 2000, 2005. And see Smith 2008 for discussions that complicate neat oppositions between the occult and local notions of "development."

10. See, e.g., Ashforth 2005; McIntosh 2010; Comaroff and Comaroff 1993; Geschiere 1997.

11. Wilson 1952: 30. Note that the term "witchdoctor" is rejected by contemporary anthropologists, in part because it conflates the positive powers of healing with the malicious powers of witchery.

12. Brantley 1979; Luongo 2006, 2011; Waller 2003.

13. Luongo 2011.

14. Ciekawy 1997.

15. Mahone 2006.

16. Luongo 2011; Waller 2003: 245.

17. Waller 2003, and see Luongo 2011 for problematic colonial glosses of the Kamba occult lexicon.

18. Ciekawy 1998.

19. Smith 2005: 154, 148–49.

20. Anderson 2005; Elkins 2005; Luongo 2011; Rosberg and Nottingham 1966.

21. Luongo 2011: 160, 174. The administration had already begun to delegate the implementation of some of its anti-witchcraft legislation to Africans. After 1933, local African tribunals were often charged with carrying out the 1925 Witchcraft Ordinance, and Africans exercised a certain amount of agency over what to count as witchery (Waller 2003: 247).

22. See, e.g., Beidelman 1982: 9; Pels 1999.

23. See Beidelman 1982: 17, 138; Chidester 1996; Nelson 1992: 35, 43; Pels 1999: 240.

24. See, e.g., Cooper and Stoler 1997; Baucom 1999: 7; Gikandi 1996: 48. Colonial regimes were always messy in practice, even if not in theory. They had to cope with tensions in their own political and religious agendas, with the unpredictability of native responses, and with the unsettling dynamics of social and sexual intercourse with the locals, as discussed in chapter 4 above. Furthermore, some have argued that these complex exchanges made their way back to the identity of those living in the metropole, and ultimately, "the colonial experience shaped what it meant to be . . . 'European' as much as the other way around" (Cooper and Stoler 1997: vii). In the view of some scholars, then (e.g., Baucom 1999; Kumar 2003), "Englishness" itself (the primary identification of Kenya's colonials) is inextricable from the experience of imperial dominance and its loss. "[E]mpire . . . is less a place where England exerts control than the place where England loses command of its own narrative of identity," Ian Baucom concludes (1999: 3), glossing Salman Rushdie. Such sweeping statements may seem vague, but when brought to bear on postcolonial European contact with the African occult, they are suggestive. Occult powers both threaten settler descendants' largely European model of personhood and force them to rearticulate its parameters.

25. Pels 1999: 240.

26. See Pels 1998. Similarly, Margaret Weiner (2003) has explored the contradictory and anxious European responses to magic in the colonial Indies, describing "the space magic occupies in the murky territory between fraud and fear." For a colonial novel set in an Indonesian context that sounds many related themes, see Couperus 1992 [1900].

27. Waller 2003: 50.

28. Luongo 2011: 214.

29. Luongo 2010: 587.

30. Ciekawy 1998

31. Malindi Municipal Council 2004: 14. In a related vein, Diane Ciekawy (1989, 1992) has demonstrated that the Independence-era witchfinding movement in coastal Kenya, led by the Mijikenda witchfinder Kajiwe, helped to facilitate the notion that witchcraft activities encourage the economic marginalization and "underdevelopment" of Mijikenda.

32. Mazera Nduyra, "Witch's Hand Seen in Coast Poverty," *Daily Nation,* June 17, 2009, quoted in Luongo 2011: 210.

33. See Cooper and Stoler 1997 for an introduction to these themes in colonial Africa and the colonial East Indies. For Kenyan settlers' anxieties about racial differentiation, see Kennedy 1987 and Shadle 2015.

34. Pieter, of course, is talking about ritual practice to *combat* witchcraft, but like many white Kenyans he conflates helpful and harmful magic. The term *mganga* typically refers to an individual practicing helpful magic, while a witchcraft practitioner would be called *mchawi* in Kiswahili or *mtsai* in the Giriama language—although any *mganga* has the potential to shift into a *mchawi*. A number of my interlocutors, too, use the terms "witchcraft" and "magic" (or "black magic") more or less interchangeably. On the displacement of the term "magic" by the term "witchcraft" in anthropological discourse in the 1930s, see Pels 1999: 239–45.

35. Dinesen 1937: 294.

36. wa Thiong'o 1981.

37. This wonderment over death by bewitchment alone dates to the colonial era, when officials puzzled over how to eradicate witchcraft and oathing so persuasive that they could cause someone to fall ill and die (Luongo 2011).

38. Capitalist accumulation, "development," and the social asymmetries and instabilities brought by colonialism and new forms of globalization have all been the targets of supernatural reprisals and rumors in sub-Saharan Africa. See Comaroff and Comaroff 1993; Auslander 1993; Ciekawy 1997, 1998, 2001; Geschiere 1997; Meyer 1992, 1995; Niehaus 2001; White 2000.

39. Cf. Brantley 1982; McIntosh 2001, 2009.

40. See Needham 1972; Tooker 1992; McIntosh 2009.

41. Luhrmann 1989: 308; Gellner 1974.

42. Tanya Luhrmann has given the name "interpretive drift" to the cognitive process by which people exposed to new situations can change their beliefs, engaging in "the slow slide from one form of explanation to another, partially propelled by the dynamics of unverbalized experience" (Luhrmann 1989: 322).

43. Perhaps this ideal core self has analogies to the Freudian superego.

44. Such phraseology is a holdover from the colonial era; Luongo quotes a colonial official writing of the Kamba in his province that "all the natives in this reserve are saturated in witchcraft" (Luongo 2011: 89).

45. See Ruel 1982 for a discussion of such distinctions in the history of Christianity. My interlocutors' use of the term "belief" is sometimes—though by no means always—inflected by a distinction between the phrases "belief that" and "belief in." Summarizing historical differences between these phrases in Christian theology, Joel Robbins argues that "belief that" has tended to imply a mental assent to an ontological proposition, while at the same time suggesting the possibility of epistemic doubt about that proposition (in contrast to "know that"),

whereas "belief in" implies trust, commitment to act a certain way toward the object of belief, and a kind of "conviction" or "certainty" about what one is saying or doing in the name of that belief (Robbins 2007: 14). Following Wilfred C. Smith 1998, Robbins also suggests that over time, Christian discourse has tended to converge on "belief that," with its attendant focus on ontology and implications of uncertainty, an unmarked subtext of the term "belief." In the context of my informants' discourse, however, "belief" and "belief in" have varying and sometimes ambiguous connotations, sometimes carving out primarily ontological stances, sometimes alluding more to trust in and social allegiance to the object of belief, and sometimes both. And while it does indeed seem that a common understanding of the term "belief" focuses upon the mental subscription to an ontological proposition, it also seems that in some narratives—in spite of the etymological history discussed by Robbins—to profess belief is *not* necessarily to index one's uncertainty, which is precisely why the metapragmatics surrounding the uses of "belief" in my data (as in James's and others' narratives) sometimes requires *marking* ambivalence or uncertainty where it obtains. Furthermore, "belief in" is sometimes more weighted toward the ontological than toward the social or moral. However, white Kenyans' aversion to making *any* kind of affirmative belief statement about the African occult—whether "believing in" or "believing that"—is perhaps the most important thing to note here.

46. Apparently having difficulty with the *mg* sound in *mganga*, Stephen inserted an *a* to smooth over it, and he also supplied an *r* to attach the English suffix "-ism" to the Kiswahili term, thus constructing the hybrid "magangarism."

47. Performing invulnerability in front of subaltern staff is an old imperial habit, dramatized in George Orwell's famous short story "Shooting an Elephant," set in colonial Burma. "A sahib has got to act like a sahib," says the narrator, a colonial police officer who kills an elephant largely to demonstrate his resolve and authority in front of the natives (Orwell [1936] 1970: 269).

48. Barber 1981.

49. McIntosh 1996: 482.

50. The speaker is Ashforth's interlocutor Modiehi (Ashforth 2000: 73).

51. For more detailed exposition of the linguistic argument here, see McIntosh 2009b.

CONCLUSION

1. Van der Merwe is one of the most common surnames in South Africa. The joke I heard from Olivia stems from a genre of *Afrikaans* van der Merwe jokes that have made their way to Kenya. Such jokes are still told in South Africa; for instance, "In [whatever year] all the van der Merwes emigrated from South Africa to Australia [or another country], raising the average IQ in both places by ten points" (Peter Dreyer, personal communication, November 17, 2015). Clearly the van der Merwe name has long been a scapegoat for various rhetorical purposes. In Kenya, imagined van der Merwe figures tend to embody intellectually lowbrow South African racists, serving as a foil to the way white Kenyans would like to be perceived.

2. Adam Hochschild, *King Leopold's Ghost: A Story of Greed, Terror and Heroism in Colonial Africa* (Boston: Houghton Mifflin, 1998).

3. Goodwin and Schiff 1995; Sharp and van Wyk 2013.

4. Hughes 2010: xvi.

5. Fisher 2011: 151.

6. Schroeder 2012: 142.

7. Shadle 2015.

8. Wander et al. 1999: 15.

9. It should be noted once again that whites are not the only group with systematic advantages in Kenya. White skin color has historically bought Kenyan whites immense privilege, in the past and in the present, but today the elite social strata include Asian and affluent black Kenyans, particularly those from political families.

10. On the perils of presuming a unified "settler culture," see Steyn 2001; Pilossof 2012: 171; Rutherford 2001: 62–63.

11. The claim of "reverse racism" has been widespread among white Zimbwabean farmers facing violent exile from their land, and among the rising numbers of impoverished Afrikaners living in squatters' encampments.

12. Pilossof 2012.

13. See, e.g., www.counterpunch.org/2009/06/09/in-south-africa-apartheid-is-dead-but-white-supremacy-lingers-on; www.telegraph.co.uk/news/worldnews/africaandindianocean/southafrica/2059457/South-Africa-AWB-leader-TerreBlanche-rallys-Boers-again.html; Goodwin and Schiff 1995.

14. Steyn 2001; Goodwin and Schiff 1995; Vice 2010. See as well Shefer 2012 on white South Africans looking back with grief at the enforced loss of intimacy with their childhood caretakers.

15. Steyn 2001: 118; see also Freedberg 2006.

16. Vice 2010: 326.

17. See http://samhopkins.org/?page_id=172.

18. See, e.g., Pilossof 2012: 17; Steyn 2001; Fisher 2011: 152. And on white South Africans' "sense of being African," see also Schroeder 2012: 7.

19. Freedberg 2006: 343.

20. Steyn 2001: 103.

21. Fisher 2011: 224.

22. "[T]he ambivalence provided by the overarching nature of the appeal enables fuzziness about partisan interests. It can render a base of privilege unassailable through adopting an alias of correct national identity" (Steyn 2001: 103).

23. www.thoughtleader.co.za/sentletsediakanyo/2010/12/28/we-are-not-all-africans-black-people-are. In a similar vein, the journalist Louis Freedberg 2006: 343 contends that some young white South Africans are engaging in a "belated embrace of their African environment" at a time when "it is least likely to be accepted by the black majority."

24. Schroeder 2012: 7.

25. Steyn 2001: 124.

References

Adams, Jonathan, and Thomas O. McShane. 1996. *The Myth of Wild Africa: Conservation without Illusion.* Berkeley: University of California Press.

Agrawal, Arun, and Clark C. Gibson. 1999. "Enchantment and Disenchantment: The Role of Community in Natural Resource Conservation." *World Development* 27, no. 4: 629–49.

Aiyar, Sana. 2015. *Indians in Kenya: The Politics of Diaspora.* Cambridge, MA: Harvard University Press.

Akama, John S. 1996. "Western Environmental Values and Nature-Based Tourism in Kenya." *Tourism Management* 17, no. 8: 567–74.

Alcoff, Linda Martin. 1998. "What Should White People Do?" *Hypatia* 13, no. 3: 6–26.

———. 2015. *The Future of Whiteness.* Cambridge: Polity Press.

Ally, Shireen. 2011. "Domestics, "dirty work" and the Affects of Domination." *South African Review of Sociology* 42, no. 2: 1–7.

Anderson, David. 1984. "Depression, Dust Bowl, Demography, and Drought: The Colonial State and Soil Conservation during the 1930s." *African Affairs* 83, no. 332: 321–43.

———. 2000. "Master and Servant in Colonial Kenya, 1895–1939." *Journal of African History* 41, no. 3: 459–85. Cambridge University Press.

———. 2005. *Histories of the Hanged: The Dirty War in Kenya and the End of Empire.* New York: Norton.

———. 2013. "Atoning for the Sins of Empire." *New York Times,* June 12, 2013. www.nytimes.com/2013/06/13/opinion/atoning-for-the-sins-of-empire.html?_r=0.

Anderson, David, and Richard Grove, eds. 1987. *Conservation in Africa: People, Policies, and Practice.* Cambridge: Cambridge University Press.

Arendt, Hannah. 1963. *Eichmann in Jerusalem: The Banality of Evil.* London: Faber & Faber.

Arhem, K. 1985. *Pastoral Man in the Garden of Eden: The Maasai of the Ngorongoro Conservation Area, Tanzania.* Uppsala Research Reports in Cultural Anthropology, Uppsala: University of Uppsala.

Ashforth, Adam. 2000. *Madumo: A Man Bewitched.* Chicago: University of Chicago Press.

———. 2005. *Witchcraft, Violence, and Democracy in South Africa.* Chicago: University of Chicago Press.

Auslander, Mark. 1993. "'Open The Wombs!': The Symbolic Politics of Modern Ngoni Witchfinding." In *Modernity and its Malcontents: Ritual and Power in Postcolonial Africa,* ed. Jean Comaroff and John Comaroff, 167–92. Chicago: University of Chicago Press.

———. 2011. *The Accidental Slaveowner: Revisiting a Myth of Race and Finding an American Family.* Athens: University of Georgia Press.

Bakhtin, M.M. 1981. *The Dialogic Imagination: Four Essays.* Edited by Michael Holquist and translated by Caryl Emerson and Michael Holquist. Austin: University of Texas Press.

Balibar, Étienne, and Immanuel Maurice Wallerstein. 1991. *Race, Nation, Class: Ambiguous Identities.* New York: Verso. Originally published as *Race, nation, classe: Les identités ambiguës* (Paris: La Découverte, 1988).

Barber, Karin. 1981. "How Man Makes God in West Africa: Yoruba Attitudes towards the 'Orisa.'" *Africa: Journal of the International African Institute* 51, no. 3: 724–45.

Barnett, Donald R., and Karari Njama. 1968. *Mau Mau from Within: An Analysis of Kenya's Peasant Revolt.* New York: Monthly Review Press.

Barrett, Rusty. 2006. "Language Ideology and Racial Inequality: Competing Functions of Spanish in an Anglo-owned Mexican Restaurant." *Language in Society* 35, no. 2: 163–204.

Baucom, Ian. 1999. *Out of Place: Englishness, Empire, and the Locations of Identity.* Princeton, NJ: Princeton University Press.

Bauman, Richard. 1986. *Story, Performance, and Event: Contextual Studies of Oral Narrative.* Cambridge: Cambridge University Press.

Beidelman, T.O. 1982. *Colonial Evangelism: A Socio-Historical Study of an East African Mission at the Grassroots.* Bloomington: Indiana University Press.

Bennett, George. 1963. *Kenya: A Political History: The Colonial Period.* Oxford: Oxford University Press.

Bennett, Huw. 2012. *Fighting the Mau Mau: The British Army and Counter-Insurgency in the Kenya Emergency.* Cambridge: Cambridge University Press.

Bennun, David. 2003. *Tick Bite Fever.* London: Ebury Press.

Berkes, F. 2007. "Community-based Conservation in a Globalized World." In *Proceedings of the National Academy of Sciences of the United States of America* 104, no. 39: 15188–93.

Berman, Bruce. 1990. *Control and Crisis in Colonial Kenya: The Dialectic of Domination.* London: James Currey.

Berman, Bruce, and John Lonsdale. 1992. *Unhappy Valley: Conflict in Kenya & Africa. Book One: State & Class. Book 2: Violence & Ethnicity.* London: James Currey.

"Betraying the Maasai." 2004. *East African.* August 13. www.theeastafrican .co.ke/magazine/-/434746/477414/-/view/printVersion/-/1l9qmx/-/index .html.

Bhaba, Homi. 1984. "Of Mimicry and Man: The Ambivalence of Colonial Discourse." *October* 28 (Spring): 125–33. https://prelectur.stanford.edu /lecturers/bhabha/mimicry.html.

———. 1994. *The Location of Culture.* London: Routledge.

Black, Marc. 2007. "Fanon and DuBoisian Double Consciousness." *Human Architecture: Journal of the Sociology of Self-Knowledge* 5, no. 3: 393–404.

Blacker, John. 2007. "The Demography of Mau Mau: Fertility and Mortality in Kenya in the 1950s: A Demographer's Viewpoint." *African Affairs* 106, no. 423: 205–27.

Blair, David. 2004. "Masai Invaders Target Last White Farmers." September 13. www.freedomunderground.org/view.php?v=3&t=3&aid=9194.

Blee, Kathleen M. 1991. *Women of the Klan: Racism and Gender in the 1920s.* Berkeley: University of California Press.

Blixen, Baroness Karen von. See Dinesen, Isak, pseud.

Bond, George Clement, and Diane M. Ciekawy, eds. 2001. *Witchcraft Dialogues: Anthropological and Philosophical Exchanges.* Athens: Ohio University Center for International Studies.

Bourgois, Philippe. 1995. *In Search of Respect: Selling Crack in El Barrio.* New York: Cambridge University Press.

Bourdieu, Pierre. 1991. *Language and Symbolic Power.* Translated by G. Raymond and M. Adamson. Cambridge, MA: Harvard University Press.

Branch, Daniel. 2009. *Defeating Mau Mau, Creating Kenya: Counterinsurgency, Civil War, and Decolonisation.* New York: Cambridge University Press.

Brantley, Cynthia. 1979. "An Historical Perspective of the Giriama and Witchcraft Control." *Africa.* 49, no. 2: 112–33.

———. 1982. *The Giriama and Colonial Resistance in Kenya, 1800–1920.* Berkeley: University of California Press.

Brennan, Denise. 2004. *What's Love Got to Do with It? Transnational Desires and Sex Tourism in the Dominican Republic.* Durham, NC: Duke University Press.

Brockington, D., and K. Homewood. 1999. "Pastoralism around Mkomazi Game Reserve: The Interaction of Conservation and Development." In *Mkomazi: The Ecology, Biodiversity, and Conservation of a Tanzanian Savanna,* ed. M. Coe, N. McWilliam, G. Stone, and M. Packer. London: Royal Geographical Society (with the Institute of British Geographers).

Brogan, Benedict. 2005. "It's Time to Celebrate the Empire, says Brown." *Daily Mail,* January 15. www.dailymail.co.uk/news/article-334208/Its-time-celebrate -Empire-says-Brown.html.

Brosius, Peter J., Anna Lowenhaupt Tsing, and Charles Zerner, eds. 2005. *Communities and Conservation: Histories and Politics of Community-Based Natural Resource Management.* Walnut Creek, CA: AltaMira Press.

Bruner, Edward M. 2001. "The Maasai and the Lion King: Authenticity, Nationalism, and Globalization in African Tourism." *American Ethnologist* 28, no. 4: 881–908

Bruner, Jerome. 1991. "The Narrative Construction of Reality." *Critical Inquiry* 18, no. 1: 1–21.

Buxton, M. Aline. 1928. *Kenya Days.* London: Edward Arnold.

Cademartori, Lorraine. 2011. "Northern Kenya." *Forbes,* December 5. www .forbes.com/forbes-life-magazine/2011/1219/escapes-northern-kenya-nairobi-sirikoi-travel.html.

Campbell, Chloe. 2007. *Race and Empire: Eugenics in Colonial Kenya.* Manchester: Manchester University Press.

Carothers, John Colin. 1954. *The Psychology of Mau Mau.* Nairobi: Government Printers

Carruthers, Susan. 2005. "Being Beastly to the Mau Mau," *Twentieth Century British History* 16.

Carrier, N. 2011. "Reviving Yaaku: Language and Identity in Kenya's Laikipia District." *African Studies* 70, no. 2: 246–63.

Carsten, Janet. 2000. *Cultures of Relatedness: New Approaches to the Study of Kinship.* Cambridge: Cambridge University Press.

Chidester, David. 1996. *Savage Systems: Colonialism and Comparative Religion in Southern Africa.* Charlottesville: University Press of Virginia.

Ciekawy, Diane M. 1989. "Witchcraft and Development in Kenyan Politics: Complementary or Conflicting Ideologies?" Paper presented at the Annual Meeting of the American Anthropological Association, San Francisco, CA.

———. 1992. "Witchcraft Eradication as Political Process in Kilifi District, Kenya, 1955–1988." PhD diss., Columbia University, New York.

———. 1997. "Policing Religious Practice in Contemporary Coastal Kenya." *PoLAR: Political and Legal Anthropology Review* 20, no. 1: 62–72.

———. 1998. "Witchcraft and Statecraft: Five Technologies of Power in Colonial and Postcolonial Kenya." *African Studies Review* 41, no. 3: 119–41.

———. 2001. "Utsai as Ethical Discourse: A Critique of Power from Mijikenda in Coastal Kenya." In *Witchcraft Dialogues: Anthropological and Philosophical Exchanges,* ed. George Clement Bond and Diane M. Ciekawy. 158–89. Athens: Ohio University Press.

Clark, Stuart, ed. 2001. *Languages of Witchcraft: Narrative, Ideology, and Meaning in Early Modern Culture.* New York: St. Martin's Press.

Clayton, Jonathan. 2005. "A Bullet in the Heart of Happy Valley." *Sunday Times.* May 1. www.thesundaytimes.co.uk/sto/news/article907020.ece.

Clayton, A., and D. C. Savage. 1974. *Government and Labour in Kenya, 1895–1963.* New York: Frank Cass.

Coetzee, J. M. 1988. *White Writing: On the Culture of Letters in South Africa.* New Haven, CT: Yale University Press.

Cohn, Bernard. 2008. "The Command of Language and the Language of Command." In *Genealogies of Orientalism: History, Theory, Politics,* ed. Edmund Burke and David Prochaska. 102–53. Lincoln: University of Nebraska Press.

Cohn, Carol. 1987. "Sex and Death in the Rational World of Defense Intellectuals." *Signs* 12, no. 4: 687–718.

Cole, Jennifer. 2002. *Forget Colonialism? Sacrifice and the Art of Memory in Madagascar*. Berkeley: University of California Press.

Cole, Jennifer, and Lynn M. Thomas, eds. 2009. *Love in Africa*. Chicago: University of Chicago Press.

Collett, David. 1987. "Pastoralists and Wildlife: Image and Reality in Kenya Maasailand." In *Conservation in Africa: People, Policies, and Practice*, ed. David Anderson and R. Grove, 129–48. Cambridge: Cambridge University Press.

Comaroff, Jean, and John L. Comaroff. 1991. *Of Revelation and Revolution: Christianity, Colonialism, and Consciousness in South Africa*. Vol. 1. Chicago: University of Chicago Press.

———. 1993. "Introduction." In *Modernity and Its Malcontents: Ritual and Power in Postcolonial Africa*, ed. id., xi–xxxvii. Chicago: University of Chicago Press.

———. 2012. *Theory from the South, or, How Euro-America Is Evolving toward Africa*. London: Paradigm.

Comaroff, John L., and Jean Comaroff. 2009. *Ethnicity, Inc.* Chicago: University of Chicago Press.

Considine, Joan, and John Rawlins, eds. 2008. *Childhood Reminiscences of Colonial East Africa, 1920–1963*. Lancaster, England: Bongo Books.

Coombes, Annie E., Lotte Hughes, and Karega-Munene. 2014. *Managing Heritage, Making Peace: History, Identity and Memory in Contemporary Kenya*. London: I. B. Tauris.

Cooper, Frederick. 1987. *On the African Waterfront: Urban Disorder and the Transformation of Work in Colonial Mombasa*. New Haven, CT: Yale University Press.

———. 2002. *Africa since 1940: The Past of the Present*. Cambridge: Cambridge University Press.

———. 2005. *Colonialism in Question: Theory, Knowledge, History*. Berkeley: University of California Press.

Cooper, Frederick, and Ann Laura Stoler, eds. 1997. *Tensions of Empire: Colonial Cultures in a Bourgeois World*. Berkeley: University of California Press.

"Corporate Social Responsibility: Woodlands Kenya Trust." 2000. www.tamarind.co.ke/csr.php.

Coulson, Andrew. 2010. "Kilimo Kwanza: A New Start for Agriculture in Tanzania?" Birmingham: Institute of Local Government Studies, University of Birmingham, England.

Couperus, Louis. 1992 [1900]. *The Hidden Force*. Translated by Alexander Teixeira de Mattos. Edited by E. M. Beekman. Singapore: Oxford University Press.

Crapanzano, Vincent. 1985. *Waiting: The Whites of South Africa*. New York: Random House.

Cronon, William. 1983. *Changes in the Land: Indians, Colonists, and the Ecology of New England*. New York: Hill & Wang.

Cuthbert, Norman, and Gillian Cuthbert. 2007. *Further Memories of Colonial East Africa*. Lancaster, England: Bongo Books.

Dangarembga, Tsitsi. 1988. *Nervous Conditions*. New York: Seal Press.

Dawes, Frank. 1974. *Not in Front of the Servants: A True Portrait of English Upstairs/Downstairs Life*. New York: Taplinger.

DePuy, Walker. 2011. "Topographies of Power and International Conservation in Laikipia, Kenya." MA thesis, University of Michigan, Ann Arbor.

Di Giovanni, Janine. 2007. "Two in the Bush." *New York Times*. February 25. www.nytimes.com/2007/02/25/style/tmagazine/25tbush.html?pagewanted= all&_r=2&.

Dinesen, Isak [pseud. Baroness Karen von Blixen-Finecke]. 1937. *Out of Africa*. London: Putnam.

Dirks, Nicholas, ed. 1992. *Cultures of Colonialism*. Ann Arbor: University of Michigan Press.

Drayton, Richard. 2005. "The Wealth of the West Was Built on Africa's Exploitation." *Guardian*, August 19. www.theguardian.com/politics/2005/aug/20/past.hearafrica05.

DuBois, W. E. B. 1996 [1903]. *The Souls of Black Folk.*. New York: Penguin Classics.

Duder, C. J. 1991. "Love and the Lions: The Image of White Settlement in Kenya in Popular Fiction,1919–1939." *African Affairs* 90: 427–38.

———. 1993. "'Men of the Officer Class': The Participants in the 1919 Soldier Settlement Scheme in Kenya." *African Affairs* 92: 69–87.

Duran, James Joseph. 1979. "Non-standard Forms in Swahili in West-central Kenya." In *Readings in Creole Studies*, ed. I. F. Hancock, E. C. Polomé, M. F. Goodman and B. Heine, 129–51. Ghent, Belgium: Story-Scientia.

East Africa Women's League [EAWL], with Elspeth Huxley and Jean Anderson. 1975 [1962]. *They Made It Their Home*. Nairobi: Print and Packaging Corp.

Eble, Connie. 1996. *Slang and Sociability: In-group Language among College Students*. Chapel Hill: University of North Carolina Press.

Ehrenreich, Barbara, and Arlie Hochschild, eds. 2004. *Global Woman: Nannies, Maids, and Sex Workers in the New Economy*. New York: Holt.

Eliot, Charles. 1905. *The East Africa Protectorate*. London: Edward Arnold.

———. 1933. *Kenya Land Commission Report*. Nairobi: Government Printer.

Elkins, Caroline. 2005. *Imperial Reckoning: The Untold Story of Britain's Gulag in Kenya*. New York: Holt.

———. 2011. "Alchemy of Evidence: Mau Mau, the British Empire, and the High Court of Justice." *Journal of Imperial and Commonwealth History* 39, no. 5: 731–48.

Errington, James Joseph. 2008. *Linguistics in a Colonial World: A Story of Language, Meaning, and Power*. Oxford: Blackwell Publishing.

Fabian, Johannes. 2000. *Out of Our Minds: Reason and Madness in the Exploration of Central Africa*. Berkeley: University of California Press.

———. 2002 [1983]. *Time and the Other: How Anthropology Makes Its Object*. Columbia University Press.

Ferguson, Niall. 2002. *Empire: How Britain Made the Modern World*. New York: Penguin Books.

Fisher, J. L. 2011. *Pioneers, Settlers, Aliens, Exiles: The Decolonisation of White Identity in Zimbabwe*. Canberra: Australian National University E Press.

Fox, Graham. 2012. "Belonging Behind Walls: Race, Security, and Citizenship amongst Euro-Kenyans in Nairobi." MA thesis, Carleton University, Ottowa, Canada.

Freedberg, Louis. 2006. "The End of 'Whiteness': The Transformation of White Identity in South Africa." In *Ethnic Identity: Problems and Prospects for the Twenty-first Century,* ed. Lola Romanucci-Ross, George A. De Vos, and Takeyuki Tsuda. Lanham, MD: AltaMira Press.

Galaty, John G. 1992. "'The Land is Yours': Social and Economic Factors in the Privatization, Sub-Division and Sale of Maasai Ranches." *Nomadic Peoples* 30: 26–40.

Garland, Elizabeth. 2006. "State of Nature: Colonial Power, Neoliberal Capital, and Wildlife Management in Tanzania." PhD diss., University of Chicago.

Gellner, Ernst. 1974. *Legitimation of Belief.* Cambridge: Cambridge University Press.

Geschiere, Peter. 1997. *The Modernity of Witchcraft: Politics and the Occult in Postcolonial Africa.* Translated by Peter Geschiere and Janet Roitman. Charlottesville: University Press of Virginia.

———. 2009. *The Perils of Belonging: Autochthony, Citizenship, and Exclusion in Africa and Europe.* Chicago: University of Chicago Press.

Geschiere, Peter, and Francis Nyamnjoh. 2000. "Capitalism and Autochthony: The Seesaw of Mobility and Belonging." *Public Culture* 12, no. 2: 423–52.

Gettleman, Jeffrey. 2006. "Kenya Killings Put Aristocrat in Racial Fire." *New York Times.* September 5. www.nytimes.com/2006/09/05/world/africa/05 kenya.html?pagewanted=all&_r=0.

Gikandi, Simon. 1996. *Maps of Englishness: Writing Identity in the Culture of Colonialism.* New York: Columbia University Press.

Gilmour, Rachel. 2006. *Grammars of Colonialism: Representing Languages in Colonial South Africa.* Basingstoke, England: Palgrave Macmillan.

Gilroy, Paul. 1991. *"'There Ain't no Black in the Union Jack': The Cultural Politics of Race and Nation."* Chicago: University of Chicago Press.

Githiora, Chege. 2002. "Sheng: Peer Language, Swahili Dialect or Emerging Creole?" *Journal of African Cultural Studies* 15, no. 2: 159–81.

———. 2008. "Kenya: Language and the Search for a Coherent National Identity." In *Language and National Identity in Africa,* ed. Andrew Simpson. 235–51. Oxford: Oxford University Press.

Githongo, John. 2000. "Why Maids Prefer White Masters." *East African,* October 5. www.hartford-hwp.com/archives/36/180.html.

Glover, P. E., and M. D. Gwynne. 1961. "The Destruction of Masailand." *New Scientist* 11, no. 249: 450–53.

Goffman, Erving. 1981. "Footing." In *Forms of Talk.* 124–59. Philadelphia: University of Pennsylvania Press.

Goldman, Mara. 2003. "Partitioned Nature, Privileged Knowledge: Community-Based Conservation in Tanzania." *Development and Change* 34, no. 5: 833–62.

Goodwin, June, and Ben Schiff. 1995. *Heart of Whiteness: Afrikaners Face Black Rule in the New South Africa.* New York: Scribner.

"Government Forces Subject Laikipia Maasai to Human Rights Abuses." 2004. *Cultural Survival,* September 17. www.culturalsurvival.org/news/michael-tiampati/government-forces-subject-laikipia-maasai-human-rights-abuses.

Gregory, Robert. 1971. *India and East Africa: A History of Race Relations within the British Empire, 1890–1939.* Oxford: Clarendon Press, 1971.

"Gun Killing That Divides the Rift Valley." 2005. *Observer,* May 8.

Hall, Catherine. 2002. *Civilising Subjects: Metropole and Colony in the English Imagination, 1830–1867.* Chicago: University of Chicago Press.

Hammer, Joshua. 2006. "The Kenyan Cowboy." *Outside.* December 5. http://outside.away.com/outside/destinations/200612/kenya-thomas-cholmondeley-1.

Hannerz, Ulf. 1996. *Transnational Connections: Culture, People, Places.* London and New York: Routledge.

Hansen, Karen Tranberg. 1989. *Distant Companions: Servants and Employers in Zambia, 1900–1985.* Ithaca, NY: Cornell University Press.

———. 1992a. "Introduction: Domesticity in Africa." In *African Encounters with Domesticity,* ed. Karen Tranberg Hansen. 1–33. New Brunswick, NJ: Rutgers University Press.

———. 1992b. "Cookstoves and Charcoal Braziers: Culinary Practices, Gender, and Class in Zambia." In *African Encounters with Domesticity,* ed. Karen Tranberg Hansen. 266–289. New Brunswick, NJ: Rutgers University Press.

Harding, Susan. 1991. "Representing Fundamentalism: The Problem of the Repugnant Cultural Other." *Social Research* 58, no. 2: 373–93.

Harries, Lyndon. 1976. "The Nationalization of Swahili in Kenya." *Language in Society* 5, no. 2:153–64.

Hartigan, John. 1999. *Racial Situations: Class Predicaments of Whiteness in Detroit.* Princeton, NJ: Princeton University Press.

Hartley, Aidan. 2004. "Cargo Cult: A Great White Hunter Takes Aim at a Few Sacred Cows in Contemporary Africa." *Spectator* August 28. www.spectator.co.uk/life/wild-life/12537/cargo-cult.

———. 2005. "Kenya Cowboy." *Spectator,* October 22. www.spectator.co.uk/the-magazine/cartoons/14359/part_2/kenya-cowboy.thtml.

———. 2007. "Home Truths." *Spectator,* August 15. www.spectator.co.uk/life/wild-life/92141/home-truths.

Haugerud, Angelique. 1995. *The Culture of Politics in Modern Kenya.* Cambridge: Cambridge University Press.

Hazzah, Leela N. 2006. "Living among Lions (Panthera Leo): Coexistence or Killing? Community Attitudes towards Conservation Initiatives and the Motivations behind Lion Killing in Kenyan Maasailand." MA thesis, University of Wisconsin-Madison.

Herzfeld, Michael. 1997. *Cultural Intimacy: Social Poetics in the Nation-State.* London: Routledge.

Hewitt, Peter. 2008 [1999]. *Kenya Cowboy: A Police Officer's Account of the Mau Mau Emergency in Kenya.* Johannesburg: South Publishers.

Hill, Jane H. 1995. "Mock Spanish: A Site for the Indexical Reproduction of Racism in American English." Language & Culture, Symposium 2. http://language-culture.binghamton.edu/symposia/2/part1/index.html.

———. 2008. *The Everyday Language of White Racism.* Oxford: Blackwell.

Hiltzik, Michael. 1991. *A Death in Kenya: The Murder of Julie Ward.* New York: Delacorte.

Hirsch, Eric, and Michael O'Hanlon, eds. 1995. *The Anthropology of Landscape: Perspectives on Space and Place.* Oxford: Clarendon Press.

Hodgson, Dorothy. 2001. *Once Intrepid Warriors: Gender, Ethnicity, and the Cultural Politics of Maasai Development.* Bloomington: Indiana University Press.

———. 2011. *Being Maasai, Becoming Indigenous: Postcolonial Politics in a Neoliberal World.* Bloomington: University of Indiana Press.

Hoffmann, Thomas. 2010. "White Kenyan English." In *The Lesser-Known Varieties of English: An Introduction,* ed. Daniel Schreier, Peter Trudgill, Edgar W. Schneider, and Jeffrey P. Williams, 286–310. Cambridge University Press.

Hofmann, Corinne. 2007 [2005]. *The White Maasai: My Exotic Tale of Love and Adventure.* New York: HarperCollins.

Homewood, K., and W. Rodgers. 1991. *Maasailand Ecology: Pastoralist Development and Wildlife Conservation in Ngorongoro, Tanzania.* New York: Cambridge University Press.

Hondagneu-Sotelo, Pierrette. 2001. *Domestica: Immigrant Workers Cleaning and Caring in the Shadows of Affluence.* Berkeley: University of California Press.

Honey, Martha. 1999. *Ecotourism and Sustainable Development: Who Owns Paradise?* Washington, DC: Island Press.

Hubinette, Tobias, and James Arvanitakis. 2012. "Transracial Adoption, White Cosmopolitanism, and the Fantasy of the Global Family." *Third Text* 26, no. 6: 691–703.

Hufford, David. 1982. *The Terror That Comes in the Night: An Experience-Centered Study of Supernatural Assault Traditions.* Philadelphia: University of Pennsylvania Press.

Hughes, David McDermott. 2006. "The Art of Belonging: Whites Writing Landscape in Savannah Africa." Paper presented to the Program in Agrarian Studies, Yale University, New Haven, CT.

———. 2010. *Whiteness in Zimbabwe: Race, Landscape, and the Problem of Belonging.* New York: Palgrave Macmillan.

Hughes, Lotte. 2005. "Malice in Maasailand: The Historical Roots of Current Political Struggles." *African Affairs* 104, no. 415: 207–24.

———. 2006a. *Moving the Maasai: A Colonial Misadventure.* New York: Palgrave Macmillan.

———. 2006b. "'Beautiful beasts' and Brave Warriors: The Longevity of a Maasai Stereotype." In *Ethnic Identity: Problems and Prospects for the Twenty-First Century,* ed. Lola Romanucci-Ross, George A. De Vos, and Takeyuki Tsuda, 264–94. Lanham, MD: AltaMira Press.

———. 2011. "'Truth be Told': Some Problems with Historical Revisionism in Kenya." *African Studies* 70, no. 2: 182–201.

Hunt, Nancy Rose. 1992. "Colonial Fairy Tales and the Knife and Fork Doctrine in the Heart of Africa." In *African Encounters with Domesticity,* ed. Karen Tranberg Hansen, 143–171. New Brunswick, NJ: Rutgers University Press.

Huxley, Elspeth. 1939. *Red Strangers*. New York: Harper & Brothers.

————. 1953 [1935]. *White Man's Country: Lord Delamere and the Making of Kenya*, vol. 1: *1870–1914*. 2nd ed. London: Chatto & Windus.

————. 1959. *The Flame Trees of Thika*. New York: Penguin Books.

Hymes, Dell. 1971. *Pidginization and Creolization of Languages*. Cambridge: Cambridge University Press.

Igoe, Jim. 2004. *Conservation and Globalization: A Study of National Parks and Indigenous Communities from East Africa to South Dakota*. Belmont, CA: Wadsworth, Cengage Learning.

Imperato, Pascal James. 2005."Differing Perspectives on Mau Mau." *African Studies Review* 48, no. 3: 147–54.

Inda, Jonathan Xavier, and Renato Rosaldo. 2002. "Introduction: A World in Motion." In *The Anthropology of Globalization: A Reader*, ed. id., 1–34. Oxford: Blackwell.

Irvine, Judith T., and Susan Gal. 2000. "Language Ideology and Linguistic Differentiation." In *Regimes of Language*, ed. Paul Kroskrity, 35–83. Sante Fe, NM: School of American Research Press.

Jackson, Stephen. 2006. "Sons of Which Soil? The Language and Politics of Autochthony in Eastern D.R. Congo." *African Studies Review* 49, no. 2: 95–123.

Jackson, Will. 2013. *Madness and Marginality: The Lives of Kenya's White Insane*. Manchester: Manchester University Press.

Jacobson, Matthew Frye. 1999. *Whiteness of a Different Color: European Immigration and the Alchemy of Race*. Cambridge, MA: Harvard University Press.

J.W. [1932?]. *Kisettla* [pamphlet]. Nairobi: East African Standard. Some sources cite reprinting in *Kenya Weekly News*, December 23, 1955, 24–25.

K'Akumu, O.A. and W.H.A. Olima. 2007. "The Dynamics and Implications of Residential Segregation in Nairobi." *Habitat International* 31, no. 1: 87–99.

Kalaora, Lea. 2011. "Madness, Corruption, and Exile: On Zimbabwe's Remaining White Commercial Farmers." *Journal of Southern African Studies* 37, no. 4: 747–62.

Kanogo, Tabitha. 1987. *Squatters and the Roots of Mau Mau, 1905–1963*. London: James Currey; Athens: Ohio University Press.

Kantai, Parselelo. 2007. "In the Grip of the Vampire State: Maasai Land Struggles in Kenyan Politics." *Journal of Eastern African Studies* 1, no. 1: 107–22.

————. 2008a. "The Maasai Invasions." In *Missionaries, Mercenaries, and Misfits: An Anthology*, ed. R. Warah. Milton Keynes, England: AuthorHouse.

————. 2008b. "Betraying the Maasai." www.theeastafrican.co.ke/magazine /-/434746/477414/-/154m3kf/-/index.html.

Kanyinga, Karuti. 2009. "The Legacy of the White Highlands: Land Rights, Ethnicity and the post-2007 Election Violence in Kenya." *Journal of Contemporary African Studies* 27, no. 3: 325–44.

Kariuki, Josiah Mwangi. 1975 [1963]. *"Mau Mau" Detainee: The Account by a Kenya African of His Experiences in Detention Camps, 1953–1960*. New York: Oxford University Press.

Keiwua, M. 2002. "Maasai Land: Part 1–A History." *whoseland*. October.

Kennedy, Dane. 1987. *Islands of White: Settler Society in Kenya and Northern Rhodesia, 1890–1939*. Durham, NC: Duke University Press.

Khan, Shamus Rahman. 2010. *Privilege: The Making of an Adolescent Elite at St Paul's School*. Princeton, NJ: Princeton University Press.

Knowles, Oliver. 2008. *Back Seat Driver*. Brighton, England: Penn Press.

Krog, Antjie. 1998. *Country of My Skull: Guilt, Sorrow, and the Limits of Forgiveness in the New South Africa*. New York: Broadway Books.

Kumar, Krishan. 2003. *The Making of English National Identity*. New York: Cambridge University Press.

Lacey, Marc. 2004. "Tribe, Claiming Whites' Land, Confronts Kenya's Government." *New York Times*. August 25. www.nytimes.com/2004/08/25/world/tribe-claiming-whites-land-confronts-kenya-s-government.html.

Leakey, Louis S. B. 1954. *Defeating Mau Mau*. Oxford: Routledge.

Le Breton, David, ed. 2010. *I Remember It Well: Fifty Years of Colonial Service Personal Reminiscences*. Kinloss, Scotland: Librario.

Le Breton, F. H. 1936. *Up-Country Swahili Exercises: For the Settler, Miner, Merchant and Their Wives, and for All Who Deal with Up-Country Natives Without Interpreters*. Richmond, Surrey, England: R. W. Simpson.

Lessing, Doris. 1992. *African Laughter: Four Visits to Zimbabwe*. New York: HarperCollins.

Letai, John. 2011a. "The Genesis of Land Deals in Kenya and Its Implication on Pastoral Livelihoods—A Case Study of Laikipia District." Presented at the International Conference on Global Land Grabbing. April 6th to 8th. www.ids.ac.uk/files/dmfile/JohnLetaiPRESENTATION3.pdf.

———. 2011b. "Land Deals in Kenya: The Genesis of Land Deals in Kenya and Its Implication on Pastoral Livelihoods—a Case Study of Laikipia District." http://landportal.info/sites/default/files/land_deals_in_kenya-initial_report_for_laikipia_district2.pdf.

Leys, Norman. 1924. *Kenya*. London: Hogarth Press.

Lindsay, W. K. 1987. "Integrating Parks and Pastoralists: Some Lessons from Amboseli." In *Conservation in Africa: People, Policies, and Practice,* ed. D. Anderson, and R. Grove, 149–67. Cambridge, England: Cambridge University Press.

Locke, John. 1690. *The second treatise of civil government and A letter concerning toleration*. Edited by J. W. Gough. Oxford: B. Blackwell, 1947.

Lonsdale, John. 1990. "Mau Maus of the Mind: Making Mau Mau and Remaking Kenya." *Journal of African History* 31, no. 3: 393–421.

———. 1992. "The Conquest State of Kenya, 1895–1905" Iin Bruce Berman and John Lonsdale, *Unhappy Valley: Conflict in Kenya and Africa,* 13–44. London: J. Currey.

Lopez, Alfred J. 2005. "Introduction: Whiteness after Empire." In *Postcolonial Whiteness: A Critical Reader on Race and Empire,* ed. id., 1–30. Albany: State University Press of New York.

———, ed. 2005. *Postcolonial Whiteness: A Critical Reader on Race and Empire,* Albany: State University Press of New York.

Lorcin, Patricia M. E. 2012. *Historicizing Colonial Nostalgia: European Women's Narratives of Algeria and Kenya, 1900–present.* Basingstoke, England: Palgrave Macmillian. 2012.

Luhrmann, Tanya. 1989. *Persuasions of the Witch's Craft: Ritual Magic in Contemporary England.* Cambridge, MA: Harvard University Press.

Luongo, Katherine. 2006. "If You Can't Beat Them, Join Them: Government Cleansings of Witches and Mau Mau in 1950s Kenya." *History in Africa* 33, no. 1: 451–71.

———. 2010. "Polling Places and 'Slow Punctured Provocation': Occult-Driven Cases in Postcolonial Kenya's High Courts." *Journal of Eastern African Studies* 4, no. 3: 577–591.

———. 2011. *Witchcraft and Colonial Rule in Kenya, 1900–1955.* New York: Cambridge University Press.

Lynch, Gabriella. 2011. *I Say to You: Ethnic Politics and the Kalenjin in Kenya.* Chicago: University of Chicago Press.

Mackenzie, John. 1988. *The Empire of Nature: Hunting, Conservation, and British Imperialism.* Manchester: Manchester University Press.

Mahone, Sloane. 2006. "The Psychology of Rebellion: Colonial Medical Responses to Dissent in British East Africa." *Journal of East African History* 47, no. 2: 241–58.

Malindi Municipal Council. 2004. *Strategic Plan, 2004–2008.* Malindi, Kenya: Malindi Printers.

Markham, Beryl. 1942. *West with the Night.* New York: North Point Press (Farrar, Straus, & Giroux).

Marks, Jonathan. 1995. *Human Biodiversity: Genes, Race, and History.* New York: Aldine de Gruyter.

Mazrui, Ali Al'Amin, and Alamin M. Mazrui. 1995. *Swahili, State and Society: The Political Economy of an African Language.* Nairobi: East African Educational Publishers; London: James Currey.

———. 1998. *The Power of Babel: Language and Governance in the African Experience.* Oxford: James Currey; Chicago: University of Chicago Press.

McElya, Micki. 2007. *Clinging to Mammy: The Faithful Slave in Twentieth-Century America.* Cambridge, MA: Harvard University Press.

McGovern, Mike. 2012. *Unmasking the State: Making Guinea Modern.* Chicago: University of Chicago Press.

McGreal, Chris. 2006. "The Lost World." *Guardian.* October 26. www.guardian.co.uk/world/2006/oct/26/kenya.chrismcgreal.

McGregor Ross, William. 1968 [1927]. *Kenya from Within: A Short Political History.* London: G. Allen & Unwin. Reprint, London: Cass.

McIntosh, Janet. 1996. "Professed Disbelief and Gender Identity on the Coast of Kenya." In *Gender and Belief Systems: Proceedings of the Fourth Berkeley Women and Language Conference, April 19, 20, and 21, 1996,* ed. Natasha Warner, Jocelyn Ahlers, Leela Bilmes, Monica Oliver, Suzanne Wertheim, and Melinda Chen, 481–90. Berkeley: Berkeley Women and Language Group, University of California.

————. 2001. "Strategic Amnesia: Versions of Vasco da Gama on the Kenya Coast." In *Images of Africa: Stereotypes and Realities,* ed. Daniel Mengara. 85–104. Trenton, NJ: Africa World Press.

————. 2004. "Maxwell's Demons: Disenchantment in the Field." *Anthropology and Humanism* 29, no. 1): 63–77.

————. 2005. "Language Essentialism and Social Hierarchies among Giriama and Swahili." *Journal of Pragmatics* 37, no. 12: 1919–1944.

————. 2006. "'Going Bush': Black Magic, White Ambivalence, and Boundaries of Belief in Post-Colonial Kenya." *Journal of Religion in Africa* 36, nos. 3–4: 254–95.

————. 2009a. *The Edge of Islam: Power, Personhood and Ethnoreligious Boundaries on the Kenya Coast.* Durham, NC: Duke University Press.

————. 2009b. "Stance and Distance: Ontological Doubt and Social Boundaries in White Kenyan Narratives about the African Occult." In *Stance: Sociolinguistic Perspectives,* ed. Alexandra Jaffe, 72–91. New York: Oxford University Press.

————. 2010. "Mobile Phones and Mipoho's Prophecy: The Powers and Dangers of Flying Language." *American Ethnologist* 37, no. 2: 337–53.

————. 2015. "Autochthony and 'Family': The Politics of Kinship in White Kenyan Bids to Belong." *Anthropological Quarterly* 88, no. 2: 251–80.

McIntosh, Peggy. 1988. "White Privilege and Male Privilege: A Personal Account of Coming to See Correspondences through Work in Women's Studies." Working Paper No. 189. Wellesley College Center for Research on Women, Wellesley, MA.

Medina, Jose. 2013. *The Epistemology of Resistance: Gender and Racial Oppression, Epistemic Injustice, and Resistant Imaginations.* New York: Oxford University Press.

Mehta, Uday Singh. 1999. *Liberalism and Empire: A Study in Nineteenth-Century British Liberal Thought.* Chicago: University of Chicago Press.

Meinertzhagen, Colonel R. 1957. *Kenya Diary, 1902–1906.* London: Oliver & Boyd.

Meiu, George Paul. 2009. "'Mombasa Morans': Embodiment, Sexual Morality, and Samburu Men in Kenya." *Canadian Journal of African Studies* 43, no. 1: 105–28.

————. 2011. "On Difference, Desire, and the Aesthetics of the Unexpected: 'The White Masai' in Kenyan Tourism." In *Great Expectations: Imagination and Anticipation in Tourism,* ed. Jonathan Skinner and Dimitrios Theodossopoulos, 96–115. New York: Berghahn Books.

Memmi, Albert. 1991[1957]. *The Colonizer and the Colonized.* Boston: Beacon Press.

Meyer, Birgit. 1992. ' "If You are a Devil You are a Witch, and If You are a Witch, You are a Devil": The Integration of "Pagan" Ideas into the Conceptual Universe of the Ewe Christians in Southeastern Ghana." *Journal of Religion in Africa* 22, no. 2: 98–132.

————. 1995. "'Delivered from the Powers of Darkness': Confessions of Satanic Riches in Christian Ghana." *Africa* 65, no. 2: 228–256.

Meyers-Scotton, Carol. 1979. "The Context Is the Message: Syntactic and Semantic Deletion in Nairobi and Kampala Varieties of Swahili." In *Readings in Creole Studies,* ed. I. F. Hancock, E. C. Polomé, M. F. Goodman, and B. Heine, 111–28. Ghent: Story-Scientia.

Michieka, Martha Moraa. 2005. "English in Kenya: A Sociolinguistic Profile." *World Englishes* 24, no. 2: 173–86.

Miller, Charles. 1971. *The Lunatic Express: An Entertainment in Imperialism.* London: Macmillan.

Mills, Charles W. 1997. *The Racial Contract.* Ithaca: Cornell University Press.

Mitchell, W. J. T. 2002. "Imperial Landscape." In *Landscape and Power,* ed. id. 2nd ed. Chicago: University of Chicago Press.

Montag, Warren. 1997. "The Universalization of Whiteness: Racism and Enlightenment." In *Whiteness: A Critical Reader,* ed. Mike Hill. 281–93. New York: New York University Press.

Moran, Mary H. 1992. "Civilized Servants: Child Fosterage and Training for Status among the Glebo of Liberia." In *African Encounters with Domesticity,* ed. Karen Tranberg Hansen, 98–115. New Brunswick, NJ: Rutgers University Press.

Mudimbe, V. Y. 1988. *The Invention of Africa,* Bloomington: Indiana University Press.

Munei, Kimpei Ole, and John G. Galaty. 2010. "Maasai Land, Law, and Dispossession." *Cultural Survival,* March 26. www.culturalsurvival.org /publications/cultural-survival   quarterly/kenya/maasai-land-law-and-dispossession.

Musila, Grace Ahingula. 2008. "Kenyan and British Social Imaginaries on Julie Ward's Death in Kenya." PhD diss., University of the Witwatersrand, Johannesburg.

Mutongi, Kenda. 2007. *Worries of the Heart: Widows, Family, and Community in Kenya.* Chicago: University of Chicago Press.

Mutonya, Mungai, and Timothy H. Parsons. 2004. "KiKAR: A Swahili Variety in Kenya's Colonial Army." *Journal of African Languages and Linguistics* 25, no. 2: 111–25.

Myers-Scotton, Carol. 1993. "Common and Uncommon Ground: Social and Structural Factors in Codeswitching." *Language in Society* 22, no. 4: 475–503.

Nabea, Wendo. 2009. "Language Policy in Kenya: Negotiation with Hegemony." *Journal of Pan-African Studies* 3, no. 1: 121–38.

Nader, Laura. 1972. "Up the Anthropologist—Perspectives Gained from Studying Up." In *Reinventing Anthropology,* ed. Dell H. Hymes, 284–311. New York: Pantheon Books.

Nagel, Joane. 2003. *Race, Ethnicity, and Sexuality: Intimate Intersections, Forbidden Frontiers.* New York: Oxford University Press.

Ndaskoi, Navaye Ole. 2006. "The Roots Causes of Maasai Predicament." *Fourth World Journal* 7, no. 1: 28–64.

Needham, Rodney. 1972. *Belief, Language, and Experience.* Chicago: University of Chicago Press.

Nelson, Jack E. 1992. *Christian Missionizing and Social Transformation: A History of Conflict and Change in Eastern Zaire.* New York: Praeger.

Neumann, R. P. 1992. "Political Ecology of Wildlife Conservation in the Mt. Meru Area of Northeast Tanzania." *Land Degradation and Rehabilitation* 3, no. 1: 85–98.

———. 1997. "Primitive Ideas: Protected Area Buffer Zones and the Politics of Land in Africa." *Development and Change* 28, no. 4: 559–82.

———. 1998. *Imposing Wilderness: Struggles over Livelihood and Nature Preservation in Africa.* Berkeley: University of California Press.

Neyfakh, Leon. 2015. "The Ethics of Ethnography." www.slate.com/articles /news_and_politics/crime/2015/06/alice_goffman_s_on_the_run_is_the_ sociologist_to_blame_for_the_inconsistencies.html.

Nicholls, C. S. 2003. *Elspeth Huxley: A Biography.* New York: Thomas Dunne Books.

———. 2005. *Red Strangers: The White Tribe of Kenya.* London: Timewell Press.

Niehaus, Isak. 2001. *Witchcraft, Power and Politics: Exploring the Occult in the South African Lowveld.* London: Pluto Press.

Nietzsche, Friedrich. 1956 [1872, 1887]. *The Birth of Tragedy and The Genealogy of Morals.* Garden City, NY: Doubleday. Reprint, New York: Anchor Books (1990).

Ntimama, William Ole. 1994. "The Maasai Dilemma." *Cultural Survival* 18, no. 1: 58–59.

Nuttall, Sarah, and Carli Coetzee, eds. 1998. *Negotiating the Past: The Making of Memory in South Africa.* Cape Town: Oxford University Press.

Nyamweru, Celia. 2001. "Letting the Side Down: Personal Reflections on Colonial and Independent Kenya." In *Global Multiculturalism: Comparative Perspectives on Ethnicity, Race, and Nation,* ed. Grant H. Cornwell and Eve Walsh Stoddard, 169–92. Lanham, MD: Rowman & Littlefield.

Ochs, Elinor, and Lisa Capps. 2001. *Living Narrative: Creating Lives in Everyday Storytelling.* Cambridge, MA: Harvard University Press.

Odhiambo, E. S. Atieno, and John Lonsdale. 2003. *Mau Mau & Nationhood: Arms, Authority, and Narration.* Oxford: James Currey.

Ogechi, Nathan Oyori. 2003. "On Language Rights in Kenya." *Nordic Journal of African Studies* 12, no. 3: 277–95. www.njas.helsinki.fi/pdf-files/vol12num3 /ogechi.pdf.

Ogot, Bethwell A. 2005. "Review Article: Britain's Gulag." *Journal of African History* 46, no. 3: 493–505.

Ortner, Sherry. "Resistance and the Problem of Ethnographic Refusal." *Comparative Studies in Society and History* 37, no. 1: 173–93.

Orwell, George. 1970 [1936]. "Shooting an Elephant." In *The Collected Essays, Journalism, and Letters of George Orwell,* vol. 1: *An Age Like This, 1920–1940,* ed. Sonia Orwell and Ian Angus, 265–72. New York: Penguin Books.

"Our Story." 2013. *Borana—The Safari and Conservation Co.* www.borana .co.ke/our-story.html.

Oyono, Fred. 2012 [1956]. *Houseboy.* Longrove, IL: Waveland Press.

Pape, John. 1990. "Black and White: The 'Perils of Sex' in Colonial Zimbabwe." *Journal of Southern African Studies* 16, no. 4: 699–720.

Parker, Ian, and Stan Bleazard, eds. 2001. *An Impossible Dream: Some of Kenya's Last Colonial Wardens Recall the Game Department in the British Empire's Closing Years.* London: Librario.

Parkipuny, M. Ole, and D. Berger. 1993. "Maasai Rangelands: Links between Social Justice and Wildlife Conservation." In *Voices from Africa: Local Perspectives on Conservation,* ed. D. Lewis and N. Carter, 113–32. Washington, DC: World Wildlife Fund.

Pels, Peter. 1997. "The Anthropology of Colonialism: Culture, History, and the Emergence of Western Governmentality." *Annual Review of Anthropology* 26: 163–83.

———. 1998. "The Magic of Africa: Reflections on a Western Commonplace." *African Studies Review* 41, no. 3: 193–209.

———. 1999. *A Politics of Presence: Contacts between Missionaries and Africans in Late Colonial Tanganyika.* Amsterdam: Harwood Academic.

———. 2003a. "Introduction: Magic and Modernity." In *Magic and Modernity: Interfaces of Revelation and Concealment,* ed. Birgit Meyer and Peter Pels, 1–38. Stanford, CA: Stanford University Press.

———. 2003b. "Spirits of Modernity: Alfred Wallace, Edward Tylor, and the Visual Politics of Fact." In *Magic and Modernity: Interfaces of Revelation and Concealment,* ed. Birgit Meyer and Peter Pels, 241–71. Stanford, CA: Stanford University Press.

Pennycook, Alasdair. 1998. *English and the Discourses of Colonialism.* London: Routledge.

Phombeah, Gray. 2004. "The Maasai's Century-old Grievance." http://news.bbc.co.uk/2/hi/africa/3614808.stm.

Pilossof, Rory. 2012. *The Unbearable Whiteness of Being: Farmers' Voices from Zimbabwe.* Harare: Weaver Press.

Planz, Mike. 2006. "Kenyan Aristocrat Arrested for Second Shooting." *Telegraph,* May 12. www.telegraph.co.uk/expat/expatfeedback/4200067/Kenyan-aristocrat-arrested-for-second-shooting.html.

Porter, Bernard. 2005. "How Did They Get Away with It?" *London Review of Books,* March 3. www.lrb.co.uk/v27/no5/porto1_.html.

Povinelli, Elizabeth. 2002. "Notes on Gridlock: Genealogy, Intimacy, Sexuality." *Public Culture* 14, no. 1: 215–38.

Pratt, Mary Louise. 1992. *Imperial Eyes: Travel Writing and Transculturation.* London: Routledge.

Ralph, Laurence. 2014. *Renegade Dreams: Living through Injury in Gangland Chicago.* Chicago: University of Chicago Press.

Ranger, Terence. 1996. "Colonial and Postcolonial Identities." In *Postcolonial Identities in Africa,* ed. Richard Werbner and Terence Ranger, 271–81. London: Zen Books.

———. 1998. "Europeans in Black Africa." *Journal of World History* 9, no. 2: 255–68.

———. 1999. *Voices from the Rocks: Nature, Culture, and History in the Matopos Hills of Zimbabwe.* Bloomington: Indiana University Press.

Refern, Paul. 2006. "Over 40,000 Britons live in Kenya, Says Survey." *Kenya Daily Nation,* August 7.

Renan, Ernest. 1990 [1882]. "What Is a Nation?" Translated and annotated by Martin Thom. In *Nation and Narration*, ed. Homi Bhabha, 8–22. New York: Routledge.

Rittenhouse, Jennifer. 2006. *Growing up Jim Crow: How Black and White Southern Children Learned Race*. Durham, NC: University of North Carolina Press.

Robben, Antonius. 1996. "Ethnographic Seduction, Transference, and Resistance in Dialogues about Terror and Violence in Argentina." *Ethos* 24, no. 1: 71–106.

Robbins, Joel. 2007. "Continuity Thinking and the Problem of Christian Culture: Belief, Time, and the Anthropology of Christianity." *Current Anthropology* 48, no. 1: 5–38.

Roberts, Sophy. 2011. "Where the Kids Can Run Wild." *Financial Times,* April 8. www.ft.com/cms/s/2/beab7504–6165–11e0-a315–00144feab49a.html #axzz2Ya3gTCgw.

Robinson, Stephen. 2009. "Saba Douglas-Hamilton on Giving Birth Outdoors." *Sunday Times,* June 18. http://women.timesonline.co.uk/tol/life_and _style/women/celebrity/article6531067.ece.

Rosaldo, Renato. 1993. "Imperialist Nostalgia." In *Culture and Truth: The Remaking of Social Analysis,* 68–87. Boston: Beacon Press.

———. 2000. "Of Headhunters and Soldiers: Separating Cultural and Ethical Relativism." *Issues in Ethics* 11, no. 1. Markkula Center for Applied Ethics, Santa Clara University. www.scu.edu/ethics/publications/iie/v11n1/relativism .html.

Rosberg, Carl G., and John Cato Nottingham. 1966. *The Myth of "Mau Mau": Nationalism in Kenya.* New York: Praeger. Published for the Hoover Institution on War, Revolution, and Peace, Stanford, CA.

Ruel, Malcolm. 1982. "Christians as Believers." In *Religious Organization and Religious Experience,* ed. John Davis. 9–31. London: Academic Press.

Rutherford, Blair. 2001. *Working on the Margins: Black Workers, White Farmers in Postcolonial Zimbabwe.* London: Zed Books.

Sanders, Todd, and H.L. Moore, eds. 2001. *Magical Interpretations, Material Realities: Modernity, Witchcraft and the Occult in Postcolonial Africa.* London: Routledge.

Sanders, Todd. 2003. "Reconsidering Witchcraft: Postcolonial Africa and Analytic (Un)Certainties." *American Anthropologist* 105, no. 2: 338–52.

Saunders, Tanya. "About the Author." 2007. In *Tales from Kulafumbi.* www .wildernessdiary.com/tanya-trevor-saunders.

Scheper-Hughes, Nancy. 2005. "The Politics of Remorse." In *A Companion to Psychological Anthropology: Modernity and Psychological Change*, ed. Conerly Casey and Robert B. Edgerton 469–93. Oxford: Blackwell.

Schieffelin, Bambi B., Kathryn Ann Woolard, and Paul V. Kroskrity, eds. 1998. *Language Ideologies: Practice and Theory.* New York: Oxford University Press.

Schmeid, Josef J. 1991. "National and Subnational Features in Kenyan English," In *English around the World: Sociolinguistic Perspectives,* ed. Jenny Cheshire. New York: Cambridge University Press.

Schmeid, Josef J. 2006. "East African Englishes." In *The Handbook of World Englishes,* ed. Braj B. Kachru, Yamuna Kachru, and Cecil L. Nelson. London: Blackwell.

Schneider, David M. 1984. *A Critique of the Study of Kinship.* Ann Arbor, MI: University of Michigan Press.

Schroeder, Richard A. 1999. "Geographies of Environmental Intervention in Africa." *Progress in Human Geography* 23, no. 3: 359–78

———. 2012. *Africa after Apartheid: South Africa, Race, and Nation in Tanzania.* Bloomington: Indiana University Press.

Scoones, Ian. 1995. "Exploiting Heterogeneity: Habitat Use by Cattle in Dryland Zimbabwe." *Journal of Arid Environments* 29: 221–37.

Scott, James C. 1972. "Patron-Client Politics and Political Change in Southeast Asia." *American Political Science Review* 66, no. 1: 91–113.

Seal, Mark. 2008. "Prisoner of Kenya." *Vanity Fair,* April. www.vanityfair.com/politics/features/2008/04/cholmondeley200804?currentPage=1.

Selva, Meera. 2005. "Woman Who Swapped London Fashion Scene for a Kenyan Warrior." *Independent on Sunday,* October 23. www.questia.com/library/1P2-1981094/woman-who-swapped-london-fashion-scene-for-a-kenyan.

Shadle, Brett Lindsay. 2012. "Cruelty and Empathy, Animals and Race, in Colonial Kenya." *Journal of Social History* 45, no. 4: 1097–116.

———. 2015. *The Souls of White Folk: White Settlers in Kenya, 1900–1920s.* Manchester: Manchester University Press.

Sharp, John, and Stephan van Wyck. 2013. "The Most Intractable Whites in South Africa? Ethnography of a Boere-Afrikaner Settlement." Paper presented at the ECAS conference, Lisbon, June 2013.

Shaw, Carolyn Martin. 1995. *Colonial Inscriptions: Race, Sex, and Class in Kenya.* Minneapolis: University of Minnesota Press.

Shefer, Tamara. 2012. "Fraught Tenderness: Narratives on Domestic Workers in Memories of Apartheid." *Peace and Conflict: Journal of Peace Psychology* 18, no. 3: 307–17.

Shipton, Parker. 2009. *Mortgaging the Ancestors: Ideologies of Attachment in Africa.* New Haven, CT: Yale University Press.

Sindiga, Isaac. 1984. "Land and Population Problems in Kajiado and Narok, Kenya." *African Studies Review* 27, no. 1: 23–39.

Smith, Andrea, ed. 2003. *Europe's Invisible Migrants.* Amsterdam: Amsterdam University Press.

Smith, Andrea. 2004. "Heteroglossia, 'Common Sense,' and Social Memory." *American Ethnologist* 31, no. 2: 251–69.

Smith, David Lovatt. 2005. *Kenya, the Kikuyu and Mau Mau.* Eastbourne, England: Anthony Rowe.

Smith, James H. 2008. *Bewitching Development: Witchcraft and the Reinvention of Development in Neoliberal Kenya.* Chicago: University of Chicago Press.

Smith, Wilfred Cantwell. 1998. *Believing: An Historical Perspective.* Oxford: Oneworld.

Sorrenson, M.P.K. 1968. *Origins of European Settlement in Kenya.* Oxford: Oxford University Press.

Southall, Roger. 2005. "Ndug'u Report Summary." *Review of African Political Economy* 103: 142–51.

Spear, Thomas, and Richard Waller. 1973. *Being Maasai: Ethnicity and Identity in East Africa*. London: James Currey.

Steinhart, Edward I. 2006. *Black Poachers, White Hunters: A Social History of Hunting in Colonial Kenya*. Oxford: James Currey.

Steyn, Melissa. 2001. *Whiteness Just Isn't What it Used To Be: White Identity in a Changing South Africa*. Albany, NY: State University of New York Press.

———. 2012. "The Ignorance Contract: Recollections of Apartheid Childhoods and the Construction of Epistemologies of Ignorance." *Identities: Global Studies in Culture and Power* 19, no. 1: 8–25.

Stoler, Ann Laura. 1997. "Sexual Affronts and Racial Frontiers: European Identities and the Cultural Politics of Exclusion in Colonial Southeast Asia." In *Tensions of Empire: Colonial Cultures in a Bourgeois World*, ed. Frederick Cooper and Ann Laura Stoler, 198–237. Berkeley: University of California Press.

———. 2001. "Tense and Tender Ties: The Politics of Comparison in North American History and (Post) Colonial Studies." *Journal of American History* 88, no. 3: 829–65. www.sscnet.ucla.edu/history/faculty/henryyu/Hist597/stoler.pdf.

———. 2002. *Carnal Knowledge and Imperial Power: Race and the Intimate in Colonial Rule*. Berkeley: University of California Press.

———. 2009. *Along the Archival Grain: Epistemic Anxieties and Colonial Common Sense*. Princeton, NJ: Princeton University Press.

Stoler, Ann Laura, and Frederick Cooper. 1997. "Between Metropole and Colony: Rethinking a Research Agenda." In *Tensions of Empire: Colonial Cultures in a Bourgeois World*, ed. Frederick Cooper and Ann Laura Stoler, 1–58. Berkeley: University of California Press.

Stoler, Ann Laura, and Karen Strassler. 2000. "Castings for the Colonial: Memory Work in "New Order" Java." *Comparative Studies in Society and History* 42, no. 1: 4–48.

Styles, Megan. 2011. "Rosy Aspirations: Work, Environment, & Global Commerce in Naivasha, Kenya." PhD diss., University of Washington, Seattle.

Sullivan, Shannon. 2006. *Revealing Whiteness: The Unconscious Habits of Racial Privilege*. Bloomington: Indiana University Press.

Suzuki, Yuka. 2007. "Putting the Lion out at Night: Domestication and the Taming of the Wild." In *Where the Wild Things Are: Domestication Reconsidered*, ed. Molly H. Mullin and Rebecca Cassidy, 229–47. Oxford: Berg.

Swigart, Leigh. 2000. "The Limits of Legitimacy: Language Ideology and Shift in Contemporary Senegal." *Journal of Linguistic Anthropology* 10, no. 1: 90–130.

Thomson, Joseph. 1885. *Through Masai Land: A Journey of Exploration among the Snowclad Volcanic Mountains and Strange Tribes of Eastern Equatorial Africa*. London: Sampson Low, Marston, Searle & Rivington.

Tidrick, Kathryn. 1980. "The Masai and Their Masters: A Psychological Study of District Administration." *African Studies Review* 23, no. 1: 15–31.

Tignor, Robert L. 1972. "The Maasai Warriors: Pattern Maintenance and Violence in Colonial Kenya." *Journal of African History* 13, no. 2: 271–90.

Tonkin, Elizabeth. 2002. "Settlers and Elites in Kenya and Liberia." In *Elite Cultures: Anthropological Perspectives,* ed. Cris Shore and Stephen Nugent, 129–44. London: Routledge.

Tooker, Deborah. 1992. "Identity Systems of Highland Burma: 'Belief', Akha Zan, and a Critique of Interiorized Notions of Ethno-Religious Identity." *Man,* n.s., 27, no. 4: 799–819.

Trzebinski, Errol. 1985. *The Kenya Pioneers.* London: Heinemann.

Tully, James. 1980. *A Discourse on Property: John Locke and His Adversaries.* Cambridge: Cambridge University Press.

———. 1994. "Rediscovering America: The Two Treatises and Aboriginal Rights." In *Locke's Philosophy: Content and Context,* ed. G. A. J. Rogers. Oxford: Clarendon Press.

Uusihakala, Katja. 1999. "From Impulsive Adventure to Postcolonial Commitment: Making White Identity in Contemporary Kenya." *European Journal of Cultural Studies* 2, no. 1: 27–45.

Van der Waal, C. S. 2012. "Creolisation and Purity: Afrikaans Language Politics in Post-Apartheid Times." *African Studies* 71, no. 3: 446–63.

Van Tol, Deanne. 2013. "The Heart of a Stranger: Voluntary Work and European Settlement in Colonial Kenya." African Studies Association 56th Annual Meeting, Baltimore, Maryland, November 23, 2013. http://papers.ssrn.com/sol3/papers.cfm?abstract_id=2252614.

Vaughan, Meghan. 1991. *Curing Their Ills: Colonial Power and African Illness.* Cambridge: Polity Press.

Vice, Samantha. 2010. "How do I live in this strange place?" *Journal of Social Philosophy* 41, no. 3: 323–42.

Vitale, Anthony J. 1980. "Kisetla: Linguistic and Sociolinguistic Aspects of a Pidgin Swahili of Kenya." *Anthropological Linguistics* 22, no. 2: 47–65.

Wadhams, Nick. 2009. "In Kenya, Can War Games Co-Exist with Wildlife?" *Time,* October 27. http://content.time.com/time/world/article/0,,1931961,00.html.

Wallace-Sanders, Kimberly. 2008. *Mammy: A Century of Race, Gender, and Southern Memory.* Ann Arbor: University of Michigan Press.

Waller, Richard D. 1985a. "Ecology, Migration, and Expansion in East Africa." *African Affairs* 84, no. 336: 347–70.

———. 1985b. "Economic and Social Relations in the Central Rift Valley: The Maa-Speakers and Their Neighbors in the Nineteenth Century." In *Kenya in the Nineteenth Century,* ed. B. Ogot, 83–151. Nairobi: Nairobi University Press.

———. 2003. "Witchcraft and Colonial Law in Kenya." *Past and Present* 180, no. 1: 241–75.

Wander, P. C., J. N. Martin, and T. K. Nakayama. 1999. "Whiteness and Beyond: Sociohistorical Foundations of Whiteness and Contemporary Challenges." In *Whiteness: The Communication of Social Identity,* ed. T. K. Nakayama and J. N. Martin, 13–26. Thousand Oaks, CA: Sage.

wa Thiong'o, Ngugi. 1981. *Detained: A Writer's Prison Diary*. London: Heinemann.

———. 1986. *Decolonising the Mind: The Politics of Language in African Literature*. London: James Currey.

Watson, Veronica T. 2013. *The Souls of White Folk: African American Writers Theorize Whiteness*. Jackson: University Press of Mississippi.

Waweru, K. 2012. "Laikipia Aspirant Fights for Land Rights." www.the-star.co.ke/news/article-2745/laikipia-aspirants-fights-land-rights.

Weiner, Margaret J. 2003. "Hidden Forces: Colonialism and the Politics of Magic in the Netherlands Indies." In *Magic and Modernity: Interfaces of Revelation and Concealment*, ed. Birgit Meyer and Peter Pels. 129–58. Stanford, CA: Stanford University Press.

Western, David. 2000. "Conservation in a Human Dominated World." *Issues in Science and Technology*, Spring. http://issues.org/16–3/western.

Weston, Kath. 1991. *Families We Choose: Lesbians, Gays, Kinship*. New York: Columbia University Press.

Williams, Ian. 2005. *Riding in Kenya*. iUniverse.

Williams, Raymond. 1977. *Marxism and Literature*. Oxford: Oxford University Press.

Wilson, Christopher. 1952. *Before the Dawn in Kenya: An Authentic Account of Life in East Africa When It Was under African Rule*. Nairobi: English Press.

White, Jenny B. 2004 [1994]. *Money Makes Us Relatives: Women's Labor in Urban Turkey*. 2nd ed. New York: Routledge

White, Luise. 1990. *The Comforts of Home: Prostitution in Colonial Nairobi*. Chicago: University of Chicago Press.

———. 2000. *Speaking with Vampires: Rumor and History in Colonial Africa*. Berkeley: University of California Press.

Whitley, Wilfred. 1969. *Swahili: The Rise of a National Language*. London: Methuen.

Whorf, Benjamin. 1956 [1939]. "The Relation of Habitual Thought and Behavior to Language." In *Language, Thought, and Reality: Selected Writings of Benjamin Lee Whorf*, ed. John B. Carroll, 134–59. Cambridge: Technology Press of Massachusetts Institute of Technology. Reprinted from *Language, Culture, and Personality: Essays in Memory of Edward Sapir*, ed. Leslie Spier (Menasha, WI: Sapir Memorial Publication Fund, 1941).

Wolf, Eric R., and Sidney W. Mintz. 1957. "Haciendas and Plantations in Middle America and the Antilles." *Social and Economic Studies* 6, no. 3: 380–412.

Wolff, Richard D. 1975. *The Economics of Colonialism: Britain and Kenya, 1870–1930*. New Haven, CT: Yale University Press.

Wouter-Kusters, Christaan. 2003. *Linguistic Complexity: The Influence of Social Change on Verbal Inflection*. Utrecht: LOT Publications. www.lotpublications.nl/publish/articles/000501/bookpart.pdf.

Wylie, Diana. 2001. *Starving on a Full Stomach: Hunger and the Triumph of Cultural Racism in Modern South Africa*. Charlottesville: University Press of Virginia.

Index

Colville, Gilbert, 56
community-based conservation (CBC), 75–78, 82–83, 241–42nn107,108
conservation: community-based conservation, 75–78, 82–83, 241–42nn107,108; Maasai involvement in, 240n85; and pastoralism, 68, 77, 241–42n107; perspectivist views of, 75, 78–79, 80–81; and romanticization of Maasai, 239–40n83; settler descendant role in, 32, 49, 52–53; and structural oblivion, 59, 77–78, 82–83, 241n99, 242n108; and tourism, 49, 77, 240n85, 241n99, 242n107
Cooper, Frederick, 7, 25
cosmopolitanism: and exit strategies, 30; and interracial relationships, 131–32; and language, 162, 170–71, 177, 254–55n71; and moral nationalism, 13, 180, 256n2; and occult, 188, 189
Crapanzano, Vincent, 15, 96, 103, 180
Crilly, Rob, 166
critical voice. See perspectivism
cultural citizenship, 4, 9, 97, 152, 158, 164, 177–78. See also moral nationalism
cultural differences discourse: and Christianity, 186; and interracial relationships, 124–25; and language, 164–65, 174–75, 255nn74,76; and language as moral nationalist tactic, 170–72, 173, 176–77, 254–55n71; and Maasai land reparation demands, 61; and marriage, 125–26, 148, 246n27; and occult, 181, 183, 184, 188–89, 199–200; and structural oblivion, 246n24. See also development ideal
cultural relativism, 15, 79, 189. See also perspectivism
Cunningham-Reid, Michael, 94, 115, 116

Dapash, Meitamei Ole, 77
Dawes, Frank, 248n53
defensiveness, 5; and Cholmondeley case, 97–99; and colonial past, 33–34; and development ideal, 97–98; and double consciousness, 6, 7, 35; and land, 50. See also white defenses of colonial past
Delamere, 3rd Baron (Hugh Cholmondeley), 23, 37, 39, 55, 88–89, 131
Delamere, 4th Baron (Thomas Cholmondeley), 37, 88, 243n4
DePuy, Walter, 57
Detained (wa Thiong'o), 107

development ideal: and colonial justifications for Maasai dispossession, 54–55, 236n11; and colonial past, 22, 55, 235n114, 241nn92,94; and conservation, 78, 79; and defensiveness, 97–98; and ethnographic approach, 17; and Independence transition, 26; and land, 54, 55, 56, 66–67, 236n11; and moral nationalism, 3, 101, 102, 243n29; and occult, 184, 187, 188–89, 199, 258n31; vs. pastoralism, 54, 55, 56, 63–65, 66–67, 68–69, 236n18, 241n94; and racism, 25, 125, 231n70, 246n24; and structural oblivion, 11, 13, 102, 113–14, 246n24; and whiteness, 214. See also cultural differences discourse
Diakanyo, Sentletse, 222
Dinesen, Isak (Baroness Karen von Blixen-Finecke), 37, 39, 71, 73, 131, 190, 233n101
domestic staff, 132–50; abuses of, 135, 136, 148, 248n54, 249n77; and Asian Kenyans, 144–45, 249n73; and autochthony, 147; and betrayal, 149, 249n78; and double consciousness, 35; and expatriates, 134, 145–46, 249n77; and fictive kinship, 132, 247–48nn50,52; handouts to, 142–44, 148, 150, 248n52, 249n69; and interracial relationships, 148–49; intimacy with, 137–38, 146–47, 248n61; and language, 170; and moral nationalism, 144, 149–50; perspectives of, 147–50; perspectivist views of, 139–40; and privilege, 4, 19; and racism, 24, 138–39; remuneration, 134, 140–42, 148, 249n66; and shared nationalist discourse, 3; and structural oblivion, 13, 132, 135–36; working conditions, 133–34, 136–37
double consciousness, 5–9, 35–36; and colonial past, 7–8, 227n16; and land, 53; and language, 158; and Maasai land reparation demands, 80; and privilege, 6, 227n9; and whiteness, 218. See also perspectivism; structural oblivion
Drayton, Richard, 235n118
Du Bois, W. E. B., 5–6, 227n9
Dudmesh, Sally, 84–85, 107, 108, 113
Dunford, Jason, 4–5, 164, 226n7
Dyer, Michael, 78

East Africa Women's League (EAWL), 51, 61

Lightning Source UK Ltd.
Milton Keynes UK
UKHW012008240121
377570UK00001B/76